THE

SELECTED

WORKS OF

GORDON

TULLOCK

VOLUME 2

The Calculus of Consent

THE SELECTED WORKS OF GORDON TULLOCK

VOLUME 1 *Virginia Political Economy*

VOLUME 2 *The Calculus of Consent: Logical Foundations of Constitutional Democracy* (with James M. Buchanan)

VOLUME 3 *The Organization of Inquiry*

VOLUME 4 *The Economics of Politics*

VOLUME 5 *The Rent-Seeking Society*

VOLUME 6 *Bureaucracy*

VOLUME 7 *The Economics and Politics of Wealth Redistribution*

VOLUME 8 *The Social Dilemma: Of Autocracy, Revolution, Coup d'Etat, and War*

VOLUME 9 *Law and Economics*

VOLUME 10 *Economics without Frontiers* (includes a cumulative index for the series)

Gordon Tullock

THE SELECTED WORKS OF GORDON TULLOCK

VOLUME 2

The Calculus of Consent

Logical Foundations of Constitutional Democracy

JAMES M. BUCHANAN *and*

GORDON TULLOCK

Edited and with an Introduction by

CHARLES K. ROWLEY

Liberty Fund

This book is published by Liberty Fund, Inc., a foundation established to encourage study of the ideal of a society of free and responsible individuals.

The cuneiform inscription that serves as our logo and as the design motif for our endpapers is the earliest-known written appearance of the word "freedom" (*amagi*), or "liberty." It is taken from a clay document written about 2300 B.C. in the Sumerian city-state of Lagash.

Printed in the United States of America

Paperback cover photo courtesy of the *American Economic Review*

Frontispiece courtesy of Center for Study of Public Choice, George Mason University, Fairfax, Virginia

14 19 20 21 22 C 6 5 4 3 2
19 20 21 22 P 9 8 7 6 5

Library of Congress Cataloging-in-Publication Data
Buchanan, James M.
The calculus of consent : logical foundations of constitutional democracy / James M. Buchanan and Gordon Tullock ; edited and with an introduction by Charles K. Rowley.
p. cm. — (The selected works of Gordon Tullock ; v. 2)
Originally published: Ann Arbor : University of Michigan Press, [1962].
Also published by Liberty Fund as v. 3 of The collected works of James M. Buchanan. ©1999. With new foreword, note on Buchanan by Tullock, and index.
Includes bibliographical references and index.
ISBN 0-86597-521-3 (alk. paper) — ISBN 0-86597-532-9 (pbk.—alk. paper)
1. Democracy. 2. Social choice. 3. Voting. I. Tullock, Gordon. II. Rowley, Charles Kershaw. III. Title.
JC423.B86 2004
321.8—dc22 2004044230

LIBERTY FUND, INC.
11301 North Meridian Street
Carmel, Indiana 46032

CONTENTS

INTRODUCTION

The Calculus of Consent: Logical Foundations of Constitutional Democracy, by James M. Buchanan and Gordon Tullock, is a classic text that played a significant role in carving out two new disciplines from economics and political science—*public choice* (the analysis of politics as it is) and *constitutional political economy* (the analysis of politics as it should be).[1] *The Calculus of Consent* is, by a wide margin, the most widely cited publication of each coauthor and, by general agreement, their most important scientific contribution.

The foundations for the book were laid during the academic year 1958–59, when Gordon Tullock was a research fellow and James M. Buchanan was joint director (with Warren Nutter) of the Thomas Jefferson Center for Studies in Political Economy at the University of Virginia. The book was written during the academic year 1959–60, while Tullock was teaching in the School of International Studies at the University of South Carolina. Both political and economic climates were favorable to a magnum opus that would focus on the gains-from-trade available from a rationally constructed constitution and downplay the notion that politics is either a conflict-ridden, negative-sum game or a quest for some collective ideal.

Politically, the world was at peace, more or less, with the Cold War stabilizing tensions between East and West. The citizens of the United States were enjoying the largely bipartisan Eisenhower presidency, constrained by a Democratic majority in Congress. Vietnam was still just a dot on the map of Indochina. Civil rights had not yet surfaced as a divisive political issue. Economically, the United States was the dominant player in world trade as Europe and Japan slowly recovered from the devastation of the Second World War; unemployment and inflation rates remained low; the dollar was the undisputed world currency; federal budgets were balanced; and the positive rate of overall economic growth dampened redistributionist pressures. In such circumstances, Americans could be forgiven the measure of myopic complacency with which they viewed their lot.

The intellectual environment, however, was decidedly less favorable. Indeed, it was sufficiently hostile to the ideas set out in *The Calculus of Consent*

1. James M. Buchanan and Gordon Tullock, *The Calculus of Consent: Logical Foundations of Constitutional Democracy* (Ann Arbor: University of Michigan Press, 1962).

that only scholars endowed with originality, courage, and entrepreneurial zeal would stand any chance of penetrating the prevailing conventional wisdom that dominated the economic and political science academies. Buchanan and Tullock combined those qualities in full measure and together constituted a formidable team that would shake the foundations of the two professions.

During the 1950s and early 1960s, the economics profession was basking in the reflected glory of John Maynard Keynes, whose own 1936 magnum opus had inspired the vision that economists could guide benevolent governments into effectively smoothing out business cycles primarily through fiscal intervention.[2] This new role of "economists as philosopher-kings," while flattering to egos and supportive of professional advancement, rendered many of them uneasy about market process and suspicious of almost all forms of constraint on the size of government.

The economics profession was dominated to a lesser extent by the new welfare economics, as best elaborated in Abba Lerner's influential 1944 book *The Economics of Control.*[3] A lifelong socialist, Lerner wrote the text in the form of a handbook, presenting his propositions as rules to be followed by the planners and plant managers of a decentralized socialist economy. In such an environment, even Milton Friedman, the most effective contemporary purveyor of free-market ideas, was forced onto the defensive, facing the almost impossible task of defending real-world private markets against idealized concepts of collective action.[4]

Political scientists were also immersed in analytical modes that *The Calculus of Consent* would challenge. Political philosophers, for the most part, remained wedded to Platonic and organic notions of benevolent government. Many political scientists, to the extent that they were interested in theory at all, were enamored of behaviorist theories and strongly hostile to the rational-choice approach that would dominate *The Calculus of Consent.* Most institutionalists simply observed the evolution and the behavior of political institutions without attempting to evaluate those institutions in terms of relevant theory. Inevitably, *The Calculus of Consent* would threaten to devalue a large stock of human capital in political science and, for this reason alone, generate hostility.

2. John Maynard Keynes, *The General Theory of Employment, Interest, and Money* (London: Macmillan, 1936).

3. Abba P. Lerner, *The Economics of Control: Principles of Welfare Economics* (New York: Macmillan, 1944).

4. Milton Friedman, *Capitalism and Freedom* (Chicago: University of Chicago Press, 1962).

The Calculus of Consent is quintessentially a joint product based on the teamwork of two very different scholars. Buchanan in 1959 was already a well-established public-finance scholar with a significant publication record. A meticulous, thoughtful, highly original, and very courageous scholar, he had already affected the economics profession with a Virginia-blend classical liberalism that infuriated the left-leaning majority and enraged the Marxist wing. Tullock in 1959 was a little-known, self-trained economist; however, he brought to the project a powerful analytical mind, a passion for understanding the political marketplace, and an unorthodox, stubborn originality that enabled him to break down strongly held conventional wisdoms. Neither Buchanan nor Tullock could have written *The Calculus of Consent* alone. The book is a blend of their diverse skills.

The Calculus of Consent is divided into four parts, each consisting of several chapters. This introduction will provide a short overview of the book and identify the key insights that would forever disturb the border between economics and political science.

Part I establishes the conceptual framework of the book in four succinct chapters. Here, a number of important challenges to conventional wisdom ("hand grenades" may be a better description) pave the way for the more formal invasion of economics and political science that comes in later chapters.

Chapter 1, the introduction, identifies the central task of the book as defining what a state ought to be. To address this issue, the authors propose to construct a theory of collective choice out of the principle of methodological individualism (i.e., focus strictly on individual motivation and individual behavior as they relate to social, as contrasted to private, activity). In their construct, individuals are assumed to be diverse, thus rendering any political process of conflict resolution difficult. The authors also indicate that the mechanism used to resolve conflict will not be the usually accepted standard of the majority vote but rather the universal consensus. The bar is thus set much higher by Tullock and Buchanan than by those who rely on the majoritarian principle alone.

Chapter 2 expands on the nature of the individualistic postulate. The authors categorically reject the organic notion of the state that dominated both economics and political science in the middle years of the twentieth century. As part of their individualistic approach, they also reject any notion of the "general will" that purports to identify the public interest as something independent of the separate interests of the individuals participating in collective-choice decisions. Similarly, they reject any theory of the collectivity that embodies exploitation by a ruling class.

Instead, they view collective action as the action of individuals choosing from within a group setting. Individuals perceive the state as an artifact created to improve their individual well-being. In this sense, the book adopts a rational-choice approach—because the criterion of goodness is universal consent, the only definition of "truth" is conceptual unanimity. In 1962, neither economists nor political scientists had any notion that political outcomes could be resolved through unanimity.

Chapter 3 expands on the nature of politics-as-exchange and thus sets the scene for the economic analysis of political markets. The authors suggest that both economic and political relationships represent cooperation on the part of two or more individuals, because individual behavior, be it private or political, does not change between markets. Of course, the economic model cannot explain all collective action any more than it can explain all private action. However, as long as some part of individual behavior in collective-choice making is motivated by utility maximization, and as long as individual-utility functions are heterogeneous, an economic theory of political behavior offers valuable insights. This chapter is important because it displaced the widely held view that politics is based on conflict with the contrary view that politics is based on cooperation.

Chapter 4 develops the rational-choice approach as the basis for analyzing individual behavior in political markets. The authors adopt the working hypothesis that individuals can rank-order the alternatives of collective as well as market choice and that this ranking is transitive. However, in analyzing the behavior of the individual in the political process, an important element of uncertainty cannot be ignored. At the moment of choice, the individual has no way of knowing the final collective-choice outcome. There is no one-to-one correspondence between individual choice and final outcome. In this sense, the individual is less responsible for final decisions than he is in the private market, and for this reason he may be less fully rational in making choices. This insight was drawn from a highly original 1954 paper by Buchanan.[5]

Part II of the book, in four path-breaking chapters, defines the realm of social choice.

In chapter 5 the authors outline an externalities-based theory to explain why individuals adopt a political constitution. They assume that the rational

5. James M. Buchanan, "Social Choice, Democracy, and Free Markets," *Journal of Political Economy* 62 (1954): 114–23.

individual acts to minimize the expected cost of social interaction in one of three ways, namely (1) purely individualistic behavior; (2) private, voluntary, but jointly organized, behavior; and (3) collective action through the political process. They emphasize that externalities are not eliminated by collective action, indeed that they may be exacerbated by them. Only if collective action is considerably more efficient in decision-making costs will the rational individual choose the collectivity in preference to the private individual or voluntary contractual alternatives. This simple concept is significant in that it effectively levels the playing field in the debate over the respective advantages of private versus political markets.

In chapter 6, arguably the most important chapter in *The Calculus of Consent*, the authors use the framework provided in chapter 5 to outline the logical foundations of constitutional democracy. To simplify the model, the authors assume that the range of collective action is predetermined and that the specific institutions through which collective action occurs are already in place. On this basis, they analyze the nature of constitutional choice confronted by any random individual.

Using the rational-choice model, they assert that every individual seeks to minimize his overall expected costs when he chooses among alternative voting rules that can range from one (random) decision maker to the rule of unanimity. The expected cost function is a combination of expected external costs (that decline monotonically) and expected decision-making costs (that increase monotonically) as the voting rule increases from one to unanimity. The rational individual seeks to minimize these (vertically summed) expected costs. The voting rule reflected in this decision may be sub-, simple-, or supra-majority. The authors suggest that unanimity over the precise rule is attainable even among diverse individuals, because each individual makes his constitutional decision behind a veil of uncertainty. This chapter shocked a large number of social scientists who were irrationally wedded to the notion of simple majority rule.

Chapter 7 refocuses attention on the central role of the rule of unanimity on the political marketplace. While recognizing that individuals may unanimously support rules of less than unanimity for collective action, for the decision-making cost reasons advanced in chapter 6, the authors emphasize that such rules are less than ideal compromises. The unanimity rule, they argue, occupies the central place in any normative theory of democratic government. At best, majority rule is just one of many practical expedients made necessary by the costs of securing widespread agreement within a diverse polity. Convinced majoritarians were irrationally infuriated by this rational constitutional statement.

Chapter 8 reexamines the nature of decision-making costs. The authors note that such costs hitherto had been ignored in all discussions of the nature of constitutional rules. Yet, because collective choices are inherently more costly than private choices, decision-making costs play a central role in determining constitutional outcomes. The authors explain the consequences of population size and degree of heterogeneity for the predictable inclusiveness of a decision-making rule as well as for the degree of restrictivity over the range of collective action.

Part III of the book, in nine chapters, applies the logic developed in Part II to describe a range of decision-making rules, the most notable being the rule of simple majority.

Chapter 9 sets the scene as one in which the constitutional rules are determined, and the expected utility-maximizing individual participates in collective action within the constitutional framework that has been established. Chapter 10 elaborates on a 1959 paper by Gordon Tullock in order to examine the operation of the simple majority rule under certain highly restricted assumptions.[6] In particular, the authors explain why logrolling is important whenever minority voters have more intensive preferences for specific collective actions than do majority voters.

In chapter 11 the authors use game theory as another means of exploring the characteristics of simple majority rule. They demonstrate conclusively that when considered in terms of individuals' own evaluations of possible social alternatives, there is nothing inherent in the operation of this rule that produces "desirable" collective decisions. Predictably, simple majority rule results in overinvestment in the public sector, at least when the investment projects provide differential benefits or are financed by differential taxation. There is nothing in the rule itself that ensures that the games are positive sum. This conclusion fundamentally challenged the prevailing consensus that majority rule was the best of all decision-making rules.

Chapter 12 relates the game theoretic analysis of the simple majority rule to the concept of Pareto optimality. The authors demonstrate that only where side payments are introduced is there any assurance that majority-rule decision making will lead to positions on the Pareto frontier. Indeed, they go fur-

6. Gordon Tullock, "Problems of Majority Voting," *Journal of Political Economy* 67 (December 1959): 571–79.

ther than that, arguing that without side payments even the rule of unanimity does not guarantee Pareto-optimal outcomes.

In chapter 13, the authors explain why their analytical model is more extensive than the Paretian construction. External costs, in their model, are either allocational or redistributional. Only the former plays a role in the Paretian construction. This insight is important because it demonstrates, in yet another dimension, that collective choices differ radically from private choices.

In chapter 14, the authors distinguish between the range and the extent of collective action and explain why this distinction is central to any rational discussion of the allocation of economic resources between the public and the private sector of the economy. Because economists were unaware of this distinction in the early 1960s, most normative analyses of whether government was too large or too small amounted to a waste of time. Individuals in their constitutional roles do not choose directly the size and scope of the public sector: first, they choose the fundamental organization of activity; second, they choose the decision-making rules.

Chapters 9 through 14 focus attention on the simplified model of direct democracy. Chapters 15 through 17 extend the constitutional model to embrace more complex models of representative democracy.

Chapter 15 identifies four basic constitutional-choice variables relevant to representative democracy, namely (1) rules for choosing representatives, (2) rules for deciding issues in legislative assemblies, (3) the degree of representation, and (4) the basis of representation. The authors explore the nature of the interrelationships between these four constitutional variables and conclude that even this much more complex constitutional environment can be analyzed in terms of the two expected cost functions outlined in chapter 6. Once again the authors provide an entirely original insight into the logical foundations of constitutional democracy.

Chapter 16 deploys the expected cost-function model to explain under what circumstances bicameral legislatures are justified. Because bicameral legislatures increase expected decision-making costs, expected external costs must be lowered significantly in order to provide a net reduction in overall expected costs. Similar arguments also apply to presidential veto powers.

In chapter 17, the authors compare and contrast their own models with the mid-twentieth-century orthodox models of political theory. Their models of politics emphasize the importance of exchange in constitutional decision making and identify the principle of unanimity as the ultimate normative benchmark. In contrast, political scientists emphasized the importance of politics as a mechanism for conflict resolution and identified the principle of majority rule as an absolute doctrine of popular sovereignty.

Part IV of the book, in three chapters and two appendixes, turns to the economics and ethics of democracy.

Chapter 18 establishes the ethical basis for economic exchange, recognizing that some forms of economic exchange (for example, prostitution) may be outlawed because they impose negative externalities. The same ethic governs the exchange of political votes. Typically, vote trading is forbidden in general elections, in part because such a mechanism enables the rich to determine election outcomes. However, logrolling within a legislature typically is allowed, in part because it offers some protection to minorities. In principle, the presence or absence of externalities, negative and positive, should govern the constitutional choice of whether or not to allow vote trading. This insight helped to reshape research in this field among both economists and political scientists.

Chapter 19 focuses attention, from a constitutional perspective, on the role and behavior of pressure and special-interest groups. The authors challenge the conventional wisdom, based on the writings of Arthur Bentley (1908) and David Truman (1951), that endorsed pressure, or special-interest, groups as inevitable, and even desirable, components of the democratic political process.[7] They note that such groups had expanded their role dramatically during the first half of the twentieth century as a profit-based response to relaxed budget constraints and to growth in the range and extent of collective choice. For the first time, the behavior of interest groups was linked to constitutional change.

Chapter 20 concludes the book with a discussion of the politics of the good society. Here it is entirely appropriate to allow the authors the final word.

> With the philosophers of the Enlightenment we share the faith that man can rationally organize his own society, that existing organization can always be perfected, and that nothing in the social order should remain exempt from rational, critical, and intelligent discussion. Man's reason is the slave to his passions, and recognizing this about himself, man can organize

7. Arthur Bentley, *The Process of Government* (1908; reprint, Bloomington, Ind.: Principia Press, 1935); David B. Truman, *The Governmental Process* (New York: Alfred Knopf, 1951).

his own association with his fellows in such a manner that the mutual benefits from social interdependence can be effectively maximized. (p. 289)

CHARLES K. ROWLEY

Duncan Black Professor of Economics, George Mason University

Senior Fellow, James M. Buchanan Center for Political Economy, George Mason University

General Director, The Locke Institute

JAMES MCGILL BUCHANAN

Jim Buchanan and I first became acquainted in 1958 when I joined him as a research fellow at the Thomas Jefferson Center for Studies in Political Economy at the University of Virginia. For forty-five years we have remained friends and colleagues, working together to promote public choice and constitutional political economy through joint publications, intellectual interaction, and organizational entrepreneurship and as coparticipants in a great intellectual journey along the less-well-traveled path. I have benefited enormously from Jim's immense intellectual reach, his generous guidance, his willingness to comment on my scholarship, and his courage and ingenuity in overcoming an adverse intellectual environment. Our joint book, *The Calculus of Consent*, is undoubtedly our greatest intellectual achievement, an outcome of highly effective team production that helped to open important new subfields of economics and political science.

GORDON TULLOCK

Fairfax, Virginia
2003

PREFACE

This is a book about the *political* organization of a society of free men. Its methodology, its conceptual apparatus, and its analytics are derived, essentially, from the discipline that has as its subject the *economic* organization of such a society. Students and scholars in *politics* will share with us an interest in the central problems under consideration. Their colleagues in *economics* will share with us an interest in the construction of the argument. This work lies squarely along that mythical, and mystical, borderline between these two prodigal offsprings of political economy.

Because it does so, the book and the work that it embodies seem closely analogous to any genuine "fence-row" effort. As almost every farmer knows, there attach both benefits and costs to fence-row plowing. In the first place, by fact of its being there, the soil along the fence row is likely to be more fertile, more productive, when properly cultivated, than that which is to be found in the more readily accessible center of the field. This potential advantage tends to be offset, however, by the enhanced probability of error and accident along the borders of orthodoxy. Many more stumps and boulders are likely to be encountered, and the sheer unfamiliarity of the territory makes unconscious and unintended diversions almost inevitable. To those two characteristic features we must add a third, one that Robert Frost has impressed even upon those who know nothing of our agrarian metaphor. "Good fences make good neighbors," and neighborly relationships stand in danger of being disturbed by furrowing too near the border line. Orthodox practitioners in both politics and economics will perhaps suggest that we respect the currently established order of the social sciences. We can only hope that the first of these three features outweighs the latter two.

The interdisciplinary nature of the book raises problems of content. Precisely because we hope to include among our readers those who are specialists in two related but different fields of scholarship, some parts of the analysis will seem oversimplified and tedious to each group. The political scientists will find our treatment of certain traditional topics to be naïve and unsophisticated. The economists will note that our elementary review of welfare theory ignores complex and difficult questions. We ask only for ordinary tolerance, that which prompts the judicious selection of the interesting elements of analysis.

What are we trying to accomplish in this book? Perhaps by answering this question at the outset, we shall be able to assist certain of our readers in understanding our analysis and also forestall misdirected criticism from others. We are not attempting to write an "ideal" political constitution for society. Therefore, the reader will find in this book little more than passing reference to many of those issues that have been considered to be among the most important in modern political theory. We do not directly discuss such things as division of powers, judicial review, executive veto, or political parties. We try, instead, to analyze the calculus of the rational individual when he is faced with questions of constitutional choice. Our main purpose is not that of exploring this choice process in detailed application to all of the many constitutional issues that may be presented. We examine the process extensively only with reference to the problem of decision-making rules. To this is added a single chapter on representation and one on the bicameral legislature. These illustrative examples of the general approach should indicate that many of the more specific issues in constitutional theory can be subjected to analysis of the sort employed in this work.

This analysis can perhaps be described by the term "methodological individualism." Human beings are conceived as the only ultimate choice-makers in determining group as well as private action. Economists have explored in considerable detail the process of individual decision-making in what is somewhat erroneously called the "market sector." Modern social scientists have, by contrast, tended to neglect the individual decision-making that must be present in the formation of group action in the "public sector." In their rejection of the contract theory of the state as an explanation of either the origin or the basis of political society, a rejection that was in itself appropriate, theorists have tended to overlook those elements within the contractarian tradition that do provide us with the "bridge" between the individual-choice calculus and group decisions.

Methodological individualism should not be confused with "individualism" as a norm for organizing social activity. Analysis of the first type represents an attempt to reduce all issues of political organization to the individual's confrontation with alternatives and his choice among them. His "logic of choice" becomes the central part of the analysis, and no position need be taken concerning the ultimate goals or criteria that should direct his choice. By contrast, "individualism" as an organizational norm involves the explicit acceptance of certain value criteria. This work is "individualist" only in the first, or methodological, sense. We hope that we have been able to make it reasonably *wertfrei* in the second, or normative, sense.

As suggested, we discuss the "constitution" at some length in this book. We shall mean by this term a set of rules that is agreed upon in advance and within which subsequent action will be conducted. Broadly considered, a preface is the constitution of a jointly written book. Since each of us must agree at this point before going on our separate ways to other works, the preface is the appropriate place to describe, as fully as possible, the contribution of each author to the final product. If we apply the calculus attributed to our representative man of this book to ourselves, we must recognize that each one of us, when separately confronted on subsequent occasions, will be sorely tempted to accept private praise for all worthy aspects of the book and to shift private blame to our partner for all errors, omissions, and blunders. To set such matters aright, a brief and jointly authorized "constitutional" preface seems in order.

In the most fundamental sense, the whole book is a genuinely joint product. The chapters have been jointly, not severally, written. We believe that the argument is co-ordinated and consistent, one part with the other. We hope that readers will agree. To some extent this co-ordination results from the rather fortunate compatibility of ideas that have been separately developed, at least in their initial, preliminary stages. Both authors have long been interested in the central problem analyzed in this book, and, from different approaches, they have independently made previous contributions. Buchanan, in his two 1954 papers,[1] tried to explore the relationships between individual choice in the market place and in the voting process. Somewhat later, in 1959,[2] he tried to examine the implications of modern welfare economics for the political organization of society. Tullock, meanwhile, has been previously concerned with constructing a general theory of political organization from motivational assumptions similar to those employed by the economist. His earlier work, which was completed in a preliminary form in 1958,[3] concentrated largely on the problems of bureaucratic organization.

1. James M. Buchanan, "Social Choice, Democracy, and Free Markets," *Journal of Political Economy*, LXII (1954), 114–23; "Individual Choice in Voting and the Market," *Journal of Political Economy*, LXII (1954), 334–43. Both of these essays are reprinted in *Fiscal Theory and Political Economy: Selected Essays* (Chapel Hill: University of North Carolina Press, 1960), pp. 75–104.

2. James M. Buchanan, "Positive Economics, Welfare Economics, and Political Economy," *Journal of Law and Economics*, II (1959), 124–38. Reprinted in *Fiscal Theory and Political Economy: Selected Essays*, pp. 105–24.

3. Gordon Tullock, *A General Theory of Politics* (University of Virginia, 1958), privately circulated.

During the academic year 1958–59, Tullock was awarded a research fellowship by the Thomas Jefferson Center for Studies in Political Economy at the University of Virginia, with which Buchanan was, and is, associated. Although no plans for this book were formulated during that year, the discussions and debates conducted at that time represent the origin of many of the specific parts of the work in its present form. During the latter part of the academic year 1958–59, Tullock completed a preliminary analysis of the logrolling processes in democratic government. This was submitted for publication in June 1959, and it was published in December of that year.[4] This preliminary version of what has now become Chapter 10 was the first organic part of the final product. Two further preliminary manuscripts were completed in the summer of 1959, although no plans for joint authorship of this book had as yet emerged. Tullock prepared and circulated a mimeographed research paper entitled "A Preliminary Investigation of the Theory of Constitutions," which contained the first elements of the important central analysis now covered in Chapter 6. Buchanan prepared a paper, "Economic Policy, Free Institutions, and Democratic Process," which he delivered at the annual meeting of the Mt. Pelerin Society in Oxford in September 1959. In this paper many of the ideas that had been jointly discussed were presented in an exploratory and tentative fashion.[5]

A final decision to collaborate on a joint project was made in September 1959, and the bulk of the book was actually written during the course of the academic year 1959–60. As previously suggested, Tullock initially developed the arguments of Chapter 10. He should also be given primary credit for the central model of Chapter 6. Insofar as the two elements of the constitutional calculus can be separated, Buchanan should perhaps be given credit for the emphasis upon the unique position occupied by the unanimity rule in democratic theory (developed in Chapter 7), while Tullock is responsible for stressing the necessity of placing some quantitative dimension on the costs of decision-making (discussed in Chapter 8). Buchanan developed the initial version of the analytical framework discussed in Chapter 5, and he is also responsible for the applications of game theory and theoretical welfare economics that are contained in Chapters 11, 12, and 13. The work on the bi-

4. Gordon Tullock, "Problems of Majority Voting," *Journal of Political Economy*, LXVII (1959), 571–79.

5. This paper is published in *Il Politico*, XXV, No. 2 (1960), 265–93. *Il Politico* is a publication of the University of Pavia, Italy.

cameral legislature of Chapter 16 is largely that of Tullock. Ideas for the remaining substantive chapters of Parts II and III were jointly derived. Insofar as the introductory, connecting, qualifying, and concluding material can be said to possess a consistent style, this is because it has at some stage passed through Buchanan's typewriter.

The two Appendices are separately written and signed. Although they discuss the argument of the book in relation to two separate and distinct bodies of literature, the discerning reader can perhaps distinguish the slight difference in emphasis between the two authors of this book. That this difference should be present and be recognized seems wholly appropriate.

We have been disturbed, disappointed, provoked, and stimulated by the comments of numerous and various critics on the book, either on its earlier separate parts or on its final totality. In almost every instance the comments have been helpful. We cannot list all of these critics, but special mention should be made of Otto Davis, Bruno Leoni, John Moes, and Vincent Thursby. Members of this group have devoted much time and effort to a rather detailed criticism of the manuscript, and in each case their comments have been constructive.

Institutional acknowledgments are also required. The Thomas Jefferson Center for Studies in Political Economy at the University of Virginia awarded Tullock the research fellowship that enabled this joint work to be commenced. The Center has also provided the bulk of the clerical assistance necessary for the processing of the book through its various stages. The cooperation of Mrs. Gladys Batson in this respect should be specially noted. Buchanan was able to devote more of his time to the project because of the award to him, during 1959–60, of a Ford Foundation Faculty Research Fellowship. Moreover, in the summer of 1961, a research grant from the Wilson Gee Institute for Research in the Social Sciences enabled him to carry the work through to final completion. Tullock was provided partial research support for the 1960–61 period by the Rockefeller Foundation, and this has enabled him to devote more time to the book than would otherwise have been possible.

JAMES M. BUCHANAN
GORDON TULLOCK

PART I

THE CONCEPTUAL FRAMEWORK

CHAPTER I

INTRODUCTION

Political theory has concerned itself with the question: What is the State? Political philosophy has extended this to: What ought the State to be? Political "science" has asked: How is the State organized?

None of these questions will be answered here. We are not directly interested in what *the* State or *a* State actually is, but propose to define quite specifically, yet quite briefly, what *we think* a State ought to be. We shall not pause to argue our case with those who might disagree, nor shall we examine in detail either the existing or some ideal organization of governmental activity.

Given an explicitly stated postulate about the objectives of collective action, we shall construct, in an admittedly preliminary and perhaps naïve fashion, a theory of collective choice. This construction will require several steps. Collective action must be, under our postulate, composed of individual actions. The first step in our construction is, therefore, some assumption about individual motivation and individual behavior in social as contrasted with private or individualized activity. Our theory thus begins with the acting or decision-making individual as he participates in the processes through which group choices are organized. Since our model incorporates individual behavior as its central feature, our "theory" can perhaps best be classified as being *methodologically* individualistic.

We shall state here what it will be necessary to reiterate: The analysis does not depend for its elementary logical validity upon any narrowly hedonistic or self-interest motivation of individuals in their behavior in social-choice processes. The representative individual in our models may be egoist or altruist or any combination thereof. Our theory is "economic" only in that it assumes that separate individuals are separate individuals and, as such, are likely to have different aims and purposes for the results of collective action. In other terms, we assume that men's interests will differ for reasons other than those of ignorance. As we shall demonstrate, more restrictive assumptions are required only when the basic theory is to be employed in developing specific operational hypotheses about the *results* of collective choice.

Any theory of collective choice must attempt to explain or to describe the means through which conflicting interests are reconciled. In a genuine sense, economic theory is also a theory of collective choice, and, as such, provides us with an explanation of how separate individual interests are reconciled through the mechanism of trade or exchange. Indeed, when individual interests are assumed to be identical, the main body of economic theory vanishes. If all men were equal in interest and in endowment, natural or artificial, there would be no organized economic activity to explain. Each man would be a Crusoe. Economic theory thus explains why men co-operate through trade: They do so because they are different.

Political theorists, by contrast, do not seem to have considered fully the implications of individual differences for a theory of political decisions. Normally, the choice-making process has been conceived of as the means of arriving at some version of "truth," some rationalist absolute which remains to be discovered through reason or revelation, and which, once discovered, will attract all men to its support. The conceptions of rationalist democracy have been based on the assumption that individual conflicts of interest will, and should, vanish once the electorate becomes fully informed. We do not deny the occasional validity of this conception, in which rules of political choice-making provide means of arriving at certain "truth judgments." However, we do question the universal, or even the typical, validity of this view of political process. Our approach to the collective decision-making processes is similar to that expounded by T. D. Weldon under the term "individualist democracy." Our assumptions are substantially equivalent to his,[1] but Weldon has emphasized the theoretical indeterminacy which such assumptions introduce. Our task, in one sense, is to provide the theoretical determinacy to the "area of human life over which a democratic government . . . can exercise control," even on the purely individualistic postulate, a determinacy that Weldon specifically states to be missing.[2]

What do we mean by theoretical determinacy here? Economic theory does not explain the organization of private choices sufficiently to enable the professional economist to predict the precise composition of the national product, the exchange ratio between any two goods or services, or the price of any one good in terms of money. Such predictions would require omni-

1. T. D. Weldon, *States and Morals* (London: Whittlesey House, 1947). For a more recent statement of a similar position, see Isaiah Berlin, *Two Concepts of Liberty* (Oxford: Clarendon Press, 1958).

2. Ibid., pp. 249 and 255.

science, not science, because we must deal with individuals as actors, not as atoms. The sciences of human choice must be modest in their aims. At best, they can provide the skilled practitioner with some ability to predict the structural characteristics of organized human activity, along with some directional effects of changes in specifically defined variables. Economic theory can help us to predict that markets will be cleared, that uniform units of product will command uniform prices in open markets, that demand will increase as price is reduced—always, of course, with the necessary *ceteris paribus* proviso attached.

The theory of political choice that we hope to construct can do even less than this. Such a theory is inherently more difficult at the outset because of the fundamental interdependence of individual actions in social choice, an interdependence which is largely absent, at least for the first level of analysis, in the market organization of economic activity. The theory of collective choice can, at best, allow us to make some very rudimentary predictions concerning the structural characteristics of group decisions.

The important choice that the group must make, willy-nilly, is: How shall the dividing line between collective action and private action be drawn? What is the realm for social and for private or individual choice? It is not the function of a theory to draw a precise line; theory assumes meaning only in terms of an analytical model which describes or explains the processes through which individuals of the group can make this all-important decision. Moreover, in deriving this model we shall be able to describe, in general terms, some of the characteristic features of a "solution."

The selection of a decision-making rule is itself a group choice, and it is not possible to discuss positively the basic choice-making of a social group except under carefully specified assumptions about rules. We confront a problem of infinite regression here. Individuals cannot competently choose between collective and private action in a particular area until the results of alternative choices are analyzed. Private action, at its simplest, presents little difficulty; the ultimate decision-maker is assumed to be the acting individual. However, collective action is wholly different. Before it can be properly assessed as an alternative to private choice, the ultimate decision-making authority must be specified. Is a simple majority to be controlling? Or must collective decisions be made only upon the attainment of full consensus? Or is there a single-minded ruling class or group? The individual's evaluation of collective choice will be influenced drastically by the decision rule that he assumes to prevail. Even when this difficulty is surmounted at the primary level, however, it allows us to analyze only the choice of the single individual in his own "constitutional" decision. When we recognize that "constitutional" decisions themselves, which are necessarily collective, may also be reached under any of several decision-making rules, the same issue is confronted all over again. Moreover, in postulating a decision-making rule for constitutional choices, we face the same problem when we ask: How is the rule itself chosen?[3]

One means of escape from what appears to be a hopeless methodological dilemma is that of introducing some rule for unanimity or full consensus at the ultimate constitutional level of decision-making. Quite apart from the relevance of this rule as an explanation of political reality, it does provide us with a criterion against which the individual person's decisions on constitutional issues may be analyzed. In examining the choice calculus of the single individual, as this calculus is constrained by the knowledge that all other individuals in the group must agree before ultimate action can be taken, we are able to discuss meaningfully "improvements" in the rules for choice-making. When will it prove desirable to shift one or more sectors of human activity from the realm of private to that of social choice, or vice versa? Implicit in our discussion is the assumption that the criteria for answering such questions as this can only be found in the conceptual unanimity among all parties in the political group. Agreement among all individuals in the group upon the change becomes the only real measure of "improvement" that may be accomplished through change.[4]

The attainment of consent is a costly process, however, and a recognition of this simple fact points directly toward an "economic" theory of constitutions. The individual will find it advantageous to agree in advance to certain rules (which he knows may work occasionally to his own disadvantage) when the benefits are expected to exceed the costs. The "economic" theory that

3. As Otto A. Davis has pointed out in his criticism of an earlier version of this manuscript, the philosophical problem discussed here is by no means confined to constitutional or political theory. Similar problems arise when any "genuine" choice is confronted. A choice among alternatives is made on the basis of some criteria; it is always possible to move one step up the hierarchy and to examine the choice of criteria; discussion stops only when we have carried the examination process back to ultimate "values."

4. The contract theory of the State can be interpreted in this manner; and, if the theory is so interpreted, our whole analysis can be classified as falling within the broad stream of contractarian doctrine. On the specific relationship between the analysis of this book and the contract theory, see Appendix 1.

may be constructed out of an analysis of individual choice provides an explanation for the emergence of a political constitution from the discussion process conducted by free individuals attempting to formulate generally acceptable rules in their own long-term interest. It is to be emphasized that, in this constitutional discussion, the prospective utility of the individual participant must be more broadly conceived than in the collective-choice process that takes place *within defined rules*.[5] Our theory of constitutional choice has normative implications only insofar as the underlying basis of individual consent is accepted.

If such a theory of the constitution is to move beyond the symbolic, some analysis of the separate decision-making rules must be attempted. The costs and the benefits from collective action, as these confront the choosing individual, can be assessed only on the basis of some analysis of the various choice processes. The central part of this book is an analysis of one of the most important rules for collective choice—that of simple majority voting. The areas of human activity that the reasonably intelligent individual will choose to place in the realm of collective choice will depend to a large extent on how he expects the choice processes to operate. Moreover, since majority rule assumes such a dominant position in modern democratic theory and practice, any theory of the constitution would be but a hollow shell without a rather careful analysis of majority rule.

Any theorizing, be it about private or collective decision-making, must initially be based on simple models which define clearly the constraints within which the individual actor operates. In a preliminary analysis, simplification and abstraction are required. The institutional constraints on human action must be stripped of all but their essentials. As noted, the central part of this book analyzes the action of individuals as they participate in group decision-making under the single constraint of simple majority rule. Existing political institutions rarely, if ever, are so simple. However, progress is made by building from the ground up, and we do not propose to present a fully developed theoretical structure. Our approach, which starts with the participation of individuals in simple voting situations, should be complementary to that which begins with existing institutional structures, such as political parties, representative assemblies, executive leadership, and other characteristics of the modern polity.

5. Cf. F. A. Hayek, *The Constitution of Liberty* (Chicago: University of Chicago Press, 1960), p. 179.

It is not surprising that a significant part of the work most closely related to this book has been done by political economists. Knut Wicksell, in his original and highly provocative work on the organization of the fiscal system, must be given much credit for inspiring many of the ideas that we develop here.[6] His work preceded by several decades the final construction of the Paretian "new" welfare economics, which is closely related although independently developed. The merit of Wicksell is that he states directly the implications of his analysis for the institutions of collective choice, a subject upon which the modern welfare economists have been rather strangely silent. Only within the last decade have serious attempts been made to analyze collective-choice processes from what may be called an "economic" approach. Recent works by Kenneth Arrow,[7] Duncan Black,[8] James M. Buchanan,[9] Robert A. Dahl and Charles E. Lindblom,[10] Bruno Leoni,[11] and Henry Oliver[12] are of direct relevance to both the methodology and the subject matter under consideration in this book. The works most closely related to this book are, however, those of Anthony Downs[13] and Gordon Tullock.[14]

6. Knut Wicksell, *Finanztheoretische Untersuchungen* (Jena: Gustav Fischer, 1896).

7. Kenneth Arrow, *Social Choice and Individual Values* (New York: John Wiley and Sons, 1951).

8. Duncan Black, *The Theory of Committees and Elections* (Cambridge: Cambridge University Press, 1958); also, Duncan Black and R. A. Newing, *Committee Decisions with Complementary Valuation* (London: William Hodge, 1951).

9. James M. Buchanan, "Social Choice, Democracy, and Free Markets," *Journal of Political Economy*, LXII (1954), 114–23; "Individual Choice in Voting and the Market," *Journal of Political Economy*, LXII (1954), 334–43; and "Positive Economics, Welfare Economics, and Political Economy," *Journal of Law and Economics*, II (1959), 124–38. Reprinted in *Fiscal Theory and Political Economy: Selected Essays* (Chapel Hill: University of North Carolina Press, 1960), pp. 75–124.

10. Robert A. Dahl and Charles E. Lindblom, *Politics, Economics, and Welfare* (New York: Harper and Bros., 1953).

11. Bruno Leoni, *Freedom and Law* (lectures delivered at Fifth Institute on Freedom and Competitive Enterprise at Claremont Men's College, 1957 [mimeographed]); "The Meaning of 'Political' in Political Decisions," *Political Studies*, V (1957).

12. Henry Oliver, "Attitudes toward Market and Political Self-Interest," *Ethics*, LXV (1955), 171–80.

13. Anthony Downs, *An Economic Theory of Democracy* (New York: Harper and Bros., 1957).

14. Gordon Tullock, *A General Theory of Politics* (University of Virginia, 1958), privately circulated.

This book differs from the work of Downs in its basic approach to the political process. Downs tries to construct a theory of government analogous to the theory of markets by concentrating his attention on the behavior of political parties. The attempt of parties to maximize voter support replaces the attempt of individuals to maximize utilities in the market process. By comparison, in this book we do not consider problems of representation (i.e., problems concerned with the selection of leaders, party organization, etc.) except at a second stage of analysis. We construct a model of collective choice-making that is more closely analogous to the theory of private choice embodied in the theory of markets than is that which Downs has produced. Tullock, on the other hand, in his preliminary version of a projected general work, concentrates his attention on the behavior of the individual in a bureaucratic hierarchy and upon the choices that such an individual faces. Our approach parallels this in its concentration upon, and its assumptions about, individual motivation, but we are interested here primarily in the behavior of the individual as he participates in a voting process and upon the results of various voting or decision-making rules.

Although developed independently, our conception of democratic process has much in common with that accepted by the school of political science which follows Arthur Bentley in trying to explain collective decision-making in terms of the interplay of group interests.[15] Throughout our analysis the word "group" could be substituted for the word "individual" without significantly affecting the results. In this way a group calculus may be developed. We have preferred, however, to retain the individualist approach. At best, the analysis of group interests leaves us one stage removed from the ultimate choice-making process which can only take place in individual minds.

The essential difference between our "economic" approach to political choice and that approach represented by the Bentley school lies in our attempt to examine the results of political activity in terms of simplified analytical models and, in this way, to suggest some of the implications of the theory that might be subjected to empirical testing.

15. The basic work in this tradition is Arthur Bentley's *The Process of Government* (Bloomington, Ind.: The Principia Press, 1935 [first published 1908]). The most important recent work is that of David B. Truman, *The Governmental Process* (New York: Alfred A. Knopf, 1951). The works of Pendleton Herring also fall within this general grouping. See his *The Politics of Democracy* (New York: W. W. Norton and Co., 1940); *Group Representation before Congress* (Baltimore: The Johns Hopkins Press, 1929).

In terms of method, our models are related to those that have been utilized in the development of the emerging "theory of teams,"[16] although, again, this development is wholly independent of our own. This theory of teams, however, has been primarily concerned with the choice of intraorganizational decision rules when the goals of an organization may be rather carefully specified. To our knowledge the theory has not been extended to apply to political decision rules.

16. See especially Jacob Marshak, "Efficient and Viable Organizational Forms," in *Modern Organization Theory*, ed. by Mason Haire (New York: John Wiley and Sons, 1959), pp. 307–20.

CHAPTER 2

THE INDIVIDUALISTIC POSTULATE

A theory of collective choice must be grounded on some assumption concerning the nature of the collective unit. What is the State? Or, to put the question more precisely, how should the State be conceived?

If an organic conception is accepted, the theory of collective choice-making is greatly simplified. The collectivity becomes as an individual, and the analyst need only search for the underlying value pattern or scale which motivates independent State action. Operationally meaningful propositions about such action may be exceedingly difficult to construct, but useful discussion may, nevertheless, proceed without much attention being paid to the manner of constructing the "bridge" between individual values and social values. The organic State has an existence, a value pattern, and a motivation independent of those of the individual human beings claiming membership. Indeed, the very term "individual" has little place in the genuinely organic conception; the single human being becomes an integral part of a larger, and more meaningful, organism.

This approach or theory of the collectivity has been of some usefulness, both as a positive interpretation of certain qualities of actual collective units and as a normative political philosophy. The conception is, however, essentially opposed to the Western philosophical tradition in which the human individual is the primary philosophical entity. Moreover, since we propose to construct a theory of collective choice that has relevance to modern Western democracy, we shall reject at the outset any organic interpretation of collective activity.[1]

1. In this, we do not go as far as Arthur Bentley, who states that this organic conception is beyond social science. His comment, however, is worth noting: ". . . we can drag in the 'social whole,' and there we are out of the field of social science. Usually we shall find, on testing the 'social whole,' that it is merely the group tendency or demand represented by the man who talks of it, erected into the pretense of a universal demand of the society; and thereby, indeed, giving the lie to its own claims; for if it were such a comprehensive all-embracing interest of the society as a whole it would be an established condition, and not at all a subject of discussion by the man who calls it an interest of society as a whole. . . ." (Arthur Bentley, *The Process of Government* [Bloomington, Ind.: The Principia Press, 1935 (first published 1908)], p. 220.)

This rejection involves something more than the mere denial that the State exists as some *überindividuell* entity. For our purposes, the contribution of the German political philosophers lies in their extension of the organic conception to its logical extremities. A meaningful rejection of the conception must go beyond a refusal to accept the extreme versions of the theory. It must extend to the more controversial issues involving the idea of the "general will." Only some organic conception of society can postulate the emergence of a mystical general will that is derived independent of the decision-making process in which the political choices made by the separate individuals are controlling. Thus, many versions of idealist democracy are, at base, but variants on the organic conception. The grail-like search for some "public interest" apart from, and independent of, the separate interests of the individual participants in social choice is a familiar activity to be found among both the theorists and the practitioners of modern democracy.[2]

In quite similar fashion, we shall also reject any theory or conception of the collectivity which embodies the exploitation of a ruled by a ruling class. This includes the Marxist vision, which incorporates the polity as one means through which the economically dominant group imposes its will on the downtrodden. Other theories of class domination are equally foreign to our purposes. Any conception of State activity that divides the social group into the ruling class and the oppressed class, and that regards the political process as simply a means through which this class dominance is established and then preserved, must be rejected as irrelevant for the discussion which follows, quite independent of the question as to whether or not such conceptions may or may not have been useful for other purposes at other times and places. This conclusion holds whether the ruling class is supposed to consist of the Marxist owners of productive factors, the party aristocracy, or the like-minded majority.

The class-dominance approach to political activity is acutely related to our own in an unfortunate terminological sense. By historical accident, the class-dominance conception, in its Marxian variant, has come to be known as the "economic" conception or interpretation of State activity. The Marxian dialectic, with its emphasis on economic position as the fundamental source of class conflict, has caused the perfectly good word "economic" to be used in a

2. For a useful critique of the more "orthodox" approach, see David B. Truman, *The Governmental Process* (New York: Alfred A. Knopf, 1951), p. 50. See also Isaiah Berlin, *Two Concepts of Liberty* (Oxford: Clarendon Press, 1958).

wholly misleading manner. So much has this word been misused and abused here, that we have found it expedient to modify the original subtitle of this book from "An Economic Theory of Political Constitutions" to that currently used.

It seems futile to talk seriously of a "theory" of constitutions in a society other than that which is composed of free individuals—at least free in the sense that deliberate political exploitation is absent. This point will require further elaboration as we proceed, because (as later chapters will demonstrate) our analysis of decision processes reveals that certain rules will allow certain members of the group to use the structure to obtain differential advantage. However, it is precisely the recognition that the State may be used for such purposes which should prompt rational individuals to place constitutional restrictions on the use of the political process. Were it not for the properly grounded fear that political processes may be used for exploitative purposes, there would be little meaning and less purpose to constitutional restrictions.

Having rejected the organic conception of the State and also the idea of class domination, we are left with a purely individualist conception of the collectivity. Collective action is viewed as the action of individuals when they choose to accomplish purposes collectively rather than individually, and the government is seen as nothing more than the set of processes, the machine, which allows such collective action to take place. This approach makes the State into something that is constructed by men, an artifact. Therefore, it is, by nature, subject to change, perfectible. This being so, it should be possible to make meaningful statements about whether or not particular modifications in the set of constraints called government will make things "better" or "worse." To this extent, the approach taken in this book is rationalist.

Again we stand in danger of slipping into a logical trap. Since we have explicitly rejected the idea of an independent "public interest" as meaningful, how can criteria for "betterness" or "worseness" be chosen? Are we reduced so early to purely subjective evaluation?

We do not propose to introduce such subjective reference, and we do not employ any "social-welfare function" to bring some organic conception in by the back door. Analysis should enable us to determine under what conditions a particular individual in the group will judge a constitutional change to be an improvement; and, when all individuals are similarly affected, the rule of unanimity provides us with an extremely weak ethical criterion for "betterness," a criterion that is implicit in the individualist conception of the State itself. We do not propose to go beyond welfare judgments deducible from a rigorous application of the unanimity rule. Only if a specific constitutional change can be shown to be in the interest of all parties shall we judge such a change to be an "improvement." On all other possible changes in the constraints on human behavior, nothing can be said without the introduction of much stronger, and more questionable, ethical precepts.

What kinds of individuals inhabit our model society? As we emphasized in the preceding chapter, the separate individuals are assumed to have separate goals both in their private and in their social action. These goals may or may not be narrowly hedonistic. To what extent must the individuals be equal? The simplest model would be one which postulates that most of the individuals are, in fact, essentially equivalent in all external characteristics. A nation of small freeholders, perhaps roughly similar to the United States of 1787, would fit the model well.[3] Such a requirement, however, would be overly restrictive for our purposes. We need make no specific assumptions concerning the extent of equality or inequality in the external characteristics of individuals in the social group. We specify only that individuals are members of a social group in which collective action is guided by a set of rules, or one in which no such rules exist. In the latter case, unlikely as it may be in the real world, the rational choice of a set of rules would seem to take on high priority. Since this case is also simpler theoretically, a large part of our discussion will be devoted to it. The more normal situation in which there exists a set of collective decision rules, but in which the question of possible improvements in these rules remains an open one, will be discussed less frequently in any specific sense. Fortunately, however, the process involved in choosing an "optimal" set of decision rules, starting *de novo*, can be extended without difficulty to the discussion of improvements in existing rules.

In discussing an original constitution or improvements in an existing constitution, we shall adopt conceptual unanimity as a criterion. That is to say, we are concerned with examining proposals that will benefit each member of the social group. There are two reasons for adopting this criterion. First, only by this procedure can we avoid making interpersonal comparisons among separate individuals. Secondly, in discussing decision rules, we get into the familiar infinite regress if we adopt particular rules for adopting rules. To avoid

3. In his careful refutation of the Beard thesis, Robert E. Brown establishes the fact that economic differences, at least in terms of class, were not important in 1787. See Robert E. Brown, *Charles Beard and the Constitution* (Princeton: Princeton University Press, 1956).

this, we turn to the unanimity rule, since it is clear that if all members of a social group desire something done that is within their power, action will be taken regardless of the decision rule in operation.

It seems futile to discuss a "theory" of constitutions for free societies on any other assumptions than these. Unless the parties agree to participate in this way in the ultimate constitutional debate and to search for the required compromises needed to attain general agreement, no real constitution can be made. An imposed constitution that embodies the coerced agreement of some members of the social group is a wholly different institution from that which we propose to examine in this book.

CHAPTER 3

POLITICS AND THE ECONOMIC NEXUS

I do not, gentlemen, trust you.
—Gunning Bedford of Delaware, Federal Convention of 1787

. . . free government is founded in jealousy and not in confidence.
—Thomas Jefferson, Kentucky Resolutions of 1798

ECONOMIC THEORY AND ECONOMIC MAN

Our purpose in this book is to derive a preliminary theory of collective choice that is in some respects analogous to the orthodox economic theory of markets. The latter is useful for predictive purposes only to the extent that the individual participant, in the market relationship, is guided by economic interest. Through the use of this specific assumption about human motivation, scholars have been able to establish for economic theory a limited claim as the only positive social science. The most controversial aspect of our approach to collective-choice processes is the assumption that we shall make concerning the motivation of individual behavior. For this reason it seems useful to discuss this assumption as carefully as possible. We may begin by reviewing in some detail the companion assumption made by the economic theorist.

The first point to be noted is that economic theory does not depend for its validity or its applicability on the presence of the purely economic man. This man of fiction, who is motivated solely by individual self-interest in all aspects of his behavior, has always represented a caricature designed by those who have sought to criticize rather than to appreciate the genuine contribution that economic analysis can make, and has made, toward a better understanding of organized human activity. The man who enters the market relationship as consumer, laborer, seller of products, or buyer of services may do so for any number of reasons. The theory of markets postulates only that the relationship be *economic*, that the interest of his opposite number in the exchange be excluded from consideration. Wicksteed's principle of "non-Tuism" is the appropriate one, and his example of Paul's tent-making is illustrative. The accepted theory of markets can explain behavior and enable the economist to make certain meaningful predictions, so long as Paul does not take into account the interest of those for whom he works in repairing the tents. Paul may be acting out of love of God, the provincial church, friends, or self without affecting the operational validity of the theory of markets.[1]

It is also necessary to emphasize that economic theory does not try to explain all human behavior, even all of that which might be called "economic" in some normally accepted sense of this term. At best, the theory explains only one important part of human activity in this sphere. It examines one relationship among individuals in isolation. No economist, to our knowledge, has ever denied that exchange takes place which is not "economic." Some individual buyers deliberately pay to sellers higher prices than is necessary to secure the product or service purchased, and some sellers deliberately accept lower prices than buyers are willing to pay. The theory requires for its usefulness only the existence of the economic relation to a degree sufficient to make prediction and explanation possible. Furthermore, only if the economic motivation is sufficiently pervasive over the behavior of all participants in market activity can economic theory claim to have operational meaning.

Even if the economic forces are not predominant enough in human behavior to allow predictions to be made, the formal theory remains of some value in explaining *one* aspect of that behavior and in allowing the theorist to develop hypotheses that may be subjected to conceptual, if not actual, testing. Reduced to its barest essentials, the economic assumption is simply that the representative or the average individual, when confronted with real choice in exchange, will choose "more" rather than "less." The only important question concerns the strength of this acknowledged force. An equally logical theory could be constructed from the opposite assumption that the average individual will choose "less" rather than "more." However, to our knowledge, no one has proposed such a theory as being even remotely descriptive of reality.

ECONOMIC AND POLITICAL EXCHANGE

This brief review of the behavioral assumption that is implicit in orthodox economic theory serves as an introduction to the question that is vital to our analysis: What behavioral assumption is appropriate for a theory of collective choice? What principle analogous to Wicksteed's principle of "non-Tuism"

1. Philip H. Wicksteed, *The Common Sense of Political Economy* (London: Macmillan, 1910), chap. V.

can be introduced to help us to develop meaningful theorems concerning the behavior of human beings as they participate in collective as contrasted with private activity?

Both the economic relation and the political relation represent co-operation on the part of two or more individuals. The market and the State are both devices through which co-operation is organized and made possible. Men co-operate through exchange of goods and services in organized markets, and such co-operation implies mutual gain. The individual enters into an exchange relationship in which he furthers his own interest by providing some product or service that is of direct benefit to the individual on the other side of the transaction. At base, political or collective action under the individualistic view of the State is much the same. Two or more individuals find it mutually advantageous to join forces to accomplish certain common purposes. In a very real sense, they "exchange" inputs in the securing of the commonly shared output.

The familiar Crusoe-Friday model may be introduced for illustrative purposes, although its limitations must be fully acknowledged. Crusoe is the better fisherman; Friday the better climber of coconut palms. They will find it mutually advantageous, therefore, to specialize and to enter into exchange. Similarly, both men will recognize the advantages to be secured from constructing a fortress. Yet one fortress is sufficient for the protection of both. Hence they will find it mutually advantageous to enter into a political "exchange" and devote resources to the construction of the common good.

The most reasonable assumption about human behavior that is suggested by this simple model is that the same basic values motivate individuals in the two cases, although the narrowly conceived hedonistic values seem clearly to be more heavily weighted in economic than in political activity. Initially, however, we might assume that the representative or the average individual acts on the basis of the same over-all value scale when he participates in market activity and in political activity.

Political theorists seem rarely to have used this essentially economic approach to collective activity.[2] Their analyses of collective-choice processes have more often been grounded on the implicit assumption that the representative individual seeks not to maximize his own utility, but to find the

2. There are, of course, exceptions. See Arthur Bentley, *The Process of Government* (Bloomington, Ind.: The Principia Press, 1935 [first published 1908]). Also note especially Pendleton Herring, *The Politics of Democracy* (New York: W. W. Norton and Co., 1940), p. 31.

"public interest" or "common good."[3] Moreover, a significant factor in the popular support for socialism through the centuries has been the underlying faith that the shift of an activity from the realm of private to that of social choice involves the replacement of the motive of private gain by that of social good.[4] Throughout the ages the profit-seeker, the utility-maximizer, has found few friends among the moral and the political philosophers. In the last two centuries the pursuit of private gain has been tolerated begrudgingly in the private sector, with the alleged "exploitation" always carefully mentioned in passing. In the political sphere the pursuit of private gain by the individual participant has been almost universally condemned as "evil" by moral philosophers of many shades. No one seems to have explored carefully the implicit assumption that the individual must somehow shift his psychological and moral gears when he moves between the private and the social aspects of life. We are, therefore, placed in the somewhat singular position of having to defend the simple assumption that the *same* individual participates in both processes against the almost certain onslaught of the moralists.

THE PARADOX EXPLAINED[5]

How is the apparent paradox to be explained? Why has the conception of man been so different in the two closely related disciplines of economic and political theory?

The first answer suggested is that man is, in reality, many things at once.[6] In certain aspects of his behavior he is an individual utility-maximizer, in a reasonably narrow hedonistic sense, and the classical economist's conception of him is quite applicable. In other aspects man is adaptive and associates or

3. For an illuminating discussion of the many ambiguities in the conception of the "public interest," see C. W. Casinelli, "The Concept of the Public Interest," *Ethics*, LXIX (1958), 48–61.

4. The following criticism of this faith seems especially interesting: "Those concerned in government are still human beings. They still have private interests to serve and interests of special groups, those of the family, clique, or class to which they belong." (John Dewey, *The Public and Its Problems* [New York: Henry Holt, 1927], p. 76.)

5. To our knowledge, the only specific recent discussion of this paradox is to be found in Henry Oliver's paper, "Attitudes toward Market and Political Self-Interest," *Ethics*, LXV (1955), 171–80.

6. For an elaboration of this point, see Frank H. Knight, *Intelligence and Democratic Action* (Cambridge: Harvard University Press, 1960). See also John Laird, *The Device of Government* (Cambridge: Cambridge University Press, 1944).

identifies himself readily with the larger organizational group of which he forms a part, including the political group. By the nature of the constraints imposed upon the individual in each case, a representative or typical man may, in fact, often switch gears when he moves from one realm of activity to another.[7] As the following chapter will demonstrate, there are reasons to suggest that the assumption of individual utility maximization will not be as successful in pointing toward meaningful propositions about collective choice as about market choice. However, the recognition that man is, indeed, a paradoxical animal should not suggest that an "economic" model of collective choice is without value. In any case, such a model should be helpful in explaining *one* aspect of political behavior; and only after the theory has been constructed and its propositions compared with data of the real world can the basic validity of the motivational assumption be ascertained.

The real explanation of the paradox must be sought elsewhere. Collective activity has not been conceived in an economic dimension, and an analysis of the behavior of individuals in terms of an economic calculus has been, understandably, neglected.[8] This emphasis on the noneconomic aspects of individual behavior in collective choice may be partially explained, in its turn, by the historical development of the modern theories of democracy. Both the theory of democracy and the theory of the market economy are products of the Enlightenment, and, for the eighteenth-century philosophers, these two orders of human activity were not to be discussed separately. The democratic State was conceived as that set of constraints appropriate to a society which managed its economic affairs largely through a competitive economic order, in which the economic interests of individuals were acknowledged to be paramount in driving men to action. The collective action required was conceived in terms of the laying down of *general* rules, applicable to all individuals and groups in the social order. In the discussion of these general rules, serious and important differences in the economic interests of separate individuals and groups were not expected to occur. Differences were foreseen

7. For a discussion of the contrast between economic and sociopsychological theories and their implied assumptions about human motivation, see Herbert Simon, *Models of Man* (New York: John Wiley and Sons, 1957), esp. pp. 165–69.

8. It is interesting to note that even when he mentions the possibility of developing a maximizing theory of political behavior in democracy, Robert A. Dahl does not conceive this in terms of maximizing individual utilities. Instead he speaks of maximizing some "state of affairs" (such as political equality) as a value or goal, and asks: "What conditions are necessary to attain the maximum achievement of this goal?" See Robert A. Dahl, *A Preface to Democratic Theory* (Chicago: University of Chicago Press, 1956), p. 2.

and the necessity for compromises recognized, but these were not usually interpreted in terms of differences in economic interest.

As the governments of Western countries grew in importance, and as economic interests began to use the democratic political process during the nineteenth century to further partisan goals (as exemplified by the tariff legislation in the United States), the continuing failure of political theory to fill this gap became more difficult to explain; and, as more and more areas of human activity formerly organized through private markets have been shifted to the realm of collective choice in this century, the lacuna in political theory becomes obvious. In the context of a limited government devoted to the passage of general legislation applying, by and large, to all groups, the development of an individualist and economic theory of collective choice is perhaps not of major import. However, when the governmental machinery directly uses almost one-third of the national product, when special interest groups clearly recognize the "profits" to be made through political action, and when a substantial proportion of all legislation exerts measurably differential effects on the separate groups of the population, an economic theory can be of great help in pointing toward some means through which these conflicting interests may be ultimately reconciled.

An individualist theory of collective choice implies, almost automatically, that the basic decision-making rules be re-examined in the light of the changing role assumed by government. There should be little reason to expect that constitutional rules developed in application to the passage of general legislation would provide an appropriate framework for the enactment of legislation that has differential or discriminatory impact on separate groups of citizens. Perhaps largely because they have not adopted this conceptual approach to collective choice, many modern students have found it necessary to rely on moral principle as perhaps the most important means of preventing the undue exploitation of one group by another through the political process. To many scholars the pressure group, which is organized to promote a particular interest through governmental action, must be an aberration; logrolling and pork-barrel legislation must be exceptions to normal activity; special tax exemptions and differential tax impositions are scarcely noted. These characteristic institutions of modern democracies demand theoretical explanation, an explanation that the main body of political theory seems unable to provide.[9]

9. The Bentley "school" represents, of course, the major exception. The important recent work of David B. Truman, *The Governmental Process* (New York: Alfred A. Knopf, 1951), must be especially noted. Truman attempts to construct a theory of representative democracy that

The Scholastic philosophers looked upon the tradesman, the merchant, and the moneylender in much the same way that many modern intellectuals look upon the political pressure group. Adam Smith and those associated with the movement he represented were partially successful in convincing the public at large that, within the limits of certain general rules of action, the self-seeking activities of the merchant and the moneylender tend to further the general interests of everyone in the community. An acceptable theory of collective choice can perhaps do something similar in pointing the way toward those rules for collective choice-making, the constitution, under which the activities of political tradesmen can be similarly reconciled with the interests of all members of the social group.

ECONOMIC MOTIVATION AND POLITICAL POWER

Some modern political theorists have discussed the collective-choice process on the basis of the assumption that the individual tries to maximize his power over other individuals. In at least one specific instance, the individual who seeks to maximize power in the collective process has been explicitly compared with the individual who seeks to maximize utility in his market activity.[10] Here it is recognized, however, that there exists no real evidence that men do, in fact, seek power over their fellows, as such.[11]

Superficially, the power-maximizer in the collective-choice process and the utility-maximizer in the market process may seem to be country cousins, and a theory of collective choice based on the power-maximization hypothesis may appear to be closely related to that which we hope to develop in this essay. Such an inference would be quite misleading. The two approaches are different in a fundamental philosophical sense. The economic approach, which assumes man to be a utility-maximizer in both his market and his political activity, does not require that one individual increase his own utility at the expense of other individuals. This approach incorporates political activity as a particular form of *exchange;* and, as in the market relation, mutual gains to all parties are ideally expected to result from the collective relation. In a

---

specifically incorporates the activities of interest groups. He does not examine the economic implications of the theory.

10. See William H. Riker, "A Test of the Adequacy of the Power Index," *Behavioral Science*, IV (1959), 120–31; Robert A. Dahl, "The Concept of Power," *Behavioral Science*, II (1957), 201–15.

11. Riker, "A Test of the Adequacy of the Power Index," 121.

very real sense, therefore, political action is viewed essentially as a means through which the "power" of all participants may be increased, if we define "power" as the ability to command things that are desired by men. To be justified by the criteria employed here, collective action must be advantageous to all parties. In the more precise terminology of modern game theory, the utility or economic approach suggests that the political process, taken in the abstract, may be interpreted as a positive-sum game.

The power-maximizing approach, by contrast, must interpret collective choice-making as a zero-sum game. The power of the one individual to control the action or behavior of another cannot be increased simultaneously for both individuals in a two-man group. What one man gains, the other must lose; mutual gains from "trade" are not possible in this conceptual framework. The political process is in this way converted into something which is diametrically opposed to the economic relation, and into something which cannot, by any stretch of the imagination, be considered analogous.[12] The contributions of game theory seem to have been introduced into political theory largely through this power-maximizing hypothesis.[13]

MADISONIAN DEMOCRACY AND THE ECONOMIC APPROACH

Robert A. Dahl, in his incisive and provocative critique, has converted the Madisonian theory of democracy (which is substantially embodied in the American constitutional structure) into something akin to the power-maximizer approach discussed above.[14] On this interpretation, Dahl is successful in showing that the theory contains many ambiguities and inconsis-

12. Bruno Leoni has questioned this discussion of the power approach. In his view, individuals entering into a political relationship exchange power, each over the other. This "exchange of power" approach seems to have much in common with what we have called the "economic" approach to political process.

13. This discussion is not to suggest that in modern political process, as it operates, elements that are characteristic of the zero-sum game are wholly absent. A single politician or a political party engaged in a struggle to win an election to office can properly be considered as being engaged in a zero-sum game, and in an analysis of this struggle the power-maximizing hypothesis can yield fruitful results, as Riker and others have demonstrated. The point to be emphasized is that our "economic" model concentrates, not on the squabble among politicians, but on the general co-operative "political" process (which includes the game among politicians as a component part) through which voters may increase total utility.

14. Robert A. Dahl, *A Preface to Democratic Theory*, esp. chap. 1.

tencies. It is not our purpose here to discuss the interpretation of Madison's doctrine. What does seem appropriate is to point out that the Madisonian theory, either that which is explicitly contained in Madison's writings or that which is embodied in the American constitutional system, may be compared with the normative theory that emerges from the economic approach. When this comparison is made, a somewhat more consistent logical basis for many of the existing constitutional restraints may be developed. We do not propose to make such a comparison explicitly in this book. The normative theory of the constitution that emerges from our analysis is derived solely from the initial individualistic postulates, the behavioral assumptions, and the predictions of the operation of rules. The determination of the degree of correspondence between this theory and the theory implicit in the American Constitution is left to the reader. Insofar as such correspondence emerges, however, this would at least suggest that Madison and the other Founding Fathers may have been somewhat more cognizant of the economic motivation in political choice-making than many of their less practical counterparts who have developed the written body of American democratic theory.

There is, in fact, evidence which suggests that Madison himself assumed that men do follow a policy of utility maximization in collective as well as private behavior and that his desire to limit the power of both majorities and minorities was based, to some extent at least, on a recognition of this motivation. His most familiar statements are to be found in the famous essay, *The Federalist No. 10*, in which he developed the argument concerning the possible dangers of factions. A careful reading of this paper suggests that Madison clearly recognized that individuals and groups would try to use the processes of government to further their own differential or partisan interests. His numerous examples of legislation concerning debtor-creditor relations, commercial policy, and taxation suggest that perhaps a better understanding of Madison's own conception of democratic process may be achieved by examining carefully the implications of the economic approach to human behavior in collective choice.

ECONOMIC MOTIVATION AND ECONOMIC DETERMINISM

The facts of intellectual history require a digression at this point for a brief discussion of a critical error that may have served to stifle much potentially productive effort in political theory. Charles A. Beard supported his "economic" interpretation of the American Constitution in part by reference to Madison's *The Federalist No. 10*. Beard's work and much of the critical discussion that it has aroused since its initial appearance in 1913 seem to have been marked by the failure to distinguish *two* quite different approaches to political activity, both of which may be called, in some sense, *economic*. The first approach, which has been discussed in this chapter as the basis for the theory of collective choice to be developed in this book, assumes that the individual, as he participates in collective decisions, is guided by the desire to maximize his own utility and that different individuals have different utility functions. The second approach assumes that the individual is motivated by his position or class status in the production process. The social class in which the individual finds himself is prior to, and determines, the interest of the individual in political activity. In one sense, the second approach is the opposite of the first since it requires that, on many occasions, the individual must act contrary to his own economic interest in order to further the interest of the social class or group to which he belongs.

Beard attempted to base his interpretation of the formation of the American Constitution on the second, essentially the Marxist, approach, and to explain the activities of the Founding Fathers in terms of class interests. As Brown has shown, Beard's argument has little factual support, in spite of its widespread acceptance by American social scientists.[15] The point that has been largely overlooked is that it remains perfectly appropriate to assume that men are motivated by utility considerations while rejecting the economic determinism implicit in the whole Marxian stream of thought. Differences in utility functions stem from differences in taste as much as anything else. The class status of the individual in the production process is one of the less important determinants of genuine economic interest. The phenomenon of textile unions and textile firms combining to bring political pressure for the prohibition of Japanese imports is much more familiar in the current American scene than any general across-the-board political activity of labor, capital, or landed interests.

The most effective way of illustrating the distinction between the individualist-economic approach and economic determinism or the class approach (a distinction that is vital to our purpose in forestalling uninformed criticism) is to repeat that the first approach may be used to develop a theory of consti-

15. Robert E. Brown, *Charles Beard and the Constitution* (Princeton: Princeton University Press, 1956).

tutions, even on the restrictive assumption that individuals are equivalent in all external characteristics.

We are not, of course, concerned directly with the history of the existing American Constitution or with the integrity of historians and the veracity of historical scholarship. This brief discussion of the confusion surrounding the Beard thesis has been necessary in order to preclude, in advance, a possibly serious misinterpretation of our efforts.

IN POSITIVE DEFENSE

This chapter will be concluded with a somewhat more positive defense of the use of the individualist-economic or the utility-maximizing assumption about behavior in the political process. There are two separate strands of such a defense—strands that are complementary to each other. The first might be called an ethical-economic defense of the utility-maximizing assumption, while the second is purely empirical.

The ethical-economic argument requires the initial acceptance of a skeptical or pessimistic view of human nature. Self-interest, broadly conceived, is recognized to be a strong motivating force in all human activity; and human action, if not bounded by ethical or moral restraints, is assumed more naturally to be directed toward the furtherance of individual or private interest. This view of human nature is, of course, essentially that taken by the utilitarian philosophers. From this, it follows directly that the individual human being must undergo some effort in restraining his "passions" and that he must act in accordance with ethical or moral principles whenever social institutions and mores dictate some departure from the pursuit of private interests. Such effort, as with all effort, is scarce: that is to say, it is economic. Therefore, it should be economized upon in its employment. Insofar as possible, institutions and legal constraints should be developed which will order the pursuit of private gain in such a way as to make it consistent with, rather than contrary to, the attainment of the objectives of the group as a whole. On these psychological and ethical foundations, the theory of markets or the competitive organization of economic activity is based. For the same reason, if it is possible to develop a theory of the political order (a theory of constitutions) which will point toward a further minimization of the scarce resources involved in the restraint of private interest, it is incumbent on the student of social processes to examine the results of models which do assume the pursuit of private interest.

As is true in so many instances, Sir Dennis Robertson has expressed this point perhaps better than anyone else:

> There exists in every human breast an inevitable state of tension between the aggressive and acquisitive instincts and the instincts of benevolence and self-sacrifice. It is for the preacher, lay or clerical, to inculcate the ultimate duty of subordinating the former to the latter. It is the humbler, and often the invidious, role of the economist to help, so far as he can, in reducing the preacher's task to manageable dimensions. It is his function to emit a warning bark if he sees courses of action being advocated or pursued which will increase unnecessarily the inevitable tension between self-interest and public duty; and to wag his tail in approval of courses of action which will tend to keep the tension low and tolerable.[16]

Once it is recognized that the institutions of collective choice-making are also variables that may be modified in important ways so as to change the tension of which Robertson speaks, the word "economist" in the citation can be replaced by the more general "social scientist." If, as Robertson continues a few pages later, "that scarce resource Love . . ." is, in fact, "the most precious thing in the world,"[17] there could be no stronger ethical argument in support of an attempt to minimize the necessity of its use in the ordering of the political activity of men.

The ultimate defense of the economic-individualist behavioral assumption must be empirical. If, through the employment of this assumption, we are able to develop hypotheses about collective choice which will aid in the explanation and subsequent understanding of observable institutions, nothing more need be thrown into the balance. However, implicit in the extension of the behavioral assumption used in economic theory to an analysis of politics is the acceptance of a methodology that is not frequently encountered in political science. Through the use of the utility-maximizing assumption, we shall construct logical models of the various choice-making processes. Such models are themselves artifacts; they are invented for the explicit purpose of explaining facts of the real world. However, prior to some conceptual testing, there is no presumption that any given model is superior to any other that might be chosen from among the infinitely large set of models within the

16. D. H. Robertson, "What Does the Economist Economize?" *Economic Commentaries* (London: Staples, 1956), p. 148.

17. Ibid., p. 154.

possibility of human imagination. The only final test of a model lies in its ability to assist in understanding real phenomena.

Models may be divided into three parts: assumptions, analysis, and conclusions. Assumptions may or may not be "descriptive" or "realistic," as these words are ordinarily used. In many cases the "unrealism" of the assumptions causes the models to be rejected before the conclusions are examined and tested. Fundamentally, the only test for "realism" of assumptions lies in the applicability of the conclusions. For this reason the reader who is critical of the behavioral assumption employed here is advised to reserve his judgment of our models until he has checked some of the real-world implications of the model against his own general knowledge of existing political institutions.

It is necessary to distinguish between two possible interpretations and applications of the general model embodying the assumption that the individual participant in collective decisions attempts to maximize his own utility. In the first, we need place no restrictions on the characteristics of individual utility functions; the model requires only that these utility functions differ as among different individuals (that is to say, different persons desire different things via the political process). This is all that is required to develop an internally consistent praxiological theory of political choice, and through the employment of this theory we may be able to explain something of the characteristics of the decision-making process itself. With this extensive model, however, we cannot develop hypotheses about the results of political choice in any conceptually observable or measurable dimension.

To take this additional step, we must move to the second interpretation mentioned above, which is a more narrowly conceived submodel. In this, we must place certain restrictions on individual utility functions, restrictions which are precisely analogous to those introduced in economic theory: that is to say, we must assume that individuals will, on the average, choose "more" rather than "less" when confronted with the opportunity for choice in a political process, with "more" and "less" being defined in terms of measurable economic position. From this model we may develop fully operational hypotheses which, if not refuted by real-world observations, lend support not only to the assumptions of the restricted submodel but also support the assumptions implicit in the more general praxiological model.

It cannot be emphasized too strongly that the moral arguments against man's pursuit of private gain, whether in the market place or in the collective-choice process, must be quite sharply distinguished from the analysis of individual behavior. Orthodox social and political theorists do not always appear to have kept this distinction clearly in mind. Norms *for* behavior have often been substituted for testable hypotheses *about* behavior. We do not propose to take a position on the moral question regarding what variables should enter into the individual's utility function when he participates in social choice, nor do we propose to go further and explore the immensely difficult set of problems concerned with the ultimate philosophical implications of the utilitarian conception of human nature. As we conceive our task, it is primarily one of analysis. We know that one interpretation of human activity suggests that men do, in fact, seek to maximize individual utilities when they participate in political decisions and that individual utility functions differ. We propose to analyze the results of various choice-making rules on the basis of this behavioral assumption, and we do so independent of the moral censure that might or might not be placed on such individual self-seeking action.

The model which incorporates this behavioral assumption and the set of conceptually testable hypotheses that may be derived from the model can, at best, explain only one aspect of collective choice. Moreover, even if the model proves to be useful in explaining an important element of politics, it does not imply that all individuals act in accordance with the behavioral assumption made or that any one individual acts in this way at all times. Just as the theory of markets can explain only some fraction of all private economic action, the theory of collective choice can explain only some undetermined fraction of collective action. However, so long as some part of all individual behavior in collective choice-making is, in fact, motivated by utility maximization, and so long as the identification of the individual with the group does not extend to the point of making *all* individual utility functions identical, an *economic-individualist* model of political activity should be of some positive worth.

CHAPTER 4

INDIVIDUAL RATIONALITY IN SOCIAL CHOICE

INDIVIDUAL AND COLLECTIVE RATIONALITY

A useful theory of human action, be it positive or normative in content and purpose, must postulate some rationality on the part of decision-making units. Choices must not only be directed toward the achievement of some objective or goal; the decision-making units must also be able to take such action as will assure the attainment of the goal. Immediately upon the introduction of the word "rationality," we encounter questions of definition and meaning. We shall try to clarify some of these below, but the first practical step is to specify precisely the decision-making unit to which the behavioral characteristic, rationality, is to apply. When we speak of private action, no difficulty is presented at this stage. The decision-making unit is the individual, who both makes the choices and constitutes the entity for whom the choices are made. A problem arises, however, when we consider collective action. Are we to consider the collectivity as the decision-making unit, and therefore, are we to scale or order collective choices against some postulated social goal or set of goals? Or, by contrast, are we to consider the individual participant in collective choice as the only real decision-maker and, as a result, discuss rational behavior only in terms of the individual's own goal achievement? It is evident from what has been said before that we shall adopt the second of these approaches. The prevalence of the first approach in much of modern literature suggests, nevertheless, that a brief comparison of these two conceptions of rationality may be helpful.

Except for the acceptance of some organic conception of the social group and its activity, it is difficult to understand why group decisions should be directed toward the achievement of any specific end or goal. Under the individualistic postulates, group decisions represent outcomes of certain agreed-upon rules for choice after the separate individual choices are fed into the process. There seems to be no reason why we should expect these final outcomes to exhibit any sense of order which might, under certain definitions of rationality, be said to reflect rational social action.[1] Nor is there reason to suggest that rationality, even if it could be achieved through appropriate modification of the rules, would be "desirable." Rational social action, in this sense, would seem to be neither a positive prediction of the results that might emerge from group activity nor a normative criterion against which decision-making rules may be "socially" ordered.

A somewhat different conception of social rationality may be introduced which appears to avoid some of these difficulties. The social scientist may explicitly postulate certain goals for the group, either upon the basis of his own value judgments or upon some more objective attempt at determining commonly shared goals for all members of the group. He may then define *rational* collective action as that which is consistent with the achievement of these goals.[2] Conceptually, it is possible to discuss collective decision-making institutions in this way; and the approach may prove of some value if the goals postulated do, in fact, represent those shared widely throughout the group, and if there is also some commonly shared or accepted means of reconciling conflicts in the attainment of the different goals or ends for the group. Note that this approach starts from the presumption that the goals of collective action are commonly shared. There is little room for the recognition that different individuals and groups seek different things through the political process. The approach offers little guidance toward an analysis of political action when significant individual and group differences are incorporated in the model.

In this book we shall not discuss social rationality or rational social action as such. We start from the presumption that only the individual chooses, and that rational behavior, if introduced at all, can only be discussed meaningfully in terms of individual action. This, in itself, does not get us very far, and it will be necessary to define carefully what we shall mean by rational individual behavior.

1. Arrow seems to suggest, implicitly, that such social rationality is an appropriate criterion against which decision-making rules may be judged. See his *Social Choice and Individual Values* (New York: John Wiley and Sons, 1951). For a more extensive critique of this aspect of the Arrow work along the lines developed here, see James M. Buchanan, "Social Choice, Democracy, and Free Markets," *Journal of Political Economy*, LXII (1954), 114–23. Reprinted in *Fiscal Theory and Political Economy: Selected Essays* (Chapel Hill: University of North Carolina Press, 1960).

2. This is the approach taken by Robert A. Dahl and Charles E. Lindblom. See their *Politics, Economics, and Welfare* (New York: Harper and Bros., 1953).

INDIVIDUAL RATIONALITY IN MARKET CHOICE

It will be helpful to review the parallel treatment of individual rationality that is incorporated in orthodox economic theory. The economist has not gone very far when he says that the representative consumer maximizes utility. Individual utility functions differ, and the economist is unable to "read" these functions from some position of omniscience. To judge whether or not individual behavior is "rational" or "irrational," the economist must try first of all to place some general minimal restrictions on the shapes of utility functions. If he is successful in this effort, he may then test the implications of his hypotheses against observed behavior.

Specifically, the modern economist assumes as working hypotheses that the average individual is able to rank or to order all alternative combinations of goods and services that may be placed before him and that this ranking is transitive.[3] Behavior of the individual is said to be "rational" when the individual chooses "more" rather than "less" and when he is consistent in his choices. When faced with a choice between two bundles, one of which includes more of one good and less of another than the bundle with which it is compared, the hypothesis of diminishing marginal substitutability or diminishing relative marginal utility is introduced. Observed market behavior of individuals does not refute these hypotheses; consumers will choose bundles containing more of everything, other things remaining the same; choices are not obviously inconsistent with each other; and consumers are observed to spend their incomes on a wide range of goods and services. With these working hypotheses about the shapes of individual utility functions, which are not refuted by testing, the economist is able to develop further propositions of relevance. In this way, the first law of demand and all of its implications are derived.

INDIVIDUAL RATIONALITY AND COLLECTIVE CHOICE

As suggested at an earlier point, all collective action may be converted to an economic dimension for the purposes of our model. Once this step is taken, we may extend the underlying economic conception of individual ra-

3. Several recent attempts have been made to test this transitivity assumption directly through experimental processes. Some results seem to undermine the validity of the transitivity assumption; others to confirm its usage. We note here only that some such assumption is required for any theory of human organization. If intransitivity (instead of transitivity) in individual preference patterns is assumed to characterize behavior, the degree of order that may be observed in either economic or political relations becomes wholly inexplicable.

tionality to collective as well as to market choices. Specifically, this involves the working hypotheses that the choosing individual can rank the alternatives of collective as well as of market choice and that this ranking will be transitive. In other words, the individual is assumed to be able to choose from among the alternative results of collective action that which stands highest in the rank order dictated by his own utility function. This may be put in somewhat more general and familiar terms if we say that the individual is assumed to be able to rank the various bundles of public or collective "goods" in the same way that he ranks private goods. Moreover, when broadly considered, all proposals for collective action may be converted into conceptually quantifiable dimensions in terms of the value and the cost of the "public goods" expected to result. We may also extend the idea of diminishing marginal rates of substitution to the collective-choice sector. This hypothesis suggests that there is a diminishing marginal rate of substitution between public and private goods, on the one hand, and among the separate "public goods" on the other.

Again it is necessary to distinguish the two separate interpretations of the "economic" approach. Individual behavior can be discussed in economic dimensions, and the processes through which differences in individual utility functions become reconciled may be predicted, without any assumptions being made concerning the externally observable results of such behavior. However, if more "positive" results are to be predicted, some specific meaning to terms such as "more collective activity" must be introduced, a meaning which will allow alternative possible results to be compared quantitatively.

The economist does, normally, attribute precise meaning to the terms "more" and "less." Moreover, if a similar model of rational behavior is extended to the collective-choice process, we are able to derive propositions about individual behavior that are parallel to those contained in economic theory. If the hypotheses are valid, the representative individual should, when confronted with relevant alternatives, choose more "public goods" when the "price" of these is lowered, other relevant things remaining the same. In more familiar terms, this states that on the average the individual will vote for "more" collective activity when the taxes he must pay are reduced, other things being equal. On the contrary, if the tax rate is increased, the individual will, if allowed to choose, select a lower level of collective activity. In a parallel way, income-demand propositions can be derived. If the income of the individual goes up and his tax bill does not, he will tend to choose to have more "public goods."

Simple propositions such as these, which will be intuitively acceptable to most economists, can be quite helpful in suggesting the full implications of the behavioral assumptions concerning individual participation in social-choice processes. However, such propositions may be extremely misleading if they are generalized too quickly and applied to the collectivity as a unit rather than to the individuals. To make such an extension or generalization without having first confronted the issue of crossing the "bridge" between individual and group choice seems likely to lead, and has led, to serious errors. Two points must be made. First, "public goods" can only be defined in terms of individual evaluations. If an individual is observed to vote in favor of a public outlay for municipal policemen, it follows that (assuming normal behavior) he would vote in favor of the municipality hiring more policemen were the wage rate for policemen to be reduced. On the other hand, another individual may not consider additional policemen necessary. The second and closely related point is that group decisions are the results of individual decisions when the latter are combined through a specific rule of decision-making. To say (as is quite commonly said by scholars of public finance) that a greater amount of collective activity will be demanded as national income expands represents the most familiar extension of this "first law of demand for public goods." In fact, if *all* individuals in the social group should happen to be in full individual equilibrium regarding amounts of public and private goods, then an increase in over-all income would suggest that individuals, acting rationally, would choose more collective as well as more private goods provided only that both sets belong to the "superior" good category. The decision-making rules under which collective choices are organized, however, will rarely operate in such a way that all members of the group will attain a position of freely chosen equilibrium. In this case, little can be said about the implications of the individual rationality assumptions and the derived propositions for collective decisions. Before anything of this nature can be discussed properly, the decision rules must be thoroughly analyzed.

The price-demand and the income-demand propositions, which are derivative from the individual-rationality hypotheses directly, apply only to the behavior of the individual. Therefore, they cannot be tested directly by the *collective* decisions which are made as a result of certain decision-making rules. This is in contrast to the situation in the market where the first law of demand and the behavioral assumptions on which it rests can be tested, within reasonable limits, against observed results. This is because of the fact that, in the market, individual choice makes up a necessary part of group choice. Individual decisions cannot be made that are explicitly contrary to decisions reflected in the movement of market variables. The "first law of demand for public goods" and similar propositions cannot be directly tested by observation of the actions of the collective unit because such results would reflect individual choices only as these are embodied in the decision-making rules. Results of collective action do not directly indicate anything about the behavior of any particular individual or even about the behavior of the average or representative individual. Therefore, we do not possess at this preliminary stage of our analysis the same degree of support for our behavioral assumptions regarding individual action in collective choice that the economist possesses. In the later development of some of our models, we hope to suggest certain implications which, when checked against real-world observations, will not be refuted, thereby providing confirmation for our original assumptions.

LIMITATIONS ON INDIVIDUAL RATIONALITY

Rational action requires the acceptance of some end and also the ability to choose the alternatives which will lead toward goal achievement. The consequences of individual choice must be known under conditions of perfect certainty for the individual to approach fully rational behavior. In analyzing market choices, in which there normally is a one-to-one correspondence between individual action and the results of that action, the certainty assumption is one that may be accepted as being useful without doing violence to the inherent structure of the theoretical model. This remains true despite the recognition that market choices are made in the face of uncertainties of various kinds.

In analyzing the behavior of the individual in the political process, there is an important element of uncertainty present that cannot be left out of account. No longer is there the one-to-one correspondence between individual choice and final action. In the case of any specific decision-making rule for the group, the individual participant has no way of knowing the final outcome, the social choice, at the time he makes his own contribution to this outcome. This particular element of uncertainty in political choice seems initially to restrict or limit quite sharply the usefulness of any theoretical model that is based on the assumption of rational individual behavior. It is difficult even to define rational individual behavior under uncertainty, although much recent effort has been devoted to this problem. Furthermore, even if an acceptable definition of rational choice under uncertainty could be made, the extension of the behavioral hypotheses to participation in group choice would make even conceptual testing almost impossible.

If our task were solely that of analyzing the results of individual behavior in isolated and unique collective choices, this uncertainty factor would loom as a severe limitation against any theory of collective choice. However, this limitation is reduced in significance to some extent when it is recognized that collective choice is a continuous process, with each unique decision representing only one link in a long-time chain of social action. Reflection on this fact, which is one of the most important bases of the analysis of this book, suggests that the uncertainty facing the individual participant in political decisions may have been substantially overestimated in the traditional concentration on unique events.

When uncertainty exists due to the impossibility of reciprocal-behavior prediction among individuals, it may be reduced only by agreement among these individuals. When the interests of the individuals are mutually conflicting, agreement can be attained only through some form of exchange or trade. Moreover, if side payments are not introduced, trade is impossible within the limits of the single decision-making act. However, if the vote of the individual in a single act of collective choice is recognized as being subject to exchange for the votes of other individuals in later choices, agreement becomes possible and, insofar as such agreement takes place, uncertainty is eliminated. So long as the decision-making rules do not dictate the expediency of such exchange among *all* participants in the group, this fundamental sort of uncertainty must, of course, remain. Nevertheless, the usefulness of rational-behavior models in analyzing political choice is limited to a somewhat lesser extent than might otherwise seem to be the case.[4]

A second and important reason why individuals may be expected to be somewhat less rational in collective than in private choices lies in the difference in the degree of responsibility for final decisions. The responsibility for any given private decision rests squarely on the chooser. The benefits and the costs are tangible, and the individual tends to consider more carefully the alternatives before him. In collective choice, by contrast, there can never be so precise a relationship between individual action and result, even if the result is correctly predicted. The chooser-voter will, of course, recognize the existence of both the benefit and the cost side of any proposed public action, but neither his own share in the benefits nor his own share in the costs can be so readily estimated as in the comparable market choices. Uncertainty elements of this sort must enter due to the necessary ignorance of the individual who

4. As we shall emphasize later in the book, the process of bargaining, of attaining agreement, itself serves to reduce significantly the range of uncertainty that may exist before bargaining.

participates in group choice. In addition to the uncertainty factor, which can be readily understood to limit the range of rational calculus, the single individual loses the sense of decision-making responsibility that is inherent in private choice. Secure in the knowledge that, regardless of his own action, social or collective decisions affecting him will be made, the individual is offered a greater opportunity either to abstain altogether from making a positive choice or to choose without having considered the alternatives carefully. In a real sense, private action forces the individual to exercise his freedom by making choices compulsory. These choices will not be made for him. The consumer who refrains from entering the market place will starve unless he hires a professional shopper. Moreover, once having been forced to make choices, he is likely to be somewhat more rational in evaluating the alternatives before him.

For these reasons, and for certain others that may become apparent as the analysis is developed, we should not expect models based on the assumption of rational individual behavior to yield as fruitful a result when applied to collective-choice processes as similar models have done when applied to market or economic choices. However, this comparatively weaker expectation provides no reason at all for refraining from the development of such models. As we have already suggested, all logical models are limited in their ability to assist in explaining behavior.

PART II

THE REALM OF SOCIAL CHOICE

CHAPTER 5

THE ORGANIZATION OF HUMAN ACTIVITY

So in all human affairs one notices, if one examines them closely, that it is impossible to remove one inconvenience without another emerging. . . . Hence in all discussions one should consider which alternative involves fewer inconveniences and should adopt this as the better course; for one never finds any issue that is clear cut and not open to question.
—Machiavelli, *The Discourses*

Is there a logical economic rationalization or explanation for the emergence of democratic political institutions? On the basis of our individualistic assumptions about human motivation can we "explain" the adoption of a political constitution? If so, what general form will this constitution take? Questions such as these have rarely been discussed carefully.[1]

If no collective action is required, there will be no need for a political constitution. Therefore, before discussing the form which such a constitution might assume, we must examine the bases for social or collective action. When will a society composed of free and rational utility-maximizing individuals choose to undertake action collectively rather than privately? Or, to make the question more precise, when will an individual member of the group find it advantageous to enter into a "political" relationship with his fellows?

THE "COSTS" APPROACH TO COLLECTIVE ACTION

The individual will find it profitable to explore the possibility of organizing an activity collectively when he expects that he may increase his utility. Individual utility may be increased by collective action in two distinct ways. First, collective action may eliminate some of the *external costs* that the private actions of other individuals impose upon the individual in question. The city policeman keeps the thief from your door. Secondly, collective action may be

1. An important exception is William J. Baumol's *Welfare Economics and the Theory of the State* (Cambridge: Harvard University Press, 1952). Starting from behavioral assumptions similar to those employed here, Baumol examines the extension of state or collective activity. He does not explore the economic aspects of the constitutional problems that are introduced in the choices among alternative collective decision-making rules.

required to secure some additional or *external benefits* that cannot be secured through purely private behavior. Individual protection against fire may not be profitable. If they are somewhat more broadly considered, these apparently distinct means of increasing individual utility become identical. Whether a specific collective effort is viewed as reducing external costs imposed on the individual or as producing an external benefit depends solely on the presumed threshold between costs and benefits. The question becomes precisely analogous to the age-old utilitarian one about the threshold between pain and pleasure.

An orthodox or standard approach would perhaps be that of taking the situation characterized by no collective action as the zero or starting point and then comparing the expected benefits from collective activity with the expected costs, the latter being measured in terms of production sacrificed in the private sector. This approach would have the advantage of being familiar to the economist who tends, professionally, to think in benefit-cost terms. The orthodox approach does not, however, lend itself well to a comparative evaluation of different methods of organizing activity. If we wish to compare collective organization with private organization, and especially if we want to analyze various collective decision-making rules, we need, even at the conceptual level, some means of comparing the *net* direct gains or the *net* direct costs of collective action with the *costs of organization* itself, that is, with *the costs of organizing decisions collectively*, a key variable in our analysis. It would be possible to use net direct gains, which could be defined as the difference between the benefits expected from collective action and the direct costs. On this basis, we could construct a "gains" or "net benefit" function, starting from a zero point where no collective action is undertaken. We shall discuss this alternative approach in somewhat more detail in a later chapter.

We propose to adopt, instead of this, a "cost" approach in our subsequent analysis of collective action. That is to say, we propose to consider collective action as a means of reducing the external costs that are imposed on the individual by purely private or voluntary action. This is identical with the net-gains approach except for the location of the zero or starting point. Instead of using as our bench mark the situation in which no collective action is undertaken at all, we shall use that situation in which no external costs are imposed on the individual because of the actions of others. Positive costs are, in this way, associated with the situation characterized by the absence of collective action in many cases, and collective action is viewed as a possible means of reducing these costs. Intuitively, this approach is more acceptable if we conceive State activity as being aimed at removing negative externalities, or external diseconomies, but it should be emphasized that the model is equally applicable to the external-economies case. The advantages of using this somewhat unorthodox method of approach will become apparent, we hope, as the analysis proceeds. We shall elaborate the methodological distinction in greater detail in Chapter 7, but a few additional points may be made at this stage.

The individual's utility derived from any single human activity is maximized when his share in the "net costs" of organizing the activity is minimized. The possible benefits that he secures from a particular method of operation are included in this calculus as cost reductions, reductions from that level which would be imposed on the individual if the activity were differently organized. There are two separable and distinct elements in the expected costs of any human activity which we want to isolate and to emphasize. First, there are costs that the individual expects to endure as a result of the actions of others over which he has no direct control. To the individual these costs are external to his own behavior, and we shall call them *external costs*, using conventional and descriptive terminology. Secondly, there are costs which the individual expects to incur as a result of his own participation in an organized activity. We shall call these *decision-making costs*.

The relationship between these two cost elements and the relevance of our approach may be illustrated with reference to an activity that is appropriately organized by purely private action. If an individual chooses to wear red underwear, presumably no other member of the social group suffers a cost. To any given individual, therefore, the organization of this activity privately involves no external costs. The individual in choosing the color of his underwear will, no doubt, undergo some decision cost. We propose, however, to ignore or to neglect this purely private cost of reaching decisions. We shall define *decision-making costs* to include only the estimated costs of participating in decisions when two or more individuals are required to reach *agreement*. This simple illustration clarifies the nature of our suggested zero point or bench mark. The *sum* of the external costs and the decision-making costs becomes *zero* for activities in which purely private action generates no external effects. The individual will, of course, reach decisions in such activities by comparing direct benefits with direct costs. However, it is precisely these direct benefits and direct costs that we may eliminate from our analysis, since these costs are not unique to particular organizational forms.

It is clear that the relevant costs with which we shall be concerned can be reduced to zero for only a relatively small proportion of all human activities. All external effects can be removed from only a small subset of the various activities in which human beings engage. Moreover, even when it is possible to remove all external effects that are involved in the organization of an activity, it will rarely, if ever, be rational for the individual to seek this state of affairs because of the decision-making costs that will be introduced. Nevertheless, the *minimization* of these relevant costs—external costs plus decision-making costs—is a suitable goal for social or political organization. We propose to call this sum of external costs and decision-making costs the costs of *social interdependence*, or, for a shorter term, *interdependence costs*, keeping in mind that this magnitude is considered only in *individual* terms. The rational individual should try to reduce these interdependence costs to the lowest possible figure when he considers the problem of making institutional and constitutional change.[2]

MINIMAL COLLECTIVIZATION—THE DEFINITION OF HUMAN AND PROPERTY RIGHTS

Individual consideration of all possible collective action may be analyzed in terms of the costs-minimization model, but it will be useful to "jump over" the minimal collectivization of activity that is involved in the initial definition of human and property rights and the enforcement of sanctions against violations of these rights. Clearly, it will be to the advantage of each individual in the group to support this minimal degree of collectivization, and it is difficult even to discuss the problems of individual constitutional choice until the range of individual power of disposition over human and nonhuman resources is defined. Unless this preliminary step is taken, we do not really know what individuals we are discussing.[3]

The interesting, and important, questions concern the possible collec-

2. Our costs approach is related to the negative version of the utilitarian principle, as formulated by Karl Popper. See his *The Open Society and Its Enemies* (2d rev. ed.; London: Routledge and Kegan Paul, 1952), Vol. II, chap. 5. Cf. also Ludwig von Mises, *Human Action* (London: William Hodge, 1949), for a general economic treatise that consistently employs the conception of the minimization of dissatisfaction rather than the maximization of satisfaction.

3. This is not to suggest that this preliminary step is unimportant or that it is not amenable to analysis. At this point, however, such an analysis would carry us too far afield. For our purposes, any delineation of property embodying separable individual or group shares provides a suitable basis.

tivization of activities beyond this minimal step of defining and enforcing the limits of private disposition over human and property resources. Why is further collectivization necessary? What are the limits of this pure *laissez-faire* model? If property rights are carefully defined, should not the pure *laissez-faire* organization bring about the elimination of all significant externalities? Why will the rational utility-maximizing individual expect the voluntary private behavior of other individuals to impose costs on him in such a world? On what rational grounds can the individual decide that a particular activity belongs to the realm of social as opposed to private choices?

THE RANGE OF VOLUNTARY ORGANIZATION

If questions such as these can be answered satisfactorily, even at the purely conceptual level, we shall have some theory of the organization of collective activity—indeed, of all human activity. For the most part, scholars who have worked in this field have approached the answering of such questions by attempting to explain the various kinds of relevant externalities that would remain in any *laissez-faire* "equilibrium." This approach seems likely to be misleading unless the equilibrium concept is defined to include the modification of private institutions. After human and property rights are initially defined, will externalities that are serious enough to warrant removing really be present? Or will *voluntary co-operative* arrangements among individuals emerge to insure the elimination of all relevant external effects? We must examine the action of private individuals in making such voluntary contractual arrangements before we can determine the extent to which various activities should or should not be collectivized.

We shall argue that, if the costs of organizing decisions voluntarily should be zero, *all* externalities would be eliminated by voluntary private behavior of individuals regardless of the initial structure of property rights.[4] There would, in this case, be no rational basis for State or collective action beyond the initial minimal delineation of the power of individual disposition over resources. The "efficiency" or "inefficiency" in the manner of defining human

4. Recall that externalities are defined in terms of reductions in individual utility, not in terms of objectively measurable criteria. Thus, our conclusion holds even though "equilibrium" may be characterized by smoke from a factory being observed to soil household laundry. Such an observation would suggest only that adequate compensations must have been, in some way, organized.

and property rights affects only the costs of organizing the required joint activity, not the possibility of attaining a position of final equilibrium.

The choice between voluntary action, individual or co-operative, and political action, which must be collective, rests on the relative costs of organizing decisions, on the relative *costs of social interdependence*. The costs of organizing voluntary contractual arrangements sufficient to remove an externality or to reduce the externality to reasonable proportions may be higher than the costs of organizing collective action sufficient to accomplish the same purpose. Or, both of these costs may be higher than the costs of bearing the externality, the spillover costs that purely individual behavior is expected to impose.

As the analysis of Chapter 6 will demonstrate, the decision as to the appropriate decision-making rule for collective choice is not independent of the decision as to what activities shall be collectivized. Nevertheless, it will be helpful if we discuss these two parts of the constitutional-choice problem separately. Here we shall assume that, if an activity is to be collectivized, the most efficient decision-making rule will be chosen. That is to say, the rule will be chosen which will minimize the expected interdependence costs of organizing the activity collectively. This assumption allows us to use a single value for the expected costs of placing any given activity in the collective sector.

This single value may be compared with two other values. First, it may be compared with the expected costs of allowing purely individualized action to organize the activity. In this case, the whole of the interdependence costs, as we have defined this term, will consist of external costs. Secondly, we may compare the expected costs of organizing the activity collectively with the expected costs of purely voluntary, but not necessarily purely individualized, action. If no collective action is introduced, the private behavior of individuals will tend to insure that any activity will be organized in such a way as to minimize the interdependence costs under this constraint. That is to say, the more "efficient" of the two alternative methods of organization will tend to be adopted in any long-range institutional equilibrium. In a real sense, therefore, it will be necessary to compare the interdependence costs of collective organization with only the most "efficient" method of voluntary organization, individual or co-operative. As the analysis will show, however, there is some usefulness in distinguishing between the two methods of organizing activity voluntarily. In many, indeed in most, cases, some jointly organized co-operative action will be found in the minimum-cost solution for non-collectivized activities. Some joint action will take place with the aim of eliminating troublesome and costly social interdependence. Individuals will, in such cases, willingly bear the added costs of these voluntary contractual arrangements in order to reduce the externalities expected to result from purely individualized action. Under other conditions, and for other activities, the minimum costs of voluntary action may be attained with little or no joint effort. Here the full external effects of individualized behavior may be retained. In either case, the relevant comparison is that to be made between the more "efficient" method of voluntary organization and the expected interdependence costs of collective organization.

One further point should be made in this introductory discussion. Voluntary action may emerge which will include all members of the social group. Here the action may be institutionally indistinguishable from political action. Governmental institutions may be employed to effect purely voluntary co-operative action. The characteristic feature would be the absence of any of the coercive or compulsive powers of the government. An example might be the organization of a village fire department.

A CONCEPTUAL CLASSIFICATION

We have assumed that the rational individual, when confronted with constitutional choice, will act so as to minimize his expected *costs of social interdependence*, which is equivalent to saying that he will act so as to maximize his expected "utility from social interdependence." We now wish to examine, in very general terms, the calculus of the individual in deciding what activities should be left in the realm of private choice and what activities should be collectivized. For any activity, the expected minimum present value of total costs expected to be imposed by collective decision-making shall be designated by the letter *g*. The individual will compare this magnitude with that which he expects to incur from the purely voluntary action of individuals. We shall make a further distinction here. We designate by the letter *a* the expected costs resulting from the purely individualistic behavior of private persons, after an initial definition of human and property rights, but *before* any change in institutional arrangements takes place. These costs represent the spillover or external effects that are anticipated to result from private behavior, given any initial distribution of scarce resources among individuals. We want to distinguish this level of expected costs, which represents nothing but external effects, from those costs that the individual anticipates to be involved in the organization of voluntary contractual arrangements that might arise to eliminate or reduce the externalities. The expected costs of an activity embodying *private* contractual arrangements designed to reduce (to internalize) externalities will be designated by the letter *b*. Note that these costs may include both external and decision-making components.

It is noted that the most "efficient" voluntary method of organizing an activity may be purely individualistic. Thus, in those cases when *a* is less than or equal to *b*, the organization represented by *b* will never be observed. The rationale for making the distinction between the individualistic organization and the voluntary, but co-operative, organization of activity stems from the analysis of those cases where *b* is less than or equal to *a*.

We now have for each activity three different expected costs which the individual may compare; these collapse to two in certain cases as indicated. There are six possible permutations of the three symbols, *a*, *b*, and *g:*

1. (a, b, g)	4. (b, g, a)
2. (a, g, b)	5. (g, a, b)
3. (b, a, g)	6. (g, b, a)

Except for the relationship between the values of *a* and *b* noted in those cases where the most efficient form of voluntary organization is the purely individualistic, these permutations may be allowed to represent strong orderings of the three values of expected costs. That is to say, the individual is assumed to be able to order the expected costs from (1) purely individualistic behavior, *a;* (2) private, voluntary, but jointly organized, behavior, *b;* and (3) collective or governmental action, *g*. We assume that the individual can order these values for each conceivable human activity, from tooth-brushing to nuclear disarmament. Since, in our approach, the objective of the individual is to minimize interdependence costs, as he perceives them, the ordering proceeds from the lowest to the highest value. We get, in this way:

1. $(a \leq b < g)$	4. $(b < g < a)$
2. $(a < g < b)$	5. $(g < a \leq b)$
3. $(b < a < g)$	6. $(g < b < a)$

We shall discuss each of these possible orderings separately.

1. In the first permutation, *a* is, by definition, equal to or less than *b*. *b* should, therefore, never be observed. *b* assumes a value different from *a* only when some voluntary organization other than that embodying purely individualized decisions becomes more "efficient."

One subset of activities characterized by this or the second ordering merits special attention. When the expected organizational costs of purely individualized behavior are zero (a = 0), there are no external effects by definition. This would be characteristic of all activities which are, in fact, "purely private," those which the individual may carry out as he pleases without affecting the well-being of any other individual in the whole social group. For this subset of human activities, no external effects are exerted by individual behavior. The obvious constitutional choice to be made by the rational individual will be to leave all such activities in the private sphere of action. This is, of course, our bench-mark case discussed above.

2. The second ordering (a < g < b) need not be separately discussed since the only relevant relationship is that between the expected costs of organizing an activity by the most efficient voluntary method, in this case represented by *a*, and the expected costs of organizing an activity collectively, *g*.

Except for the particular case noted above, where *a* = 0, note that for all of the activities contained in, or described by, the first and second orderings, and for *all* of the activities described by the remaining orderings, *some* external effects must be expected by the individual to result from purely individualized behavior. Let us now examine more carefully the remaining activities described by the first or the second ordering. By hypothesis, *a* > 0, so that some external or spillover costs are anticipated by the individual as a result of the actions of other individuals if the activity is organized through purely individualistic choices. However, since these costs are lower than those expected from either voluntary co-operative action or from governmental action, the "costs of social interdependence" are effectively minimized by leaving such activities within the sector organized by purely individualistic or private decisions. Examples are familiar here. The color of the automobile that your colleague drives certainly influences your own utility to some extent. Spillover effects are clearly present, but you will probably prefer to allow your colleague free individual choice as regards this class of decisions. You anticipate that this individualistic organization of human behavior is less costly to you, over-all, than either co-operative action organized to make all such decisions in concert or governmentally dictated regulations, which, you will recall, must apply to you as well as to your colleague.

The expected costs arising from the difficulties of organizing voluntary, but co-operative, action will be somewhat different from those expected to result from collective action. The costs of the purely voluntary co-operation that may be necessary to reduce the relevant externality are almost wholly those of decision-making: that is, such costs stem from the difficulties expected to be encountered in the reaching of agreement on joint decisions.

Since individuals will not voluntarily agree to decisions contrary to their own interests, no part of these potential costs can consist of discounted expectations of adverse decisions. Voluntary agreements need not, of course, extend to the point of eliminating the externalities expected from private action, in which case external cost elements remain in *b*. By comparison, the expected costs of collective action always involve both of the two components of costs that we have discussed. The expected value, *g*, includes two elements, as the analysis of Chapter 6 will more fully demonstrate. First, there are the costs involved in making decisions, in reaching agreement. But to these must be added the expected costs of possible decisions made adversely to the interests of the individual. Only if the unanimity rule is dictated for collective decisions will this second element, which represents a particular sort of external cost, be absent.

3. Activities characterized or described by the third ordering ($b < a < g$) are more interesting. Here the costs from the organization of the activity through voluntary contractual arrangements are expected to be less than those imposed by purely individualistic action, which are, in turn, less than those expected from collective organization. There may exist significant external effects from purely individualized behavior; if no contractual arrangements among individuals are allowed to take place, these externalities may impose considerable costs on the individual. On the other hand, the organization of such arrangements may be relatively profitable to all individuals directly affected by the externalities involved. This being true, the most efficient means of organizing these activities will be to allow them to remain in the private sector, with collective action, if any, limited to those steps that might be taken to insure freedom of private contracts. Note that this ordering suggests that the individual prefers to bear the external costs of individual behavior rather than to shift the activities in question to the collective sphere, even if there should be restrictions that prevent the desired voluntary cooperative solutions from being realized.

The set of activities described by this ordering is very important. It includes many of the activities that are embodied in the institutional structure of the market or enterprise economy. The business firm or enterprise is the best single example of an institutional arrangement or device that has as its purpose the internalization of external effects.[5] If, by combining resources

5. The fourth ordering ($b < g < a$) might, of course, also characterize the activities of a business firm, but this possibility does not modify the argument here.

into larger production units, over-all efficiency is increased, there are gains to all parties to be expected from arrangements facilitating such organization. The individual artisan is a rarity in the modern economy because there do exist increasing returns to scale of production over the initial ranges of output for almost all economic activities.[6] Voluntary private action, motivated by the desires of individuals to further their own interests, will tend to guarantee that the externalities inherent in increasing returns of this nature will be eliminated.[7]

This ordering (b < a < g) places the expected costs of purely private or individualized behavior below that of collective action (a < g) in spite of the fact that external effects are anticipated. The organization of higher education, especially professional training, may provide a helpful example. Due to the institutional restrictions on the full freedom of contract in capital values of human beings, the arrangements that might arise to insure the removal or reduction of certain externalities in higher education may be quite difficult to secure. Although students may recognize that they will be the primary beneficiaries of further professional training and that investment in such training would be financially sound, their inability to "mortgage" their own earning power may prevent them from having ready access to loan markets. Of course, collective or State action may be taken which will remove or reduce the private externalities involved here. However, many individuals may prefer to accept the expected costs of private decision-making in this area rather

6. The business firm emerges as the institutional embodiment of this fact, since co-ordination may be achieved more efficiently in this way than through the use of direct contractual relations among all parties to the co-operative endeavor. On this point, see Ronald H. Coase, "The Nature of the Firm," *Economica*, IV (1937), 386–405. Reprinted in American Economic Association, *Readings in Price Theory* (Chicago: Richard D. Irwin, 1952), pp. 331–51.

7. At first glance, it may seem awkward to fit the increasing-returns case into our general conceptual scheme. Individual production organized in small units does not normally impose external costs directly on other individuals. Instead, the combination of productive factors into larger producing units results in greater total income for all members of the group. However, stated in opportunity cost terms, any failure of production to be organized in efficient-sized units may be said to impose external costs, even if indirectly. So long as the organizing entrepreneur does not secure for himself the full value of the "surplus" resulting from combining resources, some external "benefits" from this action will be expected by all individuals; and, of course, competition among potential entrepreneurs will act to prevent any such full appropriation of the "social surplus" created by more efficient organization. The entrepreneurial behavior, therefore, may be said to reduce the "external costs" imposed on the individual by inefficient "handicraft" production.

than to undergo the expected costs of collectivization, which represent yet another kind of externality. This example is introduced here, not to provoke controversy on the merits of the position, but rather because professional education is one of the few current activities that might be described by this particular rank ordering between individualistic and collective action. Normally, if voluntary contractual arrangements are the most efficient means of organizing activity, these arrangements will tend to emerge, and the rank order of the alternative forms of organization is unimportant. In the particular case of professional education, if this ordering should be descriptive, collective action may be suggested to facilitate the emergence of the efficient private arrangements.

4. The fourth ordering (b < g < a) describes the individual assessment of a related, but distinct, set of human activities. This set is perhaps more important than the third for our purposes, since more controversial issues relating to possible collectivization may be expected to arise in the discussion of activities falling within this set. The individual expects that voluntary co-operative action will be the most efficient means of organization, and also that arrangements will tend to arise which will prove sufficient to remove or to reduce the external effects of private behavior, effects which may be slightly more serious here than in those activities described by the third ordering. Furthermore, the rank order here suggests also that the individual prefers a shift of the activities to the public sector if the voluntary arrangements required are not possible for some reason. Collective decision-making is expected to impose lower interdependence costs on the individual than purely individualistic decision-making. If care is not taken in the discussion of new activities falling within this set, the comparison that will tend to be made is between the costs of collectivization on the one hand and the costs of purely individual organization on the other, with the first, and possibly most efficient, alternative being overlooked or assumed not to exist.

Several of these points may be clarified by examples, and we can locate numerous ones in a single general set of activities encompassed by the term "municipal development." Let us first take the case of a proposed suburban shopping center. The several parcels of land are initially owned by separate individuals, but external economies are evident that may be expected to result from a co-ordinated development of the whole area. Therefore, it will be to the advantage of a developing firm, as well as to that of the separate individual owners, to organize contractual arrangements that will "internalize" most of the relevant external economies. Since the group is a reasonably small one, the costs of reaching agreement should not be overwhelming, although considerable bargaining effort may be exerted. In any case, a unified development could be predicted. No significant external economies would exist after the development is completed, and no collective action in the form of zoning ordinances or regulations will be needed. For such problems it is erroneous to contrast the expected results of purely individualistic development with development under a city plan or zoning ordinance and to opt in favor of the latter. This approach too often neglects the presence of mutual gains that may be secured by all parties from the organization of private contractual arrangements designed specifically to internalize much of the externality that initially exists.

Let us now look at the already developed residential area. Each property owner in the area will participate in the sharing of certain elements of "social surplus" which cannot be separated readily into distinguishable and enforceable property rights. This "surplus" includes such things as neighborhood atmosphere, view, absence of noise, etc. Recognizing the existence of this, each owner will seek measures through which the "surplus" may be protected against undesirable "spoilage" by the unrestricted private behavior of others. We know, of course, that the standard response of the individual in such situations is that of lending support to collective intervention in the form of municipal zoning. Let us examine here, however, whether or not voluntary arrangements may emerge which will make collective zoning action unnecessary. It seems clear that many institutional devices might be considered. If no protection against expected external diseconomies exists, a unit of property is less valuable to the owner than it would be with some protection. Without collective action the only owner who could insure this protection is the one who holds a sufficient number of single units to be able to internalize most of the expected spillover damages. It will be to the interest of a large realtor to purchase many single land units in the area. The capital value of each residential dwelling to this purchaser will tend to be greater than the capital values to the single individual owners. Mutual gains from trade will be possible. Moreover, a "solution" may emerge which will effectively eliminate the externalities or reduce these to acceptable dimensions. This shift from single ownership to corporate ownership of multiple units is only one out of the many possible institutional arrangements that might evolve. Covenants, corporate ownership of titles with individual leaseholds, and other similar arrangements might serve the same purpose.

Before he makes his constitutional choice, the rational individual should compare the expected costs of such voluntary arrangements with the expected costs of collective action. The voluntary action will always be more desirable in the sense that it cannot place any unwanted restrictions on use of property. Only if collective action is expected to be considerably more efficient will this advantage of voluntary action be overcome. Before making a permanent choice among the alternative organizations of activities, it is essential to recognize that the costs of organizing voluntary co-operative arrangements will not be so great in a dynamic situation as they will be in a static one. Over a period of development and growth, institutional changes are accomplished with much greater ease.

To continue our example, it may prove quite difficult to reorganize the developed residential area. The large realtor who desires to purchase multiple units in an area from single-unit owners may encounter prohibitive bargaining costs. The single owner-occupier who desires to do so may try to exploit his individual bargaining position to the maximum and may, in the extreme case, secure for himself the full amount of the "surplus." Faced with single owners of this persuasion, the entrepreneur will have little incentive to undertake the organizing costs that will be necessary. In such cases collective action through zoning may be indicated. The activity would be characterized by the fifth or sixth rather than the fourth ordering.

This situation in the already developed area may be compared with that in the area remaining to be developed. In the latter it will be to the advantage of the individual owner of a parcel of land to allow the whole subdivision to be developed as a single unit, at least a sufficient portion of the subdivision to secure some incremental capital value. Only through unified development can a "social surplus" be created. Individual bargaining seems likely to be considerably less intense here; costs of organizing the required internalization will be reduced. Thus, it may be quite rational for individuals in the older residential areas of a city to choose collective action in the form of zoning, and at the same time it may be irrational for the owners of undeveloped units to agree.[8]

Numerous other practical examples outside the municipal development

8. For an extended discussion of the problem of externalities in connection with municipal development, see Otto A. Davis, "The Economics of Municipal Zoning" (unpublished Ph.D. dissertation, University of Virginia, 1959). Also see the chapter on "Housing and Town Planning" in F. A. Hayek, *The Constitution of Liberty* (Chicago: University of Chicago Press, 1960).

field may be used to illustrate this fourth set of activities. Common oil pools, hunting preserves, fishing grounds, etc.: these have all provided familiar examples of external diseconomies in the literature of welfare economics. In deciding whether collective intervention is required in all such cases, the individual must try to evaluate the relative costs. Given individualized operation, production functions are interdependent; but this very interdependence guarantees that there exist profit opportunities from investment in "internalization." The capital value of the common oil pool to the single large owner, where he owns all drilling rights, must exceed the sum of the capital values of the separate drilling rights under decentralized ownership. Moreover, if the fourth ordering is descriptive, the most efficient means of organizing such activities is that of leaving such voluntary solutions full freedom to emerge.

5. The individual, at the time of the ultimate constitutional decision, should choose collective decision-making only for those activities that he describes by the fifth ($g < a \leq b$) and the sixth ($g < b < a$) orderings. The fifth ordering describes an activity for which some external effects from purely individualistic action are expected ($a > 0$), and for which the most efficient means of eliminating or reducing these effects is organization of the activity through governmental processes. Voluntary contractual arrangements among separate persons are not expected to emerge independent of collective action, since the costs of organizing decisions in this way are anticipated to be prohibitive. The relevant comparison here is between the expected costs of collective action and those expected to result from purely private behavior.

Many of the accepted regulatory activities of governments seem to fall within the set of activities described by this fifth ordering. The expected costs of organizing decisions voluntarily on the location of traffic lights, for example, may be minimized by no traffic control at all. However, this value may be much in excess of the costs that the individual expects to incur as a result of organizing traffic control collectively. The cost reduction that may be accomplished by collectivization becomes more significant when it is noted that such regulatory activities will normally be delegated to single decision-makers who will be empowered to choose rules for the whole group. Activities in this set involve high external costs if organized privately, but the external costs resulting from adverse collective decisions are not significant.

It is important to note that this set of activities can include only those which, if collective action is to be taken, will be rationally delegated to a decision-making rule requiring significantly less than full agreement among all members of the group. This conclusion will emerge from the analysis of the following chapter. At this point it is perhaps sufficient to point out that the descriptive ordering (g < a ≤ b) suggests that, while collectivization of the activities will minimize expected interdependence costs, the most efficient voluntary organization is the purely individualistic. That is to say, costs will be minimized by allowing all of the external effects of private individual behavior to continue unless collectivization is carried through. However, if the collective decision-making rule should be that of unanimity (or approximately that), *g* would surely not diverge appreciably in value from some hypothetical *b* which would represent the costs of private contractual arrangements. The reduction in expected costs by a shift from co-operative voluntary contractual arrangements to governmental organization which this ordering suggests could be expected only if the costs of bargaining should be large and the expected damage from adverse collective decisions should be small. The fifth ordering will tend, therefore, to be characteristic of all rationally chosen collective activities, which in their normal operation do not exert significant effects on the net worth of the individual.

6. The sixth ordering (g < b < a) describes those activities in which the untrammeled individualistic behavior of persons will create important spillover effects. These activities are similar to those described by the fourth ordering (b < g < a). If no collective action is taken in either case, voluntary contractual arrangements will emerge to reduce the externalities. The difference lies in the relative costs of organizing such internalization in the private and the public sectors. The individual, who is presumed able to make a comparison between these expected costs, should choose to shift to the public sector all activities that he describes by this sixth ordering.

This set includes the most important activities of governments, measured in a quantitative sense. The provision of truly collective goods, which will be discussed in some detail later, falls in this general category of activities. If no police protection were to be provided collectively, surely voluntary arrangements would be worked out to secure some co-operation in the organization of a private police force. Towns without formally organized collective fire protection organize voluntary fire departments. Numerous other examples could be cited to illustrate the activities falling within this set for the average individual.

Normally, for an activity in this set, the impact of adverse collective decisions on capital values may be significant for individual calculus; but the costs of reaching agreement, either voluntarily or collectively, may also be high. If the rule of unanimity were to be chosen as the appropriate one, the fourth and sixth orderings would become almost identical; collective action here would, in one sense, be voluntary. However, the difficulties involved in reaching general agreement among all members of the group may explain the greater efficiency of collective action for many activities. The costs of reaching agreement on decisions rise quite sharply as the unanimous support of the whole group is approached. The closer to unanimity is the rule required for decision, the greater is the power of the individual bargainer and the greater the likelihood that at least some individuals will try to "exploit" their bargaining position to the maximum extent possible. Voluntary contractual agreements sufficient to remove the externality completely may be as costly as the organization of collective action under the unanimity rule. However, the costs expected to result from adverse collection decisions, although high, may not be so great as to prevent some rational choice of a less-than-unanimity rule for decisions organizing many collective activities. The reduction in expected costs that may be secured by the change from the unanimity rule to, say, a 90 per cent rule, may more than offset the increase in total expected costs involved in discounting possible adverse decisions when the individual falls in the minority 10 per cent.

IMPLICATIONS

We have defined the possible orderings which are sufficient to describe all human activity in terms of the expected costs of private and collective organization. At the conceptual level, we may call our classification a "theory" of organization. However, in a more positive sense, we have actually done little more than to say that the individual should choose the organization that he expects to be the most efficient. Nevertheless, in specifying somewhat carefully the individual calculus in this respect, we are able to draw some important implications for a more positive interpretation of some of the real-world policy issues.

The most important implication that emerges from the approach taken here is the following: *The existence of external effects of private behavior is neither a necessary nor a sufficient condition for an activity to be placed in the realm of collective choice.* The fact that the existence of externality is not sufficient has been widely recognized, but it is clearly suggested by our classification. As indicated, externalities will continue to exist in those activities characterized by the first ordering ($a \leq b < g$), except for the subset described as "purely private" where no external effects are exerted (a = 0). Yet it will be irrational for the individual to undertake either private or collective action designed specifically to remove these externalities. The expected costs of interdependence (or the converse—the expected benefits of interdependence) are not sufficient to warrant any departure from the norm of purely atomistic-individualistic behavior.

Not so widely recognized is the fact that the existence of external effects from private behavior is not even a *necessary* condition for an activity to be collectivized on rational grounds. The activities described by the sixth ordering, which are perhaps the most important ones performed by governments, may be characterized by the absence of externalities in the final equilibrium resulting from free individual choice. Contractual arrangements will tend to be worked out on a voluntary basis which will effectively reduce and may completely remove the externalities. The advantage of collective organization for activities in this group lies wholly in its greater efficiency.

Interestingly enough, the collectivization of activities described by the sixth ordering may involve the introduction of externality—of external effects. In a final equilibrium, private contractual arrangements may remove all external effects of individual behavior, but this organization may prove quite costly to maintain. It may be quite rational in such cases for the individual to support a shift of the activity to the collective or public sector with decisions therein to be made by some less-than-unanimity rule. Moreover, under any such rule, there will exist some expected external costs of possible decisions adverse to the interests of the individual.

The description of activities by the orderings employed in this chapter broadens the meaning of the term "externality," but at the same time it serves to tie together several of the loose ends that seem to have been left dangling in much of the discussion of this subject. The classical examples of external economies and diseconomies constitute only a small set of activities, and no one has discussed carefully the criteria for determining when an externality resulting from private behavior becomes sufficiently important to warrant a shift to the public sector. Few scholars in the field have called attention to the fact that much voluntary behavior is aimed specifically at removing external effects, notably the whole economic organization of activities in business enterprises. The limits to voluntary organization, and thus the pure *laissez-faire* model of social organization, are defined not by the range of significant externalities, but instead by the *relative costs of voluntary and collective decision-making*. If decision-making costs, as we have defined them, are absent, the pure *laissez-faire* model will be rationally chosen for all activities. All externalities, negative and positive, will be eliminated as a result of purely voluntary arrangements that will be readily negotiated among private people. Almost by definition, the presence of an externality suggests that "mutual gains from trade" can be secured from internalization, provided only that the decision-making costs do not arise to interfere with the reaching of voluntary agreements.

Although it has surely been widely recognized, to our knowledge no scholar has called specific attention to the simple and obvious fact that collective organization of activities in which decisions are made through less-than-unanimity voting rules must also involve external costs for the individual.

These conclusions, which will be more firmly grounded in the analysis of the following chapters, point toward a return to an older and more traditional justification of the role of the State. Instead of advancing the discussion, the modern emphasis on externalities has, perhaps, confused the issue. The collectivization of an activity will be supported by the utility-maximizing individual when he expects the interdependence costs of this collectively organized activity (interdependence benefits), as he perceives them, to lie below (to lie above) those involved in the private voluntary organization of the activity. Collective organization may, in certain cases, lower expected costs because it removes externalities; in other cases, collective organization may introduce externalities. The costs of interdependence include both external costs and decision-making costs, and it is the sum of these two elements that is decisive in the individual constitutional calculus.

CHAPTER 6

A GENERALIZED ECONOMIC THEORY OF CONSTITUTIONS

. . . government is not something which just happens. It has to be "laid on" by somebody.

—T. D. Weldon, *States and Morals*

In Chapter 5 we have examined the calculus of the individual in determining the activities that shall be organized privately and collectively. As there suggested, the individual must consider the possible collectivization of all activities for which the private organization is expected to impose some interdependence costs on him. His final decision must rest on a comparison of these costs with those expected to be imposed on him as a result of collective organization itself. The costs that a collectively organized activity will impose on the individual depend, however, on the way in which collective decisions are to be made. Hence, as suggested earlier, the choice among the several possible decision-making rules is not independent of the choice as to the method of organization. In this chapter we propose to analyze in some detail the problem of individual choice among collective decision-making rules. For purposes of analytical simplicity we may initially assume that the organizational decision between collectivization and noncollectivization has been exogenously determined. We shall also assume that the specific institutional structure through which collective action is to be carried out is exogenously fixed.[1]

THE EXTERNAL-COSTS FUNCTION

Our method will be that of utilizing the two elements of interdependence costs introduced earlier. The possible benefits from collective action may be measured or quantified in terms of reductions in the costs that the private behavior of other individuals is expected to impose on the individual decision-

1. This particular assumption is required to avoid ambiguities that might arise concerning the possible "pricing" of collective services. As we shall discuss later, such institutional devices may, in some cases, serve as analogues to more inclusive decision rules.

maker. However, collective action, if undertaken, will also require that the individual spend some time and effort in making decisions for the group, in reaching agreement with his fellows. More importantly, under certain decision-making rules, choices contrary to the individual's own interest may be made for the group. In any case, participation in collective activity is costly to the individual, and the rational man will take this fact into account at the stage of constitutional choice.

Employing the two elements of interdependence costs, we may develop two cost functions or relationships that will prove helpful. In the first, which we shall call the *external-costs function*, we may relate, for the single individual with respect to a single activity, the costs that he expects to endure as a result of the actions of others to the number of individuals who are required to agree before a final political decision is taken for the group. We write this function as:

$$C_i = f(N_a), i = 1, 2, \ldots, N \quad (1)$$
$$N_a \leq N$$

where C_i is defined as the present value of the expected costs imposed on the *i* th individual by the actions of individuals other than himself, and where N_a is defined as the number of individuals, out of the total group N, who are required to agree before final collective action is taken. Note that all of the costs represented by C_i are external costs, even though we are now discussing collective action exclusively. It is clear that, over the range of decision-making rules, this will normally be a decreasing function: that is to say, as the number of individuals required to agree increases, the expected costs will decrease. When unanimous agreement is dictated by the decision-making rule, the expected costs on the individual must be zero since he will not willingly allow others to impose external costs on him when he can effectively prevent this from happening.

This function is represented geometrically in Figure 1. On the ordinate we measure the present value of the expected external costs; on the abscissa we measure the number of individuals required to agree for collective decision. This curve will slope downward throughout most of its range, reaching zero at a point representing the consent of all members of the group.

Note precisely what the various points on this curve represent. Point C represents the external costs that the individual expects will be imposed on him if *any* single individual in the group is authorized to undertake action *for the collectivity*. Suppose that the decision-making rule is such that collective

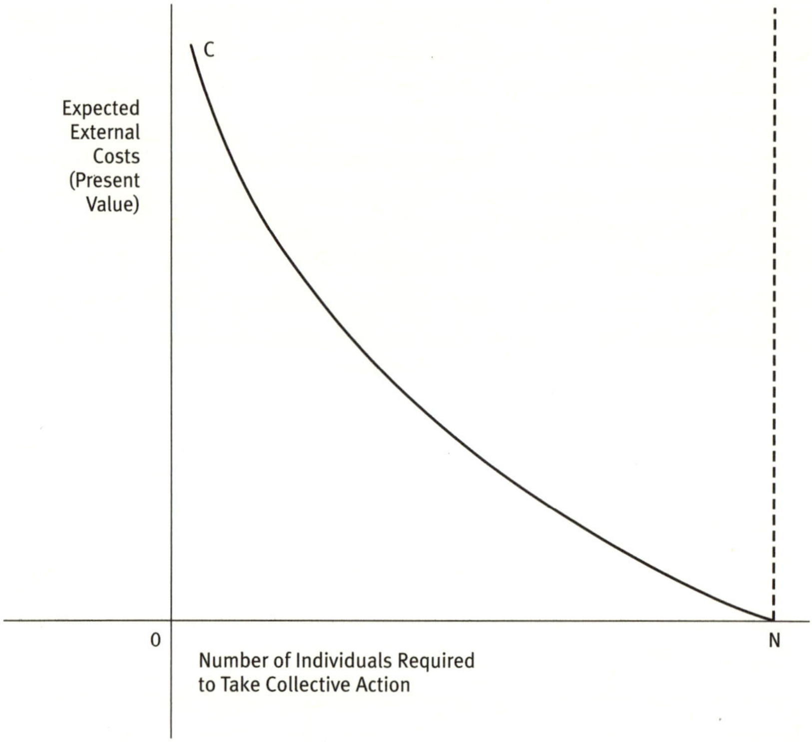

FIGURE 1

action can be taken at any time that any one member of the group dictates it. The single individual can then authorize action for the State, or in the name of the State, which adversely affects others in the group. It seems evident that under such a rule the individual must anticipate that many actions taken by others which are unfavorable to him will take place, and the costs of these actions will be *external costs* in the same sense that the costs expected from private activity might be external. The fact that collective action, under most decision-making rules, involves external costs of this nature has not been adequately recognized. The private operation of the neighborhood plant with the smoking chimney may impose external costs on the individual by soiling his laundry, but this cost is no more external to the individual's own private calculus than the tax cost imposed on him unwillingly in order to finance the provision of public services to his fellow citizen in another area. Under the extreme decision-making rule which allows any individual in the whole group to order collective action, the expected external costs will be much greater than under any private organization of activity. This is because the initial definition of property rights places some effective limits on the external effects that private people may impose on each other. By contrast, the individual rights to property against damaging State or collective action are not nearly so sharply defined in existing legal systems. The external costs that may be imposed on the individual through the collective-choice process may be much larger than those which could ever be expected to result from purely private behavior within any accepted legal framework.

Yet why must the *net* external costs expected from the various decision-making rules be positive? One of the major tasks of Part III of this book will be to demonstrate that these external costs are, in fact, positive, but a preliminary example may be quite helpful at this stage. Let us confine our discussion to the extreme decision-making rule where any individual in the group can, when he desires, order collective action. It is perhaps intuitively clear that such a rule would not be desired by the average individual, but we need to find a more rigorous proof for this intuitive observation. We shall employ a simple illustration. Assume that all local public services are financed from property-tax revenues and that the tax rate is automatically adjusted so as to cover all public expenditures. Now assume further that any individual in the municipal group under consideration may secure road or street repairs or improvements when he requests it from the city authorities. It is evident that the individual, when he makes a decision, will not take the full marginal costs of the action into account. He will make his decision on the basis of a comparison of his individual marginal costs, a part of total marginal costs only, with individual marginal benefits, which may be equal to total marginal benefits. The individual in this example will be able to secure external benefits by ordering his own street repaired or improved. Since each individual will be led to do this, and since individual benefits will exceed individual costs over a wide extension of the activity, there will surely be an overinvestment in streets and roads, relative to other public and private investments of resources. The rational individual will expect that the general operation of such a decision-making rule will result in positive external costs being imposed on him.

The decision-making rule in which *any* single individual may order collective action is useful as an extreme case in our analysis, but the model is not without some practical relevance for the real world. Specifically, such a rule is rarely encountered; but when legislative bodies, whatever the rules, respond to popular demands for public services on the basis solely of "needs" criteria, the results may approximate those which would be attained under the extreme rule discussed here. The institutional equivalent of this rule is also present in those instances where governments provide divisible or "private" goods and services to individuals without the use of pricing devices.

Before leaving the discussion of this *any person* rule, it is necessary to emphasize that it must be carefully distinguished from a rule which would identify a *unique individual* and then delegate exclusive decision-making power to him.[2] This dictatorship or monarchy model is wholly different from that under consideration here. Requiring the identification of specific individuals within the group, the dictatorship model becomes much less general than that which we use. One or two points, however, may be noted briefly in passing. To the individual who might reasonably expect to be dictator, no external costs would be anticipated. To the individual who expects, on the other hand, to be among the governed, the external costs expected will be lower than those under the extreme *any person* rule that we have been discussing. The delegation of exclusive road-repairing decisions to a single commissioner will clearly be less costly to the average taxpayer in the community than a rule which would allow anyone in the group to order road repairs when he chooses.

As we move to the right from point C in Figure 1, the net external costs expected by the individual will tend to fall. If two persons in the group, *any* two, are required to reach agreement before collective action is authorized, there will be fewer decisions that the individual expects to run contrary to his own desires. In a similar fashion, we may proceed over the more and more inclusive decision-making rules. If the agreement of three persons is required, the individual will expect lower external costs than under the two-person rule, etc. In all cases the function refers to the expected external costs from the operation of rules in which the ultimate members of the decisive groups are not specifically identifiable. So long as there remains any possibility that the individual will be affected adversely by a collective decision, expected net external costs will be positive. These costs vanish only with the rule of unanimity. This point will be discussed in greater detail in Chapter 7. Note, however, that by saying that expected external costs are positive, we are not saying that collective action is inefficient or undesirable. The existence of positive external costs implies only that there must exist some interdepen-

2. This distinction is often overlooked. See, for example, W. Starosolskyj, "Das Majoritätsprinzip," contained in *Wiener Staatswissenschaftliche Studien*, Dreizehnter Band (Wien: Franz Denticke, 1916), pp. 26–30.

dence costs from the operation of the activity considered. These costs may be minimized by collective action, but the minimum value of interdependence need not be, indeed it will seldom be, zero.

THE DECISION-MAKING-COSTS FUNCTION

If collective action is to be taken, someone must participate in the decision-making. Recognizing this, we may derive, in very general terms, a second cost relationship or function. Any single person must undergo some costs in reaching a decision, public or private. As previously noted, however, we shall ignore these costs of reaching individual decisions, that is, the costs of the subjective effort of the individual in making up his mind. If two or more persons are required to agree on a *single* decision, time and effort of another sort is introduced—that which is required to secure agreement. Moreover, these costs will increase as the size of the group required to agree increases. As a collective decision-making rule is changed to include a larger and larger proportion of the total group, these costs may increase at an increasing rate.[3] As unanimity is approached, dramatic increases in expected decision-making costs may be predicted. In fact, when unanimity is approached, the situation becomes radically different from that existing through the range of less inclusive rules. At the lower levels there is apt to be little real bargaining. If one member of a potential agreement asks for exorbitant terms, the other members will simply turn to someone else. As unanimity is approached, however, this expedient becomes more and more difficult. Individual investment in strategic bargaining becomes highly rational, and the costs imposed by such bargaining are likely to be high.

With the most inclusive decision rule, unanimity, each voter is a necessary party to any agreement. Since each voter, then, has a monopoly of an essential resource (that is, his consent), each person can aim at obtaining the entire benefit of agreement for himself. Bargaining, in the sense of attempts to maneuver people into accepting lower returns, is the only recourse under these circumstances, and it seems highly likely that agreement would normally be almost impossible. Certainly, the rewards received by voters in any

3. Note that this cost function which ranges over rules that require an increasing *share or fraction* of a total fixed-sized group to agree will be different from that function which ranges over groups of different size, each of which operates under the rule of unanimity, or indeed of any fixed decision rule. This distinction will be discussed in some detail in Chapter 8.

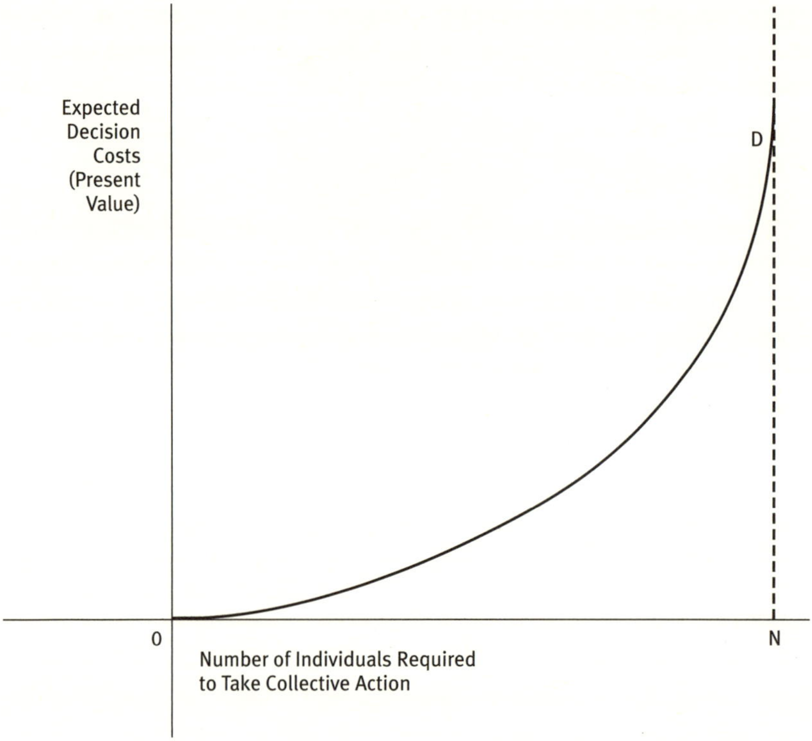

FIGURE 2

such agreement would be directly proportionate to their stubbornness and apparent unreasonableness during the bargaining stage. If we include (as we should) the opportunity costs of bargains that are never made, it seems likely that the bargaining costs might approach infinity in groups of substantial size. This, of course, is the extreme case, but somewhat similar conditions would begin to develop as the number of parties required to approve a given project approached the full membership of the group. Thus our bargaining-cost function operates in two ranges: in the lower reaches it represents mainly the problems of making up an agreed bargain among a group of people, any one of whom can readily be replaced. Here, as a consequence, there is little incentive to invest resources in strategic bargaining. Near unanimity, investments in strategic bargaining are apt to be great, and the expected costs very high.

We may write the decision-making-costs function as:

$$D_i = f(N_a), i = 1, 2, \ldots, N \qquad (2)$$
$$N_a \leq N$$

where D_i represents the present value of those costs that the *i*th individual is expected to incur while participating in the whole set of collective decisions defined by a single "activity." Figure 2 illustrates the relationship geometrically.

THE CHOICE OF OPTIMAL RULES

By employing these two functions, each of which relates expected individual costs to the number of persons in a group required to agree before a decision is made for the group, we are able to discuss the individual's choice of rules. These may best be defined in terms of the proportion of the total group that is to be required to carry a decision. For a given activity the fully rational individual, at the time of constitutional choice, will try to choose that decision-making rule which will *minimize* the present value of the expected costs that he must suffer. He will do so by minimizing the *sum* of the expected external costs and expected decision-making costs, as we have defined these separate components. Geometrically, we add the two costs functions vertically. The "optimal" or most "efficient" decision-making rule, *for the individual whose expectations are depicted and for the activity or set of activities that he is considering*, will be that shown by the lowest point on the resulting curve. Figure 3 is illustrative: the individual will choose the rule which requires that K/N of the group agree when collective decisions are made.[4]

A somewhat more general discussion of the manner in which the individual might reach a decision concerning the choice of a collective decision-making rule may be helpful. An external cost may be said to be imposed on an individual when his net worth is reduced by the behavior of another individual or group and when this reduction in net worth is not specifically recognized by the existing legal structure to be an expropriation of a defensible human or property right. The damaged individual has no recourse; he can neither prevent the action from occurring nor can he claim compensation after it has occurred. As we have suggested in the preceding chapter, it is the existence of such external costs that rationally explains the origin of either voluntarily organized, co-operative, contractual rearrangements or collective (governmental) activity. The individual who seeks to maximize his own utility may find it advantageous either to enter into voluntary contracts aimed at

4. The same results could, of course, be derived through the use of marginal costs rather than total-costs functions. The individual should choose that decision-making rule indicated by equality between the first derivatives of the two total functions, disregarding the signs.

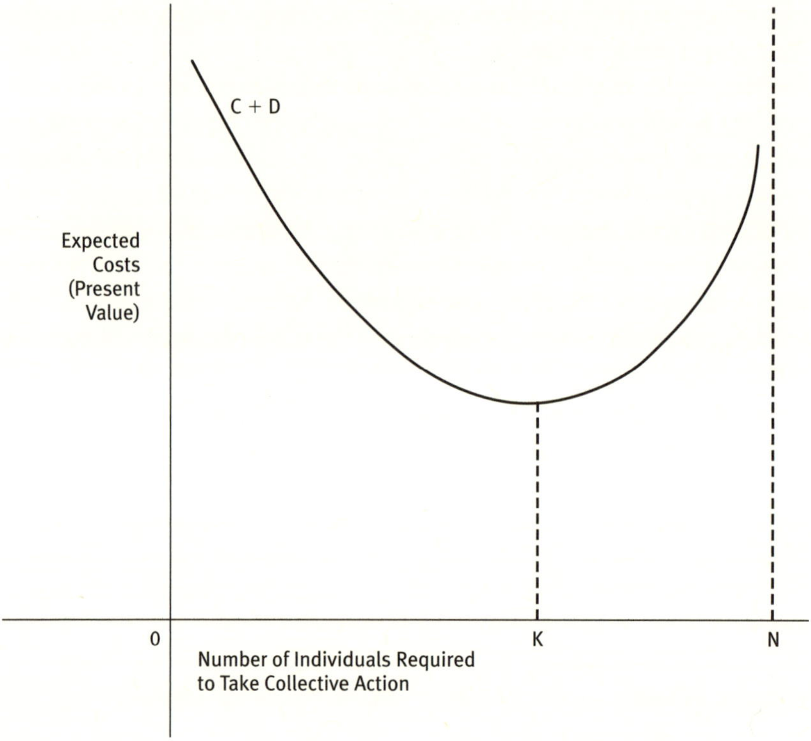

FIGURE 3

eliminating externality or to support constitutional provisions that allow private decisions to be replaced by collective decisions.

The individual will, of course, recognize that any restriction on his private freedom of action will, in certain cases, impose costs on him. Each individual will in the course of time, if allowed unrestricted freedom within the limits of the legal structure, impose certain costs on other parties; and, insofar as his own position taken alone is concerned, he will prefer to remain perfectly free to impose costs on others when he desires. On the other hand, he will recognize also that he will, on many occasions, be affected negatively by the actions of others over whom he can exert no direct control and from whom he cannot legitimately demand compensation. Knowing that he will more often be in the second situation than in the first, the fully rational individual will explore the possibility of contractual arrangements designed to protect him from external cost along with constitutional processes and provisions that may remove actions from the realm of private decision and place them within the realm of public choice.

The only means whereby the individual can insure that the actions of others will never impose costs on him is through the strict application of the rule of unanimity for all decisions, public and private. If the individual knows that he must approve *any* action before it is carried out, he will be able to remove all fear of expected external cost or damage. However, as we have already suggested, he must also consider the costs that he can expect to incur through the operation of such a rule. In small groups the attainment of general consensus or unanimity on issues thrown into the realm of collective choice may not involve overly large resource costs, but in groups of any substantial size the costs of higgling and bargaining over the terms of trade that may be required to attain agreement often will amount to more than the individual is willing to pay. The rational individual, at the stage of constitutional choice, confronts a calculus not unlike that which he must face in making his everyday economic choices. By agreeing to more inclusive rules, he is accepting the additional burden of decision-making in exchange for additional protection against adverse decisions. In moving in the opposing direction toward a less inclusive decision-making rule, the individual is trading some of his protection against external costs for a lowered cost of decision-making.

CATEGORIES OF COLLECTIVE ACTIVITY

All potential governmental or collective activity should not be organized through the operation of the same decision-making rule; this seems an obvious point which follows directly from the general analysis of the individual calculus. Even at this conceptual stage we may isolate two separate fields of potential governmental activity and discuss the decision-making rules that are applicable to each.

In the first category we may place those possible collective or public decisions which modify or restrict the structure of individual human or property rights after these have once been defined and generally accepted by the community. Property rights especially can never be defined once and for all, and there will always exist an area of quasi property rights subject to change by the action of the collective unit. The relevant point is that the individual will foresee that collective action in this area may possibly impose very severe costs on him. In such cases he will tend to place a high value on the attainment of his consent, and he may be quite willing to undergo sub-

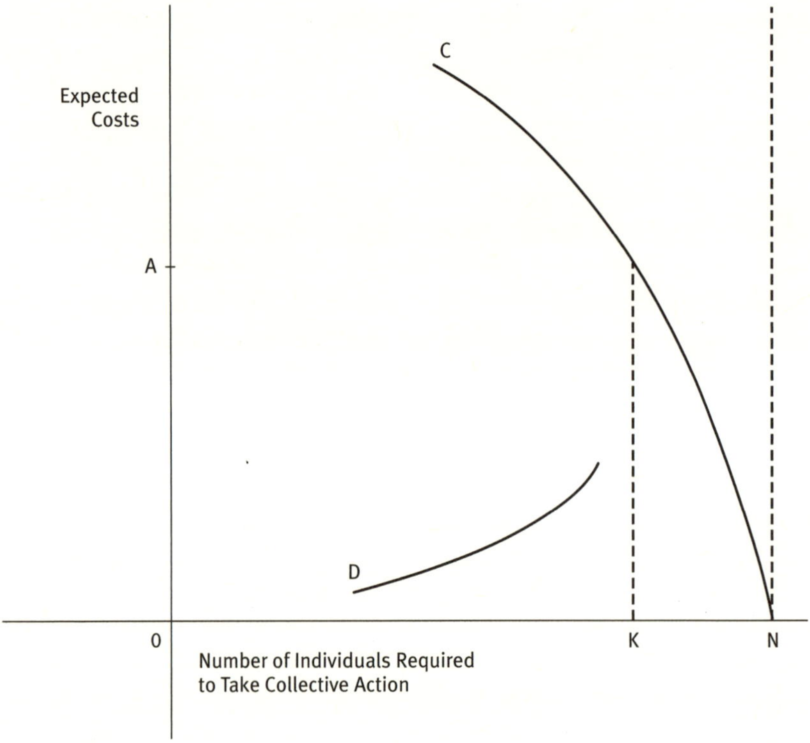

FIGURE 4

stantial decision-making costs in order to insure that he will, in fact, be reasonably protected against confiscation. In terms of our now familiar diagrams, Figure 4 illustrates this range of possible collective activities. The upper curve, that of external costs, remains relatively high throughout its range over the various decision-making rules until it bends sharply toward the abscissa when near-unanimity becomes the rule. The lower curve, that of decision-making costs, may not, in such circumstances, be a factor at all. The continuation of private action, within the restriction of property ownership as defined, may impose certain expected spillover costs, and the individual may stand to gain something by collective action. However, unless the protection of something approaching the unanimity rule is granted him, he may rationally choose to bear the continued costs of private decision-making. He may fear that collective action, taken contrary to his interest, will be more harmful than the costs imposed on him by private organization of the activity. Suppose that, for the individual whose expectations are depicted by Figure 4, the expected costs from private organization of the activity are represented by 0A. The expected external costs of collective action, independent of decision-making costs, exceed expected costs of private organization for all rules less inclusive than that shown by K/N.

The most familiar practical example of such activities is the variance provision to be found in many municipal-zoning ordinances. Property rights are defined in terms of certain specific allowable uses of land units in the zoning ordinance. If, due to the desires of a particular owner or prospective owner, the zoning board wants to change the designated usage of a piece of property, attainment of near-consensus of all the owners of nearby property may be required.[5] The primary point to be illustrated is that, when significant damage may be imposed on the individual, he will not find it advantageous to agree to any decision-making rule other than one which will approach the results of the unanimity rule in its actual operation.

The second category of potential collective activities may be defined broadly to include all of those most characteristically undertaken by governments. For most of these activities the individual will recognize that private organization will impose some interdependence costs on him, perhaps in significant amount, and he will, by hypothesis, have supported a shift of such activities to the collective sector. Many familiar examples may be introduced. The fact that individuals, if left full freedom of private choice, may not educate their own children sufficiently, may not keep their residences free of fire hazards, may not free their premises of mosquito-breeding places, may not combine in sufficiently large units to purchase police protection most efficiently, etc.: all of these suggest that such activities may rationally be thrown into the public sector. In many such cases there is a relatively sharp distinction between the expected costs from purely private organization and the expected costs from collective action, quite independent of the decision-making rule that is to be chosen.

The rational individual will also recognize that time and effort will be required on his part to participate in all such decisions and that these costs will mount as the share of the group required for decisive action is increased. Therefore, insofar as he is able to foresee the impact of such decisions, he will try to choose a decision-making rule that will minimize the total expected costs that he must incur, both the costs imposed on him by the collective de-

5. Reference here is to the so-called "20 per cent protest rule."

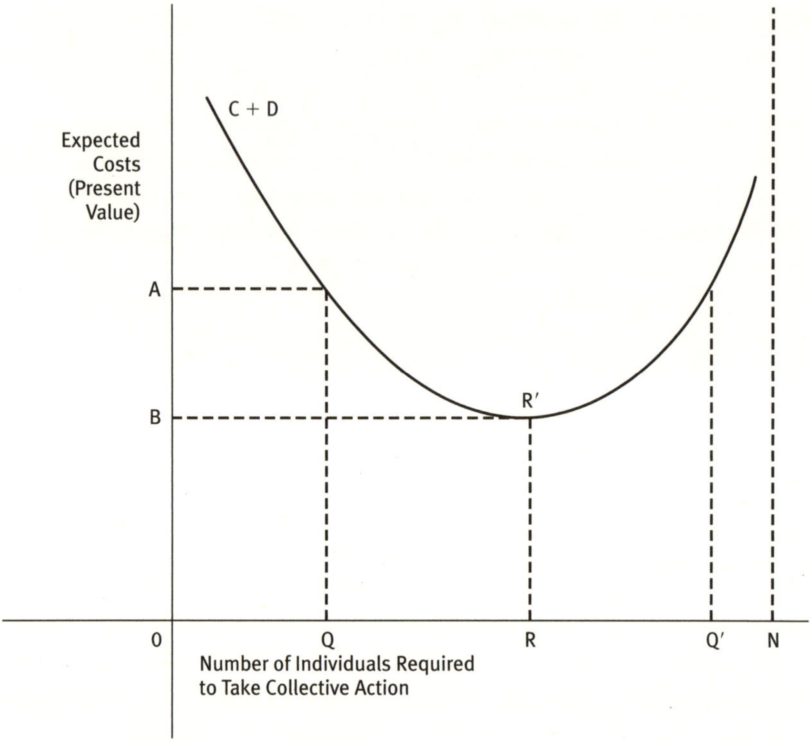

FIGURE 5

cisions taken adversely to his own interests and those which he will incur as a decision-maker. This second category is the one which the initial conceptual model analyzes well, with the appropriate rule being shown by R/N in Figure 5. Note that the set of collective activities to be operated in accordance with the R/N decision-making rule will impose some positive costs on the individual (shown by RR′ in Figure 5), but failure to restrict private activity may also be quite costly. Suppose that unrestricted private organization is expected to generate costs of 0A for the individual. The individual expects, in effect, to be able to reduce total interdependence costs from 0A to RR′ by shifting the set of decisions depicted here from private to public choice. In one sense, AB represents the "gains from trade" that the individual expects to result from his entering into a "political exchange" with his fellows for this category of decisions. Note also that gains from trade will be present from collective organization for any decision-making rule more inclusive than that shown by Q/N and less inclusive than that shown by Q′/N. However, gains are maximized only with the R/N rule.

This broad twofold classification does not, of course, suggest that all collective action should rationally be placed under one of two decision-making rules. The number of categories, and the number of decision-making rules chosen, will depend on the situation which the individual expects to prevail and the "returns to scale" expected to result from using the same rule over many activities.

INSTITUTIONAL VARIABLES AND DECISION RULES

At the beginning of this chapter we assumed not only that the decision concerning voluntary or collective organization had been made, but also that the institutional structure within which the collectively organized activity is to be performed had also been determined. It is clear that only under these restricted assumptions can the problem of deciding on the most efficient decision-making rule be discussed in isolation. Insofar as the institutional structure may be varied, it will be possible to affect the expected costs of collective organization of an activity. As the analysis of later chapters will indicate, in the extreme case it becomes possible to conceive of institutional conditions that will, in effect, largely eliminate the importance of the decision-making rule in the individual constitutional calculus. Specifically, any shift in the institutional structure of collective action toward the ideal model of "general" legislation and away from that of "differential" or "discriminatory" legislation will have the effect of reducing the extent of external costs that the individual might expect from any particular decision-making rule. Hence, other things being equal, he will tend to support less inclusive rules for decision-making as collective institutions are varied in this direction. The institutional devices that come to mind most immediately are those of user prices and benefit taxes. In effect, these devices become substitutes for more inclusive rules. Rather than introduce these specifically at this point, however, we have chosen to keep the analysis as general as possible.

SOME QUALIFICATIONS

Before we discuss some of the implications of this generalized analysis of the constitution-making process, it will be useful to emphasize some of the qualifications that must be kept in mind. First of all, the analysis describes in very general terms the calculus of the *single individual* as he confronts the question of the appropriate decision-making rules for group choices. The question as to how these constitutional choices of rational individuals might be combined has not been considered, for here we confront the infinite regression on which we have already commented. For individual decisions on constitutional questions to be combined, some rules must be laid down; but, if so, who chooses these rules? And so on. We prefer to put this issue aside and to assume, without elaboration, that at this ultimate stage, which we shall call the constitutional, the rule of unanimity holds.

This leads directly into the second qualification. Agreement seems more likely on general rules for collective choice than on the later choices to be made *within* the confines of certain agreed-on rules. Recall that we try only to analyze the calculus of the utility-maximizing individual who is confronted with the constitutional problem. Essential to the analysis is the presumption that the individual is *uncertain* as to what his own precise role will be in any one of the whole chain of later collective choices that will actually have to be made. For this reason he is considered not to have a particular and distinguishable interest separate and apart from his fellows. This is not to suggest that he will act contrary to his own interest; but the individual will not find it advantageous to vote for rules that may promote sectional, class, or group interests because, by presupposition, he is unable to predict the role that he will be playing in the actual collective decision-making process at any particular time in the future. He cannot predict with any degree of certainty whether he is more likely to be in a winning or a losing coalition on any specific issue. Therefore, he will assume that occasionally he will be in one group and occasionally in the other. His own self-interest will lead him to choose rules that will maximize the utility of an individual in a series of collective decisions with his own preferences on the separate issues being more or less randomly distributed.[6]

The uncertainty that is required in order for the individual to be led by his own interest to support constitutional provisions that are generally advantageous to all individuals and to all groups seems likely to be present at any constitutional stage of discussion. This may be demonstrated by specifying those conditions which would be necessary in the contrary case, that is, in the case

6. As Hayek suggests, the consideration of *general* rules cannot be undertaken with *particular* cases in mind. Cf. F. A. Hayek, *The Constitution of Liberty* (Chicago: University of Chicago Press, 1960), p. 210.

where the rational utility-maximizing individual will support the adoption of rules designed specifically to further partisan interests. In order for an individual to support such rules, the following conditions must *all* hold true.

1. The individual is able to predict the form of the issues that will come up for decision under whatever rule is adopted.
2. For one or more of the issues that will arise (let us call the whole set K), the outcome under the "most efficient" general rule discussed above (which we will call Rule A) is predictable.
3. For one or more of the issues in K (subset L) the predicted outcome under Rule A is expected to be less desirable to the individual than under some other decision-making rule.
4. There must exist another rule (say Rule B) under which the predicted outcome for subset of issues L is more desirable than under Rule A.
5. The advantage which the individual expects to gain from the introduction of Rule B for the issues in L exceeds the disadvantages expected to result from the possible changes in the results of the K-L subset of issues and from the use of a possibly "less efficient" rule for decisions falling outside K.
6. General agreement may be reached on the adoption of the alternative Rule B.

Of these conditions the first four may frequently be satisfied. If any single individual were allowed to be the "constitutional dictator," he might be able to adopt rules for collective decision-making that would more fully satisfy his own interest. (Obviously, in the extreme case he could adopt the rule that only he is to make decisions.) Even here, however, he would need to be almost omniscient concerning the whole set of issues that might arise under any predefined rules. Failing such omniscience (Condition 5), even the constitutional dictator may choose rules that are generally "efficient" for all groups. Moreover, Condition 6 rules out the possibility of constitutional dictatorship. The requirement that, at the ultimate constitutional stage, general agreement among all individuals must be attained precludes the adoption of special constitutional provisions or rules designed to benefit identifiable individuals or small groups as these rules operate over a time sequence of collective decisions.

This analysis does not suggest, of course, that all individuals will agree on the choice of rules before discussion. Quite clearly, individual assessments of expected costs will differ substantially. However, these differences represent conflicts of opinion about the operation or the working of rules for decision, and these differences should be amenable to reasonable analysis and discussion. This discussion should not be unlike that of the possible participants in a game when they discuss the appropriate rules under which the game shall be played. Since no player can anticipate which specific rules might benefit him during a particular play of the game, he can, along with all the other players, attempt to devise a set of rules that will constitute the most interesting game for the average or representative player. It is to the self-interest of each player to do this. Hence, the discussion can proceed without the intense conflicts of interest that are expected to arise in the later playing of the game itself.[7]

A third, and most important, qualification of our analysis is related to the second. The evolution of democratic constitutions from the discussion of rational individuals can take place only under certain relatively narrowly defined conditions. The individual participants must approach the constitution-making process as "equals" in a special sense of this term. The requisite "equality" can be insured only if the existing differences in external characteristics among individuals are accepted without rancor and if there are no clearly predictable bases among these differences for the formation of permanent coalitions. On the basis of purely economic motivation, individual members of a dominant and superior group (who considered themselves to be such and who were in the possession of power) would never rationally choose to adopt constitutional rules giving less fortunately situated individuals a position of equal participation in governmental processes. On noneconomic grounds the dominant classes might choose to do this, but, as experience has so often demonstrated in recent years, the less fortunately situated classes will rarely interpret such action as being advanced in their favor. Therefore, our analysis of the constitution-making process has little relevance for a society that is characterized by a sharp cleavage of the population into distinguishable social classes or separate racial, religious, or ethnic groupings sufficient to encourage the formation of predictable political coalitions and in which one of these coalitions has a clearly advantageous position at the constitutional stage.

This qualification should not be overemphasized, however. The requi-

7. We are indebted to Professor Rutledge Vining for this analogy with the formation of the rules of a game, and for his emphasis on the essential differences between the discussion of such rules and the discussion of the appropriate individual strategies in the playing of a defined game.

site equality mentioned above can be secured in social groupings containing widely diverse groups and classes. So long as some mobility among groups is guaranteed, coalitions will tend to be impermanent. The individual calculus of constitutional choice presented here breaks down fully only in those groups where no real constitution is possible under democratic forms, that is to say, only for those groups which do not effectively form a "society."

IMPLICATIONS

What are some of the implications of the analysis of individual choice of constitutional rules that has been developed? First of all, the analysis suggests that it is rational to *have a constitution*. By this is meant that it will be rational for the individual to choose more than one decision-making rule for collective choice-making under normal circumstances. If a single rule is to be chosen for all collective decisions, no constitution in the normal sense will exist.

The second, and most significant, implication of our analysis is that at no point in the discussion has it seemed useful or appropriate to introduce the *one* particular decision-making rule that has traditionally been very closely associated with theories of democracy. We have not found occasion to refer specifically to the rule of majority decision, or, in more definite terms, to the rule described by (N/2 + 1)/N. The analysis has shown that the rule of unanimity does possess certain special attributes, since it is only through the adoption of this rule that the individual can insure himself against the external damage that may be caused by the actions of other individuals, privately or collectively. However, in our preliminary analysis, once the rule of unanimity is departed from, there seems to be nothing to distinguish sharply any one rule from any other. The rational choice will depend, in every case, on the individual's own assessment of the expected costs. Moreover, on a priori grounds there is nothing in the analysis that points to any uniqueness in the rule that requires a simple majority to be decisive. The (N/2 + 1) point seems, a priori, to represent nothing more than one among the many possible rules, and it would seem very improbable that this rule should be "ideally" chosen for more than a very limited set of collective activities. On balance, 51 per cent of the voting population would not seem to be much preferable to 49 per cent.

To argue that simple majority rule is somehow unique, we should be required to demonstrate that one of the two costs functions developed is sharply kinked at the mid-point. Since both of the functions represent expected values, it is, of course, possible that individual utility functions embody some such kinks. Intuition suggests, however, that the burden of proof should rest with those who argue for the presence of such kinks. An alternative, and much more plausible, explanation for the predominant role that majority rule has achieved in modern democratic theorizing may be found when we consider that most of this theory has been developed in noneconomic, nonindividualistic, nonpositivistic terms. We shall explore some of these relevant points later in the book.

A third important implication of the analysis is the clearly indicated relationship between the proportion of the group required to reach agreement and the estimated economic importance of collective action. The individual will anticipate greater possible damage from collective action the more closely this action amounts to the creation and confiscation of human and property rights. He will, therefore, tend to choose somewhat more restrictive rules for social choice-making in such areas of potential political activity. This implication is not without relevance to an interpretation of the economic and social history of many Western countries. Constitutional prohibitions against many forms of collective intervention in the market economy have been abolished within the last three decades. As a result, legislative action may now produce severe capital losses or lucrative capital gains to separate individuals and groups. For the rational individual, unable to predict his future position, the imposition of some additional and renewed restraints on the exercise of such legislative power may be desirable.

Yet another implication of this general analysis is closely related to that discussed above, although it is not directly relevant to the choice of the individual for decision-making rules. Whether or not the individual will or will not support a shift of an activity from the public to the private sector or vice versa (the question already discussed in Chapter 5) will depend, as we have repeatedly stated, on the decision-making rule that is to prevail in collective choice-making. When we discussed this problem earlier, we passed over this particular aspect by postulating that the minimum-cost rule was adopted in all cases. However, in many circumstances the individual will be confronted with the choice as to the location of activity, with the rules for collective choice having been pre-established or set independently. Our analysis clearly suggests that the individual will choose to shift *more* activities to the public sector the more inclusive is the decision-making rule over some initial range of decision-making rules. In other words, there should be some direct relationship between the number of possible activities that are shifted to the pub-

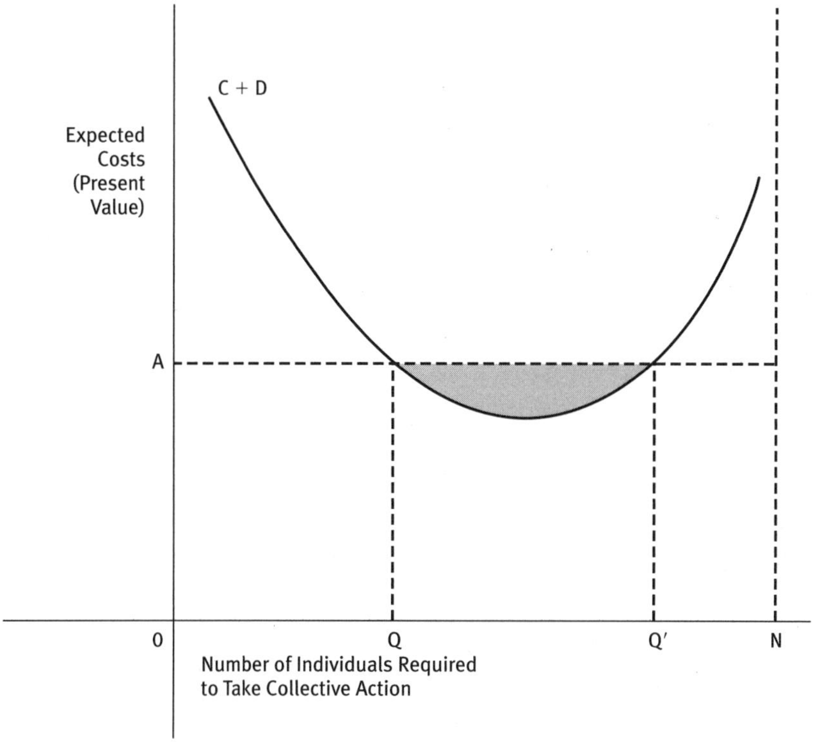

FIGURE 6

lic sector and the size of the group required to reach agreement for the whole decreasing side of the expected-costs function. This point was clearly recognized by Knut Wicksell when he suggested that many proposed public expenditure programs which could not secure even majority support if financed by standard methods might, under the rule of relative unanimity, be quickly approved by the legislative assembly.[8] By and large, scholars have assumed, without being conscious of it, that all State action takes place as if there were unanimous consent. What they have failed to recognize is that much State action, which could be rationally supported under *some* decision-making rules, cannot be rationally supported under *all* decision-making rules. Some of these points may be clarified by reference to yet another diagram, Figure 6. Note that the individual will support the collectivization of this ac-

8. Knut Wicksell, "A New Principle of Just Taxation," in *Classics in the Theory of Public Finance*, ed. R. A. Musgrave and A. T. Peacock (London: Macmillan, 1958), pp. 90–92.

tivity only if the decision-making rule falls somewhere between Q/N and Q′/N. For any collective-choice rule requiring the assent of less than Q members of the group, the expected external costs of adverse collective decisions loom large enough to make the external costs of private action, shown by 0A, bearable. On the other hand, if some rule more inclusive than Q′/N is accepted, the decision-making costs, the costs of higgling and bargaining over the terms of political exchange, become so large as to make the whole collectivization not worth the effort. Figure 6 is helpful in demonstrating clearly the essential interdependence between the choice of rules and the choice as to the location of activity in the public or the private sector.

One final point should be made before leaving this generalized theory of the constitutional-choice process. As we have emphasized, our approach has been that of analyzing the *individual's* choice among the various possible decision-making rules. It has not been necessary at any stage of the analysis to raise the problem as to the correspondence between the operation of this or that rule and the furtherance of any postulated social goal such as "social welfare" or the "common good."

CHAPTER 7

THE RULE OF UNANIMITY

We have discussed, in very general terms, the calculus of the single individual in choosing what activities are to be placed in the public sector and in choosing among the various collective decision-making rules. His final decisions have been shown to depend on some evaluation of expected relative costs from the different available alternatives. In this chapter we shall discuss certain aspects of this calculus in more detail. Before doing so, however, we shall introduce a brief methodological digression in order to attempt to justify again our "costs" approach to the constitutional-choice problem, an approach that may seem tedious in certain applications. Following this digression, we shall examine in detail the individual's estimation of the relative costs of organizational alternatives. Here it will be helpful to assume that decision-making costs are absent and to explore the unique qualities possessed by the unanimity rule, especially when compensation payments are made possible. It will also be useful to place our analysis alongside that of the modern welfare economist. Finally, we shall demonstrate that the introduction of decision-making costs is required before any departure from the adherence to the unanimity rule can be rationally supported.

THE "GAINS" APPROACH

In our discussion of the net-costs model in Chapter 5, we stated that an alternative "net gains" model could yield similar results. We may start from a zero point where no collective action is undertaken and construct a "gains" or "benefits" function. This function is illustrated by the G curve in Figure 7. This G function would attain its maximum at point M, located on a perpendicular to the abscissa directly above N.[1] That is, "net benefits" would be maximized under a decision-making rule of unanimity. This function might be compared with the costs of decision-making function D, drawn in Figure 7 in the same way that it appears in the diagrams of Chapter 6.

To the economist this approach would be the more suitable, since the

1. For a part of its range, the G curve could, of course, lie below the horizontal axis: that is to say, the "net benefits" may well be negative under certain decision-making rules.

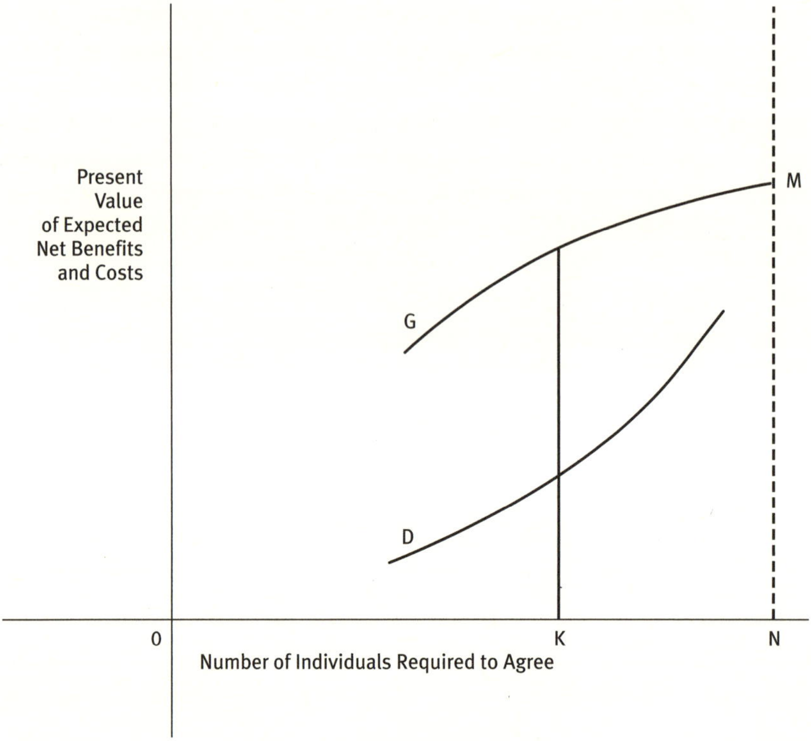

FIGURE 7

curves become fully analogous to the total-revenue and total-cost curves employed in standard price theory. The "optimum" decision-making rule for the activity depicted in Figure 7 is that shown where the slopes of the two total curves are equated, or when "marginal net benefits" equal "marginal costs of decision-making" (K/N in Figure 7). There is nothing at all incorrect in this solution. It does require an explicit use of a marginal calculus which we are able to circumvent by using the alternative, and more simplified, "net costs" approach. The "net benefits" approach is shifted to the "net costs" approach by a simple change in the zero value on the ordinate. If this is taken to be the point at which all benefits from collective action—whether in the elimination of external costs or in the utilization of potential external economies—have been realized, we may start with the recognition that the private organization of almost any activity imposes some external costs on individuals, costs that are unrelated to their own behavior. Collective action may or may not be expected to reduce these costs. The minimization of costs rather than the maximization of some difference between benefits and costs becomes the criterion for organizational and rules decisions. Moreover, in terms of the simple geometry of Chapter 6, it becomes possible to *add* the two total-costs curves vertically and to choose, or rather read off, a single low point. In the geometrical presentation no explicit reference to an equating of marginal values is required, although the solution could, of course, be defined in marginal terms. The net benefits to be secured from collective action are not neglected or overlooked in this alternative approach. They are represented clearly by the possibility and the extent of the reductions in total external costs imposed.

As suggested in an earlier chapter, this net-costs approach is intuitively more acceptable when collective action is aimed at removing negative externalities (external diseconomies) of private behavior. However, the model applies equally well in the positive, or external economies, case. The failure to undertake some sort of joint action, collectively or privately, when external economies are present is a failure to remove an external cost, expressed in an opportunity cost sense. In fact, one merit of this approach is the absence of any analytical distinction between economies and diseconomies. An additional merit, already mentioned in Chapter 5, is that, through isolating decision-making costs, we are able to compare the costs of undertaking collective action with either the costs of organizing voluntary private activity so as to eliminate a relevant externality or the costs expected to be imposed as a result of the spillover itself.

COST MINIMIZATION AND THE UNANIMITY RULE

We have discussed the individual calculus in terms of two functional relationships between the levels of expected costs and the share of individuals in the group required to agree before decisions are made. If we disregard the second relationship, that is, if we assume that the total costs of organizing decision-making are absent, the external costs from collective action expected by the individual were shown to be minimized only when the rule of unanimity prevails—when all members of the group are required to agree prior to action. (The C curves in the diagrams of Chapter 6 cut the abscissa at N.) This single decision-making rule acquires a unique position in our whole analysis which suggests that if costs of decision-making could be reduced to negligible proportions, the rational individual should always support the requirement of unanimous consent before political decisions are finally made. This conclusion follows only from the acceptance of the functional relationship as defined, that is to say, only if it is accepted that net external costs are reduced to zero by the operation of the unanimity rule. Since the reason why this must be so may not be intuitively obvious, we shall try to show that it is based strictly on the individualistic postulates and that, if these are accepted, the rule of unanimity does assume the special role assigned to it in our treatment of the constitutional problem.

Let us begin by considering a single activity that is organized by private decision-making but which does impose some external costs on the individual. The individual experiences some reduction in his utility as a result of the private behavior of other individuals. Let us further assume that these external costs are present because of spillover effects and that no effort is being made to eliminate these through voluntarily organized institutional changes. Take the common oil pool as a familiar example. We assume an initial distribution of property rights such that there are many separate owners of drilling rights to the large common pool and that there has been no joint arrangement worked out voluntarily. Recognizing the spillover costs imposed on him by the actions of others, the single owner will support some collectivization of decision-making if the costs of the latter are disregarded. He may recognize that *any* centralization of decision-making will reduce the external costs that he expects to incur, but he will also recognize that only if the consent of all members of the group is required will he be free of all expectations of external costs. Take the circumstances of the single owner whose productive equipment is somewhat more modern than that of most of his fellow drillers. Suppose that a proposal is made to set over-all limits on drilling by collective action and to allow the actual quotas to be set by a simple majority voting rule. The owner in question may rationally support the collectivization of decision-making in the first place because this will reduce the expected external costs, but he will vote against the particular quota that the majority of his fellows choose because his own interests would be better served by different limits on production. Some external costs, imposed on him by the majority in this case, can be expected to remain. Moreover, so long as there exist minorities who disagree with the decisions reached, some external costs will be expected by the individual at the time of constitutional choice because, at this time, he will be unable to determine with any degree of accuracy what his role will be in any particular decision in the future. Only the unanimity rule will insure that all external effects will be eliminated by collectivization. The member of the dissident minority suffers external effects of collective decisions enforced on him, and, so long as there remains any possibility that the individual will be a member of such a minority, expected external costs will be positive, although collectivization may reduce these expected costs substantially below those that might be expected from unrestrained private action.

All of these seem to be obvious points when considered in this fashion. This being true, it is especially surprising that the discussion about externality in the literature of welfare economics has been centered on the external costs expected to result from *private* action of individuals or firms. To our knowledge little or nothing has been said about the *external* costs imposed on the individual by *collective* action. Yet the existence of such external costs is inherent in the operation of any collective decision-making rule other than that of unanimity. Indeed, the essence of the collective-choice process under majority voting rules is the fact that the minority of voters are forced to accede to actions which they cannot prevent and for which they cannot claim compensation for damages resulting. Note that this is precisely the definition previously given for externality.

As we have already noted, the rule of unanimity makes collective decision-making voluntary in one sense. Therefore, in the absence of costs of organizing decision-making, voluntary arrangements would tend to be worked out which would effectively remove all relevant externalities. Collectivization, insofar as this is taken to imply some coercion, would never be chosen by the rational individual. As previously emphasized, the individual will choose collectivization only because of its relatively greater efficiency in the organization of decision-making. The existence of external costs (or the existence of any externality) creates opportunities for mutually advantageous "trades" or "bargains" to be made among individuals affected and also profit possibilities for individuals who are acute enough to recognize such situations. Furthermore, if we disregard the costs of making the required arrangements, voluntary action would more or less automatically take place that would be sufficient to "internalize" all externality, that is, to reduce expected external costs to zero. As implied earlier, all ordinary market exchange is, in a real sense, directed toward this end. Moreover, if there were no costs of organizing such exchanges, we could expect marketlike arrangements to expand to the point where all conceivable relevant externalities would be eliminated.

These conclusions follow directly from the underlying conception of the State itself, a conception discussed in Part I. The political mechanism in our model is viewed as a means through which individuals may co-operate to secure certain mutually desired ends. The political "game" is positive-sum, and all positive-sum games must have some "solutions" that are dominant over all participants. Since this is true, the ends are, in effect, attainable also by voluntary action if decision-making costs are neglected.

THE ROLE OF COMPENSATION

The close relationship between collective action taken under the rule of unanimity and purely voluntary action is analytically helpful since the formation of marketlike arrangements would necessarily involve the payment of compensation by some parties to others. This suggests that the positive collective action that may be justified need not directly benefit all members of the group, even if unanimous consent is required. Nothing suggests that the elimination of external costs increases the utility of each member of the social group. If this were the case, little or no action could be taken since it must be realized that externalities rarely affect all members of the group in the same way. More often, the external costs imposed by private action will be concentrated on a minority group of the total population, and other individuals in the group will receive some external benefits as a result of these external costs. If compensation payments are introduced into the model, however, the limits on the location and distribution of the externality become irrelevant.

The unanimity test is, in fact, identical to the compensation test if compensation is interpreted as that payment, negative or positive, which is required to secure agreement. Moreover, if decision-making costs are neglected, this test must be met if collective action is to be judged "desirable" by any rational individual calculus at the constitutional level. We may illustrate this point by the classical example of Pigovian welfare economics, the case of the smoking chimney. Smoke from an industrial plant fouls the air and imposes external costs on residents in the surrounding areas. If this represents a genuine externality, either voluntary arrangements will emerge to eliminate it or collective action with unanimous support can be implemented. If the externality is real, *some* collectively imposed scheme through which the damaged property owners are taxed and the firm's owners are subsidized for capital losses incurred in putting in a smoke-abatement machine can command the assent of all parties. If no such compensation scheme is possible (organization costs neglected), the externality is only apparent and not real. The same conclusion applies to the possibility of voluntary arrangements being worked out. Suppose that the owners of the residential property claim some smoke damage, however slight. If this claim is real, the opportunity will always be open for them to combine forces and buy out the firm in order to introduce smoke-abatement devices. If the costs of organizing such action are left out of account, such an arrangement would surely be made. All externalities of this sort would be eliminated through either voluntarily organized action or unanimously supported collective action, with full compensation paid to parties damaged by the changes introduced by the removal of the externalities.[2]

COMPARISON WITH THE NEW WELFARE ECONOMICS

By approaching the problem of the calculus of the single individual as he confronts constitutional choices, not knowing with accuracy his own particular role in the chain of collective decisions that may be anticipated to be carried out in the future, we arrive by a somewhat different route to a final position that is, in many respects, closely related to that taken by the "new" welfare economist. The modern welfare economist refuses to make interpersonal comparisons of utility, but yet he seeks to make some judgments concerning the welfare effects of proposed institutional changes. In order to be able to do so, he falls back on the criterion designed by Pareto. A change must be demonstrated to make at least one person in the group "better off" without making any other person "worse off," with "better off" and "worse off" being defined in terms of the voluntary preferences of the individuals as revealed by behavior. Translated in terms of decisions, this means, of course, that a change can be definitely shown to increase "total welfare" only if all persons agree, that is, only if there is the unanimous consent of all members of the group.[3] Even to be able to make this statement, the welfare economist

2. Since the conclusions here are not immediately apparent, additional comments may prove helpful. Assume that an industrial plant emits smoke which imposes real costs on local residents. Insofar as these residential property owners must undergo costs which the plant owners do not undergo, the capital value of the plant *to the group of residential owners* must exceed the capital value of the plant to its current owners. Mutual gains from trade exist, and, if we disregard all decision-making costs, trade will take place. The new owners may *not* find it profitable to introduce *complete* smoke abatement. However, since internal marginal costs of production will be increased, some reduction in output will be undertaken, provided that we assume the initial position was one of disequilibrium. For an interesting discussion of many of these points, see Ronald Coase, "The Problem of Social Cost," *Journal of Law and Economics*, III (1960), 1–44.

3. For an extended discussion of the relationship between the Pareto criterion and the unanimity rule in collective decisions, see James M. Buchanan, "Positive Economics, Welfare Economics, and Political Economy," *Journal of Law and Economics*, II (1959), 124–38. Reprinted

must accept certain ethical precepts, although these are admittedly very weak ones which should command wide assent. These precepts are those that are normally implicit in the framework of the individualistic society. To be able to go beyond the Pareto rule and to judge a change "desirable" when all parties do not agree, the economist would find it necessary to compare the utility of one individual with that of another, a comparison which must by nature introduce prospects of disagreement among separate persons. Unwilling to take this step, the welfare economist stops at the Pareto rule and disavows all claims to positive conclusions beyond its limits. He does not, however, normally suggest that collective action beyond the confines of the Pareto rule is undesirable; he is simply silent on such matters.

Some of the problems faced by the modern welfare economist are removed by our approach, but, as might be expected, others arise as more troublesome. By concentrating on the constitutional problem as faced by the individual, we need not discuss the comparability of his utility with that of others directly. We postulate only that the individual, at the time of constitutional choice, is wholly uncertain as to what his role will be in the collective-decision process in the future. If he assumes that his interests will dictate that he will more or less randomly take various positions in the decision-making process at various times, he will take this into account in choosing what activities to collectivize and what decision-making rules to adopt. Quite clearly, under such circumstances, the individual will not rationally choose to collectivize an activity under the control of any less-than-unanimity voting rule merely because he anticipates that, *if he is in the decisive group*, net costs will be reduced below those expected from private organization. He can insure his presence in the decisive group only by the voting rule of unanimity, and there will be nothing to prevent his supporting this rule if the costs of decision-making are neglected.

The approach taken here has the advantage over the new welfare economics in that it does enable us to discuss the organization of social action beyond the limits of the Pareto rule. Whereas the welfare economist either remains silent on all proposals that involve less-than-unanimous support or falls back on some nonindividualistic ethical ordering as given by a "social welfare function," we are able to describe the individual calculus on the constitutional level. The unanimity rule for reaching collective decisions will be sup-

---

in *Fiscal Theory and Political Economy: Selected Essays* (Chapel Hill: University of North Carolina Press, 1960), pp. 105–24.

ported only if the costs of decision-making are neglected. When it is recognized that resources must be used up in the process of reaching decisions and that these genuine-resource costs increase rapidly as the decision-making unit is expanded to include more members of the group, it is relatively easy to see that the rational individual will deliberately choose to collectivize certain activities and to allow these to be organized under rules that require less-than-unanimous consent of all members to decisions.

This advantage of the constitutional approach may be more apparent than real, for, while it is conceptually useful, it does move the analysis further away from any operational implications that may be tested empirically. The welfare or political economist may construct operational propositions about specifically proposed policy changes; he may advance a proposal as "presumed Pareto-optimal." This proposal then takes the form of a hypothesis subject to testing, subject to conceptual refutation. The test lies in the degree of support that the proposal obtains. The attainment of consensus in support of the change would lend support to the hypothesis; failure would tend to refute the hypothesis.

The notion that the attainment of unanimous support provides the test for the validity of specific propositions advanced by the political economist should be sharply distinguished from the notion that the rule of unanimity should be chosen at the constitutional level as the appropriate decision-making rule for collective choices.[4] It may be quite rational for the individual to choose a majority voting rule for the operation of certain collectivized activities. Once this rule is chosen, collective decisions at the legislative or policy level will be made accordingly. However, under the operation of such a rule, the political economist, trying to advance hypotheses concerning the existence of "mutual gains from trade" through the political process, is severely restricted. To insure that a proposed change is, in fact, Pareto-optimal, general agreement must be forthcoming. However, if the rule, laid down in advance by the political constitution, requires only majority approval for positive action, the compromises that might be required to attain consensus become unnecessary, and the political or welfare economist is left with no means of confirming or rejecting his hypothesis.

We have arrived at an apparent paradoxical situation, but upon closer ex-

4. The first aspect of the unanimity rule was stressed in James M. Buchanan's "Positive Economics, Welfare Economics, and Political Economy." At the time this article was written, the author did not fully appreciate the constitutional problem under discussion in this book.

amination the paradox disappears. The constitutional approach indicates clearly that the anticipated costs of reaching decisions will cause some collective activities to embody specific decisions made with less-than-unanimous approval. The welfare-political-economist approach indicates that a specific choice is Pareto-optimal only if all parties reach agreement. This suggests that even the most rationally constructed constitution will allow some decisions to be made that are "nonoptimal" in the Pareto sense. This inference is correct if attention is centered on the level of specific collective decisions. The problem here lies in determining the appropriate level at which Pareto criteria should dominate. If the constitutional decision is a rational one, the external costs imposed by "nonoptimal" choices because of the operation of a less-than-unanimity voting rule will be more than offset by the reduction in the expected costs of the decision-making. For any single decision or choice, full agreement must be possible if the action is to be justified by the Pareto rule. However, because of the bargaining range that is present, the higgling and bargaining required to reach full agreement may be quite costly. If these costs are expected to exceed those that might be imposed on potentially damaged minorities, the individual confronted with constitutional choice may decide to allow collective action to proceed under some qualified majority rule. An interpersonal comparison of utilities, of a sort, does enter into the analysis here, but note that the individual is not required to compare the utilities of A and B. He is required only to compare his own anticipated gains in utility in those situations in which he is in the decisive group with his anticipated losses in situations in which he is in the losing coalition. This calculus is made possible by the chain of separate choices that is anticipated. Moreover, since this calculus is possible for each individual, constitutional decisions to allow departures from unanimity at the level of specific collective choices may command unanimous consent.[5]

This does not suggest, however, that the less-than-unanimity rule for choice at the level of specific decisions will produce the same results as a unanimity rule or that these results are, in any sense, "optimal." As the analysis of Part III will demonstrate, all less-than-unanimity decision-making rules can be expected to lead to nonoptimal decisions by the Pareto criterion, and it remains quite meaningful to analyze these decision-making rules for their properties in producing "nonoptimal" choices. Clearly, the ultimate consti-

5. "May" is used in the permissive sense here. Sharp differences among individual-utility functions could prevent the attainment of unanimity at the ultimate constitutional level.

tutional choice must depend on a prediction of the operation of the various rules for decision-making, and if a certain rule can be shown to lead, more or less automatically, to nonoptimal choices, the costs of this property can be more accurately compared with the anticipated costs of decision-making itself.[6]

The constitutional choice of a rule is taken independent of any single specific decision or set of decisions and is quite rationally based on a long-term view embodying many separate time sequences and many separate collective acts disposing of economic resources. "Optimality" in the sense of choosing the single "best" rule is something wholly distinct from "optimality" in the allocation of resources within a given time span. The Pareto criterion itself is something different in the two cases because the individual is, in fact, different. In the first situation, the individual is uncertain as to his location along the decision-making spectrum in the chain of separate collective acts anticipated; in the second, he is located, identified, and his interests vis-à-vis those of his fellows are strictly confined. This distinction allows us to reconcile, to some considerable extent, our purely individualistic approach with the more traditional methodology of political science and philosophy. At the constitutional level, *identifiable* self-interest is not present in terms of external characteristics. The self-interest of the individual participant at this level leads him to take a position as a "representative" or "randomly distributed" participant in the succession of collective choices anticipated. Therefore, he may tend to act, from self-interest, *as if* he were choosing the best set of rules for the social group. Here the purely selfish individual and the purely altruistic individual may be indistinguishable in their behavior.

CONSENSUS AS A NORM

The individualistic theory of the constitution that we have been able to develop assigns a central role to a single decision-making rule—that of general consensus or unanimity. The other possible rules for choice-making are introduced as variants from the unanimity rule. These variants will be rationally chosen, not because they will produce "better" collective decisions (they will not), but rather because, on balance, the sheer weight of the costs in-

6. Note that by saying that less-than-unanimity rules will lead to the making of "nonoptimal" choices, we are not saying that these rules work inefficiently by any other than the simple Pareto criterion.

volved in reaching decisions unanimously dictates some departure from the "ideal" rule. The relationship between the fundamental norm here and the practical expedients deemed necessary in the operation of the State is analogous to many that are to be found in personal, social, and business life. Nevertheless, the resort to practical expedients in the latter cases does not cause the individual to lose sight of the basic rule of action appropriate to the "ideal" order of things. In political discussion, on the other hand, many scholars seem to have overlooked the central place that the unanimity rule must occupy in any normative theory of democratic government. We have witnessed an inversion whereby, for reasons to be examined later, majority rule has been elevated to the status which the unanimity rule should occupy. At best, majority rule should be viewed as one among many practical expedients made necessary by the costs of securing widespread agreement on political issues when individual and group interests diverge.

CHAPTER 8

THE COSTS OF DECISION-MAKING

In this chapter we shall examine more carefully the second cost relationship which was introduced in discussing individual constitutional choice. This relationship connects the expected costs of organizing decision-making itself with the proportion of the total group required for decision. This aspect of the constitutional-choice problem has perhaps been neglected to an even greater extent than that discussed in Chapter 7. Few scholars, to our knowledge, have explicitly analyzed decision-making costs. As a result, the only rational economic justification for constitutional selection of less-than-unanimity rules for collective action has tended to be overlooked, although, of course, the fundamental ideas have been implicitly recognized.

INDIVIDUAL AND COLLECTIVE DECISIONS

Professor Frank H. Knight has often posed the question: When should an individual rationally stop considering the pros and cons of an issue and reach a decision? This question itself suggests that purely individual decisions involve costs. For this reason the individual typically "routinizes" many day-to-day choices that he makes: that is to say, he adopts or chooses a "rule" which dictates his behavior for many single choices. This method reduces the costs of individual decision-making since it requires conscious effort, investment, only when an existing behavior rule is to be broken or modified in some way. Presumably the rational individual himself goes through a "constitutional" choice process when he chooses this basic behavior pattern, and this process can in one sense be regarded as analogous to the more complex one examined in this book. The individual may be assumed to try to extend investment in decision-making to the point where the marginal benefits no longer exceed the marginal costs.

There is no reason to expect that the individual's behavior in confronting political choices is fundamentally different from that which describes his purely private choices. In either case, he must reach a decision. The essential difference between individual choice and collective choice is that the latter requires more than one decision-maker. This means that two or more separate decision-making units must *agree* on a single alternative; and it is in the *reaching of agreement* among two or more individuals that the costs of collective decision-making are reflected, which is the reason why these costs will tend to be more than the mere sum of individual decision-making costs taken separately. On a purely individual basis each party must decide on the alternative that is more "desirable"—most likely to further his own individual goals, whatever these may be. Only after these private decisions are made does the process of reconciling divergent individual choices, of reaching agreement, begin.

As we have suggested earlier, this aspect of the political process has perhaps been neglected because of the implicit assumption that separate individuals, motivated by a desire to promote the "common good," will more or less naturally be led to agree quite quickly. However, if individuals should have different ideas about the "common good," or if, in accordance with the assumptions of our model, they seek to maximize their own utility, the costs of reaching agreement cannot be left out of account.

THE BARGAINING RANGE

If two or more individuals agree on a single decision, each of them must expect to be "better off" or at least "no worse off" as a result of the decision being carried out, with "better off" and "worse off" being defined in terms of revealed preferences in the political process. However, if all parties to an agreement expect to improve their individual positions, why is decision-making costly? Decision-making costs arise here because normally a bargaining range will exist, and, recognizing this, each individual will seek to secure the maximum gains possible for himself while keeping the net gains to his partners in the agreement to the minimum. Each individual will be led to try to conceal his own true preferences from the others in order to secure a greater share of the "surplus" expected to be created from the choice being carried out. The whole gamut of strategic behavior is introduced, with the resulting costs of bargaining. From the point of view of the individual participant, some considerable investment in "bargaining" may be quite rational. This investment of time and resources in bargaining is not productive from a "social" point of view, because the added benefits that one individual may secure represent a reduction in the potential benefits of other parties to the agreement. Given a defined bargaining range, the decision-making problem is wholly that of dividing up the fixed-sized "pie"; the game is constant-sum.

Moreover, looking backward from a decision once made, everyone in the group will be able to see that he would have been better off had the investment in "bargaining" not taken place at all provided an agreement could have been reached in some manner without bargaining. This suggests that the individual may seek to devise means of eliminating needless and resource-wasting higgling, if possible. One method of eliminating bargaining costs is to delegate decision-making authority to a single individual and agree to abide by the choices that he makes for the whole group. If we look only at the costs of decision-making (our second function), the most efficient rule for collective decision-making is that of dictatorship. This provides the element of truth in the idea that dictatorial governments are more "efficient" than democratically organized governments. However, just as the rule of unanimity must normally be tempered by a recognition of decision-making costs, so must the dictatorship rule be tempered by the recognition that external costs may be imposed on the individual by collective decisions. If the individual feels that he might possibly disagree with the decisions of the dictator, that such decisions might cause him harm, he will never rationally support the delegation of important decision-making authority to a single unit.

This point presents an interesting paradox which seems worthy of mention even though it represents a brief digression from our main argument. If the "public interest" or the "common good" is something that can be determined with relative ease, and if individual participants in collective choice act so as to promote this "common good" rather than their own interests, there seems to be little rational support for the many cumbersome and costly institutions that characterize the modern democratic process. Under such conditions the delegation of all effective decision-making power to a single decision-maker, and an accompanying hierarchy, may appear perfectly rational. If some means can be taken to insure that the dictator will, in fact, remain "benevolent," the argument becomes even stronger. Moreover, this may seem to be insured by constitutional requirements for periodic elections of rulers or ruling groups. Much of the support for the growth of modern administrative government may be based on such reasoning as this, which seems to be a rather direct implication of the orthodox assumptions in much of the literature of political science.

A positive argument for democratic decision-making institutions, beyond the election of rulers periodically, must rest on the assumptions of individualist rather than idealist democracy. Individual interests must be assumed to differ, and individuals must be assumed to try to further these by means of political as well as private activity. Only on these assumptions can the costs of decision-making be accepted as an inherent part of the process that will provide protection against the external costs that may be imposed by collective action.

A SIMPLE TWO-PERSON BARGAINING MODEL

The actual bargaining process can best be described in terms of a model. For our purposes we may use the most simple of the many bargaining models. We assume two persons and two commodities (two "goods"). There is a given initial distribution of the two commodities between the two parties. This is illustrated in the Edgeworth box diagram of Figure 8, a diagram familiar to all economists. The initial position, before trade or "agreement" is reached, is shown at α. Individual A, viewed from the southwest corner of the box, has in his possession AX_a of coconuts and AY_a of apples, coconuts and apples being used as labels for our hypothetical "goods." Individual B has in his possession the remaining amounts of the goods, DX_a of coconuts and CY_a of apples. The total amount of coconuts is shown by AD(CB) and the total amount of apples by AC(DB).

The initial combination of commodities will offer to each individual a certain amount, or level, of utility or satisfaction. Through point α we may draw indifference curves for A and B. Each point on the curve labeled *a* indicates the various combinations of commodities that provide A with the same level of satisfaction as that provided by the combination shown at α. Similarly, each point on *b* indicates combinations equally satisfactory to B. A whole family of such curves may be derived for each individual, and this family will fully describe the individual's tastes for the two goods. Moving in a northeasterly direction on the diagram, A's level of satisfaction increases; conversely, B's satisfaction increases as his position shifts in a southwesterly direction. The shaded area includes all of those combinations of the two commodities that will provide more utility or satisfaction to *both* parties (to both A and B) than is provided by the distribution shown at α. Gains from trade are possible.

The problem is that of reaching agreement on the terms of trade. Recognizing that a bargaining range exists, each individual will try to conceal his own "preference"; he will "bargain." If A can be wholly successful, he may be able to secure for himself the full amount of the "gain from trade": he may shift the distribution from α to α_1, keeping B no better off than he is without

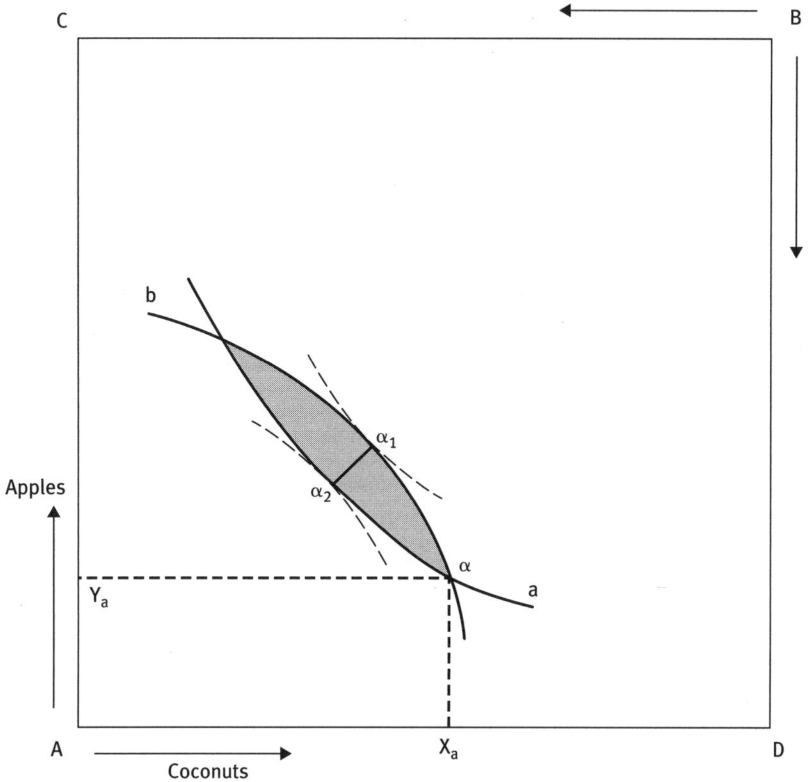

FIGURE 8

trade. Similarly, if B exploits his position fully, α_2 becomes a possible "solution." It can be anticipated that bargaining will continue until a final distribution somewhere along the line $\alpha_1\alpha_2$ is reached. This line is called the contract locus.

The shift from an initial position off the contract locus to a final position on this locus may be made in a single step or in a series of steps. Normally the second method would be followed because of the ignorance of each party concerning his adversary's preferences. The process of trading may be illustrated in Figure 9, which is an enlarged section of the earlier diagram. An initial exchange may be arranged which shifts the distribution of goods to that shown at α'. Both parties are better off than at α, A having moved to indifference curve a', and B to b'. Note that, at α', further mutually advantageous trades are possible, as is shown by the lightly shaded area. Note also, however, that the bargaining range has been substantially reduced by the initial

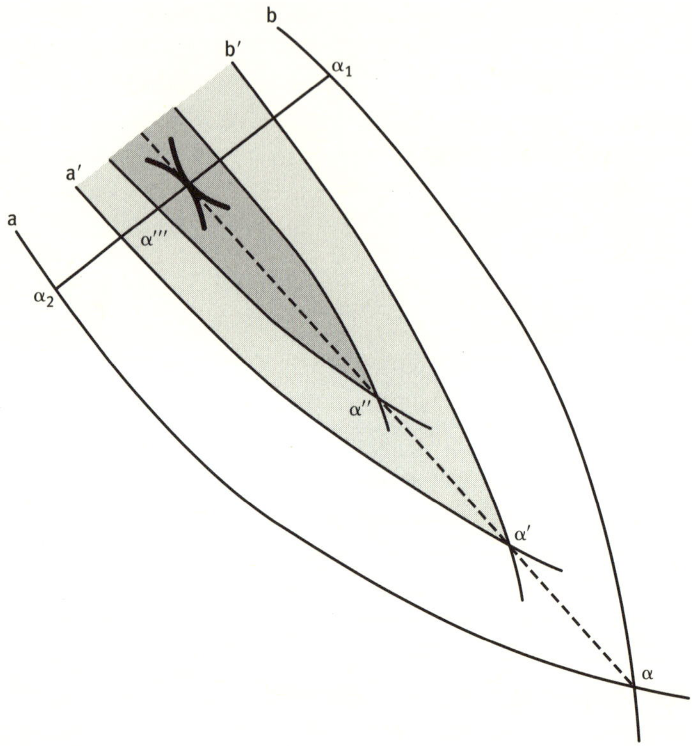

FIGURE 9

exchange. The length of the possible contract locus has been reduced. Given this reduction in the potential gains from trade, the individual will have less incentive to invest resources in strategic moves designed to exploit his bargaining position.

Suppose now that a second exchange takes place, shifting the commodity distribution to α''. The bargaining range is again drastically reduced in size, and the distribution more closely approaches the contract locus. The chances of making gains from bargaining have almost disappeared. A final exchange may be considered to place the "solution" on the contract locus at α'''. In this last step there is little or no bargaining in the usual sense since the net gains are small. Both parties are forced into a relatively complete revelation of their true preferences. At the final or "equilibrium" position, the marginal rates of substitution between the two goods must be the same for both parties.

This extremely simple bargaining model can be of some help in the analysis of constitutional choice, since it suggests that the only means of reducing the profitability of individual investment in strategic bargaining is to reduce the size of the bargaining range—to reduce the gains to be expected from such investment. In a situation where substantial gains from mutual cooperation exist, this can only be accomplished by converting *total* decisions into *marginal* ones. This can best be illustrated by reference to the organization of decisions in the market economy.

BARGAINING AND COMPETITIVE MARKETS

The *raison d'être* of market exchange is the expectation of mutual gains. Yet, insofar as markets are competitive, little scope for bargaining exists. Individuals have little incentive to invest scarce resources in strategic endeavor. As Frank Knight emphasizes, competition among individuals does not characterize truly competitive markets, which are almost wholly impersonal in operation. The market mechanism converts all decisions into marginal ones by making all units marginal units. This conversion is effected by the divisibility of goods exchanged, which is, in turn, made possible by the availability of alternatives. The individual buyer or seller secures a "net benefit" or "surplus" from exchange, but the conditions of exchange, the terms of trade, cannot be influenced substantially by his own behavior. He can obtain no incremental personal gains by modifying his behavior because his partner in contract has available multiple alternatives. Thus, the buyer who refuses to pay the competitively established price for a good can expect no concessions to his "bargaining" efforts from the seller because the latter can sell at this price to other buyers. Similarly, the seller can anticipate no bargaining advantage from the buyer because the latter can turn to alternative sellers without undue costs.

An essential difference between market and political "exchange" is the absence of alternatives in the latter case. If we disregard the marketlike elements that may be introduced by a decentralized organization of political choice, which will be discussed later in this chapter, and concentrate on the collective action of a single governmental entity, the individual participants must, by definition, reach agreement with each other. It is not easy to withdraw from the ultimate "social contract," to turn to alternative "sellers of public goods," although the possibility of "out-migration" should never be completely left out of account. For our discussion it seems best to assume that the individual must remain in the social group. This almost guarantees that there will exist some incentive for the individual to invest resources in strategic behavior, in bargaining.

The simplest market analogy to the political process is that of trade between two isolated individuals, each of whom knows that no alternative buyers and sellers exist. This is the model already discussed in some detail.

BARGAINING AND "EFFICIENT" SOLUTIONS

In a situation containing scope for bargaining, is there any assurance that an "efficient" solution will be reached at all? Will the contract locus be attained? All positions on the contract locus are defined to be "efficient" in the limited Pareto sense. Given a position on the locus, there is no other position to which a shift could be made without reducing the utility of at least one of the parties to the bargain. Thus, an "efficient" position in this sense is also an "equilibrium" position, since neither party to the bargain will have an incentive to propose further exchange. All gains from trade are secured once the contract locus is attained. The fact that mutual gains from trade will continue to exist until a solution on the locus is achieved would seem to insure that all parties will find it advantageous to continue to invest in bargaining effort until an "efficient" solution is attained. Initial investments may, of course, yield zero returns for both parties if both are stubborn and make errors in interpreting the true preferences of the other. Nevertheless, note that the failure of initial investment does not directly reduce the incentive for further investment. The possibility of mutual gains continues to exist. Moreover, failure to reach agreement may itself provide certain information to both parties which will tend to make further investments in bargaining more likely to yield returns. It seems reasonably certain, therefore, that the contract locus will be reached ultimately if the parties are rational.[1]

This is not to suggest that there may not be an overinvestment in bargaining, in decision-making, which may more than offset the total gains from trade. In a larger sense, bargaining activity may involve "inefficient" resource usage, even though the contract locus is achieved as a result of each single bargaining process.

THE MULTIPLE-PARTY BARGAIN

In the simple two-party model, each individual has some incentive to invest in strategic maneuvering. Each party can, by refusing to agree and by remaining stubborn, prevent exchange (agreement) from being made. The

1. The results of recent laboratory experiments strongly support the hypothesis that the outcome of two-person bargains will fall on the contract locus. See Sidney Siegel and Lawrence E. Fouraker, *Bargaining and Group Decision-Making* (New York: McGraw-Hill, 1960).

"marginal value" of each individual's consent is the whole of the "gains from trade," but this consent is also required if the individual himself is to be able to participate in the division of the spoils. He can forestall all benefits to others by remaining recalcitrant, but the cost of so doing is the sacrifice of all private gain. Failure to reach agreement is his responsibility as well as that of his partner.

If the size of the group is expanded, this aspect of the bargaining process is modified. Consider now a three-man, rather than a two-man, bargaining group. Here each party will realize that his own consent has a "marginal value," to the total group, equal to the full value of the total gains expected as a result of agreement or group action. Each of the three will also realize that his own consent is required for his own participation in any gain, but his private responsibility for attaining group agreement is less than in the two-man case. The single person will realize that, in addition to his own, the consent of *two others* is required. Greater uncertainty will be present in the bargaining process, and the single participant will be more reluctant to grant concessions. As in the two-party model, it seems clear that the contract plane will ultimately be reached; but it seems equally clear that the investment of each individual in decision-making will be larger than in the two-party model.

As the size of the bargaining group increases beyond three, the costs of decision-making for the individual participant will continue to increase, probably at an increasing rate. Everyday experience in the work of committees of varying size confirms this direct functional relationship between the individual costs of collective decision-making and the size of the group required to reach agreement.

MULTIPLE-PARTY BARGAINS WITHIN A TOTAL GROUP OF FIXED SIZE

We have just discussed the expected costs of decision-making when all parties to the group are required to agree before group action is taken. The dependence of the expected costs on the size of the total group is closely related to, but also quite distinct from, that which relates expected costs to the change in the number of persons required to agree *within a total group of defined size*. It is the second relationship that is important for the constitutional choice of rules, and it is in the difference between these two relationships that the explanation for much collective activity is to be found.

The distinction may be illustrated in Figure 10. The V curve represents the expected costs, to the individual participant, as the size of the group is ex-

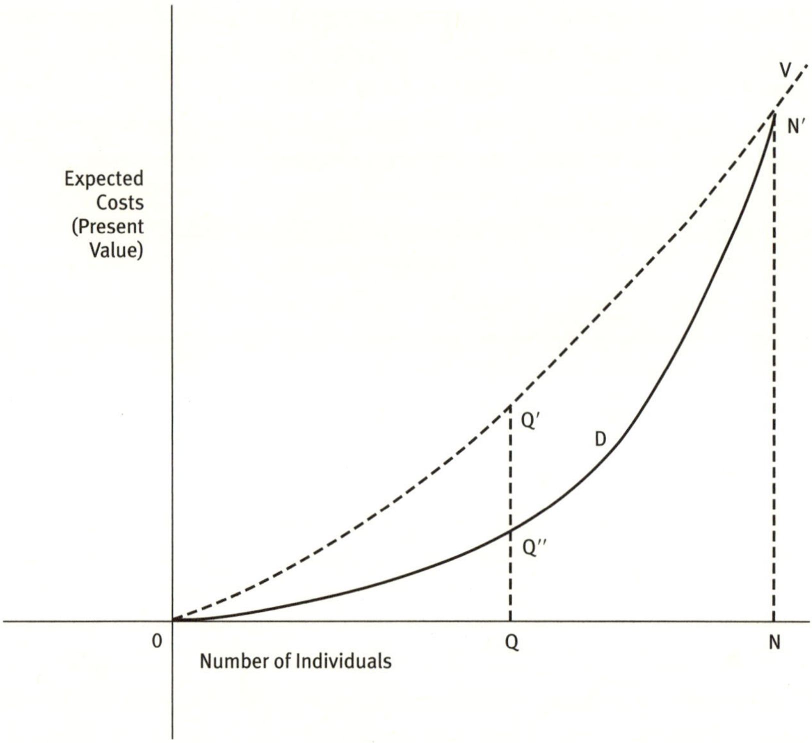

FIGURE 10

panded, always under the requirement that *all* members of the group must give consent to group action taken: in other words, under the rule of unanimity. Thus at QQ′ it represents the expected costs of obtaining unanimous agreement among a specific group of Q persons, and at NN′ the costs of obtaining unanimous agreement among N persons. By contrast, the D curve (which was employed in Chapter 6 without a full explanation) relates the expected costs of decision-making (to the individual) to the number of persons, *out of a group of N persons*, who are required by various decision-making rules to agree or consent before choices *for the whole group* are finally made. Thus QQ″ represents the expected costs of obtaining the consent of a given percentage (Q/N) of the specified group N. At point N, of course, the two curves take on identical values. For any size group there may be derived a decision-rule curve similar to the unique curve D drawn with respect to a group of size N. Note that, for any group, the D curve rises as the proportion of the group required for decision increases, but this curve does not rise so rapidly as the unanimity curve V until N is approached, and the D curve remains below the V curve throughout its range.

The two curves increase for the same reason: the costs of securing agreement, *within the decision-making group*, increase as the size of the group increases. The D curve increases less rapidly than the V curve because the adoption of less-than-unanimity rules sharply restricts the profitability of individual investment in strategic bargaining. In a real sense, the introduction of less-than-unanimity rules creates or produces effective *alternatives* for the collective-choice process, alternatives which prevent decision-making costs from reaching prohibitive heights. Let us take an example in which all members of a total group of the size (N/2 + 1), defined as equal to Q in Figure 10, are required to agree unanimously. The costs of decision-making expected by the individual participant may be quite significant (Q′ in Figure 10). Suppose we now consider the costs of decision-making expected by the individual member of a group of size N when the rule of simple majority prevails (Q″ in Figure 10). Note that this rule does not specify *which* individuals of the total population will make up the majority. The rule states only that a group of size (N/2 + 1) must agree on decision. Here the individual in the majority will have relatively little incentive to be overly stubborn in exploiting his bargaining position since he will realize that *alternative* members of the decisive coalition can be drawn from the minority. Bargaining within the majority group will, of course, take place. Such bargaining is a necessary preliminary to coalition formation. However, the bargaining range, and hence the opportunities for productive individual investment of resources in strategy, is substantially reduced.

Note that what is important here is the presence of alternative individuals outside the decision-making group who can potentially become members of the group. The D curve in Figure 10 falls quite sharply as it moves to the left of N: that is, as the decision-making rule departs from absolute unanimity. A good practical illustration of this point is provided in the requirements for approval of zoning variances in some municipalities. In some places the “20 per cent protest rule” prevails. Any 20 per cent of property owners in the relevant area can raise objection to proposed departures from the zoning ordinance. Therefore, at least four-fifths of the property owners in areas adjacent to the property, the usage of which is to be modified, must consent implicitly or explicitly before a zoning variance can be granted. It is evident that this consent of 80 per cent will be much easier to secure than the consent of

100 per cent. In the latter case, the most stubborn of the group may hold out and try to secure the whole value of the "surplus" expected. However, under the 20 per cent protest rule, even the stubborn property owner, if offered some compensation, will be reluctant to refuse consent when he fears that he will be unable to secure co-operation in making an effective protest.

This distinction between the two separate decision-making-costs functions provides an important link in our explanation for the collectivization of certain activities. If activities are left in the private sector, the securing of wholly voluntary agreements to remove existing externalities requires, in effect, that all, or nearly all, parties be compensated sufficiently to insure their consent. Such voluntary action is practically equivalent to a decision-making rule requiring unanimity for collective choice (note the coincidence of the curves V and D at N′). The bargaining costs that are involved in organizing such arrangements may be prohibitively high in many cases, with the result that, if left in the private sector, the externalities will be allowed to continue. On the other hand, the costs of organizing collective decisions under less-than-unanimity rules may be less than those expected from the continuation of the externalities. Such activities fall in the fifth ordering discussed in Chapter 6.

BARGAINING COSTS, DECISION-MAKING RULES, AND THE REVELATION OF PREFERENCES

The recognition, at the time of constitutional choice, of the costs that will be involved in securing the consent of the whole membership of the group on any single issue or set of issues is the only reason why the utility-maximizing individual will agree to place any activity in the collective sector, and, for activities placed there, will agree that operational decisions shall be made on anything less than consensus. Constitutional choices as to what activities to collectivize and what decision-making rules to adopt for these activities must depend on an assessment of the expected relative costs of decision-making on the one hand and of the operation of the activity on the other. To be able to make this assessment accurately, the individual needs to have an idea concerning the actual working of the various decision-making rules. We shall discuss some of these in detail in Part III. It is important to note here, however, that our theory of individual constitutional choice helps to explain many real-world institutions. The existence of externalities has long been used by scholars in welfare economics to justify collective action, but no one, to our knowledge, has satisfactorily provided any *economic* explanation for the general acceptance of less-than-unanimity rules for collective choice-making.[2]

In order to fully understand the theory, several separate issues relating to collective decision-making must be kept quite distinct. We have repeatedly emphasized the necessity of distinguishing between individual choice *at the constitutional level*, where the choice is among rules, and individual choice of concrete and specific action, *within defined rules*. If attention is concentrated on collective decision-making at the second, or action, level, the rule of unanimity is the only decision-making rule that is indicated by widely acceptable welfare criteria. Only under this rule will "solutions" be produced that are Pareto-optimal. The acknowledged fact that the inherent interdependence of individual choices in politics makes strategic behavior inevitable does not, in any way, invalidate this conclusion. Regardless of the number of persons in the choosing group, the contract surface will be achieved, if we assume rationality on the part of all members.

Modern welfare economics has been concerned primarily with collective action at the concrete level. Attempts have been made to devise criteria for judging specific policy measures. The reaching of unanimous agreement is the only possible test for improvement in the restricted Pareto sense, although this point has not been developed sufficiently. The recent theory of public expenditure, developed by Paul A. Samuelson and Richard A. Musgrave,[3] represents an extension of welfare-economics models to the collective-goods sector. In this discussion the distinction between the failure to attain an "optimal" solution and the failure of individuals to reveal their "true" preferences does not seem to have been made clear. As we have emphasized, whenever a bargaining opportunity presents itself, the individual will find it profitable to invest resources in decision-making, in bargaining. The two-person model above demonstrated, however, that the individual investment in strategy, which uses up resources, does not necessarily serve to reduce the attractiveness of further investment unless shifts toward the con-

2. For one of the few discussions relating to this issue, see Richard A. Musgrave, *The Theory of Public Finance* (New York: McGraw-Hill, 1959), chap. 6.

3. Paul A. Samuelson, "The Pure Theory of Public Expenditure," *Review of Economics and Statistics*, XXXVI (1954), 387–89; "Diagrammatic Exposition of a Theory of Public Expenditure," *Review of Economics and Statistics*, XXXVII (1955), 350–56. Richard A. Musgrave, *The Theory of Public Finance*.

tract locus are achieved. Bargaining ceases only during "equilibrium," that is, when the locus is attained.

In what sense does the presence of a bargaining opportunity cause individuals to conceal their "true" preferences? Each participant will try to make his "adversaries" think that he is less interested in "exchange" than is actually the case. However, in the only meaningful "equilibrium," the *marginal* evaluation of each individual must be fully revealed. On the contract surface the marginal rates of substitution among alternatives are equal for all individuals in the agreement. Note that this is the same revelation of preferences or tastes that market institutions force on the individual. There is nothing in the market process which requires the participating individual to reveal the extent of his "consumer's or seller's surplus." The market behavior of the individual reveals little information about his total demand schedule for a good; it does reveal his preferences at the appropriate *margins of decision* which he determines by his ability to vary the quantity of units that he keeps or sells. There exists, therefore, no fundamental difference between the market process, where bargaining opportunities are absent in the ideal case, and the political process, where bargaining opportunities are almost necessarily present, so far as the *revelation of individual preferences at the point of solution* is concerned. The difference in the two processes lies in the fact that bargaining opportunities afforded in the political process *cause the individual to invest more resources in decision-making*, and, in this way, cause the attainment of "solution" to be much more costly.

The adoption of specific decision-making rules is required, therefore, not because bargaining opportunities force individuals to conceal their preferences or because bargaining can be expected to yield "imperfect" solutions in particular cases, but because of the relative "inefficiency" of the process. It is easy to see that, with a generally applicable rule of unanimity, there would be relative overinvestment in decision-making. In this case the group would be devoting too much time and effort to the reaching of agreement relative to other pursuits.[4] The possible overinvestment in collective decision-making

4. The approach taken here assumes that the reduction of decision-making costs, taken independently, is desirable. Of course, if individuals secure positive utility in participating in political discussion and bargaining, the importance of decision-making costs is reduced. The analogy with ordinary games comes to mind here. If the purpose of a game is "efficiency," this could best be secured by allowing all players to get on the same "side," as Frank Knight has suggested. Specific rules are adopted which will make for an "interesting" but not an "efficient" game.

It must be acknowledged that this concept is not wholly foreign to the political process.

can be prevented only at the constitutional level. Once we are at the operational or action level, the decision-making costs will be related directly to the *rules* governing the choices. The "optimal" investment in decision-making will, of course, vary from activity to activity since, as we have shown, these costs must be combined with expected external costs before an "optimal" rule can be chosen.

GROUP SIZE AND DECISION-MAKING COSTS

The discussion of earlier chapters has shown that the theory of individual constitutional choice, although developed in purely conceptual terms, is not wholly empty. Important implications of the theory have been suggested. Additional ones may be added as a result of the more careful consideration of the second basic functional relationship between costs and the number of individuals required for agreement. The costs that the individual expects to incur as a result of his own participation in collective decision-making vary directly with the size of the deciding group in a given-sized total population. Significantly, these costs also vary directly with the size of the total population. A concrete illustration may be helpful.

Let us suppose there are two collective units, one of which has a total voting population of 100 citizens while the second has a voting population of 1000 citizens. If our hypotheses about the costs of collective decision-making are valid, there may be several activities which the rational individual will choose to collectivize in the first "country" that he will leave under private organization in the second, and larger, political unit. The expected costs of organizing decisions, *under any given rule*, will be less in the smaller unit than in the larger, assuming that the populations of each are roughly comparable. For example, simple majority rule in the first "country" will require the assent of only 51 citizens to a decision. In the second "country" the assent of 501 citizens will be needed. The differences in the costs of organizing such majority coalitions may be significant in the two cases. On the other hand, if

The idea that politics is one of the noblest endeavors is central to the Greek conception. Hannah Arendt's *The Human Condition* (Chicago: University of Chicago Press, 1958) is a modern statement of this position. For our purposes it is important to note only that, insofar as engaging in political bargaining is pleasurable in itself, the rational individual will choose to weigh the resources costs of this activity less heavily relative to the external costs of collective action. Other things being equal, he will, therefore, choose a set of more inclusive decision-making rules.

the two "countries" possess equal ultimate "sovereignty," the expected external costs of any given collective action may not be substantially different in the two units. From this it follows that, for those activities which are collectivized in both units, the smaller unit will normally have a more inclusive decision-making rule than the larger unit.

This is a very important implication which has normative value. As we have suggested, the costs of reaching agreement, of bargaining, are, from a "social" point of view, wasteful. One means of reducing these costs is to organize collective activity in the smallest units consistent with the extent of the externality that the collectivization is designed to eliminate.

THE OPTIMUM SIZE OF GOVERNMENTS

On the basis of the theory of individual constitutional choice developed in Part II, it is relatively straightforward to construct a theory for the optimum size of the collective unit, where this size is also subject to constitutional determinations. The group should be extended so long as the expected costs of the spillover effects from excluded jurisdictions exceed the expected incremental costs of decision-making resulting from adding the excluded jurisdictions.

Suppose that an activity is performed at A (see Figure 11); let us say that this represents the family unit and that the activity is elementary education. Clearly, the individuals most directly affected belong to the family unit making private decisions. It is acknowledged, however, that these decisions influence the other members of the group. Other members of the local community are most directly affected, as conceptually shown by the crosshatched area enclosed by the circle B. Costs are also imposed on individuals living in the larger community, perhaps the municipal area, shown by C. Even for individuals living in other parts of the state some external costs of educational decisions can be expected, as shown by the area D. Moreover, in a remote way, the family in Portland, Oregon, influences the utility of the family in North Carolina through its educational decisions. The question is: What is the appropriate size of the collective unit for the organization of elementary education, assuming that collectivization at some level is desirable? Conceptually, the answer is given by a comparison between the additional decision-making costs involved in moving from a lower to a higher level and the spillover costs that remain from retaining the activity at the lower level.

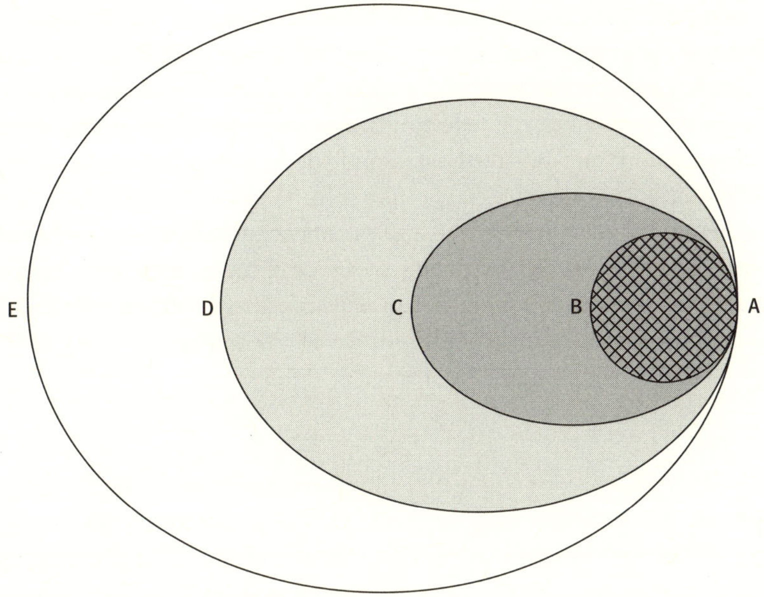

FIGURE 11

DECENTRALIZATION AND ALTERNATIVES FOR CHOICE

The preceding analysis follows directly from the theory of constitutional choice previously developed. In order to complete the picture, we must add one other element that is of significant importance. If the organization of collective activity can be effectively decentralized, this decentralization provides one means of introducing marketlike alternatives into the political process. If the individual can have available to him several political units organizing the same collective activity, he can take this into account in his locational decisions. This possibility of individual choice among alternative collective units limits both the external costs imposed by collective action and the expected costs of decision-making. Insofar as the expected external costs of collective action are due to the anticipation of decisions adverse to the interest of the individual, the limit to damages expected must be the costs of migration to another collective unit. Similarly, the limit of individual investment in bargaining will be imposed by the costs of shifting to a more agreeable collectivity. In concrete terms, this suggests that the individual will not be forced to suffer unduly large and continuing capital losses from adverse collective decisions when he can move freely to other units, nor will he find it advantageous to invest too much time and effort in persuading his stubborn fellow citizens to agree with him.

The decentralization of collective activity allows both of the basic-costs functions to be reduced; in effect, it introduces elements into the political process that are not unlike those found in the operating of competitive markets.[5]

Both the decentralization and size factors suggest that, where possible, collective activity should be organized in small rather than large political units. Organization in large units may be justified only by the overwhelming importance of the externality that remains after localized and decentralized collectivization.

DECISION-MAKING COSTS, EXTERNAL COSTS, AND CONSENSUS ON VALUES

The difficulties in reaching agreement will vary from group to group, even when all groups are assumed to contain rational individuals and no others. The second basic-costs function will be generally up-sloping for individuals in all groups, but the rate of increase will vary from one collective unit to another. The amount of investment in strategic bargaining that an individual can be expected to make will depend, to some extent, on his assessment of the bargaining skills of his fellow members in the group. It seems reasonable to expect that more will be invested in bargaining in a group composed of members who have distinctly different external characteristics than in a group composed of roughly homogeneous members. Increased uncertainty about the tastes and the bargaining skills of his fellows will lead the individual to be more stubborn in his own efforts. When he knows his fellows better, the individual will surely be less stubborn in his bargaining, and for perfectly rational reasons. The over-all costs of decision-making will be lower, given any collective-choice rule, in communities characterized by a reasonably homogeneous population than in those characterized by a heterogeneous population.

5. The aspects of decentralized collective activity discussed here have been developed by Stigler and Tiebout. See George J. Stigler, "The Tenable Range of Functions of Local Government," *Federal Expenditure Policy for Economic Growth and Stability* (Washington: Joint Economic Committee, 1957), pp. 213–16; and Charles M. Tiebout, "A Pure Theory of Local Expenditures," *Journal of Political Economy*, LXIV (1956), 416–24.

The implication of this hypothesis suggests that the more homogeneous community should adopt more inclusive rules for the making of collective decisions. However, the homogeneity characteristic affects external costs as well as decision-making costs. Thus, the community of homogeneous persons is more likely to accept less restrictive rules even though it can "afford" more restrictive ones. By contrast, the community that includes sharp differences among individual citizens and groups cannot afford the decision-making costs involved in near-unanimity rules for collective choice, but the very real fears of destruction of life and property from collective action will prompt the individual to refuse anything other than such rules. Both elements of the costs of collective action remain very high in such communities.

The difficulties involved in "exporting" Anglo-American governmental institutions to other areas of the world have been widely recognized. Our model helps to explain this phenomenon. Regardless of the compromises on decision-making rules that may be adopted, the relative costs of collective organization of activity can be expected to be much greater in a community lacking some basic consensus among its members on fundamental values. The implication of this is the obvious conclusion that the range of collective activity should be more sharply curtailed in such communities, assuming, of course, that the individualistic postulates are accepted. Many activities that may be quite rationally collectivized in Sweden, a country with a relatively homogeneous population, should be privately organized in India, Switzerland, or the United States.

PART III

ANALYSES OF DECISION-MAKING RULES

CHAPTER 9

THE STRUCTURE OF THE MODELS

The theory of individual constitutional choice developed in Part II is very general. Problems that arise in the individual's estimates of expected costs must be introduced before more useful applications of the theory can be made. Before the individual can estimate accurately the external costs that a given collective-choice rule will impose on him, he must have some idea as to how the rule itself will work. Our next step, therefore, is to analyze some of the more important decision-making rules. Most of the discussion will be concerned with a single rule—that of simple majority. However, the analysis of this rule, once completed, may be modified slightly and extended without difficulty to other more or less inclusive rules for social choice.

Before commencing the analysis proper, the underlying assumptions of our models must be stated. The restricted nature of these assumptions, their "unrealism," must appear to limit sharply the relevance of our conclusions to real-world political institutions. We shall argue, however, that such limitation is largely apparent and that, fundamentally, the conclusions are generally applicable to a wide variety of collective institutions and that they help us to understand and to explain many real-world phenomena.

We shall continue to focus our attention on the calculus of the single individual, but here we are no longer placing him at the stage of constitutional choice. We assume the existence of a constitution that lays down the rules for amalgamating individual choices into social decisions. The individual participates in taking direct collective action with a knowledge of the fixed decision-making rules. As before, he is assumed to be motivated by a desire to further his own interest, to maximize his expected utility, narrowly or broadly defined. In this stage, which we have called and shall continue to call the *operational* as opposed to the *constitutional*, the individual's interest will be more readily identifiable and more sharply distinguishable from those of his fellows than was the case at the constitutional level of decision.

DIRECT DEMOCRACY AND REPRESENTATIVE GOVERNMENT

The approach proceeds from the calculus of the individual, and it is, therefore, more concise and understandable if the individual is presumed to choose directly among the alternatives of collective action. That is to say, the analysis is sharper if we assume that collective decisions are made by rules of direct democracy. Quite clearly, this model has direct applicability only to an extremely limited set of real-world institutions. The New England town is the exceptional rather than the normal form of democratic organization. It is necessary to explain the operation of various rules at this most simple organizational level before proceeding to the more complex organizational forms contained in larger political units.

Our analysis of direct democracy can, we think, be extended to almost any set of political institutions while still retaining much of its explanatory and predictive value. We shall discuss this extension in Chapter 15, but now we shall proceed to analyze the operation of decision-making rules in terms of simple models involving individual participation in collective choices at the operational level. We shall occasionally refer to the action of legislative assemblies which seems to conform to the implications of our analysis. In one sense, these phenomena confirm the hypothesis that our model is of general relevance.[1]

THE TIME SEQUENCE OF COLLECTIVE DECISIONS

Perhaps the most distinctive feature of our models, in comparison with other analyses of collective choice-making, is the central place assigned to the plurality of collective decisions over time. The analysis is not designed to explain the operation of decision-making rules on single, isolated issues. The analytical problem posed is that of examining comparative rules for choice as these apply to many decisions spread over "time." Any rule must be analyzed in terms of the results it will produce, not on a single issue, but on the whole set of issues extending over a period of conceptually finite length.

1. Our approach is fundamentally different in this respect from that employed by Downs. He also adopts an "economic" approach to democratic process, but, instead of starting at the individual level, he starts with two-party representative democracy and analyzes the political process in terms of the attempts of governments to maximize voter support. See Anthony Downs, *An Economic Theory of Democracy* (New York: Harper and Bros., 1957).

The individual participant's recognition that issues for collective choice are not unique and isolated events imposes severe limitations on any analysis of single decisions. Issues may be wholly unrelated in their descriptive characteristics, but the rational participant will recognize the time sequence of political choice. Moreover, this will cause him to seek "gains from trade," when possible, by exchanging his vote on one issue for reciprocal support of his own interest by other participants on other issues. Thus, the time sequence of collective choice is very important in that it allows us to introduce an *economic* dimension to individual votes somewhat more handily than would otherwise be the case.

The difficulty of attributing such an economic dimension to votes in the political process has long been one of the stumbling blocks in the extension of economic reasoning to political models. The economic value of votes is confirmed by the selling and buying activities of individuals in "corrupt" circumstances, but models based on this "immoral" behavior pattern have not been considered to be useful in analyzing accepted political behavior. In the latter the essential requirement of *scarcity* has not been incorporated in the models, with the result that the applicability of an economic approach has been sharply limited. The individual participant normally has a single vote on each separate issue; votes do not "run out" or get "used up" as do the allegedly analogous "dollar votes" of individual participants in market choices. There seems to have been present a rather common failure to recognize the simple fact that if political votes did not have economic value, "corruption" would be impossible.

Individual votes result in collective decisions that exert economic effects. Each decision can be described in terms of its effects on individual incomes and wealth. So defined or described, the collective decision assumes a time dimension; it can be located in time and its impact can be measured over time. The political vote that assumes economic value can only refer to the vote exercised when *decisive* action is taken. The opportunity for the decision-making group to modify and change a provisionally approved decision through various forms of repeat voting represents yet another factor that has caused the application of an economic dimension to the political vote to be neglected.

Individuals' votes have economic value. Moreover, for any commodity or service having economic value, a market will tend to emerge from the ordinary self-seeking behavior of men unless there are strong legal or moral prohibitions against trade. Such prohibitions are, of course, present to prevent the development of open markets in individual votes,[2] but this does nothing toward removing the economic content. The absence of open markets serves only to prevent the full utilization of the pricing mechanism in allocating the scarce elements among competing alternative uses. Moreover, if pricing cannot be employed, some substitute means of *rationing* must be introduced. There are an almost infinite number of schemes that could be devised, and each scheme can be described by a set of voting rules. In each case valuable individual votes will be distributed on some basis, and this basis may be wholly *unrelated* to individual evaluations.

Let us look briefly at an example. Suppose that the group is required to make only one collective decision. It must decide how to divide up the one and only lot of manna that has fallen from heaven. There are five members of the group, and the constitution dictates that all collective decisions are to be made by simple majority rule. This means that three, any three, of the five members must agree. Since buying and selling votes is ruled out, and since there is only one decision to be made, the first three individuals who form a voting coalition will secure the manna. The two in the minority may place a much higher value on the manna than any one of the three winners, but this is irrelevant to the decision. We shall discuss models similar to this one in much greater detail later. Our purpose here is to indicate not only that any voting rule acts as a means of rationing, but that this rationing may cause a distribution of collective "goods" that is wholly unrelated to individual evaluations.

We note, however, that the introduction of a time sequence of political choices allows a market of sorts to be developed without the necessity of changing the rules for decision on single issues. If the individual participant recognizes the economic value of his own vote to others on certain issues and, in turn, recognizes the economic value of others' votes to him on separate issues, he will be motivated to engage in "trade." Moreover, if ways of "trading" can be found that do not clearly conflict with accepted standards of behavior, individuals will seek mutual advantages in this way. The possibility of exchanging votes on separate issues opens up such trading prospects. The individual may effectively, but imperfectly, "sell" his vote on a particular is-

2. At this point in our analysis we do not imply either praise or condemnation of any behavior of the individual on moral or ethical grounds. Language conventions force us to use the words "moral" and "ethical," and moral principles must be discussed later in the book, but we do not want to prejudice the analysis by moralizing at this early stage.

sue, securing in return the votes of other individuals on issues of more direct interest. This process of "logrolling" will be carefully analyzed in the following chapter, but some preliminary points should be made here.

With relatively few exceptions logrolling phenomena have been viewed as deviations from the orderly working of the democratic process. This view seems to have been adopted for two separate reasons. First, and more important, the economic motivation for political behavior reveals itself most clearly in the occasional examples of Congressional logrolling legislation. Students of the political process, who adopt the view that, at base, political behavior is not motivated by economic interest, must explain such action in terms of aberrations from more orthodox behavior. Secondly, and related to the first, there has been a failure to recognize that logrolling phenomena are much more pervasive than the more obvious examples would indicate. The phenomena surely occur at several levels of political sophistication, and the fact that the cruder instances occur at all should give the student of political process cause for looking somewhat carefully for more "acceptable" means of accomplishing similar purposes.[3]

It seems clear that, insofar as divergent interests affect the political choices of individuals and groups, the logrolling process provides the general model for analyzing the various choice-making rules.[4] Surely the individual partici-

3. An interesting recent novel about Washington politics, written by an observing journalist, includes logrolling at several levels as an important part of the political picture. See Allen Drury, *Advise and Consent* (New York: Doubleday, 1959). For the reactions of an "orthodox" liberal student of politics to this approach, see the review of the book that appeared in *The Reporter* for 11 November 1959.

4. On this point, we agree with the view of Arthur Bentley. His statement on the issue is worth noting: "Log-rolling is a term of opprobrium. This is because it is used mainly with reference to its grosser forms. But grossness as it is used in this connection merely means that certain factors which we regard as of great importance are treated by the legislator as of small importance and traded off by him for things which we regard as a mess of pottage, but which he regards as the main business of his activity. Log-rolling is, however, in fact, the most characteristic legislative process. When we condemn it 'in principle,' it is only by contrasting it with some assumed pure public spirit which is supposed to guide legislators, or which ought to guide them, and which enables them to pass judgment in Jovian calm on that which is best 'for the whole people.' Since there is nothing which is best literally for the whole people, group arrays being what they are, the test is useless, even if one could actually find legislative judgments which are not reducible to interest-group activities. And when we have reduced the legislative process to the play of group interests, then log-rolling, or give and take, appears as the very na-

pant in collective choice recognizes the time sequence of events requiring collective action, and, just as surely, he will be motivated to engage in mutually advantageous "trades" or "compromises" with his fellows. The cruder models, in which the trade is made explicit, are useful in that they are more readily subject to analysis, but the more important cases probably occur beneath the outwardly visible surface of "politics." The assumption that these crude models provide a general approach to the operation of political rules seems considerably more acceptable than the contrary one which assumes that the analysis of rules on the basis of single issues is a more satisfactory approach to a general theory of collective choice.

PERFECT AND IMPERFECT MARKETS

When a time sequence of issues is allowed for, some trading of votes takes place. No longer does the decision-making rule alone serve as the rationing device. An illustrative analogy may be helpful. Suppose that all rents on dwelling accommodations are strictly controlled, and at levels much below hypothetical "market" values. Individual landlords are subject to prosecution if they accept direct money payments ("bribes") above the controlled rents from prospective tenants. On the other hand, they are not prevented from entering into other "exchanges" with tenants at freely determined and mutually advantageous terms of trade. Landlords may "sell" furniture to tenants, or they may "purchase" other commodities. Under circumstances such as these, the expected results would be less arbitrary than under the alternative system in which no free "exchanges" between landlord and tenant are allowed, that is, in which housing is rationed solely on a nonprice basis. On the other hand, the nonprice aspects of the "market" system would make the expected results diverge significantly from that which could be predicted to emerge from a completely free market in rental units.

In our rent-control analogy, to which we shall return in a later chapter, the combination of price and nonprice rationing appears as a special institutional pattern. In the political-vote case, however, this in-between or "imperfect"

ture of the process. It is compromise, not in the abstract moral form, which philosophers can sagely discuss, but in the practical form with which every legislator who gets results through government is acquainted. It is trading. It is the adjustment of interests." (Arthur Bentley, *The Process of Government* [Bloomington, Ind.: The Principia Press, 1935 (first published 1908)], pp. 370–71.)

model represents, perhaps, the most general model of democratic process. This "imperfection," however, makes the analysis especially difficult.[5] For this reason we shall find it necessary, in the chapters that follow, to employ extremely simplified models.

Some predictions concerning the results to be expected from the operations of the in-between model may also be derived by considering the alternative models that bracket the logrolling or imperfect-vote marketing model. As we have suggested, other scholars have analyzed the nonprice model, being forced to do so by their concentration on single issues. To our knowledge, however, the full price-rationing model has not been fully developed: that is, the model in which political votes are freely marketed for money has not been subjected to rigorous analysis, even for simple voting rules. The tools supplied by modern game theory are helpful in this respect, and in Chapters 11 and 12 we analyze the operation of simple majority-rule games under the assumption of full side payments. By relaxing the full side-payments assumption, we may also compare this model with one more closely approximating the logrolling model.

THE INTENSITY OF INDIVIDUAL PREFERENCE

Much of the traditional discussion about the operation of voting rules seems to have been based on the implicit assumption that the positive and negative preferences of voters for and against alternatives of collective choice are of approximately equal intensities. Only on an assumption such as this can the failure to introduce a more careful analysis of vote-trading through logrolling be explained. If all intensities of preference are identical over all individuals and over all issues, no trading of votes is possible. In this case the individual feels as strongly on one issue as on any other, and he will never rationally agree to exchange his vote for reciprocal favors.

An example may be helpful. Consider a society confronted with three issues in sequence. The group must choose between A and $\overline{A}$, between B and $\overline{B}$, and between C and $\overline{C}$. Let us assume that the constitution dictates that each of these issues shall be decided by simple majority voting rules. Assume that, in each case, 51 per cent of the voters favor the first alternative and

5. "Imperfection" is used here only in its purely economic sense. Nothing in the discussion should be taken to suggest that a "perfect" market in political votes would be, in any sense, "perfect" in respect to some set of ideals for the organization of a political system.

49 per cent favor the second alternative, but assume also that the majorities and the minorities are not uniformly composed over the three issues. If all preferences are equal in intensity, no bargains can be struck, and A, B, and C will be chosen. Consider Voter I who favors A, B, and $\overline{\text{C}}$, and Voter II who favors $\overline{\text{A}}$, $\overline{\text{B}}$, and C. Neither would be willing to trade his vote on two issues for the other's vote on one issue, and a one-for-one trade would not be mutually advantageous.

Intuitively the assumption of equal intensity of preference seems unacceptable. Clearly the more general assumption is that individual "tastes" for collectively obtained "goods" vary in both object and intensity. In the extremes there would seem to be no question of such variance. If the issue to be decided is whether or not Voter I will or will not be executed, the intensity of preference of Voter I against this action will clearly, in some circumstances, be greater than the desires of other voters in favor of the action. As with certain other aspects of political theory, there seems to have been a failure here to distinguish between positive analysis and normative theory. Implicit in much of the discussion of majority rule has been the idea that individual votes *should* be treated as reflecting equal intensities of preference, quite independent of whether or not the norms agree with the facts in the case. This idea, in turn, probably stems from the more fundamental norm of democratic organization—that of political equality. Political equality may be fully accepted as essential to any form of democratic process, but this does not imply that individual votes on particular issues should be considered *as if* they reflect equal intensities of preferences over all participants.

The assumption of equal intensity of preference for all voters over all issues really amounts to imputing to each individual a most restricted utility function, and one that is wholly different from that which is employed in economic analysis. Not only is utility measurable; it is directly comparable among separate individuals. To the modern economist this approach to individual calculus seems anachronistic and sterile.

EQUAL INTENSITIES AND MAJORITY RULE

Although we do not propose to discuss the equal-intensity assumption in detail here, a brief digression on the relationship between it and simple majority rule may be worthwhile. When all individual preferences are of assumed equal intensity, simple majority rule will insure that the summed "benefits" from action will exceed the summed "losses." In this way simple majority rule appears to assume a unique position in terms of a very restricted "welfare" criterion.

Consider our earlier example. Recall that 51 per cent of the voters favor A and that 49 per cent favor $\bar{A}$, and that positive and negative intensities are equal. Let us interpret this equal intensity specifically as indicating that any voter would be willing to give up his preference (to accept the reverse) for $100.00. Thus, passage of the legislation in question will benefit 51 per cent of the voters by $100 each, and it will harm 49 per cent of the voters by $100 each. In the hundred-man model, A would be selected by simple majority voting, and total benefits of $5100 exceed total losses of $4900.

Note that other voting rules need not produce this result, unless compensation of some sort is allowed. For example, under a 53 per cent voting rule the project could not be approved, and, in the additive sense employed above, the community would "lose" the potential $200 in benefits. However, if individual intensities of preference are not equal over all voters, this unique feature of simple majority rule disappears. If minorities feel more strongly on particular issues than majorities, then any rule short of unanimity may lead to policies that will produce net "harm," even if the comparability of utilities among separate persons is still accepted as legitimate.

If vote-trading or compensation in any other form is allowed to be introduced, however, even this extremely restricted uniqueness of simple majority rule disappears. Let us continue to accept the equal intensity assumption. If compensation is introduced, any rule will cause A to be selected over $\bar{A}$ in the foregoing example. If the unanimity rule were in force, for example, the 51 citizens who would be the potential gainers would have to compensate the 49 potential losers by at least $4900 in order to insure the passage of the legislation.[6] The demonstration that the same results would be produced under simple majority rule and the unanimity rule can be extended to apply also to less-than-majority rules. Suppose, for example, that we reverse the arithmetical model and consider the case in which 51 voters oppose the measure while 49 voters approve, and that each voter is willing to give up his preference for $100. If, in this situation, the community operates under a rule in which any person, individually, can order collective action, the potentially damaged majority will be able, out of the opportunity "benefit" they receive from not having the action taken, to fully compensate the members of the minority who might otherwise impose the change. Thus, even with equal in-

6. We are ignoring the costs of decision-making in this example.

tensities assumed from the outset, any voting rule will produce "desirable" results as measured by the comparative utility scales that are implicit in the assumption, provided only that compensation is allowed. However, if no compensation is allowed, either directly or through vote-trading, this restricted "welfare" conclusion no longer holds, and each rule must be analyzed anew for its welfare-producing properties.

As we have suggested, moral restraints may prohibit open buying and selling of votes. However, compensations may be arranged through vote-trading over a sequence of issues. If this is allowed to take place, the uniqueness of simple majority rule disappears, even on the equal-intensity assumption. The unique features reappear only when the equal-intensity assumption is extended to apply over all issues as well as over all voters. If all individual preferences are equally intense over a single issue, and if the preferences of each single individual are equally intense over all the separate issues in which he might participate as a voter, no vote-trading will take place (as we have shown above). Under these circumstances, and under these only, can simple majority rule be said to take on particular characteristic features that distinguish it from other decision-making rules.

Some of these points will be clarified in later chapters. The main purpose here is to emphasize the overly restrictive nature of the equal-intensity assumption. In our models we propose to place no such restrictions on individual preferences for the alternatives of political choice.

EQUAL INTENSITY AND RANDOM VARIATION OF PREFERENCES

The equal-intensity assumption may be employed, without great distortion, in the analysis of the situations in which the intensities of individual preference vary symmetrically among the separate and identifiable subgroups in the population and over all issues. In effect, this situation simply translates the equal-intensity case from the individual to the group level. This situation seems rather special. Normally, an act of government will either markedly harm or markedly benefit at least one specific and identifiable group which will, accordingly, feel more strongly about the issue than will the masses of voters. There are some measures undertaken by governments, however, which are relatively general in nature, that is, which apply in a relatively nondiscriminatory fashion to all individuals and groups. For such measures, individual preferences for and against may vary, but there seems to be no particular reason to expect that such variation would systematically reflect differential intensity. If this variation is distributed in some random fashion among all groups, the employment of the equal-intensity assumption may be reasonably appropriate.

Specific minorities on issues of this sort cannot readily arrange trades to secure favorable action. Majorities will tend always to be able to secure desired action under simple majority rule, and even under other rules if compensations are allowed. The constitutional calculus discussed in previous chapters is not changed significantly in application to this case. The decision-costs function might be changed somewhat, but the appropriate method of choosing decision rules is not modified. Insofar as the equal-intensity assumption is accepted as appropriate, the low-cost point on the aggregate "cost curve" would tend to be that represented by simple majority voting. If intensities of preference are assumed equal, anything desired by a majority, by sheer arithmetic, represents, when approved, a shift to the Pareto-optimality surface. The prevention of the implementation of the will of the majority, in this special case, is never to the "interest" of "society as a whole." If simple majority rule is allowed to prevail, then "optimal" policy will always be selected.

This does not, of course, mean that majority rule will produce results that will be "optimal" for each individual in each particular case. In the case of equal intensity of preferences, the incremental payments that might be needed to obtain any qualified majority are simply transfer payments. The money would go from one man's pocket into the next man's, but there is no mutual gain from trade. In fact, there would be mutual loss when the costs of negotiating agreements are taken into account. Thus, at the time of constitutional choice, if an individual could feel confident that there would be a large number of such "equal intensity" issues to be put up for decision in the future, and if he felt that these issues would be such that his own position would fluctuate randomly between majority and minority without predictable differential intensity in the two cases, then he would expect any rule requiring compensation from the simple majority to a part of the whole of the minority to involve payments by him in some cases and payments to him by others in other cases. Over time, these could be expected to balance out. He might, therefore, wish to save himself the negotiating costs by accepting simple majority rule.

In order for this constitutional decision to be made, however, several conditions would be necessary. In the first place, there must be enough general ("equal intensity") issues expected to arise to insure that they will, with respect to the individual, be mutually canceling. Secondly, the individual must feel fairly confident that he will not tend to be in the minority more than the average number of times. Thirdly, and most restrictive, there must be some method of distinguishing these "general" cases from those clearly characterized by differential intensities of individual preference. Little comment need be added on the first two conditions, but the third may be subjected to analysis. We might try two approaches: first, we might attempt to classify legislative activities that do not seem likely to generate differential intensities of preference among separate groups, and allow decisions on these activities to be made by simple majority rule; secondly, the constitution itself might be so designed that it automatically distinguishes among issues on this basis. The first approach is clearly feasible, and to some extent it is reflected in the constitutions of Western democracies.

Designing a constitution so that it will discriminate automatically between legislation potentially affecting intense minorities and legislation on which the intensity of desires is more or less equal, or can appropriately be assumed so, may not initially seem feasible, but this is, in fact, practicable. As discussed in Chapter 16, a properly designed bicameral legislature does make this distinction automatically.

CHAPTER 10

SIMPLE MAJORITY VOTING[1]

In this chapter we propose to examine the operation of a single collective decision-making rule, that of simple majority, under certain highly restricted assumptions. Theorists of the democratic process have, traditionally, paid little attention to the actual operation of voting rules, and they seem, by and large, to have been uninterested in making generalized predictions regarding the results of actual political decision-making. This relative neglect is explained, at least in part, by the implicit assumption that participants in collective choice seek to further the "public interest," although, as we have suggested, this concept is never defined.

Quite recently a few pioneers have tried to introduce a more positive approach in political theory. Two of these, Anthony Downs and Duncan Black, have tried to develop theories of the political voting process that are based on behavioral assumptions similar to ours.[2] These contributions have been important ones, but the political process has been drastically simplified by concentration on single issues, taken one at a time and separately. Such an approach appears to have only a limited value for our purpose, which is that of analyzing the operation of voting rules as one stage in the individual's constitutional-choice problem, that of choosing the voting rules themselves. The working of a voting rule can be analyzed only as it produces results over a series of issues.

MAJORITY VOTING WITHOUT LOGROLLING

Once it is recognized that the political process embodies a continuing stream of separate decisions, the most general model must include the possibility of vote-trading, or, to use the commonly employed American term,

1. A preliminary version of this chapter has been published. See Gordon Tullock, "Problems of Majority Voting," *Journal of Political Economy*, LXVII (December 1959), 571–79. We are grateful to the editors of this journal for allowing us to reprint those parts of the earlier version that are relevant here.

2. See Anthony Downs, *An Economic Theory of Democracy* (New York: Harper and Bros., 1957) and Duncan Black, *The Theory of Committees and Elections* (Cambridge: Cambridge University Press, 1958).

"logrolling." The existence of a logrolling process is central to our general analysis of simple majority voting, but it will be helpful, by way of comparison, to consider briefly a model in which logrolling is not permitted to take place, either by legal institutions or by certain widely acknowledged moral precepts. There are certain relatively rare institutional situations in which logrolling will not be likely to occur, and in such situations the contrasting analytical model may be explanatory. The best example is the standard referendum on a simple issue. Here the individual voter cannot easily trade his own vote on the one issue for reciprocal favors on other issues because, first, he is uncertain as to when other issues will be voted on in this way, and, second, he and his immediate acquaintances represent such a small part of the total electorate that such trading effort may not be worthwhile. Furthermore, the secret ballot, normally employed in such cases, makes it impossible for any external observer to tell whether voting commitments are honored or not. Under circumstances such as these, the individual voter will make his voting decision in accordance with his own preferences on the single question posed.

In this model each voter indicates his preference, and the preference of the majority of the whole group is decisive. The defect in this procedure, a serious one that has already been mentioned in Chapter 9, is that it ignores the varying intensities of preference among the separate voters. A man who is passionately opposed to a given measure and a man who is slightly favorable but does not care greatly about it are given equal weight in the process of making final decisions. It seems obvious that both of these individuals could be made better off, in terms of their own expressed preferences, if the man strongly opposed should be permitted in some way to "trade" or exchange something with the relatively indifferent supporter of the proposed measure. Applying the strict Pareto rules for determining whether one social situation represents an improvement over another, almost any system of voting that allows some such exchange to take place would be superior to that system which weights all preferences equally on *each issue*. By way of illustration, it is conceivable that a proposal to prohibit Southern Democrats from having access to free radio time might be passed by simple majority vote in a national referendum should the issue be raised in this way. Such a measure, by contrast, would not have the slightest chance of being adopted by the decision-making process actually prevailing in the United States. The measure would never pass the Congress because the supporters of the minority threatened with damage would, if the issue arose, be willing to promise support on other measures in return for votes against such discriminatory legislation. In the complete absence of vote-trading, support for specific legislation may reach 51 per cent without much of this support being intense. In such cases a minimal introduction of vote-trading will insure defeat.

Without some form of vote-trading, even those voters who are completely indifferent on a given issue will find their preferences given as much weight as those of the most concerned individuals. The fact of voting demonstrates that an individual is not wholly indifferent, but many voters may, on referendum issues, be led to the polls more by a sense of duty or obligation than by any real interest in the issue to be determined. Interestingly enough, this "duty of a citizen to vote" is much emphasized as an essential feature of effective democratic process.[3] Even the smallest preference for one side or the other may actually determine the final choice. Permitting those citizens who feel strongly about an issue to compensate in some way those whose opinion is only feebly held can result in a great increase in the well-being of both groups, and the prohibition of such transactions will serve to prevent movement toward the conceptual "social optimality" surface, under almost any definition of this term.

Note that the results under logrolling and under nonlogrolling differ only if the minority feels more intensely about an issue than the majority. If the majority is equal or more intense in its preferences, its will must prevail in either model. It is only when the intensity of preferences of the minority is sufficiently greater than that of the majority to make the minority willing to sacrifice enough votes on other issues to detach marginal voters from the majority (intense members of the majority group may, of course, make counteroffers) that the logrolling process will change the outcome. As we have suggested, the assumption of possible differences in intensity of preferences seems more acceptable than any assumption of equal intensities, and it seems clear that on many issues specific minorities may be much more interested in the outcome of political decisions.

The above discussion suggests that a reasonably strong ethical case can be made for a certain amount of vote-trading under majority-rule institutions.

3. Owl: "We didn't hear all yo' speech—just heard yo' say git on out and vote."
Pogo: "That's enough—as long as you do that, you cannot go wrong."

(Walt Kelley, *The Pogo Papers* [New York: Simon and Schuster, 1952], p. 58.) For an excellent general comment, see Christopher Martin, "In Praise of Political Apathy," *The Listener* (23 June 1960).

We emphasize, however, that our model, which incorporates the logrolling model as the general case, is not chosen because of the ethical desirability of the institutions analyzed. Positive theory must always analyze those institutions that are, in fact, general (the test of generality being the validity of the predictions made), quite independent of ethical or moral considerations. Therefore, even if vote-trading should be viewed as morally reprehensible behavior, it might still be necessary to analyze the phenomenon carefully if it were observed in the operation of real-world political processes.

TWO TYPES OF LOGROLLING

Logrolling seems to occur in many of the institutions of political choice-making in Western democracies. It may occur in two separate and distinct ways. In all of those cases where a reasonably small number of individuals vote openly on each measure in a continuing sequence of measures, the phenomenon seems pervasive. This is normally characteristic of representative assemblies, and it may also be present in very small governmental units employing "direct democracy." The applicability of our models to representative assemblies has already been mentioned. Under the rules within which such assemblies operate, exchanges of votes are easy to arrange and to observe. Such exchanges significantly affect the results of the political process. It seems probable that this fact provides one of the major reasons for the widespread use of representative democracy.

Logrolling may occur in a second way, which we shall call *implicit logrolling*. Large bodies of voters may be called on to decide on complex issues, such as which party will rule or which set of issues will be approved in a referendum vote. Here there is *no* formal trading of votes, but an analogous process takes place. The political "entrepreneurs" who offer candidates or programs to the voters make up a complex mixture of policies designed to attract support. In so doing, they keep firmly in mind the fact that the single voter may be so interested in the outcome of a particular issue that he will vote for the one party that supports this issue, although he may be opposed to the party stand on all other issues.[4] Institutions described by this implicit log-

4. An interesting example of this is presented in the comparison of voter support for education in local communities where educational expenditures are presented along with other issues for voter approval with those communities where the educational function is organized and financed through separate decision-making units. This comparison was discussed by Julius Margolis in a paper presented before the conference on public finances by the Universities—National Bureau of Economic Research Committee, held at Charlottesville, Virginia, on 10

rolling are characteristic of much of the modern democratic procedure. Since the analysis is somewhat more incisive in the first type of logrolling, we shall not discuss the second type at this point.

A SIMPLE LOGROLLING MODEL

Let us consider a simple model. A township inhabited by one hundred farmers who own similar farms is cut by a number of main highways maintained by the state. However, these are limited-access highways, and the farmers are permitted to enter this primary network only at the appropriate intersections with local roads. All local roads are built and maintained by the township. Maintenance is simple. Any farmer who desires to have a specific road repaired is allowed to present the issue to the whole group for a vote. If the repairing proposal is approved by a simple majority, the cost is assessed against all of the farmers as a part of the real property tax, the rate of which is automatically adjusted upward or downward so as to make revenues always equal to expenditures. The principal use of the local roads by the farmers is getting to and from the major state highways. Since these major highways cut through the whole district, there are four or five farmers dependent on each particular piece of local road, and each farmer requires at least one local road to provide him with access to the main network.

In this model the simple referendum system would result in no local road being repaired because an overwhelming majority of the farmers would vote against the repairing of any given road, considered separately. A logrolling system, however, permits the local roads to be kept in repair through the emergence of bargains among voters. The actual bargaining may take a number of forms, but most of the "solutions" will tend to be unstable. In any case, "equilibrium" involves some overinvestment of resources.

One form that an implicit bargain might take is the following: each individual might determine, in his own mind, the general standard of maintenance that should be set for all local roads. That is to say, he would balance, according to his own scale of preferences, the costs of maintaining his own road at various levels of repair with the benefits expected, and try to reach a decision at the point where expected marginal costs equal marginal benefits. Generalizing this, he could then vote on each separate project to repair a

---

and 11 April 1959. See National Bureau of Economic Research, *Public Finances: Needs, Sources, and Utilization* (Princeton: Princeton University Press, 1961).

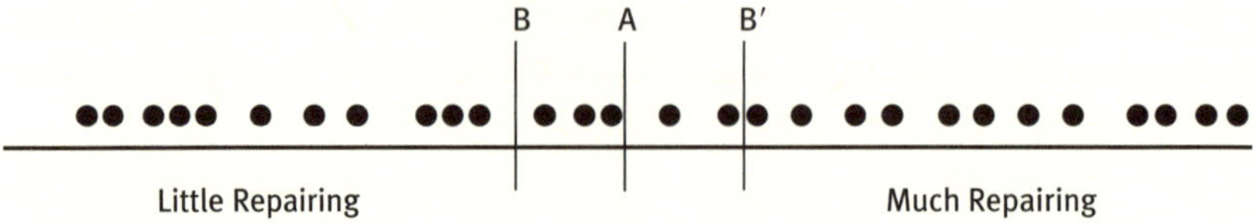

FIGURE 12

given road in the same way that he would vote for repairs on his own road. If all voters would follow this rule of reaching decisions, we would find a schedule of voting behavior such as that shown in Figure 12. Each mark or dot on the horizontal line represents the "idealized" standard of maintenance on all roads for a single voter. If a proposal for repairing a given road falls to the left of his own position on this scale, the individual will support it; if a proposal falls to the right of his own position, he will vote against it. If each road has at least one farmer living along it whose preference for general road repairs falls to the right of the median (A in Figure 12), then a proposal for road repair will be advanced as soon as any given road falls below this farmer's standard of maintenance. Successive further proposals would be made as the road deteriorated further. When the deterioration of any road reached the median level, a repair project would secure approval by simple majority vote. Hence, all local roads would, in this model, tend to be maintained up to the standard indicated by the median preference.

This result will not represent a fully "efficient" solution in any Pareto sense,[5] but it is possible to support this procedure on ethical grounds. In fact, this solution seems to be the one that most of the proponents of majoritarian democracy have in mind when they discuss democratic process. In any event, we propose to use this solution, which we shall call the "Kantian,"[6] as a more or less "correct" solution against which we shall contrast our more realistic result.[7]

5. No solution which embodies general tax financing of public services valued differently by different individuals can be Pareto-optimal, unless, of course, fully offsetting compensations are allowed.

6. Critics have objected to our usage of the word "Kantian" in this sense. We have no desire to raise complex philosophical issues here, and we point out only that the word is used solely for want of a more suitable single word describing the behavior that is adequately defined in the text.

7. As suggested in footnote 5, the postulated institutions of the model will prevent the emergence of the fully "efficient" solution in any economic sense. The Kantian solution seems, therefore, to be the most nearly "correct" one that can be attained in the model as postulated.

Note that this Kantian solution is not equivalent to our "bench mark" employed in ana-

If the farmers of the township generally follow such a policy in voting, then *any* single farmer could benefit himself simply by voting against all proposals to repair roads other than his own and by voting to repair his own road at each opportunity. This single departure from the general pattern of behavior would shift the median of the schedules slightly so that the taxes on the farmer concerned would be reduced or his road kept in better-than-average repair. If the other farmers living along this road should follow the first farmer's example (we shall call such farmers "maximizers"), they would be able to shift the standards of repair so that the road on which they live would be repaired at level B′ while reducing the standard on all other roads to B in Figure 12. Since the largest share of the costs of keeping their own road in repair would fall on other taxpayers, while the largest share of their own taxes would go to the repair of other roads, this change in behavior would be greatly to the advantage of the maximizers and greatly to the disadvantage of the "Kantians," although in the initial stages the disadvantages would not be concentrated to the same degree as the advantages.

If the farmers located on a second local road should also switch to a maximizing pattern of behavior, this action would have the effect of bringing the level of road-repairing on the two roads particularly affected down toward that which would prevail under the generalized Kantian system, while still further lowering the standards on the remaining "Kantian" roads. However, it seems probable that, finding themselves in this situation, the two groups of maximizers could benefit by forming a coalition designed to raise the standards of maintenance on the two roads. Let us consider the situation that would be confronted by an individual maximizer when he tries to decide whether or not to enter into such a coalition with other maximizers. Since he will pay only about 1/100 of the cost, almost any proposal to repair his own road will be supported by him. If, however, in order to obtain support for

---

lyzing the individual constitutional calculus in Part II, which does represent a Pareto-efficient point. The Kantian solution of this model becomes equivalent to the bench-mark solution (that is to say, it eliminates all external costs) only if one of the two following conditions is satisfied.

(1) All voters have the same conception of the idealized standard of road repair: that is, all of the dots along the horizontal line in Figure 12 fall at the median point. In this case, no one is ever disappointed by a decision. "Consensus" is automatically achieved, and, given Kantian behavior for all individuals, the actual voting rule is unimportant.

(2) The distribution of the total costs of road repair among individuals is allowed to vary to correspond with differences in "tastes" concerning the idealized standard of repair. This second condition is, of course, prevented by the assumption that general taxation is employed as the revenue-producing device.

some repair project for his own road, he must also vote for the repair of another road, the individual must also count the cost to him of other repair projects. In weighing costs and benefits, he must consider not only the tax cost to himself from a proposal to repair his own road but also the tax cost to him of the other repair jobs which he must support in order to get his own proposal adopted. In the particular situation under discussion, when the farmers on all of the local roads except two are still Kantians, this added cost consideration would put few restraints on feasible projects, but some recognition of the incremental costs of securing agreement would have to be taken into account. Furthermore, as more and more farmers became tired of being exploited by the maximizers and shifted to the maximizing pattern of behavior, this cost consideration would become more and more important.

Let us now examine a rather unlikely, but theoretically important, special case. Suppose that exactly 51 of the 100 farmers follow a maximizing policy, while 49 are pure "Kantians." Let us further suppose that all of the maximizers live on some local roads, while all of the Kantians live on other roads. Under these circumstances, the Kantians clearly would never be able to get their roads repaired at all, but the level of repairs on the maximizers' roads is more difficult to determine. In order to simplify the issue somewhat, let us assume (plausibly) that these roads are maintained on such a high level that all of the Kantian farmers would vote against all further repair proposals. In this case, it would be necessary to attain the approval of all of the maximizers to carry any single repair project. A maximizing farmer, considering the repair of his own road, would necessarily be forced to take into account his share in the costs of repairing the roads of all maximizers. He would have to consider the incremental taxes that he must pay in order to repair the roads of all other parties to the bargain. His calculus requires, however, only that he compare his own marginal benefits against his own marginal costs. No knowledge of anyone else's utility function is required. The individual need only decide whether the total bargain is or is not to his advantage.[8]

For the Kantians, note that, while no roads leading to their own farms will be repaired, they will be required to contribute toward the repair of the roads leading to the farms of the maximizers. Thus, a part of the total repair costs

8. In practice, the problem of securing the unanimous consent of the required 51 persons might be insoluble. However, since we are discussing a rather unique special model, we may ignore this possibility.

in the township will be paid by persons who are not parties to the decisive bargain, and, since the maximizers count only the costs to themselves when they make voting decisions, the general standard of road maintenance on the roads of the maximizers will tend to be higher than it would be if the Kantians were also included in the calculus. Under such conditions as these, where "virtue" so conspicuously would not pay, it seems likely that at least some of the Kantians would decide to switch to a maximizing policy. For simplicity, let us assume that they all do so at the same time. Since these reluctant maximizers would still be in a minority, their changes of heart would not immediately redound to their private benefit. However, it might be relatively easy for this minority, acting as a coalition, to find two of the original maximizers who would, in return for a promise of very good maintenance on their own roads, desert their former colleagues. It is again obvious, however, that the new majority would now be equally susceptible to similar desertions. A permanent coalition of 51 farmers formed for the purpose of exploiting the remaining 49 could not be considered to be stable in the usual sense of this term. In the terminology of game theory, which we shall use in the following chapter, any combination of 51 voters dominates any combination of less than this number, but no combination of 51 dominates all other combinations of 51.[9]

The outcome is clearly indicated. Each farmer would enter into bilateral agreements with enough other farmers on other roads to insure that his own road is repaired. The individual farmer would then be forced to include as a part of the cost of getting his own road repaired the cost (to him) of repairing the roads of 50 other farmers. These bilateral agreements would overlap, however. Farmer A (more precisely, the group of farmers living on Road A) would bargain with Farmers B, C, . . . , M. Farmer M, on the other hand,

9. In his paper, "The Theory of the Reluctant Duelist" (*American Economic Review*, XLVI [December 1956], 909–23), Daniel Ellsberg contends that accepted game-theory notions really apply only to "reluctant" players. Our case of voters is a particularly pure example. The voter must "play the game" by entering into bargains with 50 of his fellows, even though this leads to rather unsatisfactory results, simply because, given the rules, any other course of action would be worse.

This is not to suggest, however, that, *given the fiscal institutions postulated in our model*, simple majority rule is necessarily less desirable than some other decision-making rule. As the analysis of Part II demonstrates, this may or may not be the most "efficient" rule. What is clear from the analysis of our model is that the fiscal institutions postulated cannot produce "efficient" results under *any* collective decision-making rule short of unanimity.

might make up a majority bargain from an agreement with Farmer A and Farmers N, O, . . . , Z.

In counting the costs to himself involved in the repair of other roads necessary to secure the repair of his own road, each farmer would consider only the repair of those roads which he agrees to support. In this way his expenditure pattern would include as a free gift the tax payments of 49 voters. The fiscal institutions postulated insure that all 100 voters share in the costs of each repair project approved, but a minimum participation of only 51 voters in the net benefits is required by simple majority voting. The natural result would be that each road in the township would be maintained at a level considerably higher and at a greater expense than is rational from the individual standpoint of the farmers living along it. Each individual in the group would be behaving quite rationally, but the outcome would be irrational. This apparent paradox may be explained as follows: each voter pays enough in support for the repair of other roads to attain a position of equivalence between estimated individual marginal costs and individual marginal benefits, but the payments included in his private calculus make up only a part of the costs of total road repair that he must, as a taxpayer in the community, support.[10] There are other roads which will be repaired because of successful bargains to which he is not a party. Taken as a group, the road-repair projects for which he votes represent a good bargain for the individual; but other *ad hoc* bargains will also take place. The individual will, of course, vote against all projects included in these outside bargains, but he will be in the minority. Therefore, he will have to bear a part of the costs.

Any individual farmer who followed another course of action would be worse off, however, than the individual whose behavior is considered here. For example, a Kantian farmer would never have his own road repaired, but he would have to pay taxes for the support of other local roads. In any practical situation the whole decision-making process would tend to become one of elaborate negotiations, open and concealed, taking place at several levels of discourse. The man who is the most effective bargainer would have a considerable advantage. However, the general pattern of results may be less than optimal for all parties (optimal being defined here in terms of either the Kantian or the Paretian solution).

10. The fact that he is taxed for other roads not counted in his bargain reduces his real income and, hence, to some extent, reduces his desire for the consumption of road-repair services.

POSSIBLE OBJECTIONS

We may now consider certain possible objections that may be raised against the reasoning implicit in our simple logrolling model. It may be argued that those individuals whom we have called maximizers would be behaving wickedly and that ethical considerations will prevent a majority of the population in the real world from following such a course of action. Ethical and moral systems vary greatly from culture to culture, and the strength of moral restraints on private action is not readily predictable. We do not want to preclude the possible existence somewhere of a system of human behavior which could effectively restrain logrolling, but surely the American behavior pattern contains no such restraints. Under our system open logrolling is normally publicly characterized as "bad," but no real stigma attaches to those who participate in it. The press describes open logrolling arrangements without apparent disapproval, and, in fact, all of our political organizations operate on a logrolling basis.[11] Moreover, no stigma at all attaches to implicit as opposed to open logrolling.

A second argument asserts that each farmer in our model community would soon realize that if he adopted a maximizing pattern of behavior, this would lead all other farmers to do the same thing. Since the "maximizing equilibrium" is worse for almost all farmers[12] than the "Kantian median," each farmer would, on the basis of his own cold and selfish calculation, follow the Kantian system. This argument is familiar, and it is precisely analogous to the one which holds that no single labor union will force wage rates up for its own members because it will realize that such action will lead other unions to do the same and that the eventual outcome will simply be higher prices and wages without any increase in real incomes. There seems to be overwhelming empirical evidence that men do not act in this way.[13] The argument overlooks the fact that there will, of course, be short-run gains to the individuals or groups who initiate action first. In addition, the argument

11. See P. W. Bridgeman, *The Way Things Are* (Cambridge: Harvard University Press, 1959), pp. 268–69.

12. Not necessarily for all. There might be one or more farmers whose personal preferences for road-repairing called for such a large investment as to make the "maximizing equilibrium" preferable to the "Kantian median."

13. The late C. O. Hardy once referred to this argument as the one which assumes the operation of "Dr. Nourse's invisible left hand": that is, men will further their own interest by acting in the public interest.

seems to contain a logical flaw. It is based on the observation that, in any series of actions by a number of men, there must be a first step. If this can be prevented, then the whole series can be prevented. This observation is, in itself, correct; but there must also be a second, a third, and a fourth step, etc., in each series. If any one action in the series is prevented, then the whole series cannot be completed. If all of our maximizing farmers should refrain from following a maximizing course of action because each one felt that his own personal adoption of such behavior would lead to a switch to a position of "maximizing equilibrium," then, if only one of them had done so, we could construct an exactly similar argument "proving" that none of the remaining 99 would follow his example. However, if the second argument is true, the first is false; hence, the chain of reasoning contains an inconsistency.

Note that our refutation of this argument does not preclude an individual's taking the attitude: "If *no one* else acts, I shall not act." However, not only must *all* members of the group assume this attitude if the argument is to be valid, but *each* member of the group must also believe that *all* other members will take this attitude. This combination of attitudes, which would amount to complete mutual trust, seems highly improbable in any real-world situation. The argument that all individuals in the group will be worse off than if they all adopted Kantian norms of behavior does have some relevance for the support of *constitutional* changes in the decision-making rules or institutions for choice. While it may never be to the interest of the individual to refrain from adopting a maximizing attitude, given the rules as laid down, it may well be to his long-range interest to support a change in these rules themselves, which, by definition, will be *generally applicable*.

ALTERNATIVES

One means through which the separate farmers in our model might enter into a bargain so as to insure results somewhat closer to the Kantian median would be the development of a specific formula that would determine when a road should be repaired. Yet another means would be the delegation of decision-making authority to a single individual or small group. These become practicable institutions, however, only within the confines of a set of closely related issues that may be expected to arise: in our model, separate proposals for road repair. In the more general and realistic case where governmental units must consider a continuing stream of radically different projects, neither an agreed-on formula nor a single expert or group of experts would seem feasible. A formula that would permit the weighing of the costs and the benefits of such diverse programs as building irrigation projects in the West to increase agricultural production, paying farmers in the Midwest to decrease agricultural production, giving increased aid to Israel, and dredging Baltimore's harbor, is inconceivable. There could not, therefore, be any real agreement on any automatic or quasi-automatic system of allocating collective resources, and the delegation of authority to make such decisions would mean the abandonment of the legislative process as such. We are reduced to the reaching of separate decisions by logrolling processes, given the constitutional rules as laid down in advance.

MAJORITY RULE AND EXTERNAL COSTS

This is by no means so much a tragedy as our simple model may have appeared to suggest. Implicit in the comparison of the logrolling solution with the Kantian solution has been the idea that the external costs imposed on the individual by the "maximizing equilibrium" exceed those resulting from the Kantian "equilibrium." This will be true if individual farmers are primarily interested in the repair of their own roads, as our model postulates. If, by contrast, some or all of the farmers should be genuinely and intensely interested in the standards of general road repair over the whole township, the Kantian solution might be worse than the maximizing one. This is because the Kantian solution under simple majority rule can take no account of varying intensities in individual standards. For example, if there should exist a minority of farmers who feel very intensely that much more should be spent on road repairs than the majority of other voters, whose standards are somewhat indifferently held, the maximizing solution, which does result in a standard of general repair above the Kantian median, may be more "desirable" on certain commonly acknowledged welfare grounds than the Kantian solution. In this case the introduction of logrolling into the Kantian model could be beneficial to all parties.[14]

A central feature of our analysis is the demonstration that the operation of

14. As a practical example, assume that all Easterners should be intensely interested in general programs of water-resource development. Southerners are assumed to be wholly indifferent, and Westerners, by contrast, are, we assume, interested only in their own particular area projects. In this case Easterners should welcome the introduction of logrolling among the Western maximizers, since only in this way can over-all programs of water-resource development be approved.

simple majority rule, quite independent of any assumption about individual motivation, will almost always impose external costs on the individual. If more than a simple majority is required for decision, fewer resources will be devoted to road-building in our model, and the individual comparison of marginal benefits and marginal costs would tend to approach more closely the calculus required by the economists' standard criteria for attaining a Pareto-optimality surface. As the analysis of Part II has shown, however, when any consideration of more inclusive voting rules is made, the incremental costs of negotiating bargains must also be taken into account.

GENERALIZATIONS

Some of these points will be discussed later. We shall now inquire as to what extent our simple logrolling model can be generalized. It would appear that any governmental activity which benefits specific individuals or groups in a discriminatory fashion and which is financed from general taxation would fit our model well. It is not, of course, necessary that the revenues employed in paying for the projects be collected equally from all voters, either in terms of tax rates or tax collections. The minimum necessary condition is that the benefits from public activity be significantly more concentrated or localized than the costs. This is a very weak condition, and many budgetary patterns seem to meet it. If the taxes are collected by indirect methods so that individuals cannot really tell how much they individually pay for each specific public-service project, this accentuates the distortions described by our analytical model. In the marginal case the individual may be indifferent about projects benefiting others, the costs of which seem slight to him and also difficult to measure. Under these circumstances he would be particularly likely to trade his support for such projects, which may appear costless or nearly so, for reciprocal support for his own pet proposals.

Additional types of governmental activity may also be fitted into the analysis. Other forms of taxation-expenditure problems are most easily incorporated. First, we may suppose that there is some governmental activity that provides general benefit to all voters, e.g., police protection, which is financed out of general taxation. In this case the maximizing solution and the Kantian solution will tend to be identical to the extent that the benefits and the taxes are truly general. However, as soon as general taxation is departed from, parallel reasoning to that above demonstrates that special tax exemptions and favors to individuals and groups will be introduced.

On the tax side of the fiscal account, if a given sum of money is to be raised, we should expect the revenue-raising pattern to include general taxes that are, relatively, "too heavy," but which are riddled with special exemptions for all sorts of groups. The result is that of greatly reducing the efficacy of any generally accepted norms for fiscal organization (such as progression in taxes) that are supposedly adopted. The pattern that we are able to predict as a result of our analysis thus seems to be descriptive of existing fiscal institutions, quite independent of the moral justification of the behavior that our model incorporates. General and diffuse taxes, characterized by many special exemptions, finance budgets in which public services are designed, at least to a large degree, to benefit particular groups in the society. There is clearly no apparent conflict between the predictions that emerge initially from our model and fiscal reality as it is commonly interpreted.

If our analysis is to be applied even more generally to all public activity, it must be radically generalized. For any individual voter all possible measures can be arrayed according to his intensity of interest. His welfare can be improved if he accepts a decision contrary to his desire in an area where his preferences are weak in exchange for a decision in his favor in an area where his feelings are stronger. Bargains among voters can, therefore, be mutually beneficial. Potentially, the voter should enter into such bargains until the marginal "cost" of voting for something of which he disapproves but about which his feelings are weak exactly matches the expected marginal benefits of the vote or votes secured in return for support for issues in which he is more interested. Thus, he will expect to benefit from the total complex of issues which enter into his set of bargains with his fellows. In making such bargains, however, the individual must try to gain the assent of only a bare majority of other voters, not of all of them. On any given issue he can simply ignore 49 per cent of the individual decision-makers. This means that he can afford to "pay" more for other support because a part of the inconvenience caused by the measure will fall on parties who are not members of the decisive bargaining coalition.

Unfortunately, from the point of view of the individual voter, the converse also holds true. Bargains will certainly be concluded in which the single voter does not participate. Yet he will have to bear a part of the costs of action taken. As a result, the whole effect of the measures which result from his bargains and on which he votes on the winning side will be beneficial to him; but this will tend, normally, to be only slightly more than one-half of all "bargained" measures passed, and the remainder will be carried out adverse to his interest. The same result would hold true for the *average* voter under a pure referendum system. The whole problem analyzed here can be eliminated by changing the rule which compels the minority to accept the decisions of the majority without compensation. So long as this rule is employed to make collective decisions, the individual voter must expect to incur external costs as a result of public or collective action.

CHAPTER 11

SIMPLE MAJORITY VOTING AND THE THEORY OF GAMES

We shall now examine the contributions that modern game theory can make toward an analysis of simple majority voting. In one sense we shall be discussing the same problems considered in Chapter 10, but we shall use here a slightly different set of analytical tools. As will become evident to those who are even moderately sophisticated in the field, our constructions will be reasonably elementary. Our purpose is, however, not that of making any contribution to game theory itself, but rather that of applying the relevant theory to our particular problems.[1]

The application of game theory to majority voting is relatively straightforward and simple, but the limited extent to which game theory can be helpful for our purposes should be acknowledged at the outset. Most of the refinements in this theory have been developed in the analysis of two-person, zero-sum games. Quite clearly, the analysis of such games will not take us very far in predicting the outcomes of simple majority voting rules in the political process. For assistance here, we must look to the developments in the theory of *n*-person games, a theory that is considerably less sophisticated and more speculative than is that for two-person games. The zero- or constant-sum restriction is also bothersome, but, to some extent, this hurdle can be surmounted.[2]

1. The treatment will be based directly on the constructions contained in the helpful survey of Luce and Raiffa. See R. Duncan Luce and Howard Raiffa, *Games and Decisions* (New York: John Wiley and Sons, 1957).

For our particular purpose, we have not found the specific attempts to relate game theory and political theory to be useful, although these contributions may be helpful in a somewhat more general sense. See Karl Deutsch, "Game Theory and Politics: Some Problems of Application," *Canadian Journal of Economics and Political Science*, XX (1954), 76–83; Martin Shubik, ed., *Readings in Game Theory and Political Behavior* (New York: Doubleday, 1954); and Richard C. Snyder, "Game Theory and the Analysis of Political Behavior," contained in *Research Frontiers in Politics and Government* (Brookings Institution, 1955).

2. As William Riker has pointed out in his comment on an earlier version of this book, all political situations that take on genuine "game" characteristics can, for some purposes, be an-

A THREE-PERSON, CONSTANT-SUM GAME

As was the case with our model in the preceding chapter, it will be useful to "idealize" the institution under consideration, that is, to construct a model which will embody the essential characteristics of the institution without the complicating features. The model to be employed here must be even more restricted than the one used earlier. We shall initially assume that the total group is composed of three persons, equally situated. In order to relate the analysis to that of the preceding chapter, we may also assume that the individuals are farmers in a township interested in road repair. We shall assume further that the repair of one man's road produces no external or spillover effects on other members of the group.

We assume that a decision has already been made to spend a total of $1 (additional zeros will not modify our analysis) on road repair in the whole township. For simplification, let us suppose also that this sum is not raised from general taxes but is instead received in the form of an earmarked grant from some higher-level governmental unit. This assumption assures us that the game we shall consider will be one of constant-sum at $1. We continue to assume that all decisions concerning the allocation of road-repair funds are to be made by simple majority vote, and that this is the only accepted way of making collective decisions. In our first model, we analyze the operation of this rule in an isolated, single action: that is to say, the $1 grant is received only once and it must be allocated once and for all and in complete abstraction from other collective issues that may arise.

This "game" may now be normalized and put in characteristic-function form as follows:

$$\begin{aligned} &\text{i.} \quad v(1) = v(2) = v(3) = 0 \\ &\text{ii.} \quad v(1,2) = v(1,3) = v(2,3) = 1 \\ &\text{iii.} \quad v(1,2,3) = 1 \end{aligned}$$

This characteristic function states the values of the various possible coalitions that may be formed. The function clearly shows that no "coalition" composed of less than two members of the group will have value, while all coali-

---

alyzed under the zero-sum restriction. Through the interpretation of individual payoffs in a relative rather than an absolute sense, any positive-sum game can be converted into a zero-sum game. Since our purpose, however, is that of examining the economic meaning of the solutions to the various games analyzed, this conversion to a zero-sum model is not suitable.

tions of two or more members will have a value of one. If the members of a winning two-person coalition choose to share their gains symmetrically, the following three *imputations* become possible "solutions":

$$(\tfrac{1}{2}, \tfrac{1}{2}, 0) \quad (\tfrac{1}{2}, 0, \tfrac{1}{2}) \quad (0, \tfrac{1}{2}, \tfrac{1}{2})$$

This *set of imputations* will be called *F*, or the F set. This set, and this set only, satisfies the von Neumann–Morgenstern requirements for "solution" to *n*-person games, and may, in a restricted sense, be called the *solution*. The first of these requirements is that no single imputation in F either dominates or is dominated by any other imputation in the same set. (Domination is defined in terms of the effective decision-making subgroup or coalition: two in the model under analysis.) The second requirement is that any imputation not in F is dominated by at least one imputation in F.[3]

The dominance aspects of the imputations in F may be illustrated with reference to proposed shifts to imputations not in F. Suppose that the imputation (0, ½, ½) is proposed by a majority coalition (2, 3). Individual 1 can propose an alternative imputation (¼, ¾, 0), which the coalition (1, 2) can carry (which dominates the first imputation). Individual 2 might be led to abandon the first coalition with 3 and support the modified proposal since his position will be improved (¾ > ½). However, this second imputation, which is not in F, will, in turn, be dominated by the imputation (½, 0, ½), which is in F for the majority (1, 3). Individual 2 may be wary about any initial departure from the coalition with 3 if he foresees the prospect of more than one move before action is finally taken.[4] Because of this fact, the imputations in F are presumed to be more stable than those not in F, although game theorists recognize and acknowledge the limitations on the ideas of "solution" and "stability" in the *n*-person game.

The set of imputations, F, contains the imputations that we could predict from the operation of majority voting in isolated actions. Two persons would tend to secure all of the benefits while the third person would secure nothing, assuming that each individual approaches the collective decision with a view

3. See J. von Neumann and O. Morgenstern, *Theory of Games and Economic Behavior* (3d ed.; Princeton: Princeton University Press, 1953), p. 264.

4. Note that this does *not* contradict our argument of the last chapter in which it was suggested that individual farmers would not remain Kantians. The difference between the two cases is that there we were considering a whole series of separate but related actions, while here we are considering the possible shifting of coalitions prior to the taking of a single action.

toward maximizing his own expected utility, and assuming that individual utility functions are independent. Note that the set F includes imputations that dominate the "equitable" imputation (⅓, ⅓, ⅓).[5] *Any one* of the three imputations in F dominates the equitable imputation with respect to a required number of individual voters. The equitable imputation would seem, therefore, to be the most "unstable" of all imputations since *any* majority can upset it. Compare this with another "weak" imputation not in F, say, (¼, ¾, 0). This imputation is dominated only by the imputation (½, 0, ½) in F, and by a limited subset of other nonstable imputations. Hence, to change from (¼, ¾, 0) to a solution in F, a *particular* majority (1, 3) is needed, whereas to shift from (⅓, ⅓, ⅓) to a solution in F, any majority will be sufficient. Thus, the "equitable" imputation may be stabilized only by significant departures by many individuals from utility maximization.

A FIVE-PERSON, CONSTANT-SUM GAME

Let us now extend this analysis to a five-person group, with the same initial conditions assumed. We continue to assume simple majority rule so that three persons are now sufficient for decision. The characteristic function is now as follows:

i. $v(1) = v(2) = v(3) = v(4) = v(5) = 0$
ii. $v(1,2) = v(1,3) = \ldots\ldots. = v(4,5) = 0$
iii. $v(1,2,3) = v(1,2,4) = v(1,2,5) = v(1,3,4) = v(1,3,5) = v(1,4,5)$
$= v(2,3,4) = v(2,4,5) = v(3,4,5) = v(2,3,5) = 1$
iv. $v(1,2,3,4) = v(1,2,3,5) = v(1,2,4,5) = v(1,3,4,5) = v(2,3,4,5) = 1$
v. $v(1,2,3,4,5) = 1$

For the solution, set F, developed as before, we get:

(⅓, ⅓, ⅓, 0, 0) (⅓, 0, ⅓, 0, ⅓) (0, ⅓, 0, ⅓, ⅓)
(⅓, 0, 0, ⅓, ⅓) (⅓, ⅓, 0, ⅓, 0) (⅓, 0, ⅓, ⅓, 0)
(⅓, ⅓, 0, 0, ⅓) (0, ⅓, ⅓, ⅓, 0) (0, ⅓, ⅓, 0, ⅓)
(0, 0, ⅓, ⅓, ⅓)

Note that *any one* of these imputations in F dominates what we have called the equitable imputation (⅕, ⅕, ⅕, ⅕, ⅕) for the required decisive coalition

5. In this particular model, the "equitable" solution is equivalent to the "Kantian" solution discussed in the preceding chapter. We shall employ the different term here, however, because these two imputations will not be the same under different circumstances.

of three persons. On the assumption of individual utility maximization, therefore, the equitable imputation would never be chosen.

It is clear that the analysis can be extended to a group of any size. The F-set, or "solution," imputations will always contain only those involving the symmetric sharing of all gains among the members of the smallest effective coalition. In the game of simple majority rule the smallest effective set will approach 50 per cent of the total number of voters as the group is increased in size. Imputations within the solution set can always be found which will dominate, for an effective coalition, any imputation outside the set. As the size of the group is increased, however, the stability properties of the imputations in the set F seem to become less strong. In our earlier example of the three-person game, we found that the solution within the F set tends to be more stable than any similar set of imputations outside F because successful individuals might be able to foresee the consequences of departing initially from a coalition formed within F, which dictated that the gains be shared symmetrically among the members of the coalition. These consequences are, of course, that members of an apparently effective coalition might, before action is finally taken, be replaced by outsiders in a newly formed coalition.

It is perhaps useful to note that the argument for symmetry in the sharing of the gains among members of the dominant coalition rests on slightly different grounds than it does in the case with two-person co-operative games or in *n*-person games requiring that *all* participants must agree on a sharing arrangement. Schelling, in his recent argument for abandonment of symmetry, confined his discussion largely to these latter games.[6] If, as in the "majority-rule game" that we are considering here, the rules dictate that only a certain share of the total group need agree, the case for effective-coalition symmetry is stronger. The individual in the winning coalition will tend to be satisfied with a symmetrical share in total gains, not because he expects no member to concede him a larger share due to a general attitude of "fairness," but because he knows that, if he does demand more, alternative individuals stand ready and willing to join new coalitions which could effectively remove his gains entirely.

As the total group grows in size, these effective restraints on individual action are weakened. The individual will reckon his own contribution to an effective coalition at a lower value, and he will be more tempted to depart

6. T. C. Schelling, "For the Abandonment of Symmetry in Game Theory," *Review of Economics and Statistics*, XLI (August 1959), 213–24. Reprinted as Appendix B in *The Strategy of Conflict* (Cambridge: Harvard University Press, 1960), pp. 267–91.

from imputations within the "solution." The outcome of the majority-rule game in large groups seems likely to be that predicted by our model of Chapter 10. Coalitions will be formed, but any single winning coalition will be relatively unstable and impermanent. On the other hand, it should also be emphasized that as the size of the group becomes larger, any tacit adherence to moral or ethical restraints against individual utility-maximizing behavior also becomes much more difficult to secure. The deliberate exploitation of the third member by any two members of a three-man social group may be difficult to conceive, but the individual's interest in his fellow man falls off quite sharply as the group is enlarged. In this sense, therefore, the basic assumptions of the game-theory model become more relevant for large groups than for small ones. The concept of "solution" may be considerably more fuzzy in large-group situations, but the direction of effect that may be predicted to emerge seems to be of significant relevance for any study of real-world political decision-making.

THE LIMITATION OF SIDE PAYMENTS

We have analyzed the operation of majority voting in the simplest of models. We have assumed the group to be confronted with a single issue that was to be decided once and for all. As applied to real-world institutions, the limitations of this model must be carefully kept in mind. Many of these have been obscured in the analysis above, and some of them must now be mentioned. In the first place, as we have suggested in Chapter 10, logrolling or vote-trading processes would tend to arise when more than a single issue is presented to voters. We propose, however, to leave this complication aside for the time, and to assume that all forms of vote-trading are prohibited in some way. If we want to employ the terminology of game theory here, we may say that all side payments are prohibited. This prohibition effectively prevents the individual voter from being able to express his intensity of preference for or against the specific measure proposed. All that he may register is the direction of this preference, not the intensity. Implicit in the support of decision-making institutions and rules which do serve, wholly or in part, to limit side payments seems to be the psychological assumption that individual preferences are essentially symmetrical.[7]

7. This property attributed to simple majority rule has been called that of *anonymity*. May also calls it the *equality condition*. This terminology seems to be especially misleading since the psychological equality assumed is something quite different from the *political equality* insured

Let us see precisely what this complete prohibition of all side payments implies for our "solution" imputations. Consider the same three-person game discussed above, in which the $1 grant is to be divided among the three roads, with each repair project benefiting only one individual. Let us assume that, in actuality, road repair is highly productive on only one of the three roads, moderately productive on the second, and not worth the cost on the third. The values resulting from one-half (50¢) of the total expenditures on each road, respectively, are as follows: $1, 50¢, 25¢, or to use fractions: 1, ½, ¼ (note that these are *not* imputations). Simple majority voting, with all side payments (open and concealed) being prohibited, will convert all such "political games" into a fully normalized form. The solution set of imputations will be the same as before. Quantified or measured in terms of *input* or *cost* values, this set is:

$$(\tfrac{1}{2}, \tfrac{1}{2}, 0) \quad (\tfrac{1}{2}, 0, \tfrac{1}{2}) \quad (0, \tfrac{1}{2}, \tfrac{1}{2})$$

It is now necessary, however, to distinguish between input or cost values and output or benefit (utility) values. The latter become, in the same set of imputations:

$$(1, \tfrac{1}{2}, 0) \quad (1, 0, \tfrac{1}{4}) \quad (0, \tfrac{1}{2}, \tfrac{1}{4})$$

The important conclusion here is obvious. In benefit or productivity terms, the "game" is not constant-sum, and, with all side payments prohibited, there is no assurance that collective action will be taken in the most productive way. There is no more likelihood that the first imputation will be chosen than the second or third. The rule is as likely to select the least "productive" imputation as it is the most "productive."[8]

The prohibition of all side payments also prevents any imputation being selected which directly benefits less than a simple majority of the voting population, regardless of the relative productivities of public investment. For example, let us now suppose that the $1 grant, if expended exclusively on the

by the fact that each individual has one vote. Cf. K. O. May, "A Set of Independent Necessary and Sufficient Conditions for Simple Majority Decisions," *Econometrica*, XX (October 1952), 680–84.

Note also that Dahl's conception of political equality requires that each individual's preference be given equal weight. See Robert A. Dahl, *A Preface to Democratic Theory* (Chicago: University of Chicago Press, 1956), p. 37.

8. Assuming, of course, that the objective values imputed reflect accurate subjective estimates of the relative values of road repair.

first road, would yield a benefit value of \$10, on the second road \$5, and on the third road only \$1. If, in fact, all funds were expended on the first road, the imputation would be (10, 0, 0). However, note that any imputation such as (0, 2½, ½) would dominate the more concentrated, but more productive, investment. The set of imputations having the solution properties under the conditions outlined would be:

(5, 2½, 0) (5, 0, ½) (0, 2½, ½)

These rudimentary elements of game theory have helped us to demonstrate in a somewhat different, and perhaps more decisive, manner the effects of simple majority rule that were already discussed in Chapter 10. If some vote-trading is not introduced, no allowance can be made for possible variations in individual intensities of preference, a point that is rather dramatically shown in a quantitative way in the last simple model.

ALLOWANCE OF SIDE PAYMENTS

The apparent distortions that may be produced by the operation of simple majority rule without side payments suggest that the model with side payments be examined. Side payments may "improve" the results. We propose, therefore, to examine this prospect more carefully. Let us now suppose that there exists complete freedom for individuals to make all of the side payments or compensations that they choose to make. No restrictions are placed on the methods of payments, but we may think of them as being made in generalized purchasing power, or money. Such behavior of individuals is assumed not to be prohibited by either legal or moral restraints. This model allows us to introduce something akin to vote-trading in the model without departing from the confines of a single, simple issue.

Let us assume the existence of the last benefit schedule mentioned above: that is, if the whole grant were to be expended on each road, the "productivities" would be, respectively, \$10, \$5, and \$1. Simple majority voting, with full side payments, will now produce a "solution" set of imputations as follows:

(5, 5, 0) (5, 0, 5) (0, 5, 5)

In the first imputation, Individual 1 gets all of the grant expended on the repair of his own road, but he must pay Individual 2 one-half of the monetary value of the net gains for his political support. In the second imputation, Individuals 2 and 3 simply trade places. The third imputation in the solution set is most interesting. Here all road repairs are still carried out on the first road, where investment is far more productive than on the other roads, but Individuals 2 and 3 form the political majority which forces Individual 1 to pay full compensation for the road repair that he secures. Despite the fact that only his road is repaired, Individual 1 is no better off after collective action is taken than he is before.[9]

We see that the results of simple majority voting in the model where full side payments are allowed differ in several essential respects from the results of this rule when such payments are not allowed. First of all, side payments insure that the funds will be invested in the most productive manner. Secondly, there is no requirement that the projects undertaken provide physical services to more than a majority of the voters. As in all of the earlier models, the solution will embody a symmetrical sharing of total gains among the members of the smallest effective coalition, but note that the introduction of side payments tends to insure a symmetric sharing of gains measured in benefit or productivity terms.

In contrast to a logrolling model, the model which does include open buying and selling of votes (that is, full side payments in money) does not seem characteristic of modern democratic governments. We do not want to prejudge the ethical issues introduced by this model at this time, but commonly accepted attitudes and standards of behavior, as well as established legal institutions, prevent any approach to full side payments being carried out in actuality. In spite of this, the model is a highly useful one in that it does point to the type of solution attained under the more complex models which allow indirect side payments to be made.

SIMPLE LOGROLLING AND GAME THEORY

We refer, of course, to those vote-trading or logrolling models that have been discussed in Chapter 10. The simple logrolling model falls halfway between that containing no side payments and that which allows full side payments. In order to introduce logrolling, we must depart from single issues and assume that the group confronts a continuing series of separate measures. In game-theory terms, logrolling is simply an indirect means of making side payments. Individuals are unable to "purchase" voter support directly with money, but they are able to exchange votes on separate issues.

Let us continue to employ the road-repair example, with the prospect of a

9. See the discussion in Chapter 12 for some questions about this particular "solution."

$1 grant from external sources being made available to the community for disposition in each of a successive number of time periods. Let us also assume the same payoffs as before: namely, that the productivity of a $1 investment on Road 1 is $10, and on Road 2, $5, and on Road 3, $1. We must also now make some assumption about the marginal productivity functions in this model. We shall assume that, over the range of decisions considered in any bargain, the marginal productivity of investment on each road is constant: that is to say, the productivity of any $1 investment on Road 1 is $10, regardless of the amount of incremental investment undertaken on that road in previous periods.

Recall that under simple majority voting without side payments the solution set of imputations, measured in benefit terms, was:

$$(5, 2\tfrac{1}{2}, 0) \quad (5, 0, \tfrac{1}{2}) \quad (0, 2\tfrac{1}{2}, \tfrac{1}{2})$$

while in the model with full payments, this set was:

$$(5, 5, 0) \quad (5, 0, 5) \quad (0, 5, 5)$$

In the first case, the repairs would be carried out on any two of the roads represented in an effective coalition, not necessarily those roads most in need of repair. In the second case, the repairs would tend to be made where the investment is most productive, with a side payment or payments being made to insure sufficient support in the voting process.

In our simple logrolling model, the only way in which the first individual can "purchase" support for repairs on his road is by agreeing to vote for the repair of some road other than his own. He cannot substitute for this the more "efficient" transfer of money. It is difficult to present the results here in terms of a single set of benefit imputations because we must include a whole series of issues, but clearly these results must approach more closely those of the first rather than those of the second alternative model. Since some funds must be devoted to relatively unproductive investment, in some periods, the greater "efficiency" of the second model cannot be secured. We may convert simple logrolling into a political game by considering a single road-repair project in which the individual beneficiary secures majority support by giving promises of reciprocal support on future proposals, with these "promises" commanding some current economic value. The general logrolling model can then be thought of as consisting of a sequence of such games. There are, however, some differences between the simple logrolling model or its game analogue and the basic games discussed earlier. Simple logrolling, even if the issues are closely related to each other, can introduce minimal improvements in "efficiency." The process removes the necessity of insuring some physical benefits to an absolute majority for *each* single piece of legislation. Road repairs could, in any one period, be devoted exclusively to one road. Moreover, if there should exist important returns to scale of single-period investment, this could produce significant efficiencies.

Our general logrolling model can best be interpreted on the assumption that the political process embodies a continuing series of issues: in specific reference to the illustration, separate road-repair proposals. If, however, *all* road-repair projects must be voted on a single omnibus proposal, the results become equivalent to those demonstrated in the elementary games previously discussed. In this case, a minority of farmers will secure no road repairs, whereas in the general logrolling model, even under majority rule, each road would tend to be repaired because of the multiplicity of issues allowing for many separate coalitions. This difference between these two majority-rule models, however, will not affect the individual constitutional evaluation of majority voting as a means of making political decisions. In the one case, external costs will be expected because of the excessive road repairs generally carried out; in the other, external costs will be expected because of the fact that the individual might occasionally find himself in the losing coalition on a single, large, omnibus issue.

COMPLEX LOGROLLING

In our example, we have discussed the game theory aspects of logrolling phenomena that are confined to closely related issues. Instead of this, logrolling may actually take place by the trading of votes over a wide range of collective decisions, which may or may not bear physical resemblance to each other. As the "bargains" expand to include more heterogeneous issues, it seems clear that the results will begin to approach those emerging from the model which allows unrestricted side payments. If there is a sufficient number of issues confronted by voters at all times, and if the range and distribution of the individual intensities of preference over these issues are sufficiently broad, the complex logrolling process may approximate unrestricted side payments in results. Insofar as this is true, the full extent of the differential benefits from public outlay, or the differential costs of general-benefit legislation (that is, the differential intensities of individual preferences), can be exploited. The individual voter who is either strongly opposed to or strongly in favor of certain measures may, if necessary, "sell" his vote on a sufficient number of other issues to insure victory for his side in the strongly preferred outcome. His "purchasing power" is determined by the value of his support on all issues considered by other voters. Of course, the individual voter will rarely want to use up all of his purchasing power on any single measure, just as the individual consumer in the marketplace rarely uses up all his purchasing power on a single commodity or service. Complex logrolling of this type remains a "barter" system, but it merges into a pure "monetary" system (that is, one with full side payments) as the range of issues undertaken collectively is broadened. *Implicit logrolling* (discussed in Chapter 10), in which the voter is presented with a complex set of issues at the same time, is one form of the complex logrolling discussed here. If the voter is enabled to choose from among a sufficiently large number of alternative sets, his effective "purchasing power" approaches the limit that would be available to him under a "monetary" system.

THE "INDIVIDUAL RATIONALITY" CONDITION

To this point our models have been simplified by the assumption that the choice or choices facing the group involve only the final sharing of an earmarked grant or grants received from external sources. We now propose to make the models somewhat more realistic by dropping the external-grant features. Let us now suppose (just as we did in Chapter 10) that all funds for road repair are to be raised from general taxes levied uniformly on all citizens. We return to the simplest three-person game initially analyzed. This "new" game can also be discussed in the normalized form. To do so requires only that we attribute a fixed monetary sum to the various individuals at the outset. In the three-person game let us suppose that each person retains, at the beginning of "play," $\$1/3$; the beginning imputation is $(1/3, 1/3, 1/3)$. Now assume further that "play" is to involve, in every case, the disposition of $1. The form of the characteristic function is not changed:

$$\begin{aligned} &\text{i. } v(1) = v(2) = v(3) = 0 \\ &\text{ii. } v(1,2) = v(1,3) = v(2,3) = 1 \\ &\text{iii. } v(1,2,3) = 1 \end{aligned}$$

As in the earlier game, the individuals acting jointly as a group, [v(1,2,3) = 1], for example, under a rule of unanimity, cannot receive more than the gainers receive from the formation of coalitions under simple majority rule. There is, however, one major difference between the game now under consideration and the simpler one discussed earlier. In the previous game there could exist complete individual freedom to withdraw from the group. Since the funds to be expended there were assumed to come from outside the group itself, the withdrawal of a member would not serve to reduce the total gains to be secured. In other words, the earlier game satisfied a condition which may be represented as an adaptation of what Luce and Raiffa call the condition of *individual rationality*.[10] They define this condition as follows:

$$v(\{i\}) \leq x_i \text{ for every } i \text{ in } I_n. \qquad (3)$$

This condition states that no individual in the whole group, I_n, will ever receive less by being in the "game," regardless of whether or not he is in the winning or losing coalition, than he would if he "played alone" against all other members of the group. Applied to our particular problem, "playing alone" ({i}) may be interpreted as withdrawal from the game altogether.

The relevance of this condition is obvious when the purpose is that of analyzing "voluntary" games, and when it is further recognized that most of the game situations in which the individual finds himself do, in fact, represent such voluntary games. The extension of game-theory models to any analysis of political decision-making requires some consideration of "coercive" games. The condition of individual rationality, as we have stated it above, need not be satisfied at all. The individual participant in collective decision-making may, in many of the actual choices made through the political process, prefer to withdraw from "play." This does not suggest that the individual necessarily would want to withdraw from participation in the whole set of games represented by state action (although, conceptually, he could also want to do this). In any case, the individual can normally neither choose the political "games" in which he desires to participate nor can he withdraw from the ultimate social contract readily. He must remain as a participant on each issue that the group confronts.

Returning to the simple game before us, the individual, if he should be allowed to withdraw, could always retain his original value of $⅓. It follows that he would not voluntarily accept an expected value of less than ⅓ in any game if he were offered the alternative of not playing. However, in political groups, such action is not normally possible. Individuals cannot refuse to pay taxes even though they find themselves in a minority.

10. Luce and Raiffa, *Games and Decisions*, p. 193. Note that this is a much more limited usage of the term "individual rationality" than that which we have employed in Part I.

The solution set of imputations, in cost values, will be equivalent to that in the initial three-person game:

$$(\tfrac{1}{2}, \tfrac{1}{2}, 0) \quad (\tfrac{1}{2}, 0, \tfrac{1}{2}) \quad (0, \tfrac{1}{2}, \tfrac{1}{2})$$

In each of these imputations, one of the three persons will be made worse off than when play begins. However, as a member of the political unit for whom decisions are being made, he is forced to submit to the results indicated by the operation of the rules.

THE LIMITS TO "SOCIAL" WASTE

The majority-rule game considered here results in a net transfer of real income from one member of the three-person group to the other two members. Such transfers could, of course, take place directly without any necessity that tax revenues be expended in the provision of public services. In constitutional democracies, however, some limitations on majority action are almost always to be found. Moreover, since the individuals in our model are assumed equal in fiscal capacity at the outset, directly redistributive transfers would probably be prevented by constitutional provisions and traditions. If such transfers are prohibited, the majority coalition may effectively exploit the minority only through levying general taxes to provide special benefits, or through financing general benefits by special taxes. With this in mind, we shall now consider the extent to which the operation of simple majority voting rules can produce "social" wastage of resources.

If the solution set of imputations shown above is assumed to represent the imputed sets of individual evaluations of the public services (road repairs), note that there is no over-all wastage of resources. No "inefficiency" is introduced by the combined taxing-spending operation. The imputation ($\tfrac{1}{2}$, $\tfrac{1}{2}$, 0), for example, means, in this sense, that an expenditure of \$$\tfrac{1}{2}$ on the first person's road yields to him an estimated value of \$$\tfrac{1}{2}$; similarly, for the second man. The total additions to utility created by the expenditure of the \$1 are valued at the same total as are the total subtractions from utility caused by the necessary taxes ($\tfrac{1}{2} + \tfrac{1}{2} = \tfrac{1}{3} + \tfrac{1}{3} + \tfrac{1}{3}$). The "productivity" of the public expenditure is exactly equal to the alternative "productivity" of the resources should they have been left available for private disposition. This means that no introduction of side payments could modify the results, which are identical to those of purely redistributive transfers. Such transfers, by definition, involve no "social wastage" in the sense considered here, assuming, of course, that the supplies of the productive factors are not affected.

Let us now suppose, however, that the expenditure of $½ on the first person's road yields to him an incremental utility that he values at $5⁄12, and similarly for the second and third man. Under this modified assumption about the productivity of road repairs, we get a set of possible solution imputations as follows:

$$(5/12, 5/12, 0) \quad (5/12, 0, 5/12) \quad (0, 5/12, 5/12)$$

Note that it will still be profitable for the members of the winning coalition to play the game ($5/12 > 1/3$), but the total estimated value of the "gains" is less than the "losses" ($10/12 < 1$), or, in net terms, ($1/3 > 1/6$). If these individual evaluations can be compared in some way, then clearly "social wastage" of resources must be involved in the carrying out of the majority decision. One means of allowing some comparison of individual utilities is, of course, that of allowing side payments. If these are introduced, the set of imputations above cannot be said to represent any solution. Instead, in each imputation the person in the minority could always offer to compensate at least one of the others in order to get him to refrain from playing. For example, the imputation ($11/24, 11/24, 2/24$) outside the set above is dominated by no imputation in the set. Hence, the set of possible solution imputations,

$$(5/12, 5/12, 0) \quad (5/12, 0, 5/12) \quad (0, 5/12, 5/12)$$

does not satisfy the von Neumann–Morgenstern requirements. In this situation it does not seem likely that the "game," which must be *negative-sum*, will be played at all. No road repairs will be undertaken.

It should be remarked, however, that this result follows only if side payments are allowed. If neither purely redistributive income transfers nor side payments are possible, there is nothing that can arise to prevent the social process from proceeding, even if, translated into game-theory concepts, the game is one of negative-sum. Under the same productivity assumptions as before, the set of imputations,

$$(5/12, 5/12, 0) \quad (5/12, 0, 5/12) \quad (0, 5/12, 5/12)$$

now takes on all of the characteristics of the von Neumann–Morgenstern "solution." The person in a minority position can offer a maximum of ⅓ to another to refrain from playing.

It is reasonably clear from this analysis that the limits to resource wastage that could possibly result from the operation of simple majority rule will be determined by the size of the group. In our model three-person group, a "total productivity" of public investment must be at least two-thirds as great as that sacrificed in the private sector. In a five-person group this fraction becomes three-fifths. The maximum limits to resource wastage are defined by the fraction M/N, where M is the minimum number of voters required to carry a decision, and N is the number of voters in the whole group for which choices are to be made. Thus, at the limit, a public-investment project need only be slightly more than one-half as productive as the private-investment projects that are sacrificed, productivity in each case being measured in terms of the individual evaluation of benefits.[11]

This analysis is not intended to suggest that majority-rule "games" will tend to be constant- or negative-sum. In many cases, the game will, of course, be positive-sum. By altering the productivity assumptions of our simple models here, the results of positive-sum games are readily attainable. Let us suppose that the investment of $½ on each road yields $1 in benefits, as estimated by the individuals themselves. The "solution" set of imputations becomes:

$$(1, 1, 0) \quad (1, 0, 1) \quad (0, 1, 1)$$

Note that here, as in the constant-sum case, the introduction of side payments will not change this solution. Under the conditions outlined, the introduction of side payments will change the solution only if the game is negative-sum.

This limitation is no longer present, however, if we introduce some asymmetry in the benefit schedules, that is, if we assume that the productivity of public investment may vary from road to road in our model. We can, of course, conceive of games with asymmetrical benefit schedules which are positive-, constant-, or negative-sum. Moreover, a game may be switched from positive- to negative-sum within a single "solution" imputation. Consider the following set:

$$(\tfrac{11}{12}, \tfrac{1}{2}, 0) \quad (\tfrac{11}{12}, 0, \tfrac{1}{12}) \quad (0, \tfrac{1}{2}, \tfrac{1}{12})$$

Let the imputed values represent the estimated individual evaluations of the public investment of $½ on each road. Thus, the set takes on the properties of a solution unless side payments are allowed to take place. No imputation

11. In the terminology of some of the commonly used criteria for determining the allocation of public funds among separate projects, a minimum benefit-cost ratio of ½ would be required for a project to secure approval in a collective-decision process embodying simple majority rule.

in the set is more likely to be chosen than another. If the first imputation is chosen, the game, for the whole group considered as a unit, is positive-sum ($^{17}/_{12} > 1$); if the second imputation is chosen, constant-sum ($1 = 1$); if the third imputation, negative-sum ($^{7}/_{12} < 1$).

The introduction of side payments will insure that the second and the third imputations would never be produced, and even the first imputation would not exhibit the required stability properties required for solution. The F set would in this case become

$$(^{11}/_{12}, ^{11}/_{12}, 0) \quad (^{11}/_{12}, 0, ^{11}/_{12}) \quad (0, ^{11}/_{12}, ^{11}/_{12})$$

assuming constant returns to investment on the first road.

THE GENERAL BENEFIT–SPECIAL TAXATION MODEL

The previous models have incorporated the assumption that public projects providing differential benefits to individual citizens are financed by general taxes imposed equally on all citizens. The elementary propositions of *n*-person game theory applied to these models enable us to predict that serious resource wastage can result from the operation of simple majority rule. The reasons are the same as those discussed in Chapter 10. Majority rule allows members of the decisive coalition to impose external costs on other individuals in the group, costs that are not adequately taken into account in the effective decisions. Aggregate marginal costs exceed the aggregate marginal benefits from public investment. Relatively too many resources are invested in the type of public projects analyzed in the model—relatively too many as compared with both alternative private employments of resources and with alternative public employments.

The assumption that general taxation is levied to finance special benefits is clearly more descriptive of real-world fiscal institutions than the converse case. Ethically accepted principles which have long been espoused and which have found expression in modern tax institutions stress the importance of generality in the distribution of the tax burden among members of the social group. No such principles have guided the distribution of public expenditure among the several possible uses. However, in order to make our analytical models complete, it will be useful to modify our assumptions and to consider the reverse situation. Let us try to apply the elementary game-theory constructions used above to the model in which collective goods, providing general (equal) benefits to all citizens, are financed by discriminatory taxation. The analysis is relatively straightforward, but, interestingly enough, this model is not symmetrical in all respects with the one previously considered, as we shall demonstrate.

We begin, as before, with an initial imputation (1⁄3, 1⁄3, 1⁄3), which represents asset values held by the individuals. We now introduce a general-benefit situation. Suppose that the group is confronted with the opportunity to purchase a genuinely collective good, the benefits from which are not divisible; if one individual secures these benefits, each individual in the group must secure them in like amounts. As a first example, let us assume that each individual estimates his own benefits from the good to be 1⁄12. Assume further that the total costs of the collective good are 4⁄12 or 1⁄3. If the good is purchased, the final imputation of benefits, from the collective good alone, must be (1⁄12, 1⁄12, 1⁄12). However, what is relevant in this case is the "net" imputation that will result from the purchase of the collective good and the retention of shares of the initial assets.[12] The effective coalition will tend to impose special taxes on the minority, producing a "solution set" as follows,

(5⁄12, 5⁄12, 1⁄12) (5⁄12, 1⁄12, 5⁄12) (1⁄12, 5⁄12, 5⁄12)

assuming that side payments are not allowed. The over-all investment is not worth the cost ($3/12 < 4/12$); but, if taxes can be imposed in a discriminatory manner, it will still be an advantageous project from the point of view of the members of the effective coalition ($5/12 > 4/12$). The game in our illustrative example is negative-sum. Positive- or constant-sum games can also be constructed in this framework. Our purpose in this illustration is to demonstrate the possibility of negative-sum games being played and, thus, the possible wastage of resources. In the illustrative example here, the public investment should not have been undertaken since the resources employed are more productive if left in the private sector of the economy.

It can readily be seen that there are *no* effective limits to the possible extent of resource wastage under the assumptions of this model. *Any* project yielding general benefits, quite independent of cost considerations, will be supported by the dominating majority if they are successful in imposing the full tax financing of the project onto the shoulders of the minority. This feature differs substantially from the general-taxation model, where some quantita-

12. This adjustment was not necessary in the earlier models because we assumed, in each case, that the total initial assets were collected in general taxation: that is, we assumed that $1 was disposed of in each case.

tive limits could be estimated for the degree of resource wastage made possible under majority rule. Note that this feature also differs from the general implications of the logrolling analysis of Chapter 10. The analysis there implies that general-benefit projects would tend to be slighted in favor of special-benefit projects. This implication must be carefully constrained; it remains clearly true only if the assumption of general taxation is retained. If discriminatory taxation is allowed, there seems to be no a priori reason to expect special-benefit projects to take a dominating role in the operation of majority rule, except for the general presupposition that individuals may be more interested in special-benefit projects.

There is another important respect in which the general-benefit model is asymmetrical with the general-taxation model. In the latter, we have been able to demonstrate that, under the operation of simple majority rule, relatively too many resources are likely to be devoted to special-purpose public-investment projects. To be fully symmetrical with this, the general-benefit model might appear to require the conclusion that relatively too few resources be devoted to general-purpose public projects. This conclusion, however, cannot be supported. It can be demonstrated that relatively too many resources will be devoted to both special-benefit and general-benefit public projects under the operation of simple majority rule. This is an especially significant implication that emerges from our application of game theory to this voting rule, and the demonstration deserves to be carefully presented.

We shall show that every general-benefit project that is worth its cost will tend to be adopted by simple majority voting: that is to say, we shall try to prove that all possible projects involving resource investment more "productive" than the alternative investment in the private sector of the economy will tend to be adopted by majority rule. If this can be demonstrated to be true, our main point will have been established because, in the illustrative model first employed in this section, we have shown that some unproductive projects (negative-sum games) will be selected.

The proof is almost intuitive. If the dominant majority is able to impose the full costs of general-benefit projects on the minority, it follows that all projects yielding any benefits at all to the majority coalition members, *and costing no more than the maximum taxable capacity of the minority*, will be adopted without question. In our current example, any general-benefit project (any pure collective good) that costs up to ⅓ will surely be adopted. This is because, if discriminatory taxation is allowed, a sum up to this amount may be collected from the single minority member of the group. Hence, for all such projects a member of the majority coalition may secure some net benefit without cost to himself.

As the costs of collective goods move beyond the maximum taxable capacity of the minority member of the group, beyond ⅓ in our example, the individual members of the majority will be able to balance off gains against costs. Since they are the *residual* taxpayers, their own calculus will insure that a more than satisfactory balancing off will be achieved. Any project will be adopted that provides the group with general benefits valued more highly than the alternative private investments. While it is true that in making their final decisions they do not include in their calculus the full marginal benefits of the collective goods, because, by definition, these goods provide benefits to all members of the group equally, *neither* do the members of the majority include the full marginal costs. Moreover, the calculus will always reflect a more accurate estimate of marginal benefits (since the minority members will receive only an equal share) than of marginal costs (of which the minority members will bear more than an equal share).

In our analysis of the general-benefit model, we have not introduced side payments. If these are introduced, the effects are similar to those traced in the general-taxation models. Side payments will insure that no negative-sum games will ever be played: that is to say, "unproductive" public investments could never be undertaken if full side payments were to be permitted. If indirect side payments in the form of logrolling are allowed, some mitigation of the resource wastage involved in the operation of majority rule decision-making is to be expected. The extent of this mitigation will be dependent on the extent and range of the logrolling that takes place.

THE GENERAL TAXATION–GENERAL BENEFIT MODEL

Many of the modern activities of governments can be classified as falling within one of the two models previously discussed or in some combination of the two. For completeness, however, there remains the examination of those activities undertaken by governments that provide general benefits and are financed from general taxation. Let us assume that a community of identical individuals is faced with the task of providing a genuinely collective good. Benefits from this good are to be distributed equally among all citizens. This good is to be financed by taxation that is also equally distributed among all citizens.

It is immediately clear in this model that the collective-choice process does not take on the attributes of a game, regardless of the rules that may be adopted for decision-making. In this model the political process offers to the individual participant no opportunity to gain differential advantage at the expense of fellow participants. When the individual makes a decision, under any rule, he must try to compare the advantages that he will secure from the availability of the collective good and the costs that he will undergo from the increase in the general tax. His behavior can exert no external effect, either in costs or benefits, on third parties.

Communities are not, of course, made up of identical individuals. Moreover, once differences among individuals in tastes, capacities, endowments, etc., are admitted, the model for general taxation and for general benefits becomes much more difficult to discuss. It remains possible to imagine a collective decision in which the benefits from the public services provided are distributed among the membership of the group in such a manner as to precisely offset the distribution of the tax burden for this particular extension of service. In this case, where public expenditure is financed solely on some principle of marginal-benefit taxation, the conclusions reached above will hold. The individual cannot benefit at the expense of his fellows through the political process, and the game analogy breaks down. It is clear, however, that this model cannot be observed in the real world. We know that public services provided by governmental units do exert differential benefits and that these services are financed by taxation that is not general in the sense required for this extreme conceptual model.

The usefulness of this model lies in its implication that, insofar as collective action takes on such characteristics of generality (that is, nondiscrimination), the applicability of the game-theory conclusions is reduced. As we have emphasized elsewhere, the trend away from general legislation toward special legislation in modern democracies makes the conclusions drawn from the game-theory analogues more applicable than they might have been a century past.

CONCLUSIONS

The generalized conclusion that may be reached as a result of the application of elementary game theory to the institution of simple majority voting is evident. There is nothing inherent in the operation of this voting rule that will produce "desirable" collective decisions, considered in terms of individuals' own evaluations of possible social alternatives. Instead, majority voting will, under the assumptions about individual behavior postulated, tend to result in an overinvestment in the public sector when the investment projects provide differential benefits or are financed from differential taxation. There is nothing in the operation of majority rule to insure that public investment is more "productive" than alternative employments of resources, that is, nothing that insures that the games be positive-sum. Insofar as the vote-trading processes which emerge out of the sequence of separate issues confronted produce something akin to side payments, this resource-wasteful aspect of majority voting will tend to be reduced in significance.

The whole question of the relationship between the operation of simple majority voting rules and the "efficiency" in resource usage, within the context of the game-theory models, can best be discussed in terms of the constructions of modern welfare economics. In the following chapter we shall introduce these constructions in specific reference to the analysis of this chapter.

CHAPTER 12

MAJORITY RULE, GAME THEORY, AND PARETO OPTIMALITY

At several points in this book we have found, and shall find again, occasion to relate our analysis to that of modern welfare economics. This seems to be particularly useful following our application of elementary game theory to the operation of majority voting rules. By examining our results in comparison with the criteria of efficiency or optimality employed by the welfare economist, a somewhat better appreciation of the constitutional-choice problem may be achieved. To this point we have, in several instances, made reference to the Paretian criteria for efficiency. In Chapter 7 we discussed these criteria briefly. Additional discussion is wholly unnecessary for some readers, but even at the risk of introducing some redundancy, we shall first try to clarify the meaning of the fundamental Paretian construction.

PARETO OPTIMALITY

The criterion that the modern welfare economist employs in determining whether or not a given situation is "efficient" or "optimal" and whether or not a given move or change is "efficient" or "optimal" was developed by Vilfredo Pareto. We shall first define this criterion carefully, and we shall then distinguish two separate applications of the criterion.

The underlying premise of the modern Paretian construction is the purely individualistic one. The individual himself is assumed to be the only one who is able to measure or to quantify his own utility or satisfaction. No external observer is presumed able to make comparisons of utility among separate individuals. It is possible, however, even within these limits, to develop a means of evaluating either "situations" or "changes in situations" in terms of their "efficiency." To do this, a very weak ethical postulate is advanced. The "welfare" of the whole group of individuals is said to be increased if (1) every individual in the group is made better off, or (2) if at least one member in the group is made better off without anyone being made worse off. Clearly this postulate must be accepted by those who accept any form of individualistic values, that is, those who consider the individual rather than the group to be the essential philosophical entity. The ambiguities in the terms "better off" and "worse off" are removed by equating these to the individual's own preferences. If an individual shifts to position A from position B when he could have freely remained in B, he is presumed to be "better off" at B than at A.

On the basis of this construction, it becomes possible to define the property of a "social state" or "situation" that is necessary to insure its qualification as a Paretian P-point, that is, a point on a conceptual "optimality surface," a surface that will contain an infinity of such points. If, in any given situation, it is found to be impossible to make *any* change without making some individual in the group worse off, the situation is defined as Pareto-optimal or Pareto-efficient. On the other hand, if, in a given situation, it is found possible to make at least one individual better off by a change while making no individual in the group worse off, this situation is defined as nonoptimal. The first use of the Pareto norm is, therefore, to provide a means of classifying all possible social states or situations into the Pareto-optimal set and the nonoptimal set. Central to this approach is the idea that no single "most efficient" situation can be located or defined.

The second application of the Paretian construction lies in the development of a rule for classifying *changes* in social situations. A change is defined to be Pareto-optimal if, in the transition from one situation to another, either (1) every individual in the group is made better off, or (2) at least one individual in the group is made better off and no one is made worse off. It is important to note carefully just what this rule states, since much confusion has arisen in its application. It does *not* state that *any* shift from a nonoptimal to a Pareto-optimal situation is itself Pareto-optimal. The rule describes the characteristics of a *change* and does not relate directly to the characteristic of a situation or state either before or after change. A change away from an established Pareto-optimal situation cannot be itself Pareto-optimal, by definition. However, any other change may or may not be Pareto-optimal in itself. A change from one nonoptimal position to another may be Pareto-optimal, and a change from a nonoptimal position to a Pareto-optimal position may not be itself Pareto-optimal. These points can be easily illustrated in a simple diagram (see Figure 13). On the ordinate and the abscissa is measured the "welfare" or "utility" of individuals Y and X, measured in terms of their own expressions of preference. Any point along the frontier curve Y_mX_m represents a Pareto-optimal situation or state. Any movement from such a point to another point on or inside the frontier must reduce the expressed utility of one of the two individuals. Assume an initial position at A. A change from A

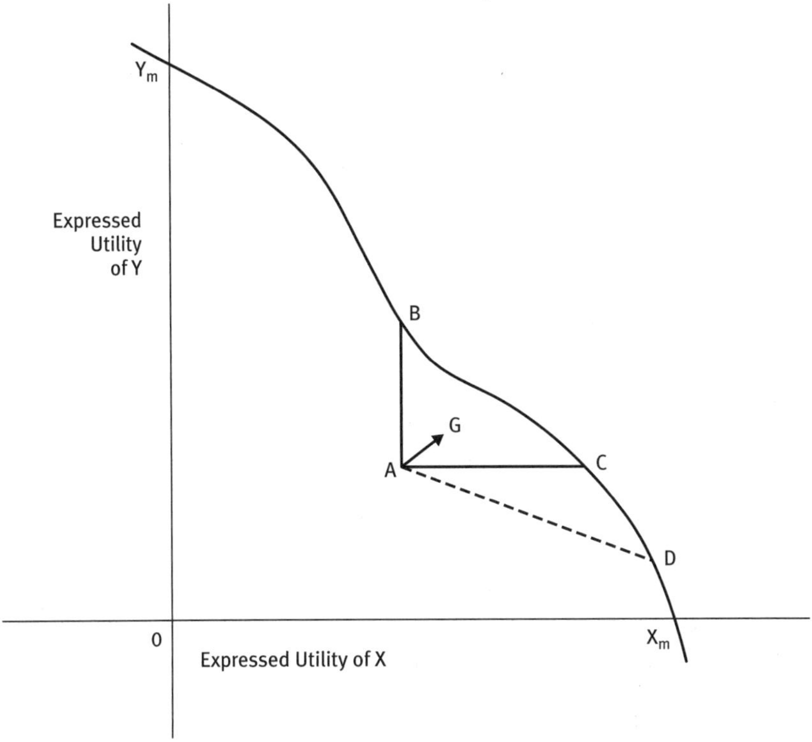

FIGURE 13

to any point on the frontier between B and C is clearly Pareto-efficient since both parties are made better off. However, a change from A to D is not itself Pareto-efficient since Y is made worse off in the process, even though the change represents a shift from a nonoptimal position A to a Pareto-optimal position D. On the other hand, a change from A to G is Pareto-optimal in itself, although it represents a shift from one nonoptimal position to another.[1]

1. We should emphasize that the graphical construction of Figure 13 is wholly conceptual. A point inside, on, or outside the frontier has *no* descriptively physical meaning. The graphical apparatus is employed solely to assist the reader in making a conceptual separation among three sets of situations or points: (1) those that are nonoptimal by the Pareto criterion, (2) those that are optimal by the same criterion, and (3) those that are unattainable. The situations or points are classified only on an observed *agreement* or a failure to agree among the individuals in the group. It is essential that these qualifications be kept clearly in mind, especially by those economist readers who may have been accustomed to discussions of the Pareto criterion in units of

This very elementary review of the Pareto criterion has been developed here because it will prove helpful to us in subsequent stages of our analysis. In the remaining parts of this chapter we shall use the Paretian conceptual apparatus in examining the results of the application of game theory to majority voting rules.

IMPUTATIONS AND PARETO OPTIMALITY

Let us recall the initial three-person game of Chapter 11, which involved the sharing of a fixed-sum external grant among three separate road-repair projects. The solution set of imputations was:

$$(\tfrac{1}{2}, \tfrac{1}{2}, 0) \quad (\tfrac{1}{2}, 0, \tfrac{1}{2}) \quad (0, \tfrac{1}{2}, \tfrac{1}{2})$$

Note that all of the imputations in F are Pareto-optimal: this is to say, there is no imputation outside the set which dominates any imputation in the set for all three individuals; there is no change from one of the imputations in F which could be made on the approval of all members of the group. This Pareto-optimality condition is imposed through the definition of the characteristic function which makes the return to the whole group,

$$v(1, 2, 3) = 1$$

along with that to any two-person majority coalition, such as

$$v(1, 3) = 1$$

In more general terms, the condition required for an imputation to exhibit Pareto optimality is that the sum of the gains to all individuals be at least as much as the whole group could gain if the members chose to act as a grand all-inclusive coalition. In more formal terms, Pareto optimality is insured by

$$\sum_{i \text{ in } I_n} x_i = v(I_n) \qquad (4)$$

where x_i is the return to an individual member of the group in a "solution" imputation, and $v(I_n)$ is the expression for the return to all individuals acting jointly as an all-inclusive coalition.[2] In our particular example, Pareto opti-

measure embodying specifically observable physical dimensions (income, goods, etc.) independent of observed agreement.

2. R. Duncan Luce and Howard Raiffa, *Games and Decisions* (New York: John Wiley and Sons, 1957), p. 193.

mality is guaranteed by the assumption that a positive-valued grant is received from some outside agency. The game here consists wholly of dividing this fixed-sized gain, and, unless wastage is involved in the process, the whole amount must be disposed. Therefore, *any* imputation, whether in the F set or not, is Pareto-optimal. Once divided, there is no way that side payments or compensations could possibly be arranged so as to move all members of the group to preferred or indifferently valued positions. This reflects the familiar point that the Pareto-optimality surface contains an infinity of points, each reflecting a separate distribution of "welfare" among members of the group.

In this initial example, the playing of the game is also Pareto-optimal, as distinct from the characteristic of the final solution: that is to say, the *change* in situation represented by the shift from the position prior to "play" to that after "play" is also Pareto-optimal. The preplay imputation is (0, 0, 0); thus, any final imputation represents individual positions which are either improvements or no worse than initial positions. The assumption that the grant is received from external sources also insures that the game itself will be Pareto-optimal. The individual-rationality condition,

$$v(\{i\}) \leq x_i \text{ for every i in } I_n$$

as we have interpreted it in Chapter 11, is satisfied.

If we now modify the game and consider that one introduced in the last part of Chapter 11 in which road-repair funds are to be raised from general taxes, the individual-rationality condition no longer holds. The majority-rule game under these circumstances is no longer Pareto-optimal. The initial imputation in this case is (⅓, ⅓, ⅓), and, in any final imputation after "play," one member of the group is moved to a less preferred position. Hence, the change represented by the game itself is nonoptimal in Pareto terms.

The solution imputation will continue to be Pareto-optimal, however, so long as condition (4) holds: that is, so long as the sum of the individual gains in any solution imputation is as much as the whole group could gain by acting through an all-inclusive coalition. However, so long as the solution imputation qualifies as a Pareto-optimal point, the playing of the game itself, *in an expectational sense*, may be considered "optimal." That is to say, this restriction on the solution insures that the payoffs to the winners of the majority-rule game are at least equal to the losses incurred by the losers. Therefore, the expected payoffs to each individual, at the start of play, must be at least equal to the value of the initially held assets. Although the game itself, as finally played, must reduce the utility of some of the players and hence be nonoptimal, the game does not involve the reduction in the expected utility of any player at the time of the participation decision, provided only that the solution imputation qualifies as Pareto-optimal. We are neglecting here the possible utility or disutility from play itself, as well as the possibility of diminishing marginal utility of income.

NEED SOLUTION IMPUTATIONS BE PARETO-OPTIMAL?

The results to this point are perhaps obvious, especially after the analysis of Chapter 11. The more interesting question is the following: Does a "solution" to the majority-rule game embody only imputations that are Pareto-optimal?

The game theorists seem to be rather unhappy about imposing this restrictive requirement on any solution to *n*-person games.[3] We may be able to shed some light on this question by a re-examination of our simple models. Suppose that the initial endowment is, as before assumed, (⅓, ⅓, ⅓). Further, let us assume that there exists no spending opportunity through which the group can increase its net real income. There are no "productive" public investments, and, in the private sector, opportunities are equalized at the appropriate margins of expenditure. In other words, the local roads simply do not need further repair, and, considered in additive cost-benefit terms, any repair project will yield less in benefits than it costs. To be specific, let us assume that the benefits yielded by repairing a road amount to only ⅚ of the costs. We shall assume full symmetry in benefit schedules: that is, public investment is equally productive on every road.

As we have put the problem, the initial imputation is Pareto-optimal. Will the group remain at this imputation? Or will majority voting move the group from an optimal to a nonoptimal position? Or from one optimal position to another?

Consider now the imputation (5/12, 5/12, 0) used before. Clearly, a shift to this imputation brings the group below the Pareto-optimality surface, but the imputation also dominates the initial one for the effective majority coalition, (1, 2) in this case. For the time being, let us label as D the set of imputations:

$$(5/12, 5/12, 0) \quad (5/12, 0, 5/12) \quad (0, 5/12, 5/12)$$

3. Ibid., p. 195.

This set seems to yield "solution" imputations although no single imputation in the set is Pareto-optimal. By proposing the imputation (0, 7/12, 3/12), the third man can form a new coalition with the second, and they could carry decision. However, as in our earlier discussion, one and three may then combine and shift to (5/12, 0, 5/12) which is in D. The stability properties of imputations in D seem to be identical to those in F.

Luce and Raiffa state that the D set, which does not contain Pareto-optimal imputations, does not represent a set of stable imputations. They argue that only that set containing Pareto-optimal imputations will exhibit the required stability of solutions. Their argument seems worth examining in some detail.

They suggest that *group rationality* (Pareto optimality), expressed in condition (4), is immaterial since all solutions that are stable must lie within the set of Pareto-optimal imputations. Basing their discussion on the work of Shapley and Gillies, they isolate four classes of *n*-tuples of payments:

$\bar{E}$ is the set of *n*-tuples in X such that

$$\sum_{i \text{ in } I_n} x_i \leq v(I_n) \qquad (5)$$

This states that $\bar{E}$ is the set of imputations for which the aggregate gains resulting from an all-inclusive coalition are greater than or equal to the summation of the gains received by the separate individuals through participation in the game, that is, in the imputations in X. In our numerical example here, the imputations listed fall within $\bar{E}$ since, by hypothesis, the aggregate real income of the group is lowered by the action taken. In numerical units, the value of the left-hand side of condition (5) would be 5/6 and the value of the right-hand side would be 1.

E is the set of *n*-tuples in X such that

$$\sum_{i \text{ in } I_n} x_i = v(I_n) \qquad (5)$$

which is the same as condition (4) above. This is the set of Pareto-optimal imputations. The first three-person game yielded imputations that necessarily fell within E, regardless of their location within or without F. Games that are purely redistributional must yield imputations in E.

$\bar{I}$ is the set of *n*-tuples in $\bar{E}$ such that

$$x_i \geq v(\{i\}) \text{ for all players in } I_n \qquad (7)$$

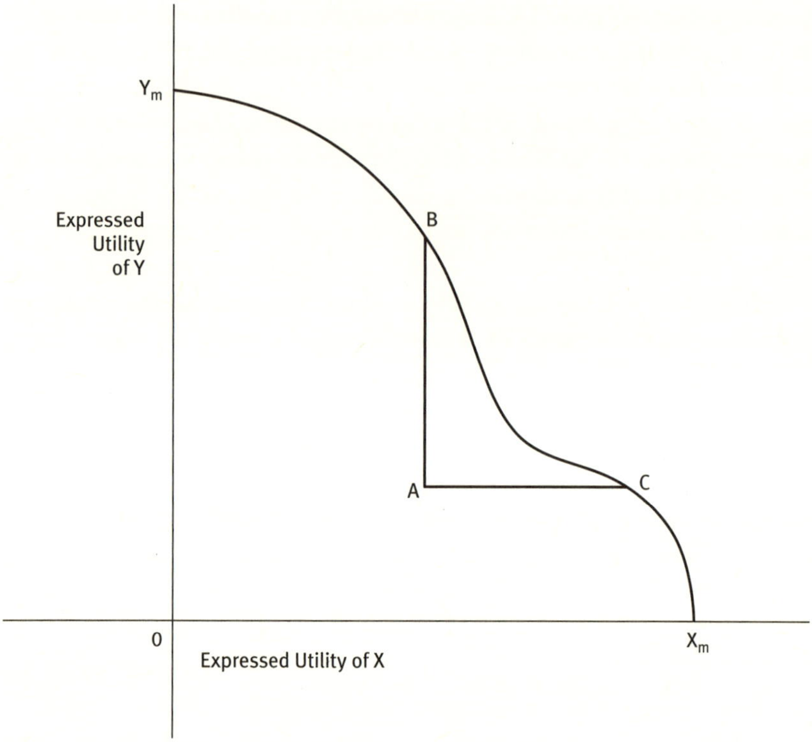

FIGURE 14

This is the subset of $\overline{E}$ which represents final imputations in which all individuals have either improved their position by participating in the game or have not been made worse off. This is the condition of individual rationality, as interpreted, which we have discussed earlier. In slightly different terminology, this condition, if satisfied, insures that the game itself is Pareto-optimal, even though a position on the optimality surface may not be achieved.

$$\text{I is the set of } n\text{-tuples in E such that} \\ x_i \geq v(\{i\}) \text{ for all players in } I_n \qquad (8)$$

This is a subset of the Pareto-optimal set of imputations. In particular, it is the subset of the Pareto-optimal set that may be attained in a Pareto-optimal manner from the initial no-play position. In other words, this set of imputations, on the Pareto frontier, can be reached by playing only "optimal" games.

In a two-person model, which can be represented on a two-dimensional surface, each set of these *n*-tuples can be shown readily. Refer to Figure 14, which is similar to Figure 13. $\overline{E}$ is represented by the whole area enclosed by the two axes and the frontier Y_mX_m. Any point along the frontier or inside the frontier satisfies the weak requirements of condition (5). E, the Pareto-optimal set, is represented by the set of points along Y_mX_m, that is, on the frontier. Note that E is a subset of $\overline{E}$. If A is defined to be the initial position, then $\overline{I}$ includes the set of points enclosed by the area ABC. I is that set of points falling along the frontier between B and C, being a subset of $\overline{I}$.

Luce and Raiffa (pp. 216–18) accept a proof by Shapley to the effect that a stable solution in E must lie within E. Hence, they conclude that no real restriction is placed on the results by assuming group rationality (Pareto optimality) in the first place. A commonsense approach may reveal the reasoning here. Why are the imputations

$$(5/12, 5/12, 0) \quad (5/12, 0, 5/12) \quad (0, 5/12, 5/12)$$

suggested as "solutions" to the particular problem considered, unstable? No element in this set, which we have called D, dominates any other element; but is every imputation not in D dominated by one in D? This second requirement is the crucial one, and D clearly does not satisfy it. Consider the imputations

$$(1/2, 1/2, 0) \quad (1/2, 0, 1/2) \quad (0, 1/2, 1/2)$$

which we recognize as the F set. One of the elements or imputations in this set dominates each imputation in D, yet no element in D dominates all of the imputations in F. This suggests that D could not represent a set of stable imputations.

Let us consider the real-world implications of this proof. Note that the imputations in F are Pareto-optimal. However, in order to attain an imputation in this set, the playing of the game must result in a shift that is equivalent to a purely redistributive transfer of real income among individual members of the group. That is to say, the game must be constant-sum, as defined by condition (6). However, given the requirement that collective decisions must involve the employment of general tax revenues to finance public services, this constant-sum restriction disappears. Moreover, when this happens, the F set of imputations remains as the solution only if full side payments are allowed. If both purely redistributive transfers and side payments are excluded, the game is severely constrained. There is no need whatever for the solution to exhibit the Pareto-optimality property. Condition (6) need not be met. The conclusion here is clearly that, if a majority is to exploit a minority, the most "efficient" means of so doing is the imposition of simple redistributive transfers (lump-sum taxes) instead of the indirect means of general-tax financing of special public-service benefits (or, conversely, special-tax financing of general-benefit public services), which may, as in our example here, involve a net cost for the group considered as a unit.

In the more constrained game without side payments, the imputations in F cannot be said to dominate those in D. Dominance has meaning only if the coalition is effective in shifting from one imputation to another. The set of imputations, F, simply does not exist in the constrained model. The D set embodies the solution with the same stability properties as the F set in the more general model, unless the human proclivities to make side payments are considered to be so strong as to rule out meaningful discussion of such constrained games.

GEOMETRICAL ILLUSTRATION

The essential points may be clarified by geometrical illustration. In Figure 15 below we measure on the ordinate the position of the dominant or the effective majority. The gains are added over the two members since we must use two-dimensional surfaces. On the abscissa we measure the position of the minority member of the three-man group. In the restricted model that we have been discussing, we assume that *no* investment in the public sector is productive. This makes the initial imputation Pareto-optimal; this imputation is (⅓, ⅓, ⅓), which becomes the point (⅔, ⅓) when plotted on the two-dimensional diagram as point I, which is, by definition, on the Pareto frontier. Since *any* division of one unit is also, by definition, on the frontier, the line AB in Figure 15 represents the whole set of Pareto-optimal points. Since we do not identify the members of the majority in the diagram and since the benefit schedules are symmetrical, if we allow individuals to shift from membership in the majority to membership in the minority, all points that are Pareto-optimal in the three-person model can be represented on AB. The set of imputations, F, the solution to the generalized game, is shown at A. At this point the member of the minority is deprived of all assets, and the two members of the majority coalition symmetrically share the gains, which are equivalent to the whole product. Again, by shifting separate individuals, A can be taken to represent all three of the imputations in F. As we have noted, if purely redistributive transfers should be allowed, a majority would immediately shift the group from I to A. Nothing would be modified except the distribution of the fixed-sum among the members of the group.

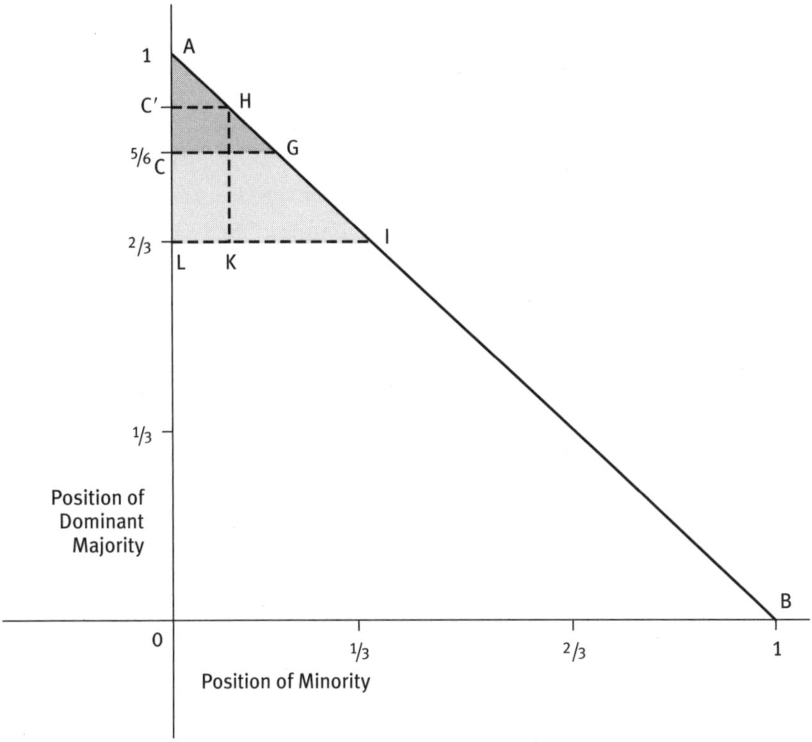

FIGURE 15

If redistributive action is excluded, the majority might still find it advantageous to take action, even though, by hypothesis, such action will be unproductive for the whole group. The point C represents the set of imputations D, defined as the solution to the more constrained model. Here the combined "gains" of the majority are ⅚, while the assets of the minority are confiscated. C is clearly beneath the optimality frontier. This suggests that, conceptually, all of the members of the group could be made better off by some change. The range of such changes is shown by the heavily shaded area in Figure 15. A shift or change from C to any point in this area would itself be Pareto-optimal. If side payments are allowed, the minority member of the group could, for example, "afford" to offer the majority IK, valued at KH by the majority, in order to allow all the group to shift to H instead of undertaking the action shown at C. The majority would, if allowed, accept this offer, but they need not stop there. They could, instead, try to outbargain the minority member and to force him to concede sufficient side payments to allow the group to move to A. The precise outcome of the actual bargaining process is unimportant; the relevant point is that such payments will insure that a final solution somewhere along the frontier will be reached. Under the specific conditions of this example, where the public project yields a total benefit value of $5/6$, the relevant range on the frontier is AG. Side payments will be paid to the majority to prevent the investment from being undertaken.

The limits to resource wastage discussed in the last chapter can also be shown readily in this diagram. If all redistributive transfers and side payments are ruled out, any collective project that yields more than $2/3$ to the effective majority will be selected. Any position on the vertical axis above L becomes a possible solution to the constrained game of majority rule.

SYMMETRY IN BENEFIT SCHEDULES

We have demonstrated clearly that majority voting rules may result in a shift of the group from a Pareto-optimal to a nonoptimal position in the constrained form of the game. It will now be useful to demonstrate geometrically that, if the initial position is nonoptimal and if an optimal position can be attained by collective action, majority voting will move the group to a Pareto-optimal position *only if the benefit schedules are symmetrical over the whole group*. Benefit schedules were assumed to be symmetrical in the previous example, where it was demonstrated that majority voting may shift the group off an initial position on the Pareto frontier. Symmetry in benefit schedules may be at most, therefore, a necessary condition for attaining a Pareto-optimal position. It can never be *sufficient* to insure the attainment of such a position. Refer to Figure 16. As before, we assume an initial (before play) position at I. However, let us assume that public investment in all three roads is equally productive, and highly productive. An investment of $\$1/2$ on each road is assumed to yield a benefit value of \$1. In this case the F set becomes

$$(1, 1, 0) \quad (1, 0, 1) \quad (0, 1, 1)$$

represented in Figure 16 as the single point A. Majority decision will tend to shift the group to A, which is on the Pareto frontier. The majority-rule game, as actually played, is not, of course, Pareto-optimal, since the minority member of the group is shifted to a lower utility level in the process of paying taxes to support the public projects beneficial to other members of the social group. In an expectational sense, however, the game is "optimal," provided, of course, that the rules are "fair." Note that, in this case, no introduction of purely redistributive transfers or side payments will change the result. The

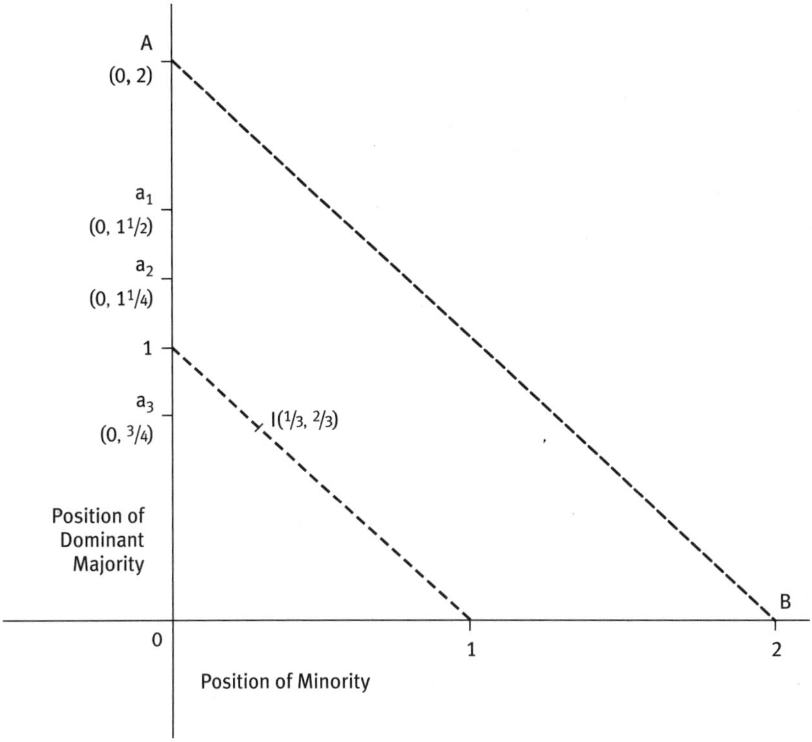

FIGURE 16

majority can reach the position shown at A only by undertaking the projects, and there is no way that the minority can make an effective counteroffer.

Note carefully, however, that this conclusion follows only when we assume symmetry in benefit schedules over all individuals.[4] If this assumption is dropped, the operation of majority-rule decision-making will not necessarily shift the group from an initial nonoptimal to a Pareto-optimal position without the introduction of side payments. For purposes of illustrating this point, we now assume that the investment of $½ on each road project will yield, respectively, $1, $½, $¼. The solution set becomes

$$(1, \tfrac{1}{2}, 0) \quad (1, 0, \tfrac{1}{4}) \quad (0, \tfrac{1}{2}, \tfrac{1}{4})$$

4. The symmetry in benefit schedules referred to here is not equivalent to the equal or symmetrical intensities of preference referred to in Chapter 9. The discussion at that point was similar to this, but note that there we postulated that the preference, negative or positive, of each individual was valued equally.

assuming no side payments. Let us assume that there exist no investments in the private economy that are more productive than investment on the first road. If individuals 1 and 2 form a dominant majority, the group will shift to point a_1 in Figure 16; if 1 and 3 form the majority, to point a_2; if 2 and 3, to point a_3. In none of these cases does majority voting shift the group to the optimality frontier, which could only be reached if all investment should be made on the first road.

When the benefits are asymmetrical, the frontier will be attained only if full side payments are allowed to take place. In the example here, Pareto optimality will be attained, after side payments, in the solution set:

$$(1, 1, 0) \quad (1, 0, 1) \quad (0, 1, 1)$$

If side payments are allowed, the first man can afford to pay the second man more than $\$1/2$, the value of repairs to the second road, for his support of a policy of exclusive investment on the first road; and the first man could clearly pay the third man more than $\$1/4$, the value of his own estimated benefits from local road repair.

This introduces an extremely interesting point that we have deliberately neglected in the discussion of Chapter 11. In a purely formal sense, the imputations in F, written above, satisfy the von Neumann–Morgenstern requirements for solution when full side payments are allowed. Moreover, since all three of the imputations satisfy the requirements jointly (that is, as a set of imputations), nothing further can be stated in terms of the formal construction. However, we have noted previously that the notions of stability and solution in *n*-person games generally are not fully satisfactory. Many games contain numerous solutions in the simple mathematical sense. Intuitively, we may see that these ideas of solution and stability are considerably less applicable to those games where benefit schedules are not symmetrical than to those in which such schedules are symmetrical. Let us consider the set F, above, more carefully. It seems clear that, of the three imputations in F, the second is more likely to emerge, or, to state this somewhat more correctly, the coalition represented by the second imputation seems more likely to emerge. Nor do some of the imputations in F seem more stable, under the restrictions of this model, than others outside the set. The second-imputation coalition between the first and the third person in the group seems more probable because the support of the third man for repair on the first road can be secured more "cheaply," even with full money payments, than the support of the second man. This is because the *relevant* alternative, as considered by the third man, may be, not his combination with the second to exploit the first to the maximum, but his combination with the second to finance repairs to their own roads. If the third imputation is not considered by 2 and 3 to be a genuine alternative, then any imputation $(c_1, 0, c_3)$, where $7/4 \geq c_1 \geq 1$, and $1 \geq c_3 \geq 1/4$, would be equally stable with (1, 0, 1). This point, which amounts to the denial that full side payments would be carried out in situations like the ones postulated, suggests the probable emergence of coalitions between those individuals and groups who are the direct beneficiaries of the most productive public projects and those individuals and groups for whom public investment is the least productive. This result will emerge, of course, only if some side payments are allowed. However, even if only limited forms of vote-trading are permitted, this general conclusion does not seem at all implausible and appears to be in accord with those reached in Chapter 10.

SIDE PAYMENTS AND PARETO OPTIMALITY

In a very real sense, the introduction of full side payments serves to create a marketable property right in the individual's political vote, his power of collective decision. If this power is marketable (that is, if it is to command a price or a market value), some element of scarcity must be present. On single issues such as those discussed in our models, the scarcity of decision-making power is evident. Only one decision can ultimately be made; only one majority can be effective. The aggregate payoff function is reduced to the (1, 0) form. If collective decisions affect the disposition of economic resources, and if resources are used up over finite time, the decision-making power over any disposition of resources is scarce indeed. Decisions become irrevocable once made.

We have shown that only if side payments are introduced is there any assurance that majority-rule decision-making will lead to positions on the Pareto-optimality frontier. It will now be shown that this property depends *solely* on the introduction of side payments and that it has no specific connection with majority rule. In order to demonstrate this, we must prove that *any* decision-making rule, with full side payments, will produce only Pareto-optimal situations.

We may take two extreme decision-making rules, those of individual dictatorship and unanimity. First, we assume that all decisions for the group are to be made by a single individual, the dictator, who is interested only in maximizing his own utility. Let us keep within the limits of our simple three-person model, and again let us assume that the group receives a grant from external sources. The benefit schedules are as follows: if all funds are spent on the first road, \$10; if all are spent on the second road, \$5; if all are spent on the third road, \$1. If Individual 1 is dictator, no question arises. However, if Individual 2 is dictator, he will find that his own utility can be maximized by "selling" his power of disposition over the external grant to Individual 1 for something in the bargaining range of \$5 to \$10. He will sell to the highest bidder, and it is evident in this model that Individual 1, for whom road repairs are the most productive, can bid highest. Similar conclusions follow if Individual 3 is dictator. A Pareto-optimal position is always attained. If the assumption of an external grant is dropped and general-tax financing assumed, this conclusion is not modified. The only difference here is that, with general-tax financing, the game itself is not Pareto-optimal. Under dictatorship, two of the individuals will tend to be made worse off as a result of any political action, always under the behavioral assumptions implicit in all of our models.

Let us now go to the opposite extreme and show that, even if a unanimity rule is adopted for collective decisions, all solution imputations will be Pareto-optimal when side payments are allowed. In the external grant case, any possible *n*-tuple or imputation dominating (0, 0, 0) for all three individuals can be attained through unanimous approval; or, if we are assuming tax financing from an initial position (⅓, ⅓, ⅓), any imputation dominating this may be a "solution." Again, however, note that all repairs will be made on the first road, if side payments can take place. The set of possible solution imputations is extremely large here. The following three imputations represent the limits in the "negotiation set":

$$(9\tfrac{1}{3}, \tfrac{1}{3}, \tfrac{1}{3}) \quad (\tfrac{1}{3}, 9\tfrac{1}{3}, \tfrac{1}{3}) \quad (\tfrac{1}{3}, \tfrac{1}{3}, 9\tfrac{1}{3})$$

If symmetry in gain is held to be characteristic of solution, a single imputation (3⅓, 3⅓, 3⅓) emerges, but, as we have noted, the argument for symmetry seems much less convincing in games of this sort where *all* participants must agree on the sharing than it does in games such as that of majority rule. The final outcome will depend on the relative bargaining strengths of the parties in negotiation, but the bargaining will take place only to determine in what proportions the gains are to be shared. The Pareto frontier will tend to be reached, and it will be reached in a Pareto-optimal manner. The latter is the unique feature of the unanimity rule. The "game" itself is Pareto-optimal. Only with the unanimity rule will collective decision-making produce changes that are necessarily Pareto-optimal.

If side payments are not allowed, neither dictatorship nor the unanimity rule will produce imputations on the Pareto frontier in all cases. The unanimity rule will always result in movement toward the frontier, but there is no assurance that the frontier or surface will be reached. Thus, we find that the Pareto criterion suggests the paradoxical conclusion that open buying and selling of political votes may actually lead to an "improvement" for the group, measured in the extremely weak ethical sense of making everyone in the group better off as a result. This conclusion deserves more careful attention, but we propose to delay this to a later point. What has been demonstrated is that, without side payments, there is nothing in any particular voting rule to insure that collective decisions will move the group to the Pareto-optimality surface or that such decisions will keep the group on this surface if it is once attained.

reaching decisions, given any decision-making rule other than unanimity. The apparent contradiction between the existence of external costs and the satisfaction of the orthodox conditions for Pareto optimality, which side payments will tend to produce, must be resolved. In so doing, we shall also be able to relate the introduction of side payments generally to the constitutional-choice models of Chapter 6. A by-product of our discussion will be the integration of income redistribution into our model of collective activity. In one sense, this chapter represents a digression from the main stream of our analysis. It seems necessary, however, to avoid certain logical pitfalls, and the material which follows will provide some foundation for the analysis of later chapters.

REDISTRIBUTIVE ELEMENTS IN MAJORITY DECISIONS

Under the behavioral assumptions of our models, majority decision-making (or any decision-making with less-than-unanimity rules for choice) will tend to produce some asymmetry in gain-sharing among the individual members of the group for which the choices are made. The members of the effective coalition will receive differentially larger shares of the benefits expected to result from collective action and/or they will bear differentially smaller shares of the costs of collective action providing general benefits for the whole group. This amounts to saying that *redistributive* elements must be a part of any collective decision reached by a less-than-unanimity rule.

What the introduction of side payments accomplishes is the conversion of all collective decisions to these *purely redistributive* elements. Unless a public investment project is "worthwhile" in a market-value sense, side payments ("bribes") will arise to prevent action from being taken, regardless of the rule for choice. What side payments cannot prevent are the net transfers of real income among the separate individuals and groups. With full side payments, the decision-making rules determine the structure of the net income transfers only; they do not influence the extent of "productive" collective activity. The latter will always be extended to the limits defined by the satisfaction of the Paretian conditions.[1] It is his inability to say anything about the distributive

1. This does not imply that the same amount of productive collective activity will be undertaken under all rules if side payments are fully effective. The distribution of real income itself influences the final allocation between public and private goods that will satisfy the full Paretian conditions. On this point, see Paul A. Samuelson, "The Pure Theory of Public Expendi-

problem that has inhibited the modern welfare economist. Since he cannot presume to make interpersonal comparisons of utility, he cannot adjudge one Pareto-optimal position to be better than any other or even adjudge one optimal position to be superior to all nonoptimal positions. A move from one point to another on the conceptual optimality surface must remain outside the analytical framework of the welfare economist. Since all decisions, public and private, leading to a point on the optimality surface must be made by a proper comparison of marginal costs with marginal benefits, no external effects of the ordinary sort can be present in the final Pareto "equilibrium." From this the inference seems clear that, under a regime with full side payments, since different decision-making rules act only to affect the location of the position on the optimality surface, the external-costs function of Chapter 6 is not applicable. This function appears from this approach to be meaningless for the analysis of purely redistributive transfers. The geometrical inference is that, for such transfers, the external-costs function would lie along the abscissa. External costs would appear to be zero under *any* rule.

Let us see precisely what the acceptance of such an inference would imply for the constitutional calculus of the individual. Recall that, under our assumptions, the individual, at the time of constitutional choice, is uncertain as to his own role on particular issues in the future. If the inference suggested here is correct, the individual, because of this uncertainty, *will not expect positive external costs to be imposed on him by purely redistributive transfers of real income*. The reason is evident: he will see that the external benefits which he may secure through imposing external costs on others on certain occasions will tend to equal the external costs which others will impose on him on different occasions. In any single action, the external costs imposed on those from whom income is taken are equal to the external benefits received by those to whom income is transferred. Since, at the constitutional stage, the individual will identify himself with neither of these groups, he will see that the effects tend to balance out as he considers the whole sequence of possible redistributive transfers.

Note carefully, however, just where this line of argument is leading us. If correct, the argument suggests that the individual, at the constitutional level, would *never choose* to collectivize the redistribution of real income among

---

ture," *Review of Economics and Statistics*, XXXVI (1954), 387–89, and "Diagrammatic Exposition of a Theory of Public Expenditure," *Review of Economics and Statistics*, XXXVII (1955), 350–56.

members of the group. If the external-costs function does not exist for such transfers, then clearly cost minimization of this activity is achieved only by allowing purely private activity. Only in this way will the decision-making costs (the costs of reaching agreement between two or more persons required to form an effective coalition for decisive collective action) be eliminated. If the distribution of real income among members of the society really does not matter, as would be implied by the argument, the most efficient way of organizing "redistribution" is to do nothing about it.

AN ALTERNATIVE EXPLANATION

There seems to be decisive empirical evidence that individuals do not behave as the above argument would indicate. In almost every society some collectivization of income redistribution is to be found; some efforts are made to accomplish real-income transfers among members of the group by collective intervention. How is this observed phenomenon to be explained in terms of our analytical approach? We shall propose an explanation which will incorporate the existence of external costs into a model restricted to purely redistributive transfers. In this explanation the extension of our analysis beyond the limits of orthodox welfare economics can be most easily made apparent.

We may assume that the marginal utility of income declines as the individual receives more income in any particular time period and that the individual recognizes this. We do not require further restrictions on the shape of the individual's utility function. If the individual recognizes that, in any given period, the marginal utility of income will decline as more is received, he will see that, *over a succession of periods*, his total utility would be increased if some means of "exchange through time" could be arranged. If some institution could be established which would add to his income during periods of bad fortune and subtract from his income during periods of good fortune, the individual's total utility over time could clearly be increased. If, in fact, he could assume that the years of good fortune would be matched by years of bad fortune within his life span, the individual could, conceptually, purchase such "income insurance" from privately organized sellers. However, at the stage of constitutional choice, the single individual cannot make this required assumption. He will recognize that, individually, he may suffer a succession of low-income periods or, alternatively, he may enjoy a succession of high-income periods. Moreover, since income is the primary economic magnitude to be considered in his over-all life planning, the individual will rarely have sufficient wealth at the outset of his life to purchase the "income insurance" that utility-maximizing considerations would dictate to be rational. Nor will potential private sellers of such insurance be in a position to enforce the sort of contracts that might be required to implement such a program in the real world. All of these obstacles to a private "income insurance" would be present even if the most fundamental obstacle were overlooked. This is the fact that the risk in question would be essentially uninsurable by ordinary standards. Since the private individual, by modifying his current behavior, is able to affect his claims for compensations, a privately organized insurance plan might be impossible.

By such considerations as these, the individual may be led to examine the prospects of collectivizing the redistribution of real income to the extent that is indicated to be rational by his utility function. In order to prevent the possibility of his falling into dire poverty in some unpredictable periods in the future, the individual may consider collective organization which will, effectively, force him to contribute real income during periods of relative affluence. Such collective redistribution of real income among individuals, viewed as the working out of this sort of "income insurance" plan, may appear rational to the utility-maximizing individual at the stage of constitutional decision. The essential "uninsurability" of the risk will not, of course, be eliminated by collectivization, but the individual may be more willing to accept the costs of such uninsurability if he knows that *all* members of the group are to be included in the plan.

Before committing himself, however, the individual must try, as best he can, to analyze the operation of the decision-making rules that may be adopted in carrying out the collective activity of redistribution. Once the constitution is established, the individual actor operates within the predefined rules; no longer must he try to reach full agreement with his fellows. Moreover, in the implementation of income redistribution through collective action, external effects become the essence of private behavior.

Let us suppose that a constitution is adopted which openly and explicitly states that net-income transfers among individuals and groups will be carried out by simple majority voting. In this situation it seems clear that the maximum possible departure from rational behavior in choosing the amount of redistribution could be present. The individuals in a successful majority coalition could impose net taxes on the minority and receive net subsidies for themselves. In the calculus of the individual participant in a majority coalition, a symmetrical share of the coalition gains will be treated as the marginal benefits of action and balanced off against zero marginal costs. It seems certain that "redistribution," considered as an activity, will be carried relatively "too far" under these conditions.

But "too far" relative to what? This is the difficult step in the analysis. Pareto criteria can be drawn in for ordinary collective action, but they are useless here. Nevertheless, the constitutional-choice model is helpful, and it allows us to answer this question, at least conceptually. Redistribution, under the circumstances postulated, will proceed "too far" relative to the amount that the individual, in the role of constitution-maker, could choose to be rational on the basis of long-run utility-maximizing considerations. In one sense, we may translate this into Pareto-optimality terms at a different level of decision-making. The amount of redistribution that unrestrained majority voting will generate will tend to be greater than that which the whole group of individuals could conceptually agree on as "desirable" at the time of constitutional choice. Since conceptual unanimity is possible on this degree of income redistribution, we may, in a certain sense, call this a Pareto-optimal amount of redistribution. The more orthodox Paretian construction applies only to the operational level of decision, that is, within the confines of established constitutional rules. If we are to discuss the formation of the rules themselves, something quite similar to the Pareto criterion emerges when we consider the "optimal" rules. However, it seems best to avoid using the same terms in both cases.

If, in fact, voting rules are expected to result in real income redistribution being extended "too far" relative to that which the individual would rationally choose, we may clearly say that the organization of this activity will be expected to impose some external costs on the individual. The external-costs function of Chapter 6 is equally as relevant in analyzing this activity as all other collective activities. In our model of collective action which allows full side payments to take place, the external costs that are expected from the operation of any decision-making rule are solely those resulting from the overextension of redistribution. Side payments will insure that the orthodox Pareto-optimality surface will be reached, but the redistribution that will take place through the collective-choice process will not represent the "optimal" shifting among positions on this orthodox optimality surface. Note that we do not require an interpersonal comparison of utility in the usual sense to be able to reach this conclusion. We require only that the individual be able to make decisions based on some presumption about his utility function in different periods of time. In a sense, of course, this does represent an interpersonal comparison of utility, but it is of a sort that individuals must, in fact, make in many everyday decisions.

We reach the conclusion that the attainment of an orthodox Pareto-optimal position is not sufficient to insure that there exist no external effects from an activity. The external costs of redistribution will remain, even if perfectly operating side payments arise to insure that the more familiar externalities are eliminated.

"INCOME INSURANCE" AND INDIVIDUAL BEHAVIOR

The expected external costs from redistributive collective action become more pronounced when it is recognized that the form of the transfers may not be at all similar to that which the rational individual, in the role of constitutional chooser, would select as the "optimal" plan of income insurance. Under the assumptions of our model, there is no reason to expect that simple majority voting, for example, would result in a net transfer of real income from the rich to the poor. There is no assurance that the dominant coalition will, in fact, be such that the transfers will provide the "insurance" considered in the constitutional calculus.

This suggests that the expected external costs of purely redistributive action may, in fact, be so high that the individual, at the constitutional level of choice, may decide that any collectivization of direct redistribution is undesirable. Because of this, he may seek to "institutionalize" the "income insurance" plan via constitutional processes.

An analogy that frequently appears in bargaining theory may prove helpful. At the outset of a hunt each of two hunters may consider that his expected utility will be maximized by agreeing on a predefined rule for sharing the day's catch. Each might realize that, only by agreeing to such a rule, could a "fair" sharing be assured. Otherwise, without rules, the hunter securing the major share of the game would probably think that his good fortune was due to his exceptional skill, and he would be extremely reluctant to part voluntarily with a share of the size that he might otherwise have agreed to under a predefined sharing rule.

Empirical evidence points strongly toward some such explanation as that developed here. Not only do most societies with democratically organized governments undertake some collective action with a view toward redistribution of real income, but the manner in which this action is taken suggests clearly that the external effects are sensed acutely by the framers of political constitutions. In the first place, arbitrary and discriminatory redistributive transfers of income and wealth among individuals and groups are normally prohibited. For direct transfers to be effected, some general bases for classifying individuals are usually required. Secondly, the whole constitutional emphasis on securing and guaranteeing the basic human rights and civil liberties can be broadly interpreted as aiming toward an equalization of opportunities rather than an equalization of rewards. If the legal and institutional framework is such that the distribution of emerging rewards is tolerably acceptable, the direct collective intervention to affect the redistribution that may be dictated is reduced. Insofar as the "income insurance" can be provided by improving the rules within which the "economic game" is played, the individual, at the stage of constitutional choice, may be spared the expected external costs of too much and possibly wrongly directed redistribution through collective action. This point was recognized by Knut Wicksell, himself a genuine humanitarian, when he suggested that efforts toward improving distributive results should be centered on reforms of the institutions of property instead of on the redistributive potential of the fiscal system.

Finally, and most importantly, redistribution of real income, per se, is rarely collectivized, in spite of the almost universal acceptance of some collective effort to intervene in the distribution process. Surely there must exist some explanation for the continuing reluctance of societies in the Western world to throw open the redistributive potential of the fiscal system to the ordinary mechanism of collective choice-making. The most plausible explanation seems to be found in the very real fear of the external effects that such an unrestricted collectivization of redistribution might generate. Instead of following this path, Western governments have opened the way for more and more effective redistribution which is accomplished indirectly through the tax financing of public goods and services. By incorporating highly progressive, but nominally general, taxes with special-benefit public services in the fiscal process, the redistribution that is carried out far exceeds that which could be accomplished directly.

This points up the difficulty of putting to practical use the conceptual separation of the allocational and the distributional aspects of the budget, a separation urged recently by R. A. Musgrave.[2] If such a separation were, in fact, required, much less effective redistribution would be carried out since the in-

2. R. A. Musgrave, *The Theory of Public Finance* (New York: McGraw-Hill, 1959).

dividual, fearful of the external costs of unrestricted redistribution, would not allow governments as much power as they now possess indirectly.

ALLOCATIONAL AND REDISTRIBUTIONAL EXTERNALITIES

From the operation of any collective decision-making rule short of unanimity, therefore, the individual normally expects two distinct sorts of external costs to be imposed on him as he considers his possible role over an extended series of issues in a sequence of time periods. If side payments ("bribes") are not allowed, or if only partially effective substitutes are sanctioned, there can be expected to arise some allocational externalities. That is to say, the collective-choice process will cause resources to be employed "inefficiently."

The effects of introducing logrolling or side payments into the collective-choice mechanism are those of "squeezing" out these allocational inefficiencies. If side payments are conceived to be perfectly organized, all such allocational inefficiencies will tend to be eliminated. There will remain only the redistributional "inefficiencies," which can also be called "externalities," with which we have been primarily concerned in this chapter.

The impact of these expected redistributional externalities (these redistributional external costs) on the individual constitutional calculus could scarcely be overemphasized, for it seems to be this expectation which causes the individual to refrain from assigning to the collective sector many activities which he would tend to collectivize if such externalities were absent. Examples are easy to come by. Full efficiency in resource usage in the United States might require the co-ordinated development of the water resources of each regional watershed. The full range of externalities in the allocational sense cannot be exploited except through the co-ordination of development extending over a geographic area encompassing several states. If we accept these presumptions as being true, does it follow that "nationalization" of this function should be supported by the rational, utility-maximizing "average" citizen of the United States, as he might be assumed to adopt a rule of making such a choice? The answer is not nearly as clear as some modern welfare economists, and applied cost-benefit analysts, would like to make it. If such projects are to be financed, or if the individual expects them to be financed, out of general tax revenues collected from the whole population of the country, the redistributional externalities expected may well be sufficiently large to offset the allocational externalities that may be continued by failure to undertake co-ordinated development.

CONCLUSIONS

As suggested at the beginning, this chapter has represented somewhat of a digression from our main line of argument. It has been designed to show that our analysis of the constitutional-choice problem (contained centrally in Chapter 6) is applicable to the collective redistribution of real income among persons, despite the apparent contradiction between the attainment of the orthodox Pareto-optimality surface and the continuing existence of net external costs. The contradiction was resolved by showing that our analytical model, extending as it does to the choice of rules for choice, is more extensive than the standard Paretian construction. External costs, in our model of constitutional choice, are made up of two elements: those resulting from what we have called allocational externalities, and those resulting from what we have called redistributional externalities.

CHAPTER 14

THE RANGE AND EXTENT OF COLLECTIVE ACTION

Implications concerning the relative size of the public and the private sectors of the economy have been suggested at several points in our analysis. These implications have not been fully explored, nor have they been related to each other. In this chapter we shall try to answer the questions: What can be said about the relative size of the public sector as a result of our analysis? Does the analysis suggest that the public sector will be "too large" with respect to the private sector, given certain decision-making rules for collective choice? Or "too small"? What criteria are to be employed in judging whether or not the sphere of collective activity is "too large" or "too small"? How do these criteria and these results compare with those that have been utilized in more orthodox or standard analyses?

MAJORITY VOTING AND EXTERNAL COSTS

The analysis of Chapters 10, 11, and 12 demonstrated that the organization of collective action through simple majority voting tends to cause a relative overinvestment in the public sector if the standard Paretian criteria are accepted. Note that the effects are always in this direction under the behavioral assumptions employed in our models. This is because the majority-voting rule allows the individual in the decisive coalition to secure benefits from collective action without bearing the full marginal costs properly attributable to him. In other words, the divergence between private marginal cost and social marginal cost (the familiar Pigovian variables) is always in the same direction.[1]

1. The direction of effect is, of course, just the opposite of that which results from the private organization of genuinely collective activities. It has been commonly recognized that, in such cases, the individual decision-maker will not be able to take into account the full benefits to the whole group when he makes his own private decisions. Therefore, the standard Pigovian analysis proceeds: there will tend to be relatively too little investment in such activities. The fact that collective decision-making, as it is organized by less-than-unanimity voting rules, has

Recognition that the rule will result in such relative overinvestment will make the individual, at the time of constitutional choice, anticipate some net external costs as a result of the operation of majority voting. A simple extension of the majority-voting model to apply to qualified majority voting yields similar results, the only difference being that expected external costs are reduced as the voting rule becomes more inclusive.

We have shown that majority voting will tend to cause overinvestment in the public sector relative to the private sector on the basis of the orthodox or standard criterion of Pareto optimality. This is a meaningful criterion for static analysis, but it is severely limited in certain important respects. In the first place, Pareto optimality, taken alone, cannot be used to assess the effects of purely redistributive transfers of real income among persons. Moreover, as we have demonstrated in Chapter 13, almost all collective decisions embody certain redistributive elements as well as allocational elements. Redistributive action can also impose external costs, costs which the orthodox Paretian criterion cannot take into account.

THE BENCH-MARK CRITERION

A more comprehensive criterion is provided by the bench mark or zero point used in the construction of the models of Chapter 6. With respect to any given activity, the bench mark is defined as that situation or position which would be achieved when all external costs are absent. In a sense, this represents an "ideally efficient" solution to the problem of organization. In those cases where decision-making costs can be neglected and where no restrictions are placed on the form that collective action is to take, this ideally efficient solution can be attained under the rule of unanimity and the characteristics of the solution are identical with Pareto optimality. Even this limited unanimity test fails, however, when we consider purely redistributive transfers of real income. This is because *all* members of the group could hardly be expected to agree on an amount of net redistribution considered "optimal" by the individual at the time of constitutional choice. Whereas majority decision-making would tend to involve redistributive "externalities" because redistribution would be extended relatively too far, the requirement of una-

---

not been recognized to produce precisely the opposite results seems to be due to the implicit assumption that collective decisions are made, if not explicitly by some voting rule of unanimity, *as if* unanimity prevails.

nimity would tend to involve redistributive "externalities" because redistribution would not be extended far enough.[2] The conceptual unanimity test is helpful, therefore, only in analyzing the allocational aspects of collective action; it is not helpful in analyzing the redistributive aspects. In any case, the test is directly useful only if decision-making costs are neglected.

These costs cannot, however, be neglected. Hence our bench-mark criterion becomes a purely hypothetical standard of achievement. For all purely allocational decisions, the bench mark becomes that position which could be attained by the operation of the rule of unanimity, with compensations as appropriate, *if individuals did not invest resources in strategic bargaining*. The position is identical to that defined more rigorously by Paul Samuelson and R. A. Musgrave in their development of the pure theory of public expenditure.[3] For such allocational decisions, the bench-mark position may be conceptualized on the assumption that individual-preference fields are fully known at a single point in time. However, for redistributive decisions, this sort of conceptualization is not possible. A hypothetical position characterized by the absence of all external effects may be imagined, but its more precise conceptualization requires the knowledge of individual utility functions at the stage of constitutional choice as well as at the stage of operational collective decision-making.

This difficulty in conceiving the existence of a bench-mark situation is actually helpful to us instead of providing a barrier to our understanding. This is because one of the main points to be emphasized is the fact that *an independent criterion for determining the appropriate allocation of resources between the public sector and the private sector does not exist*. Even if all external effects could be eliminated, the costs of agreement required might be so large that the *costs-minimizing* organization of the activity in question would require

2. The difficulty in treating redistributive transfers (even at the purely conceptual level) within the framework of our model lies in the fact that the "income insurance" calculus, outlined in Chapter 13, involves essentially an "exchange through time" among individuals rather than any "exchange among individuals at a point in time," which is central to the orthodox Paretian construction. The elimination of all external costs under the requirement of unanimity discussed in Chapter 7 follows directly from the consideration of collective allocational decisions only.

3. Paul A. Samuelson, "The Pure Theory of Public Expenditure," *Review of Economics and Statistics*, XXXVI (1954), 387–89, and "Diagrammatic Exposition of a Theory of Public Expenditure," *Review of Economics and Statistics*, XXXVII (1955), 350–56; R. A. Musgrave, *The Theory of Public Finance* (New York: McGraw-Hill, 1959), chap. 4.

the presence of some positive external costs. If this is the case, there must be an overextension of the activity, that is, too many resources utilized relative to that organization presented by the hypothetical ideal. However, these external costs, which measure the distortions caused by the relative overextension, may be more than offset by the reduction in decision-making costs below the level that full unanimity might entail. All of these points were made in Chapter 6; they are repeated here in order to show their relevance in answering the questions posed at the beginning of this chapter.

In one sense, therefore, we can quite properly say that all decision-making rules embodying less than full consensus will tend to cause relatively too many resources to be devoted to the public sector—too many relative to that idealized allocation of resources that the omniscient observer, knowing all utility functions over time, might be able to describe. In another sense, however, if we leave such omniscience out of account, no such conclusion can be reached. The alternative organization of activity—either a removal from the public sector or a change in the collective decision-making rules—might increase rather than decrease the necessary *interdependence costs* of the activity in question. At this more meaningful level of discussion, when we consider realizable organizational alternatives, no normative judgment can be formed concerning the extent of the public sector from a simple comparison of an existing organization with the bench-mark or ideal solution. Such meaningful judgments can be made only on the basis of a comparison with realizable and relevant alternatives. To say, for example, that majority rule tends to overextend the public sector relative to some idealized and unattainable benchmark allocation of resources is descriptively meaningful, but the statement is useless in answering the only important question that must confront the individual in framing constitutional decisions. The only meaningful overextension of the public sector must refer to realizable alternatives, and unless interdependence costs can be shown to be reduced under these alternatives, normative statements cannot be made. As Frank Knight has often remarked, "To call a situation hopeless is equivalent to calling it ideal."

The organization of an activity can be classified as "ideal," even though it will be overextended relative to some hypothetical ideal, only if the appropriate constitutional decisions have been made. If the organization is not that which effectively minimizes the interdependence costs, realizable alternatives are possible and normative judgments can be made. If, for those activities that have been shifted to the public sector, the costs-minimization decision-making rule has not been chosen, normative statements can be made about certain changes in organization. External costs imposed on individuals through the operation of the activity may be higher than they need be, and these costs can be reduced only by a change in the decision-making rules.

The "overextension" of collective activities relative to the hypothetical ideal is precisely equivalent in normative content to the existence of externalities resulting from individual behavior in activities appropriately organized in the private sector. As we pointed out in Chapter 5, the existence of such external effects provides neither a necessary nor a sufficient condition for a change in institutional organization.

THE RANGE AND EXTENT OF COLLECTIVE ACTION

When we discuss the allocation of economic resources between the public or collective sector and the private sector of the economy, it is essential to distinguish between the *range* of activities that may be collectivized and the *extent* to which collectivized activities may be pushed. This important distinction is often overlooked. We may clarify the distinction by a single example. Water-resource development and the provision of telephone services are two separate "activities," either of which may be organized privately or collectively. Let us assume that, as in the United States, the first is largely collectivized while the second is primarily organized in the private sector. In the terminology above, the *range* of collective action will include the activity of water-resource development but not that of telephone service.

What our analysis of the decision-making rules has shown is that, with less-than-unanimity rules, water-resource development, as a single activity, will tend to be "overextended" relative to the hypothetical bench mark. Relatively "too many" resources may be devoted to the development of water-resource projects, even though it may be "ideally" organized in a more meaningful sense. The main point is that our analysis of the operation of decision-making rules says nothing about the *range* of collectivization. This may or may not be "overextended" relative to the bench-mark criterion. This range of activities will depend on the constitutional decision that has been made concerning the organization of the activities in question.

Such constitutional decisions may or may not be appropriately made. If these decisions are made correctly, the range of collective action will be the "ideal" one, and within this range the separate activities will be organized by the costs-minimizing decision-making rules. External effects will normally be present, which is the same as saying that these activities will be "over-

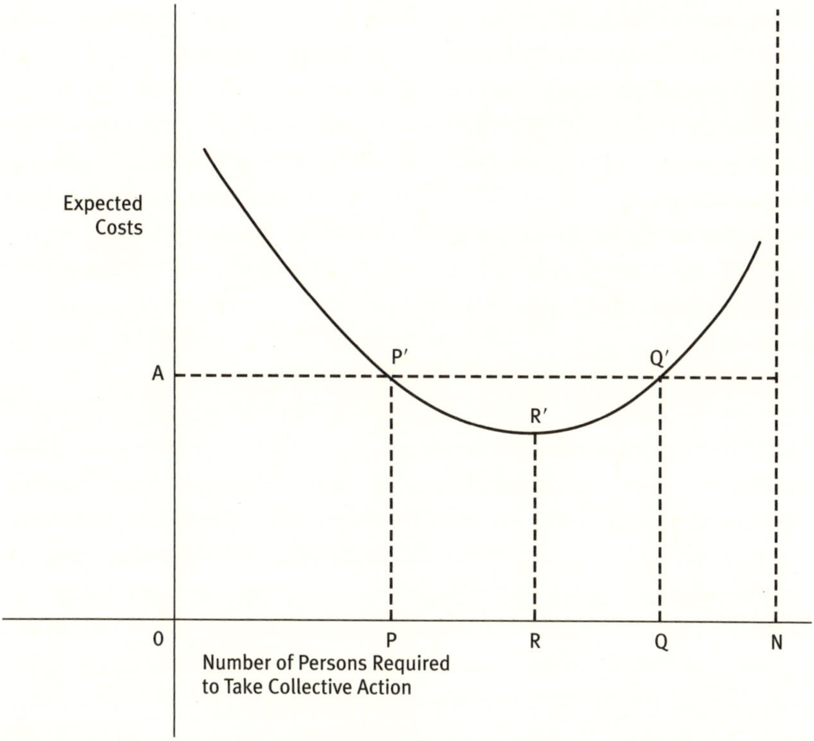

FIGURE 17

extended" relative to some hypothetical ideal, but this sort of inefficiency will be necessary to achieve an organization which will minimize over-all interdependence costs. However, if constitutional decisions are not appropriately made, either the range or the extent of collective action, or both, may be modified in the direction of improved social organization. The set of activities organized through the public sector may be either unduly restricted or unduly expanded, while the extension of the separate activities collectivized may fall short of or exceed that which would be present under more efficient costs-minimizing decision-making rules.

Several of these points may be illustrated clearly with reference to Figure 17, which is similar to Figure 6 employed earlier. The figure depicts expected costs for a single activity—external costs plus decision-making costs. For this activity collective organization is indicated. If 0A represents the expected external costs from private organization, then any collective decision-making rule between P/N and Q/N will allow collective organization to reduce interdependence costs. The appropriate constitutional decision would be to collectivize the activity and to specify that all decisions relating to it shall be taken under the rule R/N. This "ideal" organization will still involve interdependence costs of RR′, a portion of which must consist of expected external costs resulting from an overextension of activity relative to the benchmark position.

Assume now that the constitutional decision dictates collective organization of the activity under a decision rule Q/N. External costs are clearly expected to be lower (since the external-costs function slopes downward throughout its range), but decision-making costs are expected to be much higher than under the rule R/N. Under the Q/N rule, relatively fewer resources will be devoted directly to employment in the activity, say road repairs, and, measured in this dimension only, the allocation of resources would more closely approximate some "optimal" allocation. However, under Q/N, far "too many" resources will be devoted to investment in strategic bargaining. A shift from the rule Q/N to the rule R/N will cause relatively more resources to be employed directly in the carrying out of the function involved (more roads repaired to excess) and, if decision-making costs are neglected, this will represent a shift away from the "optimality" surface. However, the incremental external costs involved in this shift will be more than offset by the reduction in decision-making costs that is expected to take place.

COLLECTIVE ACTION AND RULES FOR DECISION

One of the most important conclusions stemming from our whole analysis is that the decision as to whether or not any specific activity should or should not be organized in the public sector will depend on the decision-making rules that are to be chosen. It is almost completely meaningless to discuss seriously the appropriateness or the inappropriateness of shifting any particular activity from private to public organization without specifying carefully the rules for decision that are to be adopted if the shift is made. If the rules for decision in the collective sector are assumed to be exogenously determined by constitutional provisions and by convention, the choices concerning the organization of activities will be directly dependent on these independent variables, and the whole constitutional-choice process will be severely constrained. As suggested in Chapter 6, it may be quite sensible to shift certain activities to the public sector provided certain rules for decision are adopted, and quite irrational to shift the same activities to the public sector under the expectation of still other rules. Figure 17 is again illustrative. If any decision-making rule less inclusive than P/N should be assumed to be fixed independent of the organizational decision, the individual should rationally reject all attempts to place the activity depicted in Figure 17 in the public sector. Only if the rules for decision fall within the range P/N to Q/N will collectivization of the activity be desirable.

INSTITUTIONAL VARIABLES AS ANALOGUES FOR DECISION RULES

As we have previously suggested, it will be possible in many cases to organize the operation of an activity in such a manner that analogues to decision rules may be built into the activity itself. For example, if the activity depicted in Figure 17 is expected to impose some external costs on the individual because of the differential or discriminatory nature of the benefits provided, a differential pricing or taxing scheme may be constitutionally adopted. This institutional change would, of course, modify completely the nature of the activity as conceived by the individual at the stage of constitutional choice, and, other things being equal, this would make the individual much more willing to accept both the collectivization of the activity and the operation of the activity under less-than-unanimity rules for decision-making. For our purposes, it seems best to treat activities organized through different institutional arrangements as different activities. For example, a postal system organized wholly on the basis of user pricing becomes a different activity from a postal system designed to be financed from general taxation. To the individual considering these at the stage of constitutional choice, the shape of the expected-costs functions would be so different in the two cases that it seems best to consider them as wholly distinct activities.[4]

SIDE PAYMENTS AND THE SIZE OF THE PUBLIC SECTOR

We have previously said that any form of vote-trading, extending from simple logrolling to full monetary side payments (open buying and selling of votes), tends to allow individual intensities of preference on political issues to

4. For an example of a brief but interesting discussion of some of the activities (currently undertaken by the federal government) that might be reorganized through the introduction of user pricing, see "Picking Up the Check," *The New Republic* (9 January 1961).

be more fully expressed. Any of these institutional modifications in the operation of voting rules will tend, therefore, to lower somewhat the external costs that the activity is expected to impose on the individual. If the individual knows in advance that he can, on an issue about which he feels very strongly, take some action to secure the support of less interested voters, he will expect the external costs of the activity to be less severe. In terms of our diagrammatic construction, the introduction of vote-trading in any form serves to shift downward the combined costs function shown in Figure 17.

Since the introduction of vote-trading under consideration applies only to *political* votes or political support, the expected external costs from private organization should not be modified by such an institutional difference. From this it follows that the constitutional decision as to the organization of the activity will depend also on the extent to which vote-trading is permitted and the extent to which such trading is expected to approximate perfect side payments in final results. The direction of this effect is clear. The more perfect the vote-trading "market," the wider the range of collective activities that will tend to be selected at the stage of constitutional choice. The less perfect the "market," the more restrictive must be the range and scope of collective action. The society that is characterized by strong and effective ethical and moral restraints, which prevent vote-trading, will find it more essential to place constitutional curbs on the political decisions of the majority than will the society in which these restraints are less effective.[5]

THE CHOICE OF RULES

The discussion continued in this and the preceding chapters emphasizes clearly the ambiguity that is necessarily introduced when reference is made to the "ideal" allocation of resources or, in our particular case, to the size of the public sector as being "too large" or "too small." We have demonstrated that the criteria against which the size of the public sector is usually measured are not fully appropriate. In many instances "optimal" positions represent hypo-

5. This analytical conclusion is supported by historical experience. The comparison between the government of Robespierre and the one that followed in 9 Thermidor is instructive. Of the latter it has been noted: "These men had howled with the wolves while the Reign of Terror lasted, but since their sole aim was to acquire money and to keep their skins, they were the kind of men with whom respectable people can do business." (J. Christopher Herold, *Mistress to an Age: The Life of Madame de Staël* [London: Hamish Hamilton, 1959], p. 151.)

thetical ideals impossible of attainment. Normative judgments can be made only after a comparison of realizable alternatives.

An important, and closely related, point is also illustrated here. The individual, in his role as constitution-maker, does not choose directly the size and the scope of the public sector, "the allocation of resources." Individuals choose, first of all, the fundamental organization of activity. Secondly, they choose the decision-making rules. In a somewhat broader context both of these choices can be conceived in terms of rules, and rational decisions must always be based on some comparison of the working out of alternative rules of organization over a sequence of issues. This emphasis on the fact that policy-makers always choose among organizational rules and not among "allocations" is often forcefully made by Professor Rutledge Vining. Our discussion of the constitutional calculus makes Vining's criticism of the orthodox or standard discussion of policy norms quite meaningful. To make normative statements concerning whether or not governments undertake "too much" or "too little" activity seems to be rather wasted effort unless one is prepared to suggest some possible modifications in the organizational rules through which decisions are made, aside, of course, from the purely propagandist and nonscientific effects of such pronouncements.

CHAPTER 15

QUALIFIED MAJORITY VOTING RULES, REPRESENTATION, AND THE INTERDEPENDENCE OF CONSTITUTIONAL VARIABLES

The analysis of the simple majority voting rule can be extended without difficulty to cover more or less inclusive rules for reaching collective decisions. The results from this sort of extension will be apparent to those who have understood and accepted the analytical models of the preceding chapters. If less than a simple majority should be required for carrying a decision, the expected external costs would be greater, but the costs of reaching the necessary agreement among members of the effective coalition would be lower than under the operation of simple majority rules. If more than a simple majority should be required for decision, the expected external costs would be reduced, but the decision-making costs would be increased.

Given the behavioral assumptions of our models, individuals will tend to make collective decisions by organizing themselves in the smallest coalitions defined as effective by the decision-making rules, and, for members of dominant coalitions, the gains will tend to be shared symmetrically. Larger coalitions than those necessary for decision will not tend to emerge for two reasons. First, a larger-than-necessary individual investment in strategic bargaining will be required. Secondly, a smaller individual share of the gains from collective action will result in the larger-than-necessary coalition. If we relax our behavioral assumptions or if we introduce specific uncertainties about individual bargains into the analysis, these results will be modified. However, it seems useful to remain for the time being within the strictest limits of the original analysis.

As we prohibit full side payments on single issues and introduce logrolling as an imperfect system of vote-trading, the analysis of simple majority voting can also be applied to other voting rules. Coalitions will be formed embodying reciprocal support over a sequence of issues, and these coalitions will also tend to be of the minimum effective size.

Only one interesting analytical point seems worth raising. Intuitively, it seems plausible to expect that the more inclusive voting rules will tend to produce "solutions" that are somewhat more stable than less inclusive rules. For example, a rule which requires a three-fourths majority may appear to produce more stable solutions than one which requires one-fourth. Such an inference may not, however, be correct. While larger investment in bargaining will be required the larger the coalition that is needed for decision, the reward to the individual member will also be less the larger the coalition. The "price" at which individuals can be induced to abandon the coalition will tend to be lower in the larger coalition than in smaller ones. There are thus two opposing effects on the stability of the solutions produced by the operation of voting rules, and any general conclusions relating the stability properties to the rules themselves would probably be premature.[1]

We do not propose to discuss further the extension of our analysis to *simple* voting rules, that is, to rules representing merely changes in the fraction of the total population required to reach collective decisions. The remainder of this chapter and the following chapters will be devoted to a discussion of two somewhat more complex modifications of our models. In this chapter we shall discuss the applicability of our analysis in moving beyond direct democracy to representative government. As we introduce representation, we shall find it necessary to consider *four* basic constitutional variables and their interrelationships. In Chapter 16 we shall consider the effects of introducing dual representation in two-house legislatures while retaining simple majority voting rules in each house. From these two still elementary models it should be clear that the basic analysis can be extended to a rather bewildering and complex set of possible institutional structures, many of which are to be found in real-world political systems. We do not, however, propose to make such extensions in this book.

REPRESENTATIVE GOVERNMENT

Direct democracy, under almost any decision-making rule, becomes too costly in other than very small political units when more than a few isolated

1. Note that this relationship between voting rules and the stability of solutions is not identical to the relationship between the size of the total group and the stability of solutions. As suggested earlier, game theorists argue that the stability properties of solutions to *n*-person games become less pronounced as the total group is enlarged in size. Within any group of given size, however, the change from less inclusive to more inclusive voting rules would not seem, a priori, to exert any clearly predictable effect on the stability of solutions obtained.

issues must be considered. The costs of decision-making become too large relative to the possible reductions in expected external costs that collective action might produce. If direct democracy were required, the individual, in his presumed role as constitutional choice-maker, would leave many traditional activities of the State to be organized in the private sector, and, for those few activities that he chose to collectivize, he would tend to adopt the less inclusive decision-making rules. In terms of our models, one means of reducing the *interdependence costs* generally is through the introduction of representative government. This step serves to shift downward the decision-costs function that we have previously employed several times in analyzing constitutional decisions.

If we utilize the models developed in Part II, it becomes relatively easy to construct a conceptual normative theory for the "optimal" degree of representation. At the one extreme, we have direct democracy in which the number of individuals directly participating in collective choice (the number of "representatives") and the number of individuals in the total voting population stand in a one-to-one correspondence. At the other extreme, we have a single individual who "represents" or chooses for the whole group. In either of these two extreme cases, the constitutional-choice problem is greatly simplified. In the case of direct democracy, the single choice to be made, once a basic organizational decision is assumed, concerns the rules under which collective action shall be taken. Under the other extreme dictatorship model, the rules for collective action are set; the only choice facing the conceptual constitution-maker concerns the rules for choosing the dictator. In any of the models falling between these two extremes, both of these choices must be faced. Rules for choosing representatives must be determined, and rules for deciding issues in legislative assemblies must also be laid down. In addition, there is a third choice that must be faced, a choice that is assumed to be resolved in the two extreme models. The degree of representation must be chosen: that is to say, the proportion of the total population to be elected to the representative assembly must be selected. Finally, to all of these choices a fourth must be added: namely, the selection of the basis for representation. We shall refer to these as the four essential constitutional variables.

Consideration of the complexities introduced by these several constitutional-choice problems reveals the abstract and highly simplified nature of our direct democracy models, in which we were able to eliminate all of the choices except the one relating directly to decision-making rules. In a more general context it is evident that the four constitutional problems are interrelated, and, ideally, the individual should reach a decision on all four variables simultaneously. The basis of representation and the degree of representation indicated to be most "efficient" will depend surely on the rules through which representatives are to be selected and the rules which are to be required to carry decision in the legislative assembly. The separate variables can only be discussed individually in partial terms: that is, we may assume three of the variables to be fixed while discussing the fourth. Essentially this is what we have done in our earlier chapters. If we assume that the rules for selecting representatives are given, and that the degree of representation and the basis of representation are predetermined, our models may be applied directly to the setting of the rules for decision in legislative assemblies. On the other hand, if we assume these latter rules to be given, along with the degree and the basis of representation, we may apply our analysis to the selection of rules for selecting representatives without major analytical changes being required. The problems of determining the degree and the basis of representation are similar, but they seem sufficiently different to warrant some detailed consideration.

THE DEGREE OF REPRESENTATION

We now want to consider only the choice concerning the degree of representation. Let us assume that representatives are to be chosen by simple majority voting rules, that the basis of representation is geographical, and that the unicameral legislature is to reach all decisions by majority voting. All of the constitutional variables are thus fixed except that which defines the proportion of the population that will sit as "representative" for the whole population in the assembly.[2]

2. The following reference to Washington's position on this issue is revealing: "On the final day, after the constitution had been engrossed, and the printers had begun printing 500 copies, a motion was made to reduce the congressional constituencies from 40,000 to 30,000. 'When the President rose,' as Madison's notes record, 'for the purpose of putting the question,' he said that 'although his situation'—as president—'had hitherto restrained him from offering his sentiments on questions pending in the House, and it might be thought, ought now to impose silence on him, yet he could not forbear expressing his wish that the alteration proposed might take place. It was much to be desired that the objections to the plan recommended might be as few as possible.—The smallness of the proportion of representatives had been considered by many members of the Convention, an insufficient security for the rights and interests of the people. He acknowledged that it had always appeared to himself among the ex-

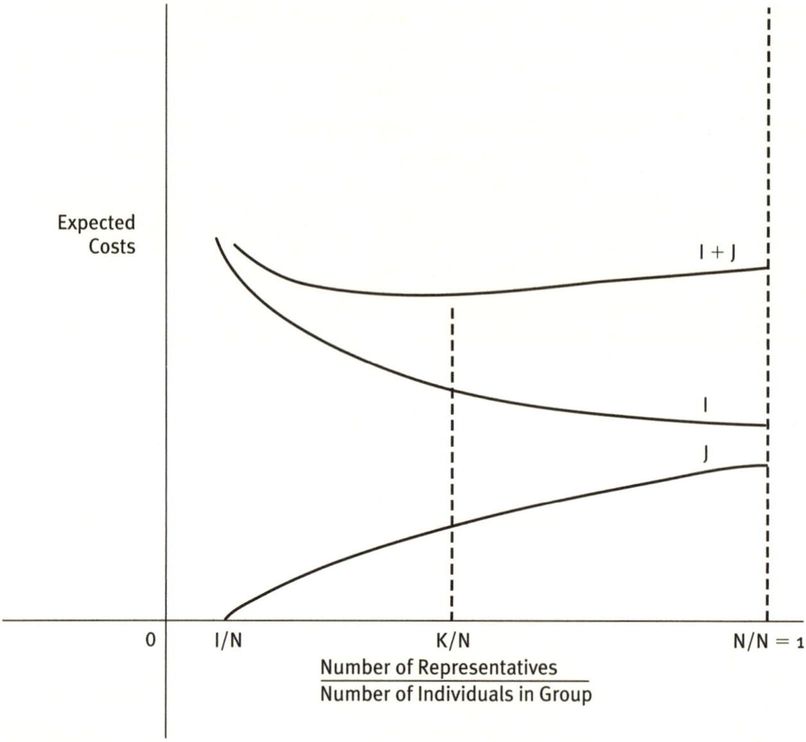

FIGURE 18

Within the restrictions of this model, we can derive costs functions that are quite similar, but not identical, to those which we have previously employed. Figure 18 illustrates. On the ordinate we measure expected costs, as before, but on the abscissa the quantity measured is different from that of earlier models. Here we measure the proportion of the group to be selected as members of the representative assembly. As before, we may now derive an external-costs function and a decision-making-costs function. They will have the same general shape as before. Let I represent the expected external-costs function. This will tend to slope downward because surely the individual will recognize that his own interests will be represented more adequately and more faithfully the more closely the representation approaches the full mem-

ceptionable parts of the plan; and late as the present moment was for admitting amendments, he thought this of so much consequence that it would give him much satisfaction to see it adopted.'" (Carl Van Doren, *The Great Rehearsal* [New York: Viking Press, 1948], p. 170.)

bership of the group. Note that, even at N/N, external costs are expected to be positive. This is because we have assumed a single rule, majority voting, in the legislative assembly. The positive value of the function at N/N, therefore, suggests that even with direct democracy the individual will expect to be in the losing coalition on some occasions.

Let J represent the decision-making-costs function. This will rise as the legislative assembly becomes larger because, given any rule, the costs of securing agreement increase. For example, let us suppose that the total group is made up of 100 persons. If one representative in 20 is selected, we should have a legislature composed of 5 persons, and, under simple majority rule, the agreement of 3 persons would be required for decision. On the other hand, if one representative in 10 is selected, we should have a legislature of 10 members, and a majority of 6 persons would be needed for decision. Clearly, the costs of securing agreement among 6 persons are greater than those of securing similar agreement among 3. As before, we may now add these two costs functions vertically, securing the curve I + J in Figure 18. The "optimal" degree of representation is shown where K/N of the total group are chosen to sit in the legislative assembly.

This analysis is simple and straightforward, but unfortunately it is also rather useless as it stands. Nevertheless, some interesting implications do emerge. First of all, the functional relationships described above are clearly affected by the size of the total group. As N becomes larger, the decision-costs function in Figure 18 will tend to shift upward. By comparison, the external-costs function, I, seems likely to be more directly influenced by the *proportion* of the population sitting in the assembly than by the *size* of the total population. If this is true, this function will be less affected by shifts in the over-all size of the group than the decision-costs function. The implication seems to be that the costs-minimizing solution is reached at a lower fraction of the total group in larger groups than in smaller groups. This implication seems intuitively obvious, but it does provide us with a quasi-empirical check on the conceptual validity of our general analytical models. It also helps to rationalize the common practice of democratic governments to lower the fraction of the population in the representative assembly as the population grows. They tend to do this by maintaining approximately fixed-sized representative assemblies.

A second, and less obvious, implication follows directly from the first. Since decision-making costs increase as the group grows larger, and since there seems to be no reason to expect that external costs will decrease, the total costs expected to arise from collective organization of activity, under any given rules for legislative decision-making, will tend to be higher in large groups than in small groups. This suggests that the basic organizational decisions will be affected by the size of the group; *ceteris paribus*, the larger the size of the group, the smaller should be the set of activities undertaken collectively.

THE BASIS OF REPRESENTATION

The constitutional variable that we have called "the basis of representation" is difficult to analyze in precise quantitative terms. Meaningful analysis does seem possible, however. First of all, let us "freeze" the other three constitutional variables. We shall assume that a simple majority of constituents is required to elect a representative who can normally be expected to act in a manner that will please a majority of his constituents. We shall also assume that the number of representatives in the legislature is fixed, and that a simple majority rule is to be adopted for decision-making in the legislature. The only variable left free for determination is the one that defines the basis upon which the representatives are to be selected from among the whole population.

We may proceed by examining the extreme cases. Conceptually we can think of a basis for representation that embodies a deliberate attempt at randomizing individual variations of political interest. For example, suppose that individuals should be classified into constituent groups solely on the basis of beginning letters of their surnames. Each group, appropriately adjusted in size with other groups, would be authorized to elect a single representative to the legislative assembly. Under this or any other roughly similar basis for representation, we should expect little or no convergence of special-interest groups behind particular representatives on any continuing or permanent pattern. Relatively, the most important stage for coalition formation in these circumstances would be at the level of electing the representative. The individual would anticipate significant external costs at this level of the political process; his own "representative" would effectively support his interest (would "represent" him) only if the individual voter should belong to the winning or majority coalition. Different coalitions would, of course, emerge in different constituencies, and some external costs would be expected to be produced by the actions of the legislative assembly. However, under the circumstances postulated, the individual citizen should be, relatively, more interested in the rules under which representatives are to be selected and in the degree of representation than in the rules for final legislative decision.

In this model (which we will call the "randomized-basis" model) vote-trading would take place at all levels, but it would be most pronounced at the level of electing representatives and would take the form of *implicit* log-rolling. The individual who sought to be elected to the representative assembly would find it necessary to offer a "package" program sufficiently attractive to encourage the support of a majority of his constituents. Since, by hypothesis, the separate interests of his constituents correspond in range to those of the whole social group, he will include in the "package" many special programs designed to appeal to the strongly expressed interests of minority groups.

In the simplest "randomized-basis" model, there would be no assurance that similar "packages" would even be presented to each group of constituents, and very slight probability that the elected representatives to the assembly could be grouped readily into identifiable positions. Each representative might reflect a wholly different configuration of interests.

Certain statements can be made concerning the over-all characteristics of such a system of representation. By and large, it would seem that the expected external costs of collective action should be lower than under alternative bases of representation. The randomized basis would probably offer somewhat greater protection against the deliberate exploitation of specific minority interests, assuming fixed values for the other three constitutional variables. On the other hand, the costs of reaching collective decisions would probably be quite high in this model. Bargains of complex nature would have to be arranged at the level of selection of representatives, and exceedingly complex bargains might be required for the functioning of the legislative process.

Let us now consider a model at the opposite extreme. Assume that a purely functional basis for representation is selected. That is, assume that each definable interest group in the population is allowed to select a representative or representatives as members of the legislative assembly. The contrast with the first model is sharp and clear. If individual interests are homogeneous over reasonably large groups of individuals by identifiable functional characteristics, there will be relatively little difference in the various rules for electing representatives. The individual, in making constitutional choices, will only be interested in seeing that a member of his group (union, trade association, or professional society) sits in the assembly and that the membership of the latter is distributed over the different groups so that "adequate" representation is provided his own group. The expected external costs in this model will be concentrated on the prospects of adverse legislative decisions, not on the prospects of electing representatives who will not effectively act on behalf of individual voters. From this it follows that the rules for legislative decision will be the important constitutional variable under this basis for representation.

It seems obvious that decision-making costs will be considerably lower in this than in the randomized-basis model. On the other hand, expected external costs will surely be higher, assuming, of course, that the rules for selection and for decision are fixed. If we should want to diagram the selection of a basis for representation in terms of two costs functions similar to those employed several times before, we could, conceptually, think of starting at the left with the functional representation basis and proceeding to the right as we approach the purely randomized basis. If this were done, the curves so drawn would slope in the same directions as in the earlier problems, and, conceptually, an "optimal" basis of representation could be chosen—"optimal" being defined here in terms of the "ideal" mix of random and functional elements in the basis.

Geographic representation, the standard basis for at least one house in the legislatures of most Western democratic countries, falls somewhere between the two extreme models discussed above—between purely randomized representation and purely functional representation. If, in fact, individuals and groups were distributed randomly over space with reference to their political interests, geographical representation would approximate the first model. On the other hand, if separate political interests should prove to be primarily geographical, the second model would be more closely approached. We know, of course, that elements of both random and functional representation are present in the geographical basis. Within single constituencies there is normally to be found a reasonably wide range of voter interests, but there also remain many political issues which involve differential geographical impact. On such issues the geographical basis becomes similar to the purely functional in effect. Geographical representation is similar to majority voting in that, a priori, there is nothing that can be said for it as regards superiority over other possible bases.

THE STRUCTURE OF CONTROL IN REPRESENTATIVE DEMOCRACY

The costs implicit in the substitution of representative democracy for direct democracy are of the category that we have denominated "external costs." Bargaining costs are reduced by the use of the representatives. The costs which

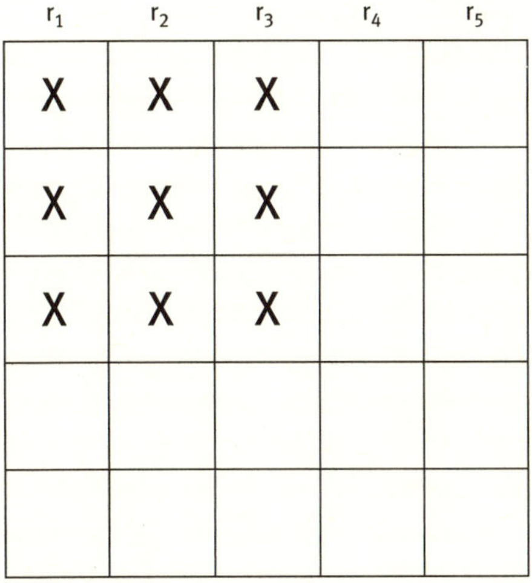

FIGURE 19[4]

would arise from attempting to govern the whole United States through direct majority voting are so extreme that the representative system is acceptable even though it does markedly increase the external costs. In order to examine the external costs created by the representation device, let us construct a simple model. Consider a society composed of 25 voters who organize themselves into 5 constituencies of 5 each for the purpose of appointing representatives to conduct their mutual affairs (Figure 19).[3]

As a first approximation, let us suppose that the representatives, $r_1 \ldots r_5$, simply vote as the majority of their constituents want them to. Under these circumstances a measure favored by nine voters, arranged like those marked X in the diagram, will be adopted. In the real world, as the number of voters and constituencies increases, the minimum-sized coalition required for dominance under simple majority voting approaches ¼ of all voters as a limit. For example, if there should be 39,601 voters arranged in 199 constituencies of 199 voters each, only 10,000 voters would have to favor an issue to secure passage (only 100 more than ¼ of all the voters). Thus, a logrolling bargain

3. Actually, with such a small group, the costs of bargaining would be quite modest and direct democracy would be more efficient. Larger and more realistic models, however, are harder both on the draftsman and the reader.

4. The voters do not, of course, necessarily form the square submatrix shown. Any combination of nine voters distributed three each in three constituencies is sufficient to constitute a dominant coalition.

to obtain benefits from the political process need only involve about 1/4 of the voters under a representative system. Therefore, representative institutions of this type are almost equivalent to permitting any group of 1/4 of the voters in direct democracy to form a logrolling coalition empowered to determine what roads will be repaired, which harbors dredged, and which special interest groups will receive government aid. At this stage in the book it should not be necessary to point out how great the external cost imposed by such a procedure would be.

These external costs imposed by representative voting would be moderated by two factors. In the first place, not just any group of 1/4 of the voters could win. It would be necessary for the group to be approximately equally distributed among a bare majority of the constituencies and absent in the remainder of the constituencies. This fact (which has already been discussed) would presumably put some, although not very onerous, restrictions on the bargains which could be struck. The type of project which is traditionally associated with the pork barrel—a small item benefiting a small group of voters, most of whom are within one constituency—would be little handicapped by this factor. Bargains intended to benefit groups spread through several constituencies, however, will be harder to negotiate, and groups spread through more than a majority of the constituencies will find profitable bargains extremely hard to arrange.

The second limiting factor lies in the organization of the bargaining process. Instead of each voter entering into bargains with other voters, the bargains are negotiated entirely by the representatives. This undoubtedly reduces the total-bargaining cost as compared with attempting to make bargains directly among millions of voters, but it also introduces sizable imperfections in the "market," and these may affect (either positively or negatively) the external costs. In offering themselves for election, representatives offer to the voters in their constituencies a "platform" embodying that which they propose to accomplish. The individual voter then judges which of the competing candidates' platforms is most to his liking, discounting this judgment by his estimate of the likelihood of the various candidates' succeeding in making their promised bargains in the representative body, and casts his vote accordingly. The result is not precisely equivalent to that which would be expected under direct bargaining, but we do not propose to consider the differences in this work.

In general, legislative bodies are designed with two chambers (a subject discussed in the following chapter), but there are some countries which have either a one-chamber legislature or a two-chamber legislature with one chamber having greatly restricted powers. We might expect governments depending on this device to be highly inefficient, but an examination indicates that they frequently have mechanisms which, in essence, change the nature of the system enough to avoid the consequences that we have been discussing. Most of the small North European democracies, for example, follow a voting system under which the voter opts for a party and then the parties are given votes in the legislature in proportion to their respective totals. Although this system has its disadvantages,[5] it does have the advantage of providing what amounts to a unanimity system in selecting members of the representative body. All voters, not just the majority of each constituency, are represented in the legislature. Consequently, a majority of the legislature represents a majority of the voters, not just ¼+ as may be the case in a logrolling or party coalition when the members are elected from single-member constituencies.

INTERDEPENDENCE AMONG CONSTITUTIONAL VARIABLES

We have emphasized that the four basic constitutional variables introduced by representative government are interdependent. The "optimal" or "equilibrium" value for any one variable will depend on the values for the remaining variables, and, conceptually, the fully rational constitutional choice will embody the results of a simultaneous determination of all four variables, along with the more fundamental organizational decision concerning whether or not an activity or a set of activities is to be collectivized at all. We know, of course, that the variables may not be set simultaneously at their "optimal" values. Even at the highly abstract level of analysis characterizing our discussion, it will be useful to examine more carefully the interdependence among these variables. This examination will be helpful in demonstrating that our basic model may be applied to a wide range of constitutional-choice problems. We should be able to indicate some of the directions of change in the "equilibrium" values for remaining variables that would result from exogenous or externally imposed changes in single variables. In terms of a specific illustration, we should try to predict the direction of change in, say, the legislative-assembly rules for decision that would be suggested as a result of

5. See Anthony Downs, *An Economic Theory of Democracy* (New York: Harper and Bros., 1957), pp. 142–64.

an externally imposed shift from a randomized basis to a functional basis of representation in the assembly. Or, to introduce a second illustration, we may be able to suggest the "desirable" change in the degree of representation indicated as a result of changing the rules for electing representatives.

In order to discuss these interrelationships carefully, we shall find it useful to define the separate constitutional variables:

X_1: defined as the variable that describes the rules for electing members to the legislative assembly. It will assume fractional values ranging from 1/N to N/N or 1 as the election rule becomes more inclusive. An increase in X_1 shall be interpreted as a shift from a less inclusive to a more inclusive rule for electing a representative, say, from a simple majority to a two-thirds majority.

X_2: defined as the variable that describes the basis of representation of members of the assembly. As suggested, this variable is somewhat more difficult to conceive in quantitative terms than the others, but we may think of various "mixes" of functional and random elements. An increase in X_2 shall be interpreted as a change in the weights of the two elements, with functional aspects becoming less pronounced and randomized aspects becoming more pronounced. By way of illustration, an increase in X_2 would result from an increase in the number of delegates-at-large in a state assembly.

X_3: defined as the variable that describes the degree of representation. It will assume fractional values ranging from 1/N to N/N or 1 as the degree of representation ranges from dictatorship to direct democracy. An increase in X_3 shall be interpreted as an increase in the numerical value of the fraction, that is, as a move in the direction of direct democracy.

X_4: defined as the variable that describes the rule through which the legislative assembly shall reach its decisions. It will assume fractional values ranging from 1/N to N/N or 1 as the rule becomes more inclusive. An increase in X_4 shall be interpreted as a shift from a less inclusive to a more inclusive rule for decision, that is, as a shift toward the rule of unanimity.

Our whole analysis here is normative in the sense that we are considering the calculus of the individual as he faces constitutional choices. The four variables are interdependent in this rational calculus. There is no necessary interdependence in any other institutional sense. This individual, as he considers these variables, will be able to construct four independent relationships which will, in turn, enable him to solve the system for four unknowns. We may summarize this set of relationships by (9) given below.

$$F(X_1, X_2, X_3, X_4) \tag{9}$$

We may assume that the individual whose calculus we consider is initially in full "constitutional equilibrium." This means simply that we assume that he has selected values for the four variables that seem most suitable from his own point of view. In mathematical terms, he has minimized total interdependence costs as a function of the four variables.

$$\mathit{min}\ y = F(X_1, X_2, X_3, X_4) \tag{10}$$

This function is, of course, minimized when the set of simultaneous equations represented by (11) is solved.

$$\begin{aligned} \frac{\partial y}{\partial X_1} &= 0 \\ \frac{\partial y}{\partial X_2} &= 0 \\ \frac{\partial y}{\partial X_3} &= 0 \\ \frac{\partial y}{\partial X_4} &= 0 \end{aligned} \tag{11}$$

We want now to examine the effects on these "equilibrium" values that will be exerted by imposing exogenous changes on the variables, one at a time. That is to say, let us suppose that an exogenous change forces X_1 to take on some value other than its "equilibrium" value. Let us label this exogenously determined, nonequilibrium value for X_1 as $\overline{X}_1$. We ask the question: Granted this change in the value for X_1, what values should the other variables, X_2, X_3, X_4, take in order to minimize total interdependence costs in the new situation, that is, in that situation where $\overline{X}_1$ cannot be modified? The problem is the same as before. We seek to minimize total interdependence costs; but, since one of our four constitutional variables is fixed exogenously, we must solve a system of simultaneous equations in only three variables.

$$\mathit{min}\ z = F(\overline{X}_1, X_2, X_3, X_4) \tag{12}$$

This is accomplished when the following set of equations is solved.

$$\frac{\partial z}{\partial X_2} = 0$$
$$\frac{\partial z}{\partial X_3} = 0 \tag{13}$$
$$\frac{\partial z}{\partial X_4} = 0$$

What we want to determine now is the difference in the solution values for X_2, X_3, and X_4 in equations (11) and in equations (13). Since these differences are generated by the initial exogenously imposed change on X_1, we may represent them in the following form.

$$\frac{\delta X_2}{\delta \overline{\overline{X}}_1}, \frac{\delta X_3}{\delta \overline{\overline{X}}_1}, \frac{\delta X_4}{\delta \overline{\overline{X}}_1} \tag{14}$$

These symbols represent the changes in the "equilibrium" values for X_2, X_3, and X_4 that are generated when X_1 is exogenously changed from its initial "equilibrium" value, X_1, to its new value, $\overline{X}_1$.

To bring this discussion back to our basic constitutional problem, suppose that a satisfactory constitution exists but that the migration of persons over space shifts the established geographical basis of representation from one that was close to the randomized-basis model to one that is significantly more functional in nature. What should the rational individual, if he were confronted with the opportunity to choose, do as regards the possible changes in the rules for selecting representatives, the possible changes in the size of the representative assembly, and the possible changes in the rules for decision in the assembly?

The whole set of effects that we want to examine may be summarized in the form of the following matrix, (15) below, using the symbols as developed in (14).

$$\begin{matrix} \frac{\delta X_2}{\delta \overline{\overline{X}}_1}, \frac{\delta X_3}{\delta \overline{\overline{X}}_1}, \frac{\delta X_4}{\delta \overline{\overline{X}}_1} \\ \frac{\delta X_1}{\delta \overline{\overline{X}}_2}, \frac{\delta X_3}{\delta \overline{\overline{X}}_2}, \frac{\delta X_4}{\delta \overline{\overline{X}}_2} \\ \frac{\delta X_1}{\delta \overline{\overline{X}}_3}, \frac{\delta X_2}{\delta \overline{\overline{X}}_3}, \frac{\delta X_4}{\delta \overline{\overline{X}}_3} \\ \frac{\delta X_1}{\delta \overline{\overline{X}}_4}, \frac{\delta X_2}{\delta \overline{\overline{X}}_4}, \frac{\delta X_3}{\delta \overline{\overline{X}}_4} \end{matrix} \tag{15}$$

Each element in this matrix represents the effects on one variable that will result from changing the value of one other variable, assuming that the individual whose calculus we are considering reacts to the exogenous change by seeking to minimize total interdependence costs. For example, let us look at the last entry in the first row, $\frac{\delta X_4}{\delta \overline{X}_1}$. This represents the change in the equilibrium or optimal value for X_4 that would result from the exogenous change represented by shifting X_1 to some arbitrarily determined value, $\overline{X}_1$. In terms of the specific meaning attached to these symbols, $\frac{\delta X_4}{\delta \overline{X}_1}$ indicates the change in the rules for decision in the legislative assembly that the individual might consider desirable as a result of an exogenously imposed change in the rules for electing representatives.

It is clear that we cannot expect to do more with this analysis than to indicate the directions of change: that is, we cannot do more than to insert the signs for the symbols in matrix (15). However, this in itself can possibly provide us with a significant amount of information.

Let us now concentrate on the first row. The elements, $\frac{\delta X_2}{\delta \overline{X}_1}, \frac{\delta X_3}{\delta \overline{X}_1}, \frac{\delta X_4}{\delta \overline{X}_1}$, represent the changes that would be generated in X_2, X_3, and X_4, respectively, by externally imposed changes in X_1, defined as the rule for electing representatives to the legislative assembly. As this rule is made more inclusive (for example, as X_1 increases in value from $\frac{N/2 + 1}{2}$ to $2N/3$), the decision-making costs at this level of collective action will increase.

We may note first of all that any exogenously imposed change from the initially assumed "equilibrium" set of values for the constitutional variables must result in an increase in over-all interdependence costs. This follows from the fact that the initial situation is, by definition, "optimal" for the individual in question. In responding to the exogenously imposed change in the single variable under consideration, the individual will, however, attempt again to minimize interdependence costs, within the limits of the new set of constraints. As we have suggested above, the increase in X_1, defined as the inclusiveness of the rule for electing representatives to the legislative assembly, will increase decision-making costs. The change will also reduce external costs,[6] but not to the extent that decision-making costs are increased. If no change

6. The more inclusive rule for selecting representatives will guarantee to the individual that his own interest will be more likely to be "represented" in the assembly. This being true, his own interest stands a greater chance of being represented in any decisive coalition in the assembly. The danger of adverse collective actions is clearly reduced.

in the other constitutional variables is allowed to occur, the individual will find himself devoting more resources to the making of collective decisions than he would choose if given the opportunity. While he will be somewhat more protected than before the change from the dangers of adverse collective action, he will want to consider how he might modify those constitutional variables remaining within his control. Specifically, what changes will the individual desire to make in X_2, X_3, and X_4 in response to the change imposed on X_1?

Note that we have specifically defined each of the constitutional variables in such a manner that an increase involves an addition to decision-making costs and a reduction in external costs. We are now inquiring about the changes in X_2, X_3, and X_4 that will result from an *increase* in X_1. The direction of change in the three variables will depend on the type of relationship that exists among the separate variables. It seems reasonable to suppose that these variables are mutually compensating in the individual's calculus: that is to say, he will try to shift to a new position of equilibrium by changing those variables remaining within his power of choice in such a manner as to compensate or to offset the initial change imposed on X_1. More specifically, he will try to shift the values for the variables X_2, X_3, and X_4 in the directions that will represent *decreases* in decision-making costs and *increases* in external costs. For a decrease in X_1, changes in the other directions would be suggested. As we have defined the four variables, the direction of change in X_2, X_3, and X_4 would, in each case, be opposite to the change imposed on X_1. Thus, we fill in the first row of matrix (15) with minus signs.

$$(-) \quad (-) \quad (-)$$

These signs indicate that, if the rule for the election of representatives to the assembly becomes more inclusive (if X_1 increases), the basis of representation will tend to become somewhat more functional (X_2 will be decreased), the degree of representation will tend to be decreased, that is, the assembly can be made smaller (X_3 will be decreased), and the rule for decision-making in the assembly itself will tend to be made less inclusive (X_4 will be decreased).

In a similar fashion we may examine the remaining rows in matrix (15). Look at the second row. Here we examine the effects on X_1, X_3, and X_4 that might be predicted to result from a change imposed on X_2, which measures the basis of representation. As the earlier discussion has suggested, a shift from a functional basis for representation to one that contains more randomized elements (an increase in X_2) probably increases decision-making costs but decreases expected external costs. If this is correct, and if the variables are related in a compensating rather than a complementing way, the appropriate changes in the other variables will involve decreases in decision-making costs and increases in external costs. The signs in the second row of the matrix will also be negative. As the basis for representation in the assembly is increasingly randomized (as X_2 is increased), the rational constitutional choice will tend to embody less inclusive rules for selecting representatives (lower values for X_1), smaller representative assemblies (lower values for X_3), and less inclusive rules for decision-making within the assembly itself (lower values for X_4). Accordingly, two rows in the matrix can now be filled in, at least as to sign.

$$\begin{matrix} (-) & (-) & (-) \\ (-) & (-) & (-) \end{matrix}$$

We now move to the third row, which relates to the effects on the "equilibrium" values for X_1, X_2, and X_4 that are produced by independent changes imposed on X_3, defined as the degree of representation. As X_3 increases, that is, as direct democracy is approached, decision-making costs increase sharply, but, of course, expected external costs decrease. The rational individual, assumed to have some opportunity to choose values for the remaining variables, will tend to bear additional external costs (expected) at the other stages of the collective-decision process in order to "save" some decision-making costs (expected). He will tend to select some less inclusive rule for electing representatives (lower values for X_1), a more functional basis for representation (lower values for X_2), and some less inclusive rule for decision-making in the assembly (lower values for X_4). The signs in the third row of the matrix are also negative.

$$\begin{matrix} (-) & (-) & (-) \\ (-) & (-) & (-) \\ (-) & (-) & (-) \end{matrix}$$

The last row involves changes exogenously imposed on X_4, the variable that describes the rules for making choices in the legislative assembly itself. For the same reasons as before, the signs of the symbols in the row will be negative. As the decision-making rule is made more inclusive (as X_4 increases), rational constitutional choice should dictate a somewhat smaller assembly (lower values for X_3), a somewhat more functional basis for representation (lower values for X_2), and somewhat less inclusive rules for selecting representatives to the assembly (lower values for X_1). The whole sign matrix may now be filled in.

$$\begin{matrix} (-) & (-) & (-) \\ (-) & (-) & (-) \\ (-) & (-) & (-) \\ (-) & (-) & (-) \end{matrix}$$

If the relationships among the constitutional variables are those that we have assumed in constructing this matrix, the information contained in the matrix is of considerable importance.[7] The fact that all of the elements in the matrix should prove, on the basis of reasonable assumptions about the relationships among the variables, to have negative signs is relevant, methodologically, for our whole analysis of the constitutional-choice process.

The negative signs arise because we have been able to define each of the four constitutional variables in such a manner that an increase in each variable must involve higher decision-making costs and lower external costs—both of these cost elements being considered in an expected sense. This, in turn, depends on our ability to describe each variable (and others that might be potentially considered) in terms of these two basic cost functions. We conclude, therefore, that the highly abstract and simplified analytical model of Chapter 6 is far more powerful than might have been anticipated at first. At the outset the model may have appeared to be applicable only to direct democracy; but, because the other constitutional variables can be readily translated into the same functional variables, the basic analytical model can be employed as the *general* model for constitutional choice.[8] We have shown that

7. It should be emphasized that the derivation of the sign matrix depends strictly upon the relationships among the variables that we have assumed to be present. These relationships are based on what seem to be reasonable assumptions about individual constitutional calculus. Essentially, we have assumed that the constitutional variables, as defined, are compensating rather than complementing. It seems rather difficult to imagine the complementary relationship as applying *generally*, although it would not, of course, be difficult to imagine a complementary relationship between two narrowly defined constitutional variables. However, it should be noted that there is no *mathematical* reason why the general relationship among the variables considered need be compensatory.

8. Research now in progress suggests that the general analytical model is also useful in application to other problems of social organization. For example, the problems of the usage of common-property resources and of the degree of decentralization within a unified organizational structure can both be analyzed with essentially the same model as that introduced in this book.

the four constitutional variables introduced by representative government can be reduced in form to a single model that embodies the two essential cost functions.

This point may be clarified if we introduce an analogy with economic theory. Economists recognize that, in the real world, most business firms produce and market several products simultaneously. A full and complete analysis of the firm's calculus would require an examination of many variables, and, conceptually, the fully rational firm must arrive at a determination of all of the variables under its control simultaneously. In spite of this recognition, economists can explain a great deal about the decision-making process of business firms by simplifying this process. By assuming that the firm produces and markets a single product, all of the analysis needed for a broad general understanding of the operation of business firms can be presented. Our model of the constitutional-choice process seems quite similar in this respect. In the real world there are many constitutional-institutional variables which the individual must rationally consider when he is given the opportunity of reflecting on the prospects of alternative political organizations. However, if our purpose is the relatively limited one of analyzing the essential decision-making processes through which all constitutional choices must be made, the simplified construction that we have emphasized seems quite helpful. Perhaps the absence of such models in the literature of political science is to be explained, in part at least, by an overconcentration on the apparent complexities of real-world political processes.

CHAPTER 16

THE BICAMERAL LEGISLATURE

The two-house or bicameral legislative assembly is a common institution in Western democracies. This institution represents a particular configuration of the constitutional variables discussed in Chapter 15, and it may be analyzed, up to a point, in terms of our models. We shall proceed first to postulate an extreme case. Let us assume that a social group is composed of 9 persons, whom we shall designate by numbers 1 to 9. Further, we assume that these persons may be easily classified into three distinct interest or pressure groups, which, for convenience, we shall call: Labor, Property, and Trade. We shall use the subscripts L, P, and T to classify the numbered individuals.

Let us assume that the group has adopted a political constitution. All constitutional decisions have been made. (After analyzing the operation of the two-house system, we shall return to discuss the constitutional issue concerning the "efficiency" of this system.) The constitution calls for a bicameral legislature. There are to be three representatives in each house, and simple majority decision is required for action in each house. Final collective decision requires the approval of both houses.

Representatives to the first house, which we shall call the "House," are to be elected on a functional basis. The three interests are each allowed to elect a single representative by simple majority vote. We may diagram the constituents of each representative to the House in the following way:

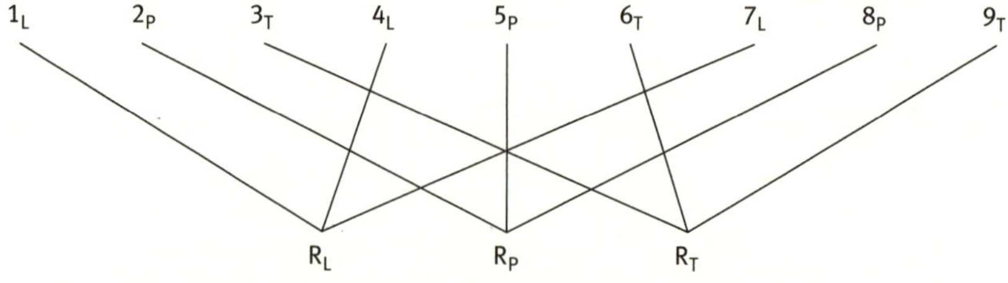

In the second house of the legislature, which we shall call the "Senate," the basis of representation is fully randomized, that is, each constituency includes within it each of the defined interest groups. We may diagram the constituents of each representative to this house as follows:

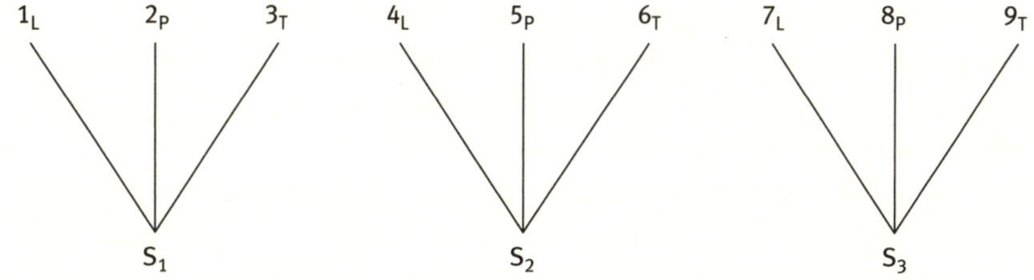

The question is that of determining how this two-house legislature will work in producing collective decisions. To carry decision, a majority of each house is required. The minimum effective coalition would be composed of four members, two from each house. Let us initially confine our attention to a single, isolated issue. Suppose that R_L and R_P form a majority in the House, and S_1 and S_2 form a majority in the Senate. Let us look carefully at the combined coalition: R_L, R_P, S_1, S_2. No difficulty arises when we consider the first two members. These representatives will try to further the interests of Labor and Property, which, for current purposes, we assume to be well-defined and homogeneous over individuals in the groups represented. The interests represented by S_1 and S_2, however, will depend on the effective voting coalitions that have been successful in local elections. In order for the two-house legislature to yield results similar in nature to the single-house legislature, both S_1 and S_2 must represent coalitions of Labor and Property interests. In specific terms, S_1 must be elected by the coalition of 1_L and 2_P, and S_2 must be elected by the coalition of 4_L and 5_P. Under these highly restricted conditions, collective action would tend to promote the interests of Labor and Property at the expense of Trade. This result is identical to that which would arise from the operation of a single legislative body operating under the same decision-making rules. To be generally true, however, this requires that a majority of the representatives in the randomized-basis house, the Senate, be elected by the same coalition of interests that forms the majority in the functional-basis House. This requirement would appear to be rarely met, especially as we move beyond the abstract models and consider a world in which interests are many, changing, and ill-defined.

Returning to the coalition R_L, R_P, S_1, S_2, now assume that *either* S_1 or S_2 should be elected by a majority that includes a voter from the Trade group. In this case no legislation could find majority support in both houses unless it was genuinely to the "general" interest of the whole social group. "Class" or "discriminatory" legislation, such as that which could be predicted to arise under the previously discussed configuration, is no longer possible. If, in order to pass both houses, the "representative" of each interest group must participate in an effective coalition, the two-house system introduces a qualified rule of unanimity into the collective-choice process.

It seems clear that the two-house system of representation introduces an element of uncertainty that was not present in our other models. Whereas we could not, in the analysis of a single group, predict the identity of the members of the winning and the losing coalitions in single issues, we were able to indicate the size of the minimum effective coalition that would be required to carry legislation. Moreover, from this limited amount of information some predictions could be made about the degree of minority exploitation and the degree of possible social waste. This is no longer possible under the two-house system, even when we continue to employ the same basic behavioral assumptions. As our examples have shown, the two-house legislature may produce results ranging from those equivalent to simple majority voting in a single house to those equivalent to the operation of the unanimity rule in a single house. The precise results will depend in each case on the overlapping of the interest-group coalitions in each house.

A few points seem worth noting. It is evident that the two-house system will involve considerably higher decision-making costs than the single-house system, given the same rules for choice under each alternative. From this it follows that, unless the two-house system is expected to produce some offsetting reduction in external costs, there is little reason for its rational support. Translated into more practical terms, this means that unless the bases for representation are significantly different in the two houses, there would seem to be little excuse for the two-house system. On the other hand, if the bases of representation can be made significantly different in the two houses, the institution of the bicameral legislature may prove to be an effective means of securing a substantial reduction in the expected external costs of collective action without incurring as much added decision-making costs as a more inclusive rule would involve in a single house. For example, to produce the same results in a single-house legislature, a rule of ¾ majority might be required under certain circumstances. However, the decision-making costs involved in the operation of this majority might be significantly greater than those involved in the two-house legislature with each house acting on simple-majority voting principles. A priori, it does not seem possible to make such comparisons readily.

Vote-trading will, of course, take place in the two-house legislature, as we

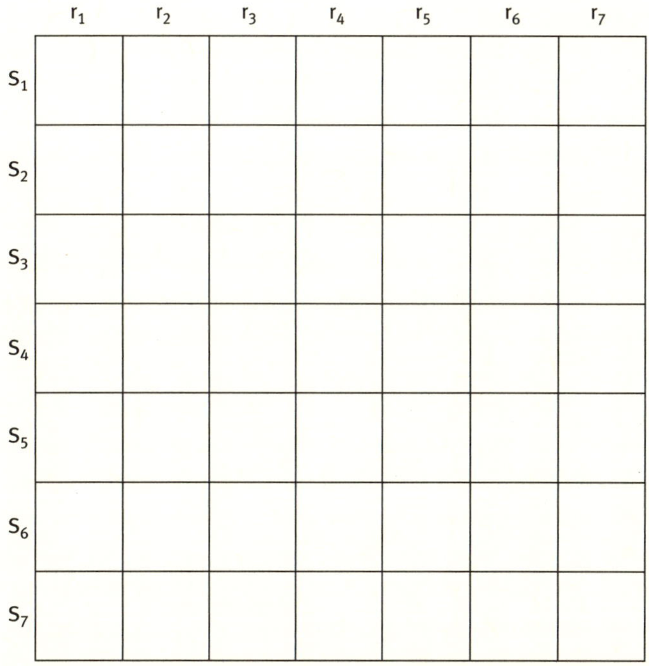

FIGURE 20

all must recognize. The process of vote-trading through logrolling becomes somewhat more complex and its analysis considerably more difficult. In order to undertake this analysis, let us consider briefly a group of 49 voters who have organized themselves in 7 constituencies of 7 voters each for the purpose of electing one house of a legislature, and in another set of 7 constituencies of 7 each for the purpose of electing the other. Let us suppose the constituencies consist, respectively, of the columns and rows of the square in Figure 20.

This is a system which follows the organizational principle which we may call "complete diversity." Although complete diversity is unknown in political practice, it provides an excellent starting point for further analysis. The system, of course, is not limited to a group of 49 members. The 9-man electorate discussed above was also organized according to this rule, and a group that may be shown by a square of 199 by 199 will be used later in the chapter. Nor is it necessary that the illustrative diagram be a square; an oblong rectangle, with more representatives in one house than in the other, would be perfectly acceptable. Finally, our reasoning would not be changed if there

	r_1	r_2	r_3	r_4	r_5	r_6	r_7
s_1							
s_2							
s_3	X	X	X	X			
s_4	X	X	X	X			
s_5			O				
s_6	X	X	X′	X		O	
s_7	X	X	X	X			

FIGURE 21

were more than one voter reflected in each square of the diagram. Thus, we can consider a situation in which each square contains, say, 10,000 voters as one of complete diversity. *The only requirement for complete diversity is that the members of the constituency of a representative in one house be distributed evenly among all of the constituencies for the other house.*

The smallest bargain which could enact a group of measures in this type of legislature would involve a coalition of 16 voters, arranged generally like the X's in Figure 21. The coalition must include 4 voters in each of 4 constituencies of each legislative chamber. At first glance, it might appear that voting under a two-house legislative system leads to the same results as a one-house legislature, since this coalition is also that necessary to get a measure through a one-house legislature.[1] In fact, this coalition would get a measure through either of the two houses which are elected by the completely diverse electorates shown on our diagram. A little further consideration, however, indicates that this form of bargaining would not be feasible.

Suppose, for example, that voter X′ on the diagram decided that he was

1. See Figure 19 and the discussion relevant to it.

not being fairly treated and asked for a change which would lead to higher compensation for himself. The remaining members of the coalition would either have to give in or else construct a radically different bargain. If X′ were left out of the bargain, it would be necessary to drop either the row s_6 or the column r_3 and substitute another row or column for it. In other words, any member of such a coalition can be replaced only by radically changing the form of the coalition. In the mathematically convenient 199 by 199 square, a coalition of 10,000 voters organized like the X's in Figure 21 could control the votes of both houses. However, if one member of the coalition demanded more compensation, then his coalition partners would have the choice of either giving in to his demands or of dropping him *and 99 other members* of the coalition. This situation is one in which substantial unanimity among a specified group is required to form the coalition, and the difficulties of getting unanimity in practice have been previously discussed. For each individual member of the coalition, investment of resources in strategic bargaining with the objective of getting much more than an equal share of the total returns from the coalition would be rational. In situations where large investments in strategic bargaining are rational, the cost of bargaining becomes prohibitively high. Thus we have an interesting situation in which, in essence, there are two costs-of-higgling functions. In addition to the decision-costs curve associated with changing voting rules, there is also a cost-of-higgling curve associated with the type of bargain to be struck. Although a minimum-membership bargain of the sort shown in Figure 21 would be the most economical from the standpoint of its members, the bargaining costs involved in making it up are prohibitive and this type of coalition can, therefore, be ruled out.

If X′ decides that he is not receiving favorable enough consideration from his coalition partners, they have yet another alternative to paying him what he asks or radically reconstructing the organization of the bargain. They could replace X′ by two other voters, who are located like the two O's in Figure 21. A coalition constructed by this method, however, will be larger than one composed of people in the arrangement of the X's and will also be composed of two classes of voters: those whose favorable consideration of the bargain is necessary to obtain approval in each one of both chambers, and those like the O's whose vote is necessary only to obtain a majority in one or the other of the two chambers.

Leaving aside, for the time being, the question of the size of the new coalition, let us consider the bargaining problems raised by the existence of two classes of members of the coalition. There are two possible ways of dealing with the matter. Leaders may try to treat all members of the coalition equally, or they may choose to "compensate" the members of the two classes differently. The first leads to impossible difficulties. For example, if a policy were adopted of compensating the O's equally with the X's, then any X would know that the cost of replacing him would be two times the current "payment" received by the members of the coalition. It would only be rational for him to insist on receiving, say, 1.9 times the amount that others were receiving. If this offer were refused by the other members of the coalition, then they would have to obtain two replacements, and this is even more expensive than meeting his offer. Thus, each voter whose vote is required for approval of the measure in two houses would, if he were rational, hold out for about twice the standard "rate" of compensation. However, it is obviously impossible for a coalition to pay all of its members equally and at the same time pay some of them twice as much as others. The result would be that coalitions which attempted to stick to the system of making equal payments would find themselves, once again, confronted with members who invested sizable amounts in strategic bargaining, and the costs of bargaining would be too high for such a system to be feasible.

The contrary system of "paying" the members of the two classes differently does not raise this kind of problem. If each member of the coalition whose vote is necessary in both houses gets twice what a member whose vote is necessary in only one house does, then members of the coalition should get merely the marginal value of their votes. Any member withdrawing from the coalition can be replaced readily by one or two other voters, and there is, therefore, no incentive to invest excessive resources in strategic bargaining. However, if this two-category system is adopted, then there is no particular reason why coalition managers should favor voters whose votes are necessary in two houses, and who cost twice as much, over voters whose votes are necessary in only one house. The coalition can be made up just as "cheaply" from one type or from the other. This being so, there is no particular reason to expect that people trying to make up such a coalition will concentrate on voters who are necessary in both houses. Moreover, if they do not follow a conscious policy of trying to get such voters into the coalitions, then there would be only a random overlap between the voters in the coalitions which control the majority in each house.

This may be illustrated in Figure 22. The crosshatched squares represent the minimum-sized coalition (5 by 5 in the 81-voter group with two houses of 9 constituencies each) that would be necessary to secure a majority in both houses. This coalition, however, would be no more likely to arise than that

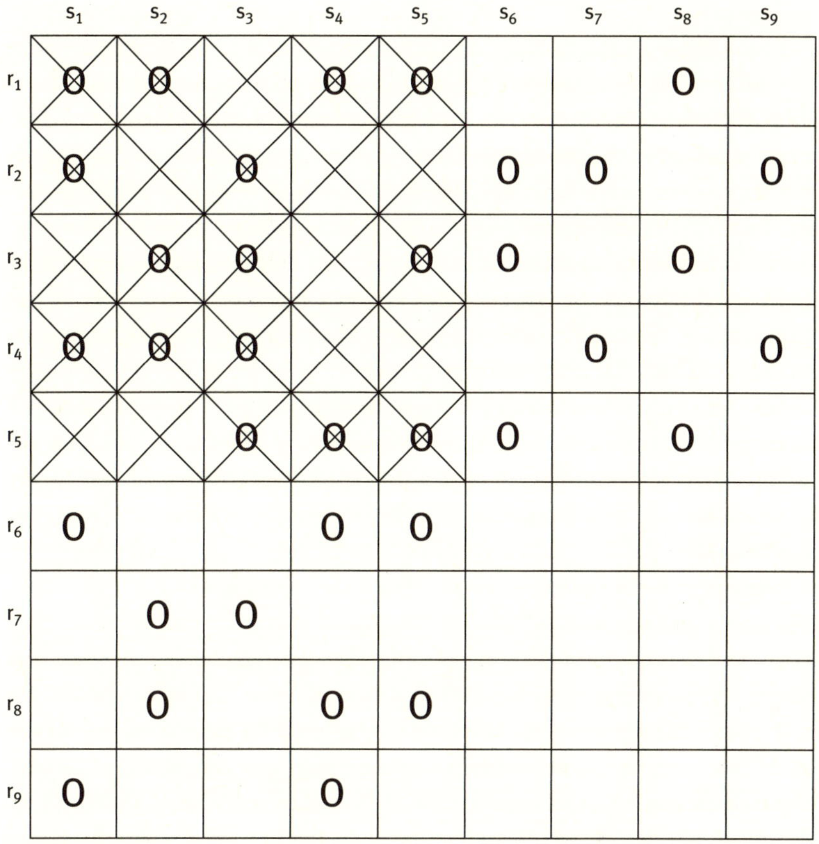

FIGURE 22

shown by the squares marked "O" if the support of the "less powerful" voters (those marked "O" which fall outside the 5 by 5 crosshatched matrix) can be secured at a lower bargaining "price" than the "more powerful" voters. This suggests that in the two-house system the minimum-sized coalition (in terms of numbers) need not arise, even on the assumption of fully rational behavior on the part of all members. Instead, the agreement finally reached will represent the minimum number of voters required to form that effective coalition which involves a minimization of bargaining costs.

We have no historical experience with systems which involve representation through two houses that are completely diverse in their constituencies, and therefore we cannot check our conclusions by examining data from the real world. However, it is possible to get the same general result by another line of reasoning, which may serve as a partial check. In representative government the negotiating is done by the representatives. Each representative should vote for any measure or combination of measures which will be approved by a majority of his constituents and should attempt to arrange bargains satisfactory to such a majority. Given the arrangements of the constituencies with complete diversity, this simple policy on the part of each representative would lead to the same result that we obtained by analyzing the coalition formation in the two-house legislature. This is because the constituents for a single representative in each house include members of all constituencies in the second house, randomly distributed. The end result, in a system in which the representation is like that shown in Figure 21 but in which the square is 199 by 199, would be that in the mean case approximately 17,500 out of the 39,601 voters would have to approve a measure before it was passed. Of these about 2500 would be situated so that their votes would be necessary in both houses, and these voters would tend to be suitably rewarded for their luck.

Compared with the 10,000 voters necessary to control a one-house representative assembly, 17,500 is a distinct "improvement"—although it is still less than a majority of the voters; 17,500, in fact, is the number of voters that would be needed to pass a measure through a one-house legislature if a ⅞ legislative majority were required. Requiring a ¾ legislative majority in both houses would mean that a little over 24,000 voters would be necessary to pass a measure, of whom almost 6000 would be required in both houses. This is more than a majority and better than could be obtained by requiring unanimity in one house. That is to say, the over-all result would reflect a more inclusive "rule" than would the requirement of legislative unanimity in a one-house legislature, where each representative is elected by a simple majority of constituents.

In Chapter 9 it was stated that the bicameral legislative system automatically discriminates between measures in which the intensities of the desires or antipathies of the voters are equal and measures in which the minority has stronger feelings than the majority. We have thus far been discussing the latter case; let us now turn to the equal-intensity situation. The reader will remember from the discussion in Chapter 9 that, although equal intensities of feelings are most unlikely, the situation could arise if the differences in intensities among the voters were to be symmetrically distributed among subgroups of voters. Studies of the equal-intensity situation, therefore, are useful for such issues as were involved in the traditional idea of general legislation. In matters concerned with foreign policy, the criminal code, and promotion of scientific discovery, etc., it is possible that differences of opinion may well exist, and there is no reason to believe that all opinions will be held with equal intensity, but there is also no particular reason to expect the differences in intensity to be systematically distributed among particular groupings. Although such matters are a relatively minor part of the activities of most modern governments, they are of considerable importance and may well deserve special handling.

In this chapter we have thus far been discussing the intense-minority case; let us now turn to an equal-intensity case. Suppose that in a representative government which uses a single-house legislature, the members of which are elected by simple majority vote from separate constituencies, some issue comes up in which the intensities of the feelings of the voters are equal. Given that the electorate in each constituency is large and that there are quite a number of constituencies (which is the situation in real life), it is highly likely that a majority of the constituencies will have a majority reflecting a majority of the whole electorate. If this is so, then the representative assembly should vote in accordance with the wishes of the majority of the people, which is the "correct" decision in this case. In those cases (and they would be much less common) where the majority was concentrated in a minority of the constituencies, the representatives of those constituencies would be motivated to enter into bargains with the representatives of other districts with the result that the measure would still be disposed of as the majority wished. All of this follows from the fact that, in the equal-intensity case, minorities are unable to compensate members of the majority for changing their votes, while the members of the majority can readily compensate the minority for such changes.

If we consider the changes in this picture which would result from a bicameral legislature with complete diversity of representation, they turn out to be small. Again, if the number of voters is very large and the number of constituencies quite large, the laws of combinations and permutations would result in a majority of constituencies in both houses being in agreement with the majority of the whole population, so in most cases the two houses would simply enact the will of the majority. Cases in which the voters were distributed in such a way that they failed of a majority in one house or the other would be commoner than with a one-house legislature, but still relatively uncommon. As in the one-house system, bargains would not be particularly hard to arrange in such a case. Thus the switch from single-house to two-house representative government makes only a very slight difference in the way that equal-intensity issues are treated. There is a small increase in the cost of higgling, but that is all.

This contrasts sharply with the results for cases where the minority is more intense in its desires than the majority. As we have seen, in such cases logrolling leads to only a little more than 1/4 of the voters being able to control a one-house legislature, while over 7/16 are necessary to control a two-house legislature. A rule which required the organizers of a logrolling coalition to obtain the approval of 7/16 of the voters in a one-house legislative system of representative government would require that the legislature, if it were elected by simple majority in individual constituencies, operate on a 7/8 majority rule, i.e., pass only bills which are approved of by 7/8 of its members. The 7/8 rule, however, would impose quite a heavy bargaining cost on equal-intensity measures. The two-chamber legislature, by automatically distinguishing between the two cases and imposing much greater restraints on the erection of coalitions by members of intense minorities than on majorities in equal-intensity cases, can perform a very valuable function.

The advantage gained by the use of the two-house legislature, however, is rather dissipated by the simple majority method of voting. Even in the two-house legislature the intense minority can pass its measures with less popular support than can an equal-intensity majority. This appears the opposite of what should be the case, but given the simple-majority voting rule nothing can be done about it. Departures from the simple majority rule, however, can improve the situation. For example, if methods of election of the representatives should insure that each house represents the whole people, not just a majority in each constituency, then a two-house legislature with simple majority voting in each house would require 3/4 of the people to approve bargains of intense minorities, while still permitting passage of equal-intensity measures which were approved of by only simple majorities. This sounds utopian, but conceivable practical arrangements to obtain comparable results would be possible.

So far we have been discussing a two-house legislature in which there is "complete diversity" in the constituencies of the representatives in the two houses. In practice this situation is never found; however, partial diversity is almost universal in governments which use the two-house system. Partial diversity takes many forms, and for purposes of analysis we shall divide it into two subtypes: "arrangement" and "number" diversity. Number diversity is fairly common in its pure form in the real world (the United States legislative branch is an example), while arrangement diversity is almost never found in its pure form. In most cases the two are intermixed in two-house legislatures. We shall examine them in their pure form largely for simplicity, and we shall start with "arrangement" diversity for the same reason.

We have covered a completely diverse system of constituencies for a two-house legislature. At the other extreme we can easily imagine a completely nondiverse system. If the members of each house were elected from the same constituencies (that is, if each constituency sent a representative to each house), then the two houses would be identically constituted, and the situation, from our present standpoint, would not differ from a one-house legislature.[2] Using our diagram, it is possible to construct systems of representation which form a continuum from complete diversity to complete non-diversity. To illustrate "arrangement" diversity, see Figure 23. In this square matrix representing 49 voters, the columns denote constituencies in one house. A particular configuration can then be chosen to represent each constituency in the second house. Each senator shares 2, 3, 4, . . . 7 voters with some given representative. In Figure 23 we have chosen to give each senator 4 constituents in common with some single representative. For example, the blank squares represent the first senate constituency. Here the senator shares 4 voters with r_1 and 1 voter each with r_2, r_3, and r_4.

Obviously, as we proceed by small steps from complete diversity to complete nondiversity, the features of completely diverse systems which we have discussed gradually fade away. Semidiverse systems, however, have a special feature which neither completely diverse nor completely nondiverse systems share. Such systems, in effect, classify the voters into categories. For example, in Figure 23 the voters in the bottom four rows are represented in the Senate and in the House by representatives elected from the same constituencies, while the voters in the upper three rows are represented by diversely based legislators. The result is that it is much easier to work out coalitions which will benefit the people in the lower four rows than in the upper three. The costs of bargaining are lower because part of the bargain is already implicitly made by the arrangement of constituencies. Further, bargains involving only voters in the lower four rows will operate on a basis similar to that of the single-house legislature, while those involving voters in the top three rows will have to operate on the same basis as in a completely diverse system.

2. This is not to deny that such a system might have some advantages over a single house. In particular, it might provide for more careful consideration of issues.

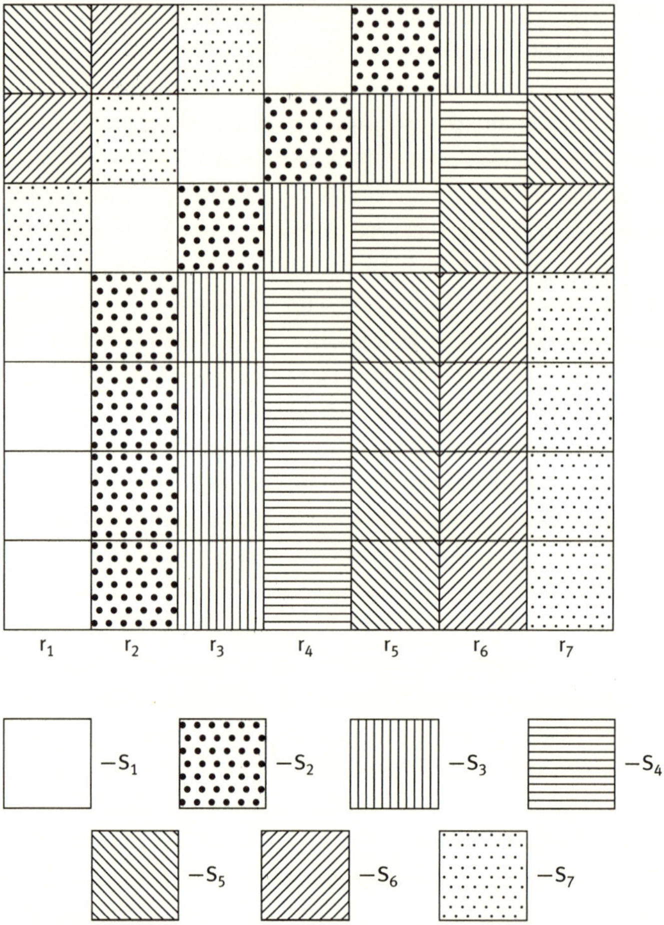

FIGURE 23

Clearly, this system greatly favors the voters who are so arranged as to have the advantage of a sort of prefabricated bargain.

Although this situation is never exactly duplicated in real-life political organizations, something very like it is quite common. The American farmers, for example, possess what amounts to a built-in coalition in the two houses of our legislature. This gives them a great advantage over less fortunately situated groups.

Our second type of partial diversity is "number" diversity. Under the American constitution many Western voters are much more heavily represented in the Senate than the inhabitants of the more populous states. In the

House, on the other hand, people from different parts of the country are more or less equally represented. This situation arises from the fact that each state has two senators, regardless of how sparse its population, while the representatives are distributed among the states according to population. The system has been criticized for giving the voters in the thinly populated states an unfair advantage. This “unfairness,” however, is not intrinsic in number diversity as a concept. It is easy to conceive of a system under which area A elects 5 representatives to the “House” and 1 to the “Senate,” while area B elects 1 to the “House” and 5 to the “Senate,” thus obtaining the advantages of number diversity without giving any voter more power than any other.

The system to which we are accustomed, however, does give the voters in some states an advantage over those in others. In the American system the constituency of most senators “includes” the constituencies of a number of representatives. As illustrated in Figure 24, the constituency for senator s_1 includes the constituencies of representatives r_1, r_2, and r_3. This type of diver-

r_1	r_2	r_3	r_4	r_5	r_6	r_7
	X		O		O	O
	X	X	X	O	O	O
X		X	X			O
	X	X	O	O	O	O
X		X	O		O	
X	X		X	O		
X			X	O		
	s_1			s_2		s_3

FIGURE 24

sity also leads to some improvements over the single-chamber legislature. Many coalitions which would pass in the House will fail in the Senate. For example, the voters marked X in Figure 24 could maneuver their bill through the House, but it would fail in the Senate. On the other hand, there would still be some bills that would be passed by this type of two-chamber legislature which would require only the very minimum of voter support in a one-chamber legislature, e.g., the one shown by the O's on the diagram.

Two chambers differing from each other only in this way offer much less of a safeguard against the imposition of excessive "external cost" on the citizen than organization in accordance with what we have called "arrangement" diversity. Further, if the number of constituents varies from "senator" to "senator," it may introduce an element of discrimination among the voters. Those who are in small constituencies have an advantage over those who are in large ones. Nevertheless, the device does, to some extent, improve the operating characteristics of a system of representative government.

There is also another phenomenon in the real world which can be regarded as an extreme version of number diversity. The President of the United States and many other "executives" are equipped with the veto power. This, in effect, constitutes them as a third house of the legislature. In this case, however, the "third house" represents the entire body of voters in one grand constituency. The President should, insofar as he uses his veto power as a simple legislative tool, follow the preferences of the majority of the voters. Therefore, he would accept only bargains which meet the approval of the majority of the populace, and hence could considerably raise the minimum size of the logrolling coalitions. Normally, of course, the President tends simply to sign most bills, and vetoes only a minority. Nevertheless, he has the power to constitute himself as a third legislative house, and the exercise of this power, whether explicit or implicit, materially improves the functioning of the American Constitution.

CHAPTER 17

THE ORTHODOX MODEL OF MAJORITY RULE

The crux of the question is not whether the majority should rule but what kind of majority should rule.
—Walter Lippmann, *The Washington Post*, 5 January 1961

We have made no attempt to relate our analysis directly to the history and development of political theory. We propose to leave this for somewhat extended development in an appendix. The "economic" approach to both the problem of constitutional choice and the analysis of decision-making rules is perhaps sufficiently differentiated from what has been the mainstream of political scholarship to warrant independent treatment before the doctrinal setting has been completed. Moreover, in this respect the preliminary and exploratory nature of our whole analytical inquiry must be doubly emphasized.

Nevertheless, it will be useful at this stage to try to compare and contrast our models with the orthodox models of modern political theory, *as we conceive the latter*. We take this step, not for the purpose of comparison per se, but because in this way the content of our own analysis may be more clearly demonstrated, especially to noneconomist readers. We stand, of course, in danger of having our descriptions of the orthodox models labeled as straw men. Whether the constructions are straw or stone (and we are willing to leave this decision to others), we observe merely that, methodologically, straw men may also be useful.

As implied in Chapters 1 and 2, our approach to collective action is avowedly individualist, rationalist, and secular. At the ultimate stage of constitutional choice, when decisions must be made among alternative means of organizing human activity and among rules for collective decision-making, full consensus of unanimity among all members of the social group seems to us to be the only conceivable test of the "rightness" of the choices made. This postulated unanimity rule for ultimate constitutional decisions allows us to divorce much of our analysis from the long and continuing debate concerning the validity of majority rule as an absolute doctrine of popular sovereignty.

UNANIMITY AND "POLITICAL EXCHANGE"

In our view, both at the level of ultimate constitutional choice and at the level of analyzing the operation of particular rules, the issues have often been posed in terms of false alternatives. The alternatives are not those of majority rule or minority rule. One of the great advantages of an essentially economic approach to collective action lies in the implicit recognition that "political exchange," at all levels, is basically equivalent to economic exchange. By this we mean simply that *mutually* advantageous results can be expected from individual participation in community effort. Much of the debate surrounding the majority-rule doctrine seems to deny this possibility implicitly, even if such a denial is not explicitly stated. In this sense the discussion seems closely akin to the medieval arguments about the "just price." If, in market or exchange transactions, the loss to one trader must be offset by gains to the other, some rational basis for philosophical argumentation about the "justice" of prices would be present. However, the simple fact is, of course, that in normal trade *all* parties gain; there exist *mutual gains from trade*. The great contribution of Adam Smith lies in his popularization of this simple point, but the full import of this conception for democratic political theory does not seem to have yet been appreciated.

Insofar as participation in the organization of a community, a State, is mutually advantageous to *all* parties, the formation of a "social contract" on the basis of unanimous agreement becomes possible. Moreover, the only test of the mutuality of advantage is the measure of agreement reached. Modern political theorists have perhaps shrugged off the unanimity requirement too early in their thinking. By noting that the attainment of unanimity is infeasible or impossible, they have tended to pose the false dilemma mentioned above. The early theorists (Hobbes, Althusius, Locke, and Rousseau) did assume consensus in the formation of the original contract. They did so because the essence of any contractual arrangement is *voluntary* participation, and no rational being will voluntarily agree to something which yields him, in net terms, expected damage or harm. The categorical opposition of interests that many theorists assume to arise to prevent unanimity is much more likely to characterize the operational as opposed to the constitutional level of decision, and it is essential that these two levels of decision be sharply distinguished. It is at the operational level, where solidified economic interests of individuals and groups are directly subjected to modification and change by State action, that violent conflicts of interest can, and do, arise. At the "higher" constitutional level the problem confronted by the individuals of the group is that of choosing among alternative *rules* for organizing operational choices, and the discussion at this level will be concerned with the predicted operation of these rules. By a careful separation of these two levels of decision, much of the confusion inherent in modern interpretations of the contract theory of the State can be removed. Conceptually, men can reach agreement on rules, even when each party recognizes in advance that he will be "coerced" by the operation of agreed-on rules in certain circumstances. A potential thief, recognizing the need for protecting his own person and property, will support laws against theft, even though he will anticipate the probability that he will himself be subjected to punishment under these laws. Individuals at the level of operational decisions may accept results that run contrary to their own interest, not because they accept the will of the decision-making group as their own in some undefined, metaphysical manner, but simply because they know that the acceptance of adverse decisions (in our terminology, the bearing of external costs) is inherent occasionally in the "bargain" or "exchange" which is, in the long run, beneficial to them. The expected external costs caused by adverse decisions may fall short of the added costs that would be involved in the participation in the more complex political bargaining process that might be required to protect individual interests more fully. In our construction, therefore, there is no necessary inconsistency implied in the adoption of, say, simple majority rule for the making of certain everyday decisions for the group with respect to those activities that have been explicitly collectivized, and the insistence on unanimity of consensus on changes in the fundamental organizational rules. The organizing principle or theme of our whole construction is the concentration on the individual calculus, and it is easy to see that both the unanimity rule at the constitutional level and other less-than-unanimity rules at the operational level of decisions may be based directly on this calculus.[1]

While it is clear that something akin to the doctrine of inalienable rights—institutionally embodied in constitutional provisions limiting the authority

1. Note that essentially the same position has recently been taken by Morton A. Kaplan: "Thus social rules may often be considered as game payoffs, and we are willing to take lower contract payoffs at any particular time or to take risks of lower payoffs that we would be unwilling to accept if we had not internalized these social rules. And most men also have an interest in supporting the socialization process, for, although it constrains them, they are better off than if none was constrained." (Morton A. Kaplan, *Some Problems in the Strategic Analysis of International Politics*, Research Monograph No. 2, Center of International Studies, Princeton [12 January 1959], p. 9.)

of legislative majorities—can easily be reconciled with our construction, we should emphasize that this doctrine is not central to our construction. The fact that much of our construction can be reconciled with a strain of orthodox democratic theory, and vice versa, should not obscure the profound differences between our approach and the one which has been implicit in much political theory and philosophy, both ancient and modern. The most basic difference lies in the incorporation into our models of the economic meaning of the unanimity rule, a part of our construction previously discussed in Chapter 7.

Much political discussion seems to have proceeded as follows: "If the interests of two or more individuals conflict, unanimity is impossible. Some interests must prevail over others if action is not to be wholly stifled." This line of reasoning seems quite plausible until one confronts ordinary economic exchange. Note that in such an exchange the interests of the two contracting parties clearly conflict. Yet unanimity is reached. Contracts are made; bargains are struck without the introduction of explicit or implicit coercion. In this case, no interest prevails over the other; both interests are furthered. Our continued repetition of this simple analogy stems from our conviction that, at base, it is the failure to grasp fully the significance of this point that has retarded progress in political theory.

The "social contract" is, of course, vastly more complex than market exchange, involving as it does many individuals simultaneously. Nevertheless, the central notion of mutuality of gain may be carried over to the political relationship. When it is translated into individual behavior, mutuality of gain becomes equivalent to unanimous agreement among the contracting parties. The *only* test for the presence of mutual gain is *agreement*. If agreement cannot be reached, given adequate time for discussion and compromise, this fact in itself suggests the absence of any mutuality of gain. Moreover, where mutuality of gain is not possible, no criteria consistent with the individualistic philosophical conception of society can be introduced which will appropriately weight gains and losses among the separate parties to the institution taking the place of a contract (clearly, a relationship that does not embody unanimous consent is not a contract).

There may, of course, exist situations in which the formation of a "social contract" is not possible. When the negotiating parties are divided into groups that are classified on bases which seem reasonably certain to remain as permanent, independently of the decision-making rules that might be adopted, a "constitution" (in the sense that we have used this term throughout) may not be possible. The individual may never get the opportunity to participate (at the level of the Nation-State) in the choice process that we have been discussing. Under such conditions societies will tend to be controlled by some groups which will tyrannize over other groups. Such a situation must continue to exist, so long as genuinely mutual arrangements cannot be made.

MUTUALLY EXCLUSIVE ALTERNATIVES

Situations such as these are not, however, what the orthodox theorist seems to have in mind when he makes statements like the one which we have attributed to him above. Implicitly, the orthodox theorist conceives all relevant political choice to take the form of selection between two mutually exclusive alternatives. An appropriate analogue is the choice confronted by the traveler at a fork in the road. He must either take one road or the other; the only other alternative is to stop. If, indeed, political decisions should assume this form, the statement imputed to the orthodox theorist above would be somewhat meaningful; but are the decisions that are confronted in the political process properly conceived as choices among mutually exclusive alternatives? Once more, let us turn to the analogy with market exchange. Such exchange could be converted into choices among mutually exclusive alternatives only if one partner to the bargain or contract should be required to secure gains *at the direct expense of the other party*. If such a rule were laid down in advance, any "solution" would require that the interests of one or the other of the parties prevail and the interests of the "loser" be subjected to "defeat." In game-theoretic terms, the assumption of mutually exclusive alternatives is equivalent to assuming that the game is zero-sum. The winnings must match the losings. If, in fact, this is the appropriate conception of the political "game," it is relatively easy to see that, once several persons (several players) are introduced, and if symmetry in preferences among individuals is postulated, the interests of the larger number (the majority) "should" or "ought" to prevail over the interests of the lesser number.

Clearly this would represent a wholly incorrect and misleading way of analyzing economic or market transactions. The implication of the approach would be that no exchange should take place at all because gainers balance losers in two-person trades and symmetry in preference is to be assumed present. Is this approach, by contrast, the appropriate means of analyzing political transactions? By now it is perhaps obvious that we do not think that political choices should, at base, be conceived in terms of selection among mutually exclusive alternatives. The essence of the contractual conception of the collectivity, quite independent of the empirical validity of this construction, involves the mutuality of gain among all members of the group. However, *all* participants in a zero-sum game cannot win simultaneously. Games of zero-sum are played, and political choices on many occasions do reduce to mutually exclusive alternatives; but why do we observe zero-sum games being played in the real world? The answer is that such games are played because each and every participant has, implicitly, accepted the "contract" embodied in the rules of the game when he chooses to play. The zero-sum characteristic applies to the "solution" of the game; it does not apply to the "contract" through which all participants agree on the rules. At this second level there must be mutual gains, and the rule of unanimity must apply. At this level there is no way in which a zero-sum solution could apply; the game simply would not be played unless all participants expected some individual benefit at the time of entry.

This reference to game theory may be helpful, but we have not yet clearly shown the statement of the hypothetical orthodox theorist to be demonstrably false. Let us turn to a simple model of a three-man society, engaged in the formation of a "social contract." Let us call the three men A, B, and C. Suppose that the discussion is proceeding on the fundamental organizational rules that entering into a community or group life might involve. Let us assume that A is very interested in insuring that fishing is collectively organized, because he likes fish and because he also realizes that joint effort is much more productive than individual effort. If we limit our attention to this decision, we may reduce it to a yes-or-no question. Either the catching of fish will be collectively organized or it will not. These appear to be mutually exclusive alternatives, and it seems impossible that agreement could be reached unanimously if, say, C, who does not like fish anyway, does not agree to collective organization of this activity. This is the point at which our hypothetical orthodox theorist of the constitutional process seems to have stopped, but this represents the central error of his interpretation. Let us say now that C, in turn, is interested in insuring that the group allow the gathering of coconuts to be privately organized because he thinks he is a much better climber of trees than A or B. On the other hand, A and B both want to collectivize this activity as well as fishing. Suppose that B, in contrast to A and C, is really more interested in securing some defense against external attack than he is in either fish or coconuts. He wants, first of all, to organize some standing patrol or watch. Under these circumstances it becomes conceivable that the group can reach unanimous agreement of a "constitution" or contract. They can do so by making the appropriate compromises or "trades" among themselves. The process would be equivalent to the logrolling process discussed in Chapter 10, and the only test for determining whether or not the organization of the community is or is not mutually desirable to all parties lies in the possibility that such an agreement can be reached. Our hypothetical orthodox theorist, therefore, errs in not following through beyond the confines of a single issue. Once several issues are introduced, and the variance of interests among individuals and over separate issues is allowed for, trades become possible. Moreover, when trade can take place, the analogy with economic or market exchange is appropriate. No longer must the group reach yes-or-no decisions at the constitutional level; no longer must alternatives be mutually exclusive. The existence of conflicts of interest does not preclude the attainment of unanimity; this merely makes it necessary that discussion proceed until the appropriate compromises are found.

If direct side payments among individuals are allowed for, even this modification is not needed. Return to our illustrative model. Suppose that the only decision confronted is that concerning the organization of fishing. A and B desire collectivization because of the greater efficiency, but C, not liking fish, is opposed. If side payments are allowed, the support of C for the collectivization of fishing for the group may be secured by the transfer of some item possessing real value to C by A and B (e.g., a few cigarettes); and only if C can be so convinced to support the collectivization of fishing will the entering into the agreement with A and B be worthwhile to him.

THE MEANING OF "MAJORITY RULE"

We have shown that the attainment of unanimity is always possible if there exist mutual gains from entering into the "social contract," and that the orthodox theorist has tended to dismiss unanimity as a possible alternative to majority or minority rule too hurriedly because of a concentration on mutually exclusive alternatives. Our earlier models have shown, however, that the group may rationally choose less-than-unanimous decision-making rules for the carrying out of operational decisions for the collectivity. We now want to isolate a second major fallacy in the orthodox position. Even in these cases when unanimity is either not possible or not chosen as the rule by the group, we shall try to demonstrate that the dilemma posed by a a majority rule–minority rule dichotomy remains a false one.

Recall that the unique feature of our models for constitutional choice was the demonstration that, unless equal intensity of preferences is postulated, there are no particular characteristics attributable to the 51 per cent rule for choice. This is only one out of many possible decision-making rules. The peculiar position that this proportion has assumed in orthodox thinking seems to be due to the idea that if less than 50 per cent are allowed to make a decision, the more than 50 per cent will be "concluded" or "coerced" into acceptance. Thus, the requirement of a qualified majority really amounts to allowing a minority to rule. If we may again put the words into the mouth of our hypothetical orthodox theorist, he might say: "If more than 51 per cent are required for political decision, this will really allow the minority to rule since the wishes of the 51 per cent, a majority, can be thwarted." In this construction there is no difference between the qualified majority of, say, 75 per cent and the simple minority rule of 26 per cent. Whereas in our constitutional models there may be a great difference in the external costs expected to be incurred under the 26 per cent minority rule and the 75 per cent majority rule, the orthodox theorist would deny this difference. Moreover, he would claim that the existing provisions for amending the United States Constitution embody the rule of the minority.

Does the requirement of a qualified majority amount to the rule of the minority? Here, as before, the error of the orthodox theorist seems to reflect his emphasis on reducing all decisions to the yes-no, mutually exclusive type, and the implied failure to put quantitative significance on alternatives confronted. If we come to an issue analogous to the fork in the road mentioned above, and if this is the only issue, and if no side payments are allowed, the orthodox theorist would seem to be on reasonably safe ground in saying that the requirement of 75 per cent agreement would allow the 26 per cent to be really controlling for decisions.

However, if the requirement of a qualified majority of, say, 75 per cent is really equivalent to the minority "rule" of 26 per cent, what sort of decisions must be involved? Not only must the alternatives of choice be conceived as being mutually exclusive, but the alternative of inaction must be counted as equivalent to action. The fork-in-the-road analogy mentioned above becomes too general because the alternative represented by stopping the journey is precluded. One way or the other must presumably be chosen. Suppose that there are 100 persons on a hayride and such a fork in the road looms ahead. Suppose that 74 of these persons choose to take the right-hand fork; 26 of them want to go to the left. With the 75 per cent rule in effect, neither road could be taken until and unless some compromises were made. With a 27 per cent rule in effect, the right-hand road would be taken without question in these circumstances. Surely these two rules produce different results.

Failure to secure the required 75 per cent is not equivalent to granting "rule" to 27 per cent. If the third alternative of stopping the journey is allowed for, the 75 per cent rule will not allow action to be taken. The orthodox theorist would argue that such inaction, in this case, amounts to "victory" for the "recalcitrant" 26 persons making up the minority. Taken individually, however, these persons are thwarted in their desires in precisely the same way that the individual members of the larger group are thwarted. These individuals must also bear the costs of inaction. The argument may be advanced that, in such hypothetical situations as this, the interests of the greater number should be counted more heavily; but this, presumably, is a question that is appropriately answered only at the time when the decision-making rules are chosen. In our construction it seems wholly inappropriate to introduce this essentially irrelevant ethical issue at the stage of operational decision-making. When it is recognized at the ultimate constitutional stage that the larger the majority required for decision, the lower are the expected external costs that the individual expects to incur as a result of collective decisions being made adversely to his own interest, we may discuss the operation of the various rules quite independently of all attempts to measure utilities and to compare these interpersonally.

The orthodox theorist will not, however, accept this line of reasoning. He will say that the question to be decided in our illustration should be put as follows: Shall the group take the right-hand road or not?—Vote yes or vote no. In this way the qualified majority rule is made to appear equivalent to "minority rule." A minority of 26 per cent is empowered to block action desired by 74 per cent.

This argument is more sophisticated than the one considered previously, and it is more difficult to refute convincingly. To do so, we must, first of all, clarify the meaning of the terms "majority rule" and "minority rule." We have used these terms throughout our analysis to describe decision-making processes. Such general usage is no longer sufficient. We must sharply differentiate between two kinds of decisions: (1) the positive decision that authorizes action for the social group, and (2) the negative decision that effectively blocks action proposed by another group. If a group is empowered to make decisions resulting in positive action by/for the whole group, we shall say that this group effectively "rules" for the decisions in question. It does not seem meaningful to say that the power to block action constitutes effective "rule."

This relevant distinction between the power of determining action and the power of blocking action has not been sufficiently emphasized in the literature of political science.[2] The reason for this neglect seems to be an overconcentration on the operation of simple majority rule. If a simple majority is empowered to determine positive action, there can be no other simple majority empowered to block the action proposed. Two simple majorities cannot simultaneously exist. The distinction becomes clear only when we consider "minority rule." If we adopt the meaning of this term suggested above, a group smaller than one of simple majority must be empowered to make positive decisions for the collectivity. For example, suppose we choose to consider a 40 per cent decision-making rule. This rule, under our definition, would be operative when 40 per cent of the voters, *any* 40 per cent, are empowered to take action positively for the whole group. It is clear that the *same* rule could not also be applied to *blocking* action. If 40 per cent were also required to block action, then 40 per cent could not be defined as the "rule of the minority" at all. The rule for blocking action must always be $[(N + 1) - X]$ per cent, X being the percentage of the total group empowered to institute or to conclude positive action. Effective minority rule, therefore, must require a *majority* to block legislation proposed by the minority. Effective "rule" by the 40 per cent minority must involve the requirement that 61 per cent of the voters are required to veto action proposed by a minority.

When the orthodox theorist suggests that qualified majority voting amounts to "rule" by the minority, he is referring to the rule for blocking action. If this line of reasoning is carried to its logical conclusion, we get the paradoxical result *that the rule of unanimity is the same as the minority rule of one*. Thus the rule of requiring unanimity among members of a jury to acquit or to convict becomes equivalent to the rule that would permit any individual juror to convict or to acquit. Instead of being at the opposing ends of the decision-making spectrum, as our whole construction suggests, the unanimity rule and the rule of one become identical. This paradoxical result suggests clearly that the power of blocking action is not what we normally mean, or should mean, when we speak of "majority rule" or "minority rule."[3]

2. This is not to suggest that the distinction has not been clearly understood by political theorists and that its recognition has not affected political institutions. The executive power to veto legislation adopted by a representative assembly finds its basic rationale in the recognition of this distinction. Cf. Benjamin Constant, *Réflexions sur les Constitutions* (Paris: Nicolle, 1814), pp. 50f.

3. The tendency to slip inadvertently from one meaning into the other is well illustrated by a recent statement made by Anthony Downs: ". . . it is better for more voters to *tell fewer what to do than vice versa*. The only practical arrangement to accomplish this is simple majority rule. Any rule requiring more than a simple majority for passage of an act allows a minority *to pre-*

The distinction between the power of taking action and of blocking action proposed by others is an essential one; it represents the difference between the power *to impose external costs on others* and the power *to prevent external costs from being imposed*.

We may illustrate with reference to our familiar road-repair example. Let us assume that the constitution of our model township dictates that all road-repair decisions are to be made by a two-thirds majority. Under these conditions the power to institute action, lodged in any effective coalition of two-thirds of the voters, involves the power to impose external costs on the other one-third, either through the levy of taxes or the failure to repair certain roads to standard. One-third of all voters plus one have the power to veto or block any proposed repair project, but this power is effective only in the sense that a group of this size can prevent the additional taxes being levied. In no way can this minority group impose additional external costs on the other members of the group.[4]

THE PROBLEM OF BIASED RULES

We have not yet satisfied the hypothetical orthodox theorist.[5] He may conceivably accept all of our previous arguments but still try to stop us short by saying: What about the situation in which the issue confronted is whether

---

vent action by the majority. . . ." (Italics supplied.—Anthony Downs, "In Defense of Majority Voting," unpublished mimeographed paper written as a general critique of Gordon Tullock's paper, "Problems of Majority Voting," which was an early version of Chapter 10. In Downs' favor, however, it might be noted that he supports present procedures for the amending of the Constitution.)

On this general issue, see also Willmoore Kendall, *John Locke and the Doctrine of Majority Rule* (Urbana: University of Illinois Press, 1941), p. 116.

4. This conclusion assumes that individuals of the blocking coalition are rationally motivated. If, instead, these individuals should *all* be irrational, they might refuse to enter into "bargains" advantageous to them, and, by this refusal, they might be said to impose "external costs" on others. For example, suppose that a two-thirds majority rule is in operation. Suppose now that 66 out of 100 voters propose a project that will be genuinely beneficial to *all 100 voters*. To prevent this project from being adopted *all 34* other voters must be irrational. If only a few are irrational, the project will be carried. This example suggests that the rationality assumption is not important for the conclusions reached. Individuals will, by and large, tend to approve all proposals that provide them with expected net benefits. This relatively weak version of the rationality assumption seems to be all that is required.

5. Note that we refer to the orthodox *theorist*, not orthodox institutions. In the real world the overwhelming majority of democratic constitutions cannot, in fact, be amended by simple majorities. Many theorists simply refuse to apply their theoretical structure to constitutions.

or not a change in the rules should be made? Here the alternatives are mutually exclusive: change or no change. Moreover, should the established order (the *status quo*) operate in such a way as to benefit special minority interests, then surely the qualified majority rule for changing the "constitution" will allow the blocking power of the minority to be controlling. In effect, the maintenance of things as they are amounts to genuine "minority rule."

This argument gets us to the heart of the whole discussion of majority rule as a doctrine of popular sovereignty, to which we referred earlier in this chapter to some extent. We have discussed the applicability of the unanimity rule at the stage of making original constitutional decisions. At any point in time subsequent to the formation of the original "contract," the social organization must be presumed to be operating within the framework of certain established rules. These organizational rules define the way in which certain collective decisions will be made, including decisions to change the "contract." If these basic rules suggest that, for some decisions, more than a 51 per cent majority is required for positive action, it is surely the established order of affairs that may be said to be "ruling," and not the particular minority that may or may not be securing "benefits" through the continuance of this established order.

This is not to suggest that the established order must prevail for all time, once it is accepted, nor that, either at its beginning or at any particular moment in time, this order is necessarily "optimal." The "social contract" is best conceived as subject to continual revision and change, and the consent that is given must be thought of as being continuous. However, the relevant point is that change in this "contract," if it is desirable at all, can always find unanimous support, given the appropriate time for compromise.

Again we revert to the game analogy. We may, if we like, think of players as being continually engaged in two kinds of mental activity. First, they are trying to figure out moves or strategies with which their own interests can be advanced within the context of a well-defined game. Secondly, and simultaneously with this activity, they can be conceived as trying to figure out a possible change in the rules that would make for a better game. In this second activity they will realize that they must choose rule changes on which all players can agree if the game is to continue. A proposed change in the rules (or in the definition of the game) designed especially to further individual or group interests, majority or minority, would be recognized to be impossible. The other players could simply withdraw from the game.

Our conception of the constitutional-choice process is a dynamic one quite analogous to the game mentioned above. We do not conceive the "constitution" as having been established once and for all. We conceive the contractual aspects to be continuous, and the existence of a set of organizational rules is assumed to embody consensus. We think of the individual as engaging continuously both in everyday operational decisions within the confines of established organizational rules and in choices concerned with changes in the rules themselves, that is, constitutional choices. The implicit rule for securing the adoption of changes in these organizational rules (changes in the structure of the social contract) must be that of unanimity. This is because only through the securing of unanimity can any change be judged desirable on the acceptance of the individualistic ethic.

This does not imply, as is so often suggested, that the requirement of unanimity on changes in the rules (on the constitution) embodies an undue or unwarranted elevation of the *status quo* to a sacrosanct position. In the first place, the idea of *status quo* in terms of established organizational rules is hazy at best. The stability of the established rules for organizing public and private decisions does not, even remotely, tend to stabilize the results of these decisions measured in terms of the more standard variables such as income, wealth, employment, etc. The municipal-zoning ordinance may be accepted by all parties until someone has the opportunity to sell his own property to a developer at a huge capital gain. At this point in the sequence, the individual standing to gain would certainly desire a change in the rules to allow him to exploit this unforeseen opportunity, but it is precisely because this sort of thing is unforeseen that the zoning ordinance can be adopted in the first place. *Ex post*, the individual faced with the opportunity to gain is likely to object strenuously to the *status quo* (that is, to the zoning ordinance), but securing a variance for one individual alone is equivalent to changing the rules of the ordinary game to the strategic advantage of one player. In the continued playing of the "social game," individuals will each confront situations in which they desire, strategically, to change the rules; but it is because these situations are distributed stochastically that agreement becomes possible. If a change in the rules (a change in the *status quo*) is mutually beneficial, it will, of course, be adopted. Empirical evidence from the operation of voluntary organizations suggests that rules are often changed.

An individual need not, of course, accept the "contract" that exists. He may rationally consider the rules to be undesirable. Faced with this conclusion, two choices remain open to him. He may seek to convert others to his point of view, and, if arrangements can be worked out through which all others come to agree, the "constitution" can be changed. Secondly, the individual may choose to reject the "contract" entirely; he may revert to a "state of nature"—in this case a revolt against established social order. On ethical grounds the individual must always be granted the "right" to make such a choice, but, once he has done so, the remaining members of the group have no contractual obligation to consider the revolutionary to be subject to the protections of the "contract." This "right of revolution" is not modified as it extends beyond the single individual to a minority or even to a majority of the population. In this, as in other aspects of our construction of the constitutional implications of a consistent individualistic philosophy, the shifts in the fraction of the population approving or disapproving certain changes are not of central importance.

PART IV

THE ECONOMICS AND THE ETHICS OF DEMOCRACY

CHAPTER 18

DEMOCRATIC ETHICS AND ECONOMIC EFFICIENCY

Are politics an attempt to realize ideals, or an endeavor to get advantages within the limits of ethics? Are ethics a purpose or a limit?
—Lord Acton

The failure to separate positive analysis and normative ethical statements has been one of the major barriers to scientific progress in political theory. Rarely does one encounter so much confusion between "what is" and "what ought to be" as in this field of scholarship. Our analysis is not, of course, free of value judgments. In the introductory chapters we have explicitly stated the fundamental postulates on which our construction is based. We have tried to outline, in an admittedly preliminary and exploratory fashion, the calculus of the rational utility-maximizing individual as he confronts what we have found useful to call constitutional choices. This whole calculus has meaning only if methodological individualism is accepted, and this approach must embody philosophical commitments. Unless the individual human being (or family unit) is accepted as the central philosophical entity, and this acceptance requires an ethical judgment, our analysis is of little value. Many scholars refuse to accept this premise, and propose instead to adopt some organic conception of the social group. This alternative conception embodies the individual as a part of a larger whole and attributes to him varying degrees of ethical independence. Under this conception several theories of political constitutions may be developed, and these theories may be useful in explaining and predicting the evolution of certain political institutions in certain circumstances. We do not propose to argue in favor of our own individualistic conception or against the organic one. We repeat merely that, having stated our premises explicitly in this respect, no objection should be raised against our construction on the grounds that it neglects the "ethos of group life."

THE BEHAVIORAL ASSUMPTIONS

We must also emphasize that our behavioral assumptions do not properly introduce an ethical question. We have tried to apply the economist's assumptions about human behavior in an analysis of political choice. There is nothing moral or ethical about an analytical assumption. Disagreement may appropriately arise concerning the empirical validity of the utility-maximizing assumption, but this is a matter that may conceptually be subjected to empirical testing through the comparison of the real-world implications of hypotheses developed on the basis of this assumption and real-world observations. No issue of "right" or "wrong" in an ethical sense need be introduced at all.

Compared with the more standard works in political science, our analysis may seem to involve a "pessimistic" view of human nature. For scientific progress, however, it is essential that all conceivable assumptions about human behavior be tested. If our models provide some explanations of real-world events, and we believe that they do, our assumptions must have some empirical validity, quite apart from the "attractiveness" of the human characters that inhabit our hypothetical model world.[1]

In one sense our approach taken as a whole is more "optimistic" than that taken by standard writers in political theory. Our assumptions about human nature may be judged "pessimistic," but our conception of the political process, as such, is surely more congenial to those seeking "sweetness and light," "peace," and all such good things than the conception usually implicit in political discourse. We view collective decision-making (collective action) as a form of human activity through which mutual gains are made possible. Thus, in our conception, collective activity, like market activity, is a genuinely *co-operative* endeavor in which *all* parties, conceptually, stand to gain. By contrast, much of orthodox political thought seems to be based on the view that the collective-choice process reflects a partisan struggle in which the beneficiaries secure gains solely at the expense of the losers. If the political "game" should be, in fact, similar to that conception which seems to be implicit in much discussion, especially that concerned with the doctrine of majority rule, the maintenance of political order must depend, in fact, on the strength of moral restraints placed on human actors. If, by contrast, a broader and, we think, a more "correct" conception of political choice is adopted, there need be less reliance on moral restraints of individuals.

1. The persons in our analytical models may seem to be ethically unattractive, but it should be noted that intellectually they are considerably more "attractive" than the human beings included in more orthodox models of political behavior.

THE ETHICS OF TRADE

In our analysis we have assumed that individuals are motivated by utility-maximizing considerations and that, when an opportunity for mutual gains exists, "trade" will take place. This assumption is one of the foundations on which economic theory is constructed. Let us examine some of the ethical issues that may arise in the operation of ordinary market exchange before considering the much more complex problems inherent in this approach to the political-choice process.

Initially it seems useful to distinguish two separate stages in the organization of economic exchange, although in practice these two stages are simultaneous and the two decisions made by the individual participant are interdependent. First, the individual must decide to enter into an exchange relationship, and, secondly, he must agree to the specific terms at which exchange shall take place. The point to be made here is that, in normal discussion, ethical issues are considered to arise in the second decision, but not in the first. In Chapter 8 we discussed the simple two-person bargaining model in some detail. Where a bargaining range exists, the terms of trade will determine the division of the total benefits among the participating parties. Moreover, since this division is essentially a distributional question, the whole problem of "fair shares" arises, a problem that can only be discussed in terms of ethical norms.

As we suggested in our earlier discussion, this admittedly ethical problem is reduced to a minimum in the operation of competitive markets because the proper functioning of a market organization will insure that the single buyer or the single seller has little control over the terms of trade. If the terms of trade (the conditions of exchange) are set independent of the individual participant's own behavior, no ethical question can arise concerning his "fairness" in dealing with other parties to exchange, ruling out fraudulent behavior. Thus we find that ethical issues about market behavior present themselves only when individuals or groups are in noncompetitive positions, when they possess some power to influence the terms of trade in their favor.

In ordinary exchange no ethical question is presumed to arise concerning the decision of the individual to *engage in trade*, regardless of whether or not he possesses independent power to influence the terms of trade. Moreover, a moment's reflection suggests that there could hardly be an ethical issue posed regarding this sort of behavior. Not only is the individual presumed to secure some benefit by entering into trade, but he must also be providing benefit to the other parties in the contract. On almost any set of ethical norms, trade would seem to be an activity that would be accepted as fully consistent with the moral standards of the community.

It is difficult for the modern student of social progress to keep in mind the fact that this apparently obvious interpretation of trading activity has only been dominant since the eighteenth-century Enlightenment. Before that time, "trade," as an activity, was suspect; and, implicitly, individuals engaged in trade were somehow supposed to be following less moral pursuits than other members of society. This suspicion of trade, as an activity, still dominates the non-Western world and has not yet entirely disappeared from Western thought. Some of the elements of such suspicion can perhaps explain the neglect of the study of the political process in terms of an "exchange" relationship.

Under what conditions is "trade" or "exchange," even in the modern world, considered to be immoral in and of itself and quite apart from the terms of trade? To begin with, we must recognize that each person has certain moral standards, and these normally will include certain criteria for human behavior. An individual may consider it perfectly moral behavior to sell his own labor services to a business firm, but he may think that it is grossly immoral for a woman to sell the services of her body to a man. An economist may consider it morally acceptable to sell his educational services to a university, but morally unacceptable to sell his professional services to a political party. Each person will have a set of such moral values, and these may include attitudes toward certain commodities or services that other people "ought" not to sell for "money." There is nothing inconsistent between the existence of such moral standards and an individualistic ethic until and unless the individual desires to *constrain others to conform to his own moral standard of behavior*. It is quite consistent for the individual to hold a set of values which dictates that a woman ought not to sell her body on the market, and at the same time to include within this set of values the attitude that he should not attempt to constrain the prostitute and her client from exercising their own free choices. In evaluating behavior in others which he thinks morally wrong, the individual, in effect, says: "I think that they are doing themselves harm by such actions; but, since I value freedom of individual choice and since there is no harm imposed on me by their actions, I do not wish to interfere by placing constraints on their behavior."

Note that this attitude is to be distinguished from a second one in which the individual thinks that other individuals, through behaving in a way that he considers immoral or unethical, are actually reducing his own utility. If an individual interprets the prostitute plying her trade in this way, her activity is, in a real sense, imposing external costs on him. However, even when external costs are imposed on third parties, we must distinguish two separate reactions. The individual may recognize that the activity is imposing external costs on him, but he may also recognize that constraints on this activity may open up the way for other collectively imposed constraints, some of which may affect him directly and adversely. Looking at the problem in this way, the individual may rationally choose to accept the external costs (the reductions in his own utility) which the free play of individual choice in the activity under consideration introduces.

We must distinguish this attitude from that of another individual who holds somewhat stronger views on the immorality of the activity in question, say, prostitution. This individual may rationally seek collective action aimed at preventing the activity from taking place. In reaching a decision of this kind, the individual evaluates the external costs that the activity imposes on him and estimates that these are sufficiently great to offset all possible adverse collective decisions that might be taken against some of his own accepted practices were the State allowed to legislate on moral issues. In this case the individual must consider the external costs to be high enough that he is willing to pay some positive sum in order to secure elimination of the activity. In this sense he must be willing to "trade" something in return for the elimination of the activity under consideration. In many cases, of course, moral standards would become significantly weaker than they initially appear if those who hold them were asked to contribute positive sums toward the elimination of that behavior in others which they condemn as immoral.

Normally, of course, there is sufficient standardization of moral values over the population of a community to prevent serious issues of the sort posed from arising. Most trade falls within the accepted moral schemata of the great majority of the population. Nevertheless, it should be acknowledged that there is never a sharp dividing line between the many trading or exchange activities that are generally accepted and the relatively few genuine trading activities that may be suspect.

EXCHANGE OF POLITICAL VOTES

This discussion of the morality of exchange is helpful because it points directly toward one interpretation of prevailing attitudes on the exchange of votes in Western societies. Individual votes on political issues seem to be among the scarce commodities or services that many members of the community consider inappropriate for open buying and selling. The free marketing of votes, either by an individual or by a member of a legislative assembly, is considered to be an activity in which individuals "ought not" to engage. This attitude toward the marketability of political votes, interpreted in the sense of outright vote-buying and vote-selling, seems to be an empirical fact. The attitude toward vote-trading through indirect methods is considerably different.[2] Our task, therefore, is to examine the logical basis for this combination of attitudes, if indeed one exists.

Why should the rational individual consider the sale and purchase of votes among his fellow citizens to impose external costs on him, that is, to reduce his own utility? Suppose that A observes B selling his political vote on an issue to C. Why should A's utility be affected by this transaction? B and C mutually gain from the exchange, or else it would not take place. One approach would suggest that A's utility is reduced (that he bears external costs) because the transaction gives to C political power that C would not otherwise possess. If open buying and selling were to be permitted, A could have an equal opportunity with C to purchase the vote of B. However, what is meant by "equal opportunity" in this case? If the distribution of *economic* power among the citizens is unequal, open buying and selling of political votes might be said to give "unfair" advantages to the richer members of the group. To be sure, both the poor (exemplified by B), who would find their over-all economic position improved by selling their political decision-making power, and the rich (exemplified by C) would gain from the vote exchange. However, *if majority voting prevails*, A can be more readily exploited by the votes of B and C in a coalition "owned" and organized by C.

This argument, which is probably characteristic of much orthodox thinking, would seem to contradict some of the conclusions reached earlier to the effect that full side payments (that is, open vote-buying and vote-selling) would tend to *reduce*, not to increase, expected external costs from the operation of decision-making rules. We are obliged, therefore, to examine the argument quite carefully. Again we may use a simple illustrative example. Figure 25 shows the location of three families, A, B, and C, in a community. The

2. The prevailing attitude seems to be quite closely related to the "grossness" of the form that vote-trading activity takes. Truman notes that legislatures and constitutional assemblies have, on occasion, defined vote-trading as a crime, and the Mississippi constitution of 1890 required all legislators to take an oath that they would not engage in vote-trading activity. (David B. Truman, *The Governmental Process* [New York: Alfred A. Knopf, 1951], p. 368.)

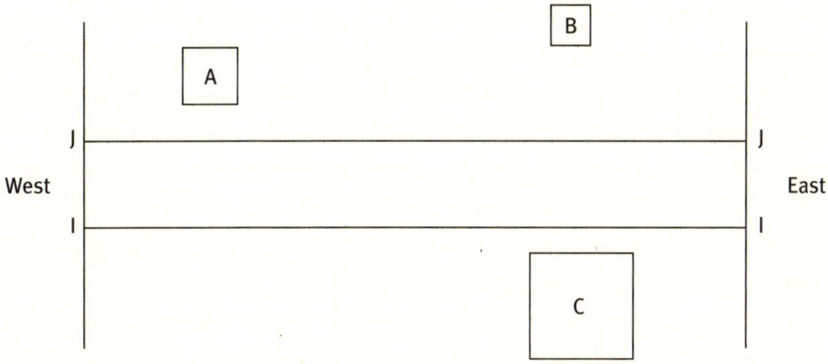

FIGURE 25

sizes of the squares indicate the economic position of the three families; for simplicity, assume these to be houses. Suppose now that the community is granted sufficient outside funds to construct one road to be run horizontally from the western to the eastern boundary of the territory. If open vote-buying is allowed, C may purchase B's vote and, by *majority rule*, choose the road shown as II in Figure 25. On the other hand, if all vote-buying and vote-selling should be prohibited, A and B might form the majority and construct the road shown at JJ. This road, being closer to both A and B, would seem to be a more "desirable" choice on the grounds that "political equality" is more nearly satisfied by this decision than by the alternative one.

This line of reasoning is quite convincing, up to a point, and it does tend to contradict some of our earlier conclusions. It does so, however, only because *the market is assumed to be imperfect*. If, instead, the vote market is assumed to be perfect in all respects, A and B might well form the majority coalition, as in the no-trade case, but *they would still construct the road at II*. They could, by acting as a coalition, force C to purchase both of their votes (or to pay as much for one as if two were purchased) and to pay an amount sufficient to reduce his own net gain to zero (a negative sum if the road is to be tax financed). A, acting as a "political entrepreneur," could offer B just as much for his vote as does C under these circumstances, because he would be aware that he will have the opportunity to sell both votes (as one) to C. One additional transaction or "bargain" would be required in this solution, but with perfect markets this will be no barrier.

It seems evident, however, that some *imperfection* in the vote market might arise, and, in this case, bargains or trades between C and B would seem much more likely to emerge. Expecting this, the rational individual may consider the open buying and selling of votes to impose an external cost on him.

If we consider the question of vote-marketing at the time of constitutional choice, differences in economic position are not predictable. Therefore, to generalize our discussion we need to allow, not for predictable differences in economic position, but for differences in interest on particular issues, which may or may not be based on differences in economic status. The individual, considering organizational rules, may well think that vote-marketing, if it could operate perfectly, would reduce expected external costs. However, he may also predict imperfections in this market which may more than offset this advantage. With expected market imperfections of a certain type, the individual may choose rationally to try to prohibit the open buying and selling of political votes.[3]

If the market imperfections are expected to take the form of the exclusive exchange of votes between the most interested and the least interested groups, with the absence of "political entrepreneurs" or "vote brokers" in the mildly interested groups, the individual may expect interest coalitions to solidify and to become permanent. The basis on which his constitutional decisions rest may be changed if he does, in fact, expect permanent coalitions to form.

Closely analogous to this is the operation of competitive markets. If, in fact, markets could be expected to work perfectly, there would never be any need for the State to intervene with antimonopoly legislation. The firm securing a monopoly position temporarily would tend to be restrained in its efforts by the emergence of other firms producing closely related goods and services. Any restriction on the freedom of firms to merge, to enter into pricing agreements, etc., would, under these conditions, amount to a denial of "gains from trade." However, when it is recognized that certain types of agreement may lead to the establishment of market-power positions that are not readily displaced due to the imperfect operation of the mechanism of adjustment, it becomes reasonable to seek prohibitions on such agreements.

There are two separate reasons why such agreements should be prohibited under these circumstances. First, once attained, the firms may be able to ex-

3. Note that the central point made here is precisely equivalent to that raised in connection with the symmetry in gains among the members of a dominant majority coalition in Chapter 12. Symmetry may only be predicted with reasonable certainty if side payments operate perfectly. With partial, but incomplete, side payments, symmetry no longer seems essential for "solution."

ploit their bargaining advantage; they may be able to secure an "unfair" share of the total gains from trade by manipulating the terms of trade in their favor. This is not, however, the relevant part of the antimonopoly analogy for our purposes. Here the aim of intervention is not that of prohibiting trade, but rather that of insuring more acceptable terms of trade. The second reason for trying to prevent the attainment of positions of dominant market power lies in the expected ability of firms, once having attained this power, to prevent the emergence of other rival groups (competitors). This reason, which is the central theme in the legal if not in the economic history of the antimonopoly laws, seems closely analogous to the argument that we have developed above regarding the open buying and selling of votes in the market. The individual may not have sufficient confidence in the perfection of the vote-market's operation; he may fear that open buying and selling will quickly lead to the emergence of specific interest-group coalitions, which will tend to become permanent and which will possess the power to prevent the emergence of alternative patterns of coalition formation.

The whole institution of vote-buying and -selling is exceedingly difficult to analyze because of the unique nature of the items traded. A vote in the collective-choice process, operating under less-than-unanimity rules, represents potential power to impose external costs on other individuals. There are few fully acceptable analogies in the operation of ordinary markets. The potential power exists, of course, whether or not the individual holder places it on the market. Thus it is relatively easy to see why moral and ethical questions of major import tend to arise when any consideration of vote-trading is introduced.

THE IMPERFECT IDEAL

We recognize, however, that some forms of vote-trading are accepted as being consistent with the prevailing moral standards in Western democracies. The individual calculus in this respect—if prevailing attitudes can be taken to reflect rationally reached conclusions—suggests that, in reference to the whole issue of vote-trading, the "ideal" is neither "none" nor "all" but somewhere in between. As the analysis above indicates, if market imperfection is expected to be present and if the results of this imperfection can be predicted in advance, the placing of prohibitions on open buying and selling of political votes may be quite rational. If a full and open vote-trading market, where transactions take place in money, could be predicted to result in the most interested individuals and groups purchasing votes from the least interested on all or a substantial number of issues, then the rational utility-maximizing individual might expect such an institution to result in unbearable external costs or even in the overthrow of the constitutional system, the "social contract." On the other hand, the individual might also recognize the advantages to be secured from vote-trading under certain circumstances. Indeed, if all vote-trading were prohibited, he would probably be unwilling or at least quite reluctant to agree to any less-than-unanimous decision-making rules for collective choice.[4] He may consider, therefore, that the "optimal" amount of vote-trading is provided by that system which prohibits open markets in political votes as such but which sanctions indirect methods of accomplishing roughly the same purposes. The opportunity to trade votes on separate issues through logrolling, explicit and implicit, provides an essential protection to interested minorities against discriminatory legislation. The value of this protection may be widely acknowledged, and at the same time the "open" sale of votes may be condemned as immoral. We have shown that this attitudinal pattern need not be internally inconsistent, even within the limited framework of the individualistic ethic.

The conflict between democratic ethics and economic efficiency need not, therefore, exist in so distinct a form as it might have appeared at earlier stages of our construction. Economists recognize that unrestricted trade can be guaranteed to lead to greater "efficiency" in resource usage only if markets are expected to operate perfectly. If imperfections are predicted and the characteristics of these imperfections can be identified, specific restrictions on trade may, under certain conditions, actually increase "efficiency." These restrictions will rarely, however, extend to the prohibition of all trade.

This is not to imply that the existing set of legal prohibitions and restrictions (along with the existing moral attitudes toward the exchange of votes) is necessarily that set which the rational utility-maximizing individual "should" support. Our purpose has been that of indicating that this set is not necessarily inconsistent in itself, and that the possible conflict between ethical standards and economic efficiency is not demonstrated.

We are aware, of course, that other arguments can be developed to justify the moral attitudes on vote-trading that seem to exist. We neither wish to deny the value of these arguments nor to compare them with those we have presented. For our purposes, which are those of developing the implications

4. Alexander Hamilton is said to have remarked that the British Constitution would fall when corruption came to an end. See Sir Henry Maine, *Popular Government* (New York: Henry Holt, 1886), p. 102.

of rational individual behavior in political choice-making, the other arguments are irrelevant. Much of the orthodox discussion has been based, as we have suggested, on different assumptions about the behavior of the human actor in the political process. If individuals are assumed not to try to further their own interests but instead to seek some "public interest" or "common good" when they participate in collective choice, the sale of a vote becomes clearly immoral since the receipt of a money payment provides definite proof that the individual is receiving "private" gains from his power to participate in political action. Much of the standard attitude toward vote-trading probably stems from this approach to the governmental process. We note only that the immorality of vote-trading in this context is wholly different from that which we have considered in some detail above, and much behavior which seems to be accepted as standard practice in modern democratic institutions must also be held to be immoral on this alternative approach. It would be interesting to examine the full implications of the behavioral assumption which holds that the individual always seeks the "public interest," but, as Frank Knight has often observed, no one has yet provided us with an analysis of the organization of a society of angels.

VOTE-TRADING AND THE RULE OF UNANIMITY

The analysis of vote-trading above applies only when collective decisions are made under less-than-unanimity voting rules. If the unanimity rule is required for collective action, the political vote of an individual no longer represents the potential power to impose external costs on other individuals. Here the vote represents only the "right" or the "permit" to participate in the division of the mutual gains that collective organization and action can secure. This major change in the very meaning and significance of the political vote of the individual modifies the analysis of vote-trading.

If, for all collective decisions, all members of the group are required to agree, there would seem to be no rational basis for imposing any prohibition on the purchase and the sale of political votes of individuals. The dangers discussed above, those of permanent power blocs being formed, no longer can exist since the effective coalition on all issues must always consist of all members of the group. Prohibitions on vote-trading under the unanimity rule serve only to create inefficiencies in the use of collective resources. An illustrative example may be helpful. Suppose that all vote-trading were to be strictly prohibited and that the rule of unanimity is operative for all collective action. Any proposal that stands a chance of adoption must include within a single "package" elements that provide net benefits to each individual and group in the community. In order to organize such a "package" proposal, many rather wasteful and inefficient projects may have to be included. If open vote-trading were to be allowed, there would be no need for any genuinely inefficient projects to be undertaken. True "pork-barrel" legislation would never be observed under this institutional scheme. With vote-trading prohibited, this sort of "pork-barrel" legislation would be quite prevalent under the operation of the unanimity rule, although it would be present under other voting rules also. However, under these other voting rules this "pork-barrel" inefficiency must be compared with the greater danger of permanent coalition formation that open vote-buying and vote-selling might encourage. This second danger, or cost, is wholly absent when the rule of unanimity is operative.

THE RENT-CONTROL ANALOGY

We may construct, without difficulty, an economic analogue to the prohibition of vote-trading. This analogue serves perhaps to bring out clearly the nature of the questions raised by our whole approach to the political process.

Assume that, in a ten-man (family) community, a new apartment unit is to be made available by the municipal government. There are six units in this apartment building, and the rentals are strictly controlled, being established at a predetermined level. Suppose further that this rental price is below the demand price of each of the ten families in the group. In other words, every one of the families will desire to move into the new subsidized housing if possible. We should also expect, however, that demand prices for this opportunity will vary over the ten individuals in the group. Some families will be relatively satisfied with their current accommodations and thus would secure relatively little net advantage from the new opportunity. Other families will find that the net advantages from residence in the community housing project would be substantial.

Now assume that no plan for rationing the six available units is adopted. The municipal authority simply announces that the first six families to sign up on a particular morning will be assigned the units. It is clear that a queue will form on the designated day, and also that no predictable configuration can be placed on this queue. Let us suppose that a queue forms which is like that shown in Figure 26. Individuals 5 through 10 will be successful in securing the desired housing, and Individuals 1 through 4 will be left to live in their current residences. This result seems to be almost precisely equivalent

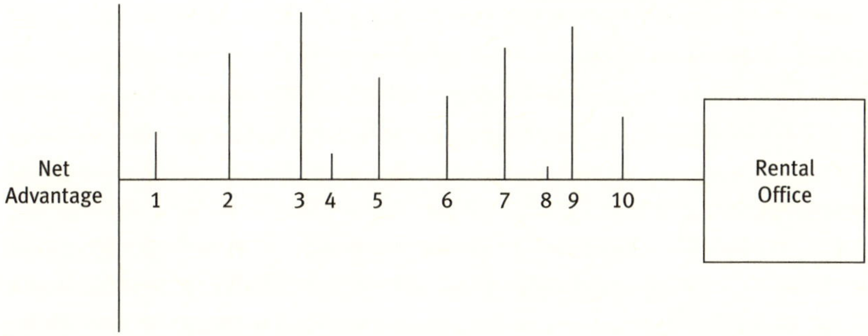

FIGURE 26

to the operation of simple majority voting when no vote-trading of any kind is allowed to take place. Individual 8, for example, who receives only a slight net advantage, secures, nevertheless, one of the municipal units. Similarly, in the analogous political process the individual who cares relatively little about the outcome on a particular issue counts for as much as any other individual.

Let us now modify our example. Suppose that housing permits are to be issued. Since only six units are present, permits totaling to six are to be made available. However, assume also that the municipal authority does not choose to discriminate among the various citizens. Following the principle of "housing equality," the authority therefore issues a permit of 6⁄10 to each family, but it encourages the buying and selling of these permits among families. No one can secure an apartment unit unless he presents to the authority one full permit; no family can secure an apartment under these circumstances unless it purchases additional permits from others. We assume that fractional permits are marketed in units of 1⁄10. The result is readily predictable; queuing will no longer determine the outcome. Individuals 2, 3, 5, 6, 7, and 9 will secure the apartments. Individuals 1, 4, 8, and 10 will sell all of their permits. All members of the group are better off as a result, and a Pareto-optimal solution is attained Pareto optimally (if we neglect the costs of organizing the exchanges). This example seems precisely analogous to that political voting rule which requires unanimity but which allows for full side payments (full vote-buying and vote-selling). Note especially that "political equality" is maintained in the sense that each man is given an equal "vote" at the outset.

Let us now introduce a third version of our rent-control illustration which will be analogous to simple majority voting with full side payments (open vote-trading). As before, assume that housing permits are issued equally to all families. However, assume that, instead of 6⁄10 being issued to each family, each family is now given one full permit. Thus, the authority issues more permits than there are apartments available for disposition. Full purchase and sale of permits is encouraged during a period prior to the announcement of a date for distributing units among permit holders. As in the first case, units will be allocated to the first six individuals presenting permits on one designated day. However, prior to this time, those persons desiring the community housing most strongly will be able to "purchase" additional permits to prevent their losing out in an allocation solely by queue. It is easy to see that this "market" will not work nearly so smoothly as in the previous example. While the market in permits will tend to insure that the six families desiring the municipal housing most strongly will end up with the available units, there is nothing in the operation of this market that will insure that each of the ten families gains in the over-all operation. Only six of the families will be certain to secure net gains (although more could do so), and these six need not be the same ones who finally secure the housing units. They may be fully "squeezed" by other families who are better "vote brokers." The reason for this difference in result is that, finally, four of the permits originally issued will prove to be of zero value at the time of assignment. Those families caught holding the worthless permits will gain nothing at all.

These rent-control analogies seem helpful in pointing up the issues of democratic ethics. In the second example, full vote-trading would seem to be desirable, and little ethical argument could be advanced against it. This is because the institution of trading here not only insures greater efficiency in the allocation of housing space but it also insures that every family in the group secures some positive benefits. This last result is due to the equivalence with the unanimity rule of choice. If we move to the third example, the analogue with simple majority voting, the case for allowing open vote-trading is considerably less strong. While the open marketing of votes may insure increased measured "efficiency" by guaranteeing that those families securing the apartments will be those desiring them most strongly, this advantage may be more than offset by the secondary inefficiencies stemming from the free operation of the vote market.

CONCLUSIONS

The interesting conclusion is reached that, under our behavioral assumptions, vote-trading per se cannot be condemned on the basis of a rational individualistic ethic but that *vote-trading under rules for collective choice requiring less than full agreement* among all members of the group may be condemned. The fact that the political vote of the individual is wholly different in these two cases makes for an extremely important difference in the attitude of the rational individual toward vote-trading. In the one case, the vote represents the potential power to impose external costs on other individuals in the group, and it is because of the fear that market imperfections may cause this power to become solidified into permanent or quasi-permanent coalitions that the individual may choose to restrict in some way the institution of vote-trading. In the other case, when unanimity is required for action, the vote does not represent the potential power to impose costs on others. No offsetting reason arises to oppose the efficiency reason for allowing full and free marketing of political votes.

This distinction is very similar to that made in discussing ordinary economic transactions. For the most part, these transactions directly affect the parties participating in exchange to the exclusion of third parties. Such transactions are, therefore, fully accepted as falling within the standard behavior patterns of democratic society. Trade is not suspect under these conditions. This is equivalent to saying that the group unanimously approves trade of this sort. Ordinary market exchange is, in a real sense, equivalent to the political rule of unanimity. On the other hand, trade does become subject to question when the services exchanged (produced) come to represent the power to affect third parties adversely, that is, to impose spillover or external costs on individuals outside the contractual relationship. Somewhat interestingly, however, the form of the suspicion is rather different in the two cases of political and economic decision-making. When economic or market activity is observed to result in the imposition of costs on parties outside the exchange relationship, economists have tended to call attention to the "inefficiency" in over-all resource usage that this organizational arrangement generates. They seem rarely to have brought into question the morality or ethics of the individuals participating in such activity. Individuals are assumed to seek to maximize their own utility within the limits of the effective constraints imposed on their action. Not bringing the underlying motivational assumptions into question, the economist tends, therefore, more or less automatically to think in terms of modifying the set of constraints on individual action (the redefining of property rights, the changes in the legal structure, etc.) with a view toward eliminating the inefficiencies, if possible.

By contrast, the student of political processes, observing what is essentially the same phenomenon in another form (that is, the imposition of external costs on third parties), has not considered the inefficiency aspects seriously. Instead he has—through his emphasis on moral restraints on self-interest, his concept of the "public interest," etc.—sought to accomplish reform through a regeneration of individual motives. Ethical and not structural reforms tend to be emphasized. Breakdowns and failures in the operation of the system are attributed to "bad" men, not to the rules that constrain them.

CHAPTER 19

PRESSURE GROUPS, SPECIAL INTERESTS, AND THE CONSTITUTION

Perhaps the clearest answer offered was . . . by Mr. Bane . . . there is no public interest in the sense of being an interest of the whole public. There are only particular interests. . . . The panel did not accept this solution, and Mr. Bane did not defend it.

. . . Mr. Larsen asked whether it was not true that the means of obtaining the objectives, rather than the objectives themselves, was the issue. . . . Perhaps the process, the means of compromise and agreement, are themselves a large part of the public interest.

—*Major Economic Groups and National Policy*,
The American Round Table, Digest Report

In large political units the institutional manifestation of the active promotion of economic interest is the pressure group. The reason for the very existence of such groups lies in their ability to promote and to further, through the political-choice process, the particular functional interests represented. The emergence of such groups to positions of dominant importance during the last half century has been one of the most significant developments in the American political scene. This fact, which can no longer be hidden from view or considered as an aberration to orderly political process, has understandably weakened the predominance of the traditional model of democratic choice-making institutions. In the face of observable pressure-group activity with its demonstrable results on the outcome of specific issues presented and debated in legislative assemblies, the behavioral premise that calls for the legislator to follow a selfless pursuit of the "public interest" or the "general welfare" as something independent of and apart from private economic interest is severely threatened. Empirical reality must have its ultimate effect on analytical models, even if this reality contains implications about human behavior that scholars with strongly held ethical ideals find difficult to accept.

In recent years the role of the pressure or special-interest group in democratic political process has come to be more widely accepted as inevitable, if not "desirable." In 1951 David B. Truman, building on the earlier work of

Arthur Bentley and to some extent on that of E. Pendleton Herring, made a bold attempt to construct a positive theory of American politics on the basis of an acknowledged interplay of group interests.[1] In 1958 an interesting, if abortive, effort to examine the role of the pressure group was undertaken in a round-table discussion at the University of Chicago.[2]

SPECIAL INTEREST AND THE "PUBLIC INTEREST"

Most attempts to examine the role of pressure groups have bogged down in their efforts to define the "public interest." If this cannot, in fact, be defined, it becomes impossible to determine, even conceptually, the extent to which the activity of special-interest groups either advances or retards progress toward the "general welfare." Analysis becomes impossible without a well-defined criterion. Our essentially economic approach to the political process is useful in that it allows us to escape from the ambiguities surrounding the concept of the public interest. The literature of modern welfare economics is especially helpful in this respect. The discussion in this field has clarified some of the more troublesome issues that seem to arise. One approach recognizes that definitive meaning can be attached to "social welfare" or the "public interest" only if a social-welfare function is fully described. This function conceptually orders all possible states of society, and quite unambiguously allows for the selection of the "best" or from a restricted set of available alternatives, the relatively "best." However, in order to describe this function, some individual must make quite explicit his own value judgments. There is no escape from the responsibility of individual ethical decision. In this construction the "public interest" is what the individual says it is. Moreover, each individual will have a meaningful conception of what he conceives to be the public interest; there will be as many social-welfare func-

1. David B. Truman, *The Governmental Process* (New York: Alfred A. Knopf, 1951). See also Arthur Bentley, *The Process of Government* (Bloomington, Ind.: The Principia Press, 1935 [first published 1908]), and Pendleton Herring, *The Politics of Democracy* (New York: W. W. Norton and Co., 1940).

For a discussion of recent European works on the problem of pressure groups, see Wilhelm Röpke, " 'I gruppi di pressione' e l'ultima istanza," *Studi economici*, XIV (1959), 480–85. See especially Joseph H. Kaiser, *Die Repräsentation organisierter Interessen* (Berlin: Duncker and Humblot, 1956).

2. *Major Economic Groups and National Policy*, The American Round Table, Digest Report (Chicago, 1958).

tions as there are individuals in the group. "Social welfare" or the "public interest" does exist, for the individual, as something apart from and independent of special group interests, but the usefulness of this approach disappears when we come to those issues on which individual evaluations of alternatives differ.

We have rejected this approach. Instead of initially developing a social-welfare function which unambiguously orders all social situations, we start from the presumption that we are quite ignorant as to what is "better" or "worse" for the group. Falling back on the Pareto criterion for assessing changes, we admit as "better" only those changes that are observed to be approved unanimously by all members of the group. Any change that secures unanimous support is clearly "desirable," and we can say that such a change is "in the public interest." Few would, we suspect, dispute this half of our criterion for evaluating social changes. However, we go further and state that, for *any* change *in* the public interest, unanimous support can be achieved. This half is perhaps less acceptable until the economic meaning of "improvement" is fully understood. If the political process is conceived as one means through which individuals co-operate to attain mutual advantage, it is clear that, conceptually, all persons can be made "better off" by any change that does, in fact, produce sufficient "improvement" for mutual advantage to be possible.

Our unanimity criterion does not, however, seem to get us very far toward a definition of the public interest in any practical applications of this term. Actually we observe day-to-day decisions being made on other-than-unanimity rules for choice. Is there no criterion by which we may judge whether or not specific changes are or are not "desirable"?

At this point our construction becomes equivalent to that conception of the public interest raised by Mr. Roy Larsen in the Chicago round-table discussion and cited at the beginning of this chapter. There is clearly no way of determining the degree to which the public interest is advanced by the operation of ordinary rules for legislative decision-making on any single issue. Here we should expect only particular or group interests. We expect that some of these will be advanced and that others will be thwarted. The "public interest" becomes meaningful only in terms of the operation of the rules for decision-making, and these rules can be evaluated only over a long and continuing series of separate issues. Our conceptual and analytical separation of the constitutional and the operational level of collective decision allows us to discuss the unanimous choice of rules and at the same time to recognize the arbitrary results that will be produced by the operation of any given rule on specific issues.

At the ultimate constitutional level of decision, the implied requirement of consensus prevents the partisan struggle among group interests that characterizes operational decisions. If identifiable and permanent coalitions are expected, genuine constitutional process, as we have defined this term, is not possible. We do not, of course, deny that conditions may be present in which separate class or group interests are so solidified that no democratic constitution can be chosen for the community. However, we should emphasize that at the ordinary operational level of decision, within defined constitutional rules, pressure-group conflicts are fully consistent with the democratic process. Indeed it is precisely because the individual anticipates that economic interest will manifest itself in the operation of ordinary collective choice-making rules that he is willing to choose processes that involve considerable investment of resources in strategic endeavor. Our analysis is not, therefore, inconsistent with a structure of political institutions closely approximating those found in Western democracies. If, in fact, the individual could be "trusted" not to follow economic interest, and if all pressure groups could be assumed away, there might be, on some grounds, considerably less strength in the argument for many of the checks and balances that characterize modern democratic process.

PRESSURE GROUPS AND BIG GOVERNMENT

The activities and the importance of special-interest groups in the political process are not independent of either the over-all size or the composition of the governmental budget. A hypothesis explaining the increasing importance of the pressure group over the last half century need not rest on the presumption of a decline in the public morality. A far simpler and much more acceptable hypothesis is that interest-group activity, measured in terms of organizational costs, is a direct function of the "profits" expected from the political process by functional groups. In an era when the whole of governmental activity was sharply limited and when the activities that were collectivized exerted a general impact over substantially all individuals and groups, the relative absence of organized special interests is readily explainable. However, as the importance of the public sector has increased relative to the private sector, and as this expansion has taken the form of an increasingly differential or discriminatory impact on the separate and identifiable groups of the population, the increased investment in organization aimed at securing differential gains by political means is a predictable result.[3]

This relationship is not, however, one-sided. While the profitability of investment in organization is a direct function of the size of the total public sector and an inverse function of the "generality" of the government budget, both the size and the composition of the budget depend, in turn, on the amount of investment in political organization. The organized pressure group thus arises because differential advantages are expected to be secured through the political process, and, in turn, differential advantages for particular groups are produced because of the existence of organized activity. A spiral effect comes into play here, the results of which may be observed in the federal income-tax structure, federal tariff legislation, federal resource-development projects, and many other important areas of economic legislation in particular. This spiral effect has an important bearing on the individual constitutional calculus, and it is therefore worth discussing in some detail.

Conjecturally, and certainly not without considerable historical validity, we may imagine a government that undertakes only those activities which provide *general* benefits to all individuals and groups and which are financed from *general* tax revenues. Under these conditions there would be relatively little incentive for particular groups of individuals to organize themselves into associations designed specifically to secure special advantages through governmental action. Suppose now that this institutional "equilibrium" is disturbed through the efforts of one particular interest group, which organizes in an attempt to secure the adoption of favorable legislation. Assume that, through some means of side payments, this group is successful in its activity. It secures the passage of legislation which provides the group represented with special benefits that are not applied *generally* to the whole population. The measure adopted protects a specific industry, exempts a particular form of association from the antimonopoly laws, grants differential tax privileges, or any of the many other commonly accepted current practices.

The results will be that total collective action is increased and, secondly, that the door is opened for differential class-, group-, or sectional-interest legislation. Other functional or interest groups, observing the success of the first, will now find it profitable to invest resources (funds) in political organization. The pressure group, as such, will rapidly become a part of the political decision-making process. Moreover, because of the activities of such

3. Cf. Röpke, "'I gruppi di pressione' e l'ultima istanza," 484.

groups, the range and the extent of collective action will tend to be increased. As more and more groups come to recognize the advantages to be secured by special political dispensation, this organizational process will continue. The ultimate "equilibrium" will be reached only when all groups have become fully organized.[4]

PLURALISTIC EQUILIBRIUM

Many modern students of pressure-group phenomena seem to rely on this "equilibrium" and expect it to produce, if not "optimal," at least "satisfactory" results. It is often noted that the individual will simultaneously be a member of several organized interest groups: his trade union, his church, his local political unit, etc. Moreover, because of this multiple membership he will restrain the self-seeking activities of any particular group to which he belongs. Some such restraint cannot be overlooked, but it must also be acknowledged that few, if any, single individuals will be members of *all* groups simultaneously, and, even disregarding this, membership in separate groups will generate *different degrees of individual interest*. The fact that the member of the trade association or the trade union is also a consumer will not effectively restrain his activities in seeking differential advantage for his particular producer group because of the predominant importance of his producer role with respect to any single decision that the government might confront relating to the specific industry.

The difficulty is not removed if we postulate that each functional group has "equal power." In this case mutual "exploitation" will proceed to take place under ordinary democratic processes. Discriminatory legislation will continue to be adopted. The only difference between this situation and that in which "power" is distributed unequally among organized groups, and between organized groups and the unorganized members of the community, is that the costs will tend, over time, to be distributed over the whole population somewhat more "equitably." In this "equal-group-power" model, all groups will, over a whole sequence of issues, bear roughly the same share of the total costs of pluralistic organization. This conclusion is readily demon-

4. For an instructive analysis of the modern pressure-group problem in terms of its historical development out of economic liberalism, see Professor Goetz's briefs paper, "Some Economic Aspects of Pluralistic Society," delivered at the meeting of the Mt. Pelerin Society in Oxford in September 1959.

strated by referring to the simple logrolling model developed in Chapter 10. In that model we may substitute a single group interest for each individual farmer, thus guaranteeing "equal power" to each group, and then examine the results. Given any collective decision-making rule other than that of unanimity, external costs will tend to be imposed by collective action. Differential or group legislation is precisely equivalent to the special road-repair projects financed out of general-tax revenues which were introduced in the model of Chapter 10.

EXTERNAL COSTS AND "OPTIMAL" ORGANIZATION

As we have repeatedly emphasized, the existence of external costs imposed by the operation of the rules for making collective decisions is neither a necessary nor a sufficient condition for "nonoptimality" in an organizational sense. The advantage of our construction lies in the fact that we are not required to explain away the effects of the special-interest groups in describing the "optimal" organization of collective decisions. Pressure- or interest-group activity is one institutional manifestation of external costs, and external costs are expected to be present even in the "ideal" organization. The question remains, however, as to whether or not the existing organization reduces the over-all interdependence costs (external costs plus decision-making costs) to the lowest possible level. Saying that external costs will be present in the "ideal" organization is not equivalent to saying that any organization embodying pressure-group activity is, in any sense, "ideal."

No direct measurement of the total interdependence costs under existing or alternative decision-making rules is readily available. Certain conclusions can be drawn, however, on the basis of the facts of history. We may observe a notable expansion in the range and extent of collective activity over the last half century—especially in that category of activity appropriately classified as differential or discriminatory legislation. During the same period we have witnessed also a great increase in investment in organized interest-group efforts designed specifically to secure political advantage. These facts allow us to reach the conclusion that the constitutional rules that were "optimal" in 1900 are probably not "optimal" in 1960. If we may assume that the fundamental rules for organizing collective decisions were more closely in accordance with the "ideal" in 1900 than in 1960, these same rules will tend to produce a higher level of interdependence costs than necessary. This suggests that some shifting in the direction of more inclusive decision-making rules for collective choice and some more restrictive limits on the range of collective activity might now be "rational" to the individual considering constitutional changes. The contrary possibility, of course, also exists. If the operation of existing constitutional rules produces roughly "optimal" results today, clearly these *same* rules were overly restrictive in earlier stages of development marked by relatively less organized pressure for differential legislation.

We express an explicit value judgment here, but we consider the first alternative interpretation to be more applicable to American society. Moreover, because of this judgment we consider the external costs imposed by the operation of existing rules to be excessive. Nevertheless, we can also be somewhat optimistic, over the long run, regarding the prospects for securing some genuine improvements in political organization. If, in fact, the organization of special interests has advanced to the point at which no one interest can expect, in the long run, to secure differential advantage, the way may be open for some changes in the organizational rules themselves. Each interest group will, of course, turn every effort toward improving its own position, *within the limits of the prevailing rules;* but if, in fact, all interests come to recognize that the external costs involved in this continuous struggle of interests are excessive, all might agree on some changes in the rules that allow such behavior to take place. It seems doubtful whether American democracy has as yet reached this point of mutual recognition of the advantages to be secured from the requisite constitutional changes. However, as more and more groups organize to secure political support, and as more and more discriminatory action does come to characterize separate political decisions, reaction will surely set in at some point. We begin to see, perhaps, the beginnings of such reaction today with respect to income-tax legislation. More and more criticism is being raised against the maze of special exemptions and deductions that has come to characterize income-tax laws. Although the brief experience of late 1959 showed that, when actual changes of a more general sort are proposed, the special beneficiary groups are still sufficiently strong to retain the currently existing structure, the criticism is still likely to mount. While the excessive external costs involved in discriminatory tax legislation are perhaps more likely to be recognized than those involved in other legislation, the current discussion of tax policy does seem to bear out the prediction that could be made on the basis of our construction.

Ultimately the hope for some "improvement" must lie in the mutual consent of the special interests themselves for constitutional changes which will act so as to reduce the excessive costs that discriminatory legislation imposes on all groups over time. It is in seeking such changes in the organizational rules themselves that genuinely enlightened self-interests of these groups may be expressed. It seems sheer folly to expect that the interest groups will, unilaterally and independently, exercise sufficient self-restraint, given existing rules. To expect them to do so amounts to expecting them to act contrary to their *raison d'être*.

GENERAL AND SPECIAL LEGISLATION

If all collective action should be of such a nature that the benefits and costs could be spread equally over the whole population of the community, no problem of the interest group, and indeed few of the problems of government, would arise. If each individual, in his capacity as choice-maker for the whole group, could, in his calculus, balance off a pro-rata share of the total benefits against a pro-rata share of the total costs, we could expect almost any collective decision-making rule to produce reasonably acceptable results. Under these relatively "ideal" circumstances, individuals and groups would have relatively little incentive (because there would not exist much genuine possibility) to utilize the political process to secure advantage over their fellows. However, few collective decisions, if any, can be reduced to such general dimensions. Almost any conceivable collective action will provide more benefits to some citizens than to others, and almost any conceivable distribution of a given cost sum will bear more heavily on some individuals and groups than on others. As the analyses of Chapters 10 through 15 have shown, it is the opportunity to secure differential benefits from collective activity that attracts the political "profit-seeking" group. Moreover, these differential benefits may be secured in either of two ways. First, activities may be approved which cause benefits to accrue to selected individuals and groups but which impose costs generally on all members of the community. This was illustrated by our initial road-repair examples. Secondly, activities may be approved which provide general benefits to all members of the community but which impose costs on certain selected individuals and groups. The necessary condition for the presence of external costs, as we have used this term, is some difference in the distribution of the benefits and costs of collective action among members of the community.

One means of modifying the organizational rules so as to produce results akin to those that would be produced under truly "general" legislation would be to require that those individuals and groups securing differential benefits also bear the differential costs. This legislative generalization of the benefit principle of taxation would, in effect, produce results similar to those that would take place under "general" legislation. Note that this change in the rules need not be equivalent to requiring a larger majority or unanimity, although the results need not be significantly different from those produced by such changes. While the requirement of unanimity would tend to insure that all collective action is based on a "benefit principle" of sorts, the requirement that the benefit principle be followed need not insure that all proposals receive unanimous support. The reason for this difference is that presumably in the second case "benefits" would be measured or estimated in some manner that would be independent of the individual's own evaluations. Therefore, a practical equivalent to the unanimity rule might be, say, majority voting under reasonably strict constitutional requirements about the matching of special benefits and special costs, as measured in some reasonably objective manner. This inversion of the Wicksell scheme, in which he proposed the rule of relative unanimity in order to insure the matching of benefits and costs, would, in any case, reduce the external costs imposed by the operation of any given rule for collective decisions other than the unanimity rule. Moreover, for all issues of collective choice other than those in which redistributive objectives are of primary importance, some improvement could, conceptually, be achieved along these lines.

A practical example may be helpful here. Suppose that a constitutional requirement is adopted to the effect that all irrigation projects, all river-valley-development and flood-control projects, all harbor and inland waterway developments, and the like must be financed, at least in part, by the levy of a special income tax on residents of those areas directly benefited by the projects in question. The number of such projects approved, even under unchanged voting procedures, could either be reduced or increased. It would be clear that those projects failing to win support would be "inefficient" and should therefore be eliminated, provided only that the differential benefits and differential costs are measured with some degree of accuracy. If all areas of the country should become sufficiently "organized" in support of such localized federal resource-development projects, and if all units were in some proximate equality as to power, it would be in the genuine interest of all groups to implement constitutional changes of the sort illustrated. The fact that the interest or pressure group *as such* tends to develop an interest in continuing to exist will, of course, be a real barrier to such reform.

Analogous but different constitutional changes could be instituted which would reduce the excessive external costs imposed by the operation of special-interest groups in those cases where over-all redistribution objectives cannot be put aside. Many collective projects are undertaken in whole or in part primarily because they do provide benefits to one group of the people at the expense of other groups. These objectives may be quite legitimate ones, and they may be accepted as such by all, or nearly all, members of the community. However, the difference in the distribution of benefits and costs may result in excessive external costs quite independent of the accomplishment of the distributional objectives. For example, suppose that the issue confronted should be that of providing some federal funds to aid the depressed coal-mining area of West Virginia. For such a measure the levy of special taxes on citizens of West Virginia would be largely self-defeating. Nevertheless, it is relatively easy to see that, if such aid is to be financed out of general-tax revenues, a veritable Pandora's box may be opened. Depressed fishing villages along the Gulf coast, depressed textile towns in New England, depressed automobile production centers in Michigan, depressed zinc-mining areas in Colorado, etc., may all demand and receive federal assistance. As a result, excessive costs will be imposed on the whole population.

One means of eliminating this sort of distortion, which may appear somewhat farfetched because it is novel, would be to require that all such projects be financed out of taxes levied on specific groups in the total population, although *not* on the same group securing the benefits. For example, if the funds designed for aid to West Virginia were to be collected from special taxes levied on citizens of Oklahoma only, then we could be assured that roughly balancing political forces would determine the final outcome. Excessive external costs world be substantially reduced in this manner, and something roughly similar to the pattern of "general" legislation would emerge. Genuinely depressed areas, considered as such by the whole population, would tend to be provided with assistance without at the same time opening up the whole set of grants to areas not considered to be deserving of assistance. Congressmen from, say, North Dakota or Minnesota, in our example, would be confronted with two opposing partisan interests. Those representing West Virginia would try to secure favorable votes; those from Oklahoma would try to influence the Congressmen in the offsetting manner. Through the logrolling process some solution would be reached, and this solution would more nearly reflect "the public interest" than the alternative one which requires general-tax financing. There could, of course, be no assurance that "optimal" individual decisions would be reached, but it seems relatively certain that a somewhat closer approach to a set of "optimal" collective decisions over time could be produced in this way than under existing rules.

These suggestions are highly tentative and preliminary, as indeed are many which have been advanced elsewhere in this book. The consideration of mutually beneficial constitutional changes aimed at reducing the external costs imposed by the operation of special-interest groups in modern democratic process would seem to represent an extremely important and worthwhile activity for scholars in political science.

THE ETHICS OF PRESSURE-GROUP ACTIVITY

An analysis requires, first of all, a somewhat more widespread acceptance of special-interest or pressure-group activity as an inherent and predictable part of modern democratic process. In our analysis this activity is a predictable outcome of our fundamental behavioral assumptions. At least in this one respect, the facts of the real world lend support to the confirmation of our assumptions. Scientific progress in the analysis of politics cannot be made until this widespread activity is fully incorporated in the analytical models. Such an incorporation need not commit the analyst to either an acceptance or a rejection of the activity as morally "good" conduct on the part of the practitioners. The economist does not need to say that the individual "should" or "ought to" maximize his own utility; he starts from the assumption that the individual does do so, and that is all there is to it. The student of the political-choice process should do as much; if he does so, the pressure or interest group becomes an essential building block in any political "science."

CHAPTER 20

THE POLITICS OF THE GOOD SOCIETY

Political society is complex and many-sided; perhaps the first thing that should be said about any "theory" concerning the organization and the operation of this society should be to stress the limitations that any single explanation must embody. The theory that we have developed in this book has been based on the assumption that individuals are the only meaningful decision-making units, that these individuals are motivated by utility-maximizing considerations, and that they are well informed and fully rational in their choices. Yet we know that "groups" do exist as something apart from the individual members, that individuals are motivated by many considerations, and that individuals are far from being either well informed or rational in their political behavior. The apparently extreme assumptions of our analytical models would seem to restrict severely the descriptive, explanatory, and predictive value of our theory.

We are encouraged, however, when we observe the scientific progress that has been made in the study of natural phenomena and also in the study of economic organization. The real world of nature is also highly complex, and the assumptions introduced into the model of the physical scientist appear to be as remote from observable factual reality as those that we have introduced. Despite the apparent unrealism of his models, the physical scientist has been able to make significant progress toward uncovering laws that govern the natural world, and upon these laws he has been able to provide explanations and to make predictions that are verified by real-world events. The physical scientist is not, however, dealing with man, and the study of human beings in association with each other introduces a whole set of complexities that remain outside his realm. Social science can never be "scientific" in the same sense as the physical sciences. Nevertheless, the study of economic organization does have some legitimate claim to the status of a "science." Economic theory starts from basic assumptions about human behavior; each individual is assumed to attempt to maximize his own utility. Individuals are also assumed to be fully informed and to be rational in their behavior. On the basis of these assumptions a body of theory has been developed which does provide some satisfactory explanations of real-world phenomena. We know, of course, that in the economic as well as the political relationship, individuals are not entirely rational, they are not well informed, and they do not follow self-interest in all circumstances. Yet we can observe that people purchase more goods at lower prices, that wage rates for similar occupations tend to equality, that the return on investment will tend to be equalized in different employments, and many other propositions of "positive" economics that can be subjected to empirical testing.

In this book we have tried to extend the assumptions of the economist to the behavior of the individual as he participates in the political process. As we have suggested at several points, the explanatory value of our preliminary theory is considerably more limited than that of economic theory. We think, however, that the "theory," as developed here, does provide some "explanation" of certain aspects of political organization.

THE LOGICAL MODEL

Relevant theory is made up of two parts, and our construction embodies both of these. First, on the basis of certain initial postulates and assumptions, the logical consequences can be developed. This sort of theorizing is purely logical in nature and has no empirical relevance in the direct sense. Herein, theory resembles mathematics. Our approach to individual constitutional choice can be interpreted in this way. On the basis of the assumption that individuals do follow utility-maximizing rules of behavior and that they are fully informed and rational, we can work out the consequences of the various rules for making collective choices. To some extent this is what we have done in our simple models in earlier chapters. In this respect we should emphasize that the conclusions depend strictly on the assumptions introduced, and, barring logical errors in the reasoning, there can be no question as to the "truth" or "falsity" of the theory.

This pure logic of constitutional choice is unique only in that we have introduced assumptions that are different from those of other scholars. The important thing to note in this respect is that an infinite number of theories of this purely logical sort can be developed. The usefulness of the logical model depends solely on the relevance of the model to real-world issues.

THE OPERATIONAL MODEL

The only means of testing or verifying the logical structure lies in comparing some of the predictions that can be made on the basis of the theory with observations of the real world. At several points in the analysis we have referred to certain institutional facts that seemed to lend support to the theoretical model under construction. By and large, the operation of the political process in Western democracies suggests to us that our theoretical model does have explanatory value, but what is meant by explanatory value in this respect? If our theory is capable of explaining all conceivable configurations that might be observed in the real-world political process, then it is no theory at all. Adopting the conception of the logical positivists for the moment, we could then say that the construction is meaningless. In order to maintain that our construction has some operational validity, we must show that there are conceivable observations that would refute the fundamental hypotheses.

What observable real-world events could refute the hypotheses of the model? Obviously, we cannot directly observe whether or not individuals maximize their own utility. The statement that they do so is, in one sense, meaningless, or, to use a more acceptable term, nonoperational. Nor can we readily observe whether or not individuals act rationally. To test the empirical relevance of our construction we must, therefore, turn to the implications of these behavioral assumptions for the operation of political-choice processes and the evolution of political institutions. We should stress that we do not intend to develop in any exhaustive way the operational implications of our analysis at this point. We may, however, suggest a few tests.

If, for example, we should observe a social group operating under less inclusive rules for constitutional change than for day-to-day operational decisions, this would seem clearly to refute the central hypothesis of our theory. If we should observe single groups deciding unilaterally to give up special-privilege legislation, our hypotheses are refuted. If we could observe the oil industry pressure group petitioning Congress for an elimination of the depletion allowance, if we could observe the American watchmakers unilaterally petitioning the President to lower the tariff rates on Swiss and Japanese watch imports, if we could observe the California farmers actively opposing federal irrigation projects, then we should have clear evidence that some conception of the political process alternative to our own should be sought. These few examples are sufficient to suggest that our theory is an operational one; the hypotheses are conceptually refutable, and we can easily imagine observable events that would refute particular elements of the theory. The fact that the required events seem only remotely possible in our examples provides some indication that empirical support for our construction is relatively strong.

There exist, of course, certain other observable phenomena that clearly refute the testable version of our hypotheses. Insofar as these can be found and observed, our hypotheses are weakened. We have nowhere proposed or suggested that the "economic" approach can explain all aspects of the complex political process. We suggest only the much more limited hypothesis that the approach does explain certain elements of modern political activity that have previously been unexplainable with standard models.

THE IMPERFECT IDEAL

One of the more significant doctrinal implications of our construction lies in its implicit rationalization of a political structure that has never seemed to possess rigorous theoretical foundation. The analysis shows quite clearly that the "ideal" organization of activity may embody many and varying rules for making collective decisions, may involve considerable investment in decision-making costs, may include many of the so-called checks and balances, may allow considerable administrative authority on certain matters, may be quite restrictive as regards amendments to a written constitution, and may provide quite rigid protections to the so-called inalienable rights. The apparent inefficiency that this over-all system may seem to introduce when other criteria of organization are employed disappears in the construction that has been developed in this book.

This is not, of course, to suggest that the American experiment in constitutional democracy is the best of all possible political worlds. The purpose of this construction has not been to provide this sort of rationalization. It remains true, however, that in the course of this work the authors have come to appreciate more fully the genius of the Founding Fathers in the construction of the American system. We do not think that this genius can be wholly separated from its environment, which was also that in which the ideas of economic theory were initially developed. The rather bewildering complex of institutions that makes up the American decision-making system does not seem openly to contradict the fundamental hypotheses of our model. This is the extent to which our construction serves as a rationalization for what is, or perhaps more aptly stated, what is supposed to be.

We think, nevertheless, that this point in itself is a useful one. Our analysis, broadly interpreted, is quite similar in many respects to that of those scholars who have continued to express an implicit faith in the pragmatic, groping process that has characterized American democratic institutions. In an unsystematic way many of these writers have perhaps sensed the essential approach that we have been able to make somewhat more rigorous in this work. At the outset we suggested that our purpose was to provide some "theoretical determinacy" to the working of "individualist democracy." If we have done so, the supporters of this conception of democratic process will perhaps have a somewhat stronger theoretical base from which to defend their position against the continuing onslaughts of the proponents of "idealist democracy."

We hope especially that our theoretical construction will cause the student of political process, as well as the man in the street, to consider more carefully and more cautiously the proper place of majority rule in the constitutional system. The discussion surrounding this conception has been perhaps the most confused part of political theory. The failure to distinguish between the power of a majority to take positive action and the power to block action has caused qualified majority rule to be equated with minority rule. All of such arguments would have been more fruitful if it had been recognized that any decision-making rule, other than that of unanimity, is itself a choice that the group must make at the constitutional level. Moreover, it must be recognized that any rule imposes some costs. Once these simple elements of our theory are understood, majority rule becomes simply one rule among a continuous set of possible rules for organizing collective decisions.

THE POLITICS OF THE GOOD SOCIETY

We have argued that our theoretical structure does have some operational relevance in the understanding of modern political institutions and that it does provide some conceptual rationalization for the type of political complex represented by American constitutional democracy. We have not specifically answered the question as to whether or not the politics of the sort embodied in our theory is a part of the operation of a "good" society, and we should stand properly accused of intellectual cowardice if we should end this book without further comment on this matter. Accept the fact that some men, some of the time, do act so as to promote partisan private or group interests through political means; accept that our models do help to explain many of the results. However, are we prepared to say that these results are "desirable" attributes of the social order?

We do not intend to evade this question, but, before answering it, we should insist on some clarification of the issues. It is essential that it be understood that those characteristics which are "desirable" in the behavior of a person or persons are wholly independent of those characteristics that are "desirable" in an institutional structure. The moralist must be distinguished from the social philosopher. Our whole approach has concentrated on the institutional organization of social activity.

If we start from a rigidly conceived institutional organization, the only relevant variable becomes the behavior of individual human beings. Given any organization of social life, there are certain moral or ethical standards of conduct, and these may be discussed objectively and dispassionately. Under certain circumstances, widespread agreement may be reached regarding the content of a set of moral precepts or principles. For centuries the Judeo-Christian world has accepted certain ethical ideals, at least to some degree. Among these ideals has been the responsibility of the individual to make choices on the basis of an interest broader than that which is defined by his own selfish short-run gains. The familiar golden rule and the admonition to "Love thy neighbor" both express this principle.

Insofar as these ideals do motivate individuals, the differences among the results produced by separate organizational systems are reduced. Moreover, given any social organization that does allow for some "exploitation" of man by man (and none exists that does not), more acceptable results will follow from a greater devotion to these moral ideals. Indeed, a widespread adoption of Judeo-Christian morality may be a necessary condition to the operation of any genuinely free society of individuals.

Several qualifying points need to be introduced before proceeding further. Behavior in accordance with the precepts of the golden rule, literally interpreted, can lead to a conflict of individual interests that is equally as intense as that which would arise under the operation of pure self-interest. Christian idealism, to be effective in leading to a more harmonious social order, must be tempered by an acceptance of the moral imperative of individualism, the rule of equal freedom. The acceptance of the right of the individual to do as he desires so long as his action does not infringe on the freedom of other individuals to do likewise must be a characteristic trait in any "good" society. The precept "Love thy neighbor, but also let him alone when he desires to be let alone" may, in one sense, be said to be the overriding ethical principle for Western liberal society.

If we are to allow the individual to be free, however, we cannot be assured that he will always follow the moral rules agreed on by the philosophers as being necessary for harmonious social life. The individual may behave "badly," and, if he does so, he may gain "unfair" advantages over his fellows. This brings us squarely to the central issue. Should the social order be organized to allow moral deviants to gain at the expense of their fellows? Or instead, should the institutional arrangements be constructed in such a way that the "immoral" actor can gain little, if at all, by his departure from everyday standards of behavior? These questions are based on the acceptance of the "idea of progress" as applied to social organization, that is, on the assumption that social organization is subject to criticism and to change and that it can be "improved"—and presumably such change can modify the degree to which the individual actor who departs from morally acceptable behavior patterns can exploit his fellow men.

It should be emphasized that no social organization in which men (some men or all men) are allowed freedom of choice can prevent the exploitation of man by man and group by group. Our construction is helpful in that it enables us to illustrate this point quite clearly. The relevant choice among alternative institutions reduces to that of selecting that set which effectively minimizes the costs (maximizes the benefits) of living in association. The shift from market organization to political organization does not, in any way, eliminate the opportunity for specific individuals and groups to impose external costs on others. This extremely simple conclusion, which we have repeated many times, has not been adequately recognized. Market organization, however, is based on the idea that individuals will tend, by and large, to seek their own interest. This does not suggest that each and every participant in the marketplace is assumed to try to exert the maximum effort to secure short-run gains. It does suggest that the social philosophy of market organization recognizes this behavior as a possibility and that the organizational norms are based on the view that this sort of behavior can be channeled in such a direction that it becomes beneficial rather than detrimental to the interests of all members of the community. These organizational norms are misunderstood and grossly misrepresented in much of the critical discussion of the market order. This order is not, in any sense, organized on the principle that self-seeking activity is morally "good." There is no conflict between the philosophy of the market, which is a philosophy of social organization, and that of Christianity, which is a philosophy of individual behavior. The market order is founded on the empirical reality that not *all* men renounce self-interest, and that, because of this, the pursuit of private gain should be put to social use where this is possible.

The question that we have posed in this work concerns the possibility of extending a similar approach to political organization. Can the pursuit of individual self-interest be turned to good account in politics as well as in economics? We have tried to outline the sort of calculus that the individual must undergo when he considers this question. We have discussed the formation of organizational rules that might result from such a rational calculus. In our more rigorous analytical models we have adopted the extreme assumption that each participant in the political process tries, single-mindedly, to further his own interest, at the expense of others if this is necessary. We were able to show that, even under such an extreme behavioral assumption, something closely akin to constitutional democracy as we know it would tend to emerge from rational individual calculus. We believe that this in itself is an important proof that should assist in the construction of a genuine theory of constitutional democracy.

In developing this analysis we are not, in any way, glorifying the pursuit of self- or group interest by political means. Empirical evidence does seem to point toward this pursuit as an important element in modern democratic process. Our approach is based on the idea that, insofar as this pursuit of self-interest does take place, it should be taken into account in the organization of the political constitution. Only in this way can the institutional setting for collective choice-making be constructed so as to confine the exploitation of man by man within acceptable limits. We are convinced that man can organize his political society better by putting checkreins on his behavior in advance, checkreins which effectively restrain the behavior of the deviant from the "moral way"—behavior that may be observed only occasionally and temporarily but which may also be quite characteristic of real-world human beings.

To the extent that the individual, in his capacity as decision-maker for the group, is able to divorce himself from his own interests (his own set of values) and to take a broadly based attitude of Kantian scope, the external costs that any decision-making rule is expected to impose are reduced. We do not deny this possibility or even the common appearance of such an attitude on the part of individual electors or on that of legislators and administrators. Moreover, insofar as this attitude exists, somewhat fewer constitutional constraints on the operation of ordinary rules for collective choice may be dictated than would otherwise be indicated as rational. It should be stressed that moral restraint is a substitute for institutional-constitutional restraint, and in a society with more of the former there will be less need for the latter, and vice versa. Our quarrel with those who would rely primarily on the moral restraint of individuals to prevent undue exploitation of individuals and groups through the political process is, therefore, at base, an empirical one. The assessment of the nature of man himself will, or should, determine the respective importance that is placed on institutional-constitutional restraint and on moral limitations on the behavior of individuals in political society.

The assessment of human nature that is required here cannot, however, be limited to an observation of man's activity in the political process to the exclusion of his activity elsewhere. The modern critic of constitutional democracy who calls for more direct operation of majority rule cannot, at the same time, rationally condemn modern man for his attention to selfish and short-run interests in the nation's marketplace. If modern man is unduly interested in the emoluments of the affluent society (in creature comforts), he is not likely to shed this cloak merely because he is placed in a slightly different institutional complex. A shift of activity from the market sector cannot in itself change the nature of man, the actor in both processes. The individual who seeks short-run pleasures through his consumption of modern "luxury" items sold in the market is precisely the same individual who will seek partisan advantage through political action. The man who spends his time at the television set or in his automobile in private life is not the man who is likely to vote for more taxes to finance libraries, concerts, and schools. This simple point seems to have been almost entirely overlooked in the so-called "great debate" of the 1960's.

It is not surprising that our conception of the "good" political society should resemble that held by the philosophers of the Enlightenment. Our analysis marks a return to an integration of the political and the economic problems of social organization, and constitutional democracy in its modern sense was born as a twin of the market economy. With the philosophers of the Enlightenment we share the faith that man can rationally organize his own society, that existing organization can always be perfected, and that nothing in the social order should remain exempt from rational, critical, and intelligent discussion. Man's reason is the slave to his passions, and recognizing this about himself, man can organize his own association with his fellows in such a manner that the mutual benefits from social interdependence can be effectively maximized.

APPENDIX 1

MARGINAL NOTES ON READING POLITICAL PHILOSOPHY

by James M. Buchanan

Neither of the authors of this book is a full-fledged political scientist by disciplinary specialization and training. Moreover, even within the ranks of the acknowledged professionals, political theory and political philosophy constitute subdisciplines of substantial independence. It would, therefore, be presumptuous in the extreme for us to claim here that we have mastered even the accepted "classics" of political philosophy sufficiently to measure our own preliminary investigations and analysis against some wider criteria than our own subjective standards.

We are well aware, however, that the problems of social organization discussed in this book are among the most important that learned philosophers have debated throughout recorded history. Our work could, quite properly, be charged with serious omission if we should fail to include what must be, at best, relatively uninformed commentary on the classical treatment of some of these problems. Therefore, it appears useful in this Appendix to offer some marginal comments that have been prompted by a reading of some of the selected works in political philosophy. We hope that these notes will be helpful in relating our analysis to what has gone before and in pointing up the differences which, in our view, make the analysis contained in the main text of this book essentially unique.

POLITICS, MORALS, AND THE METHODOLOGY OF POLITICAL SCIENCE

"What ought to be" is the primary normative question. "What is" remains the basic positive one. The distinction has separated the moral philosopher on the one hand from the scientist on the other, but the dichotomy so achieved is too simple in relation to the problems that arise in political theory and philosophy. At the beginning of the text of this book, we stated that political philosophy has been concerned with what the State ought to be while political theory has been concerned with what the State is. Note that, even in such a purely introductory and nonrigorous statement, it was necessary to move beyond the simple form of the normative-positive dichotomy. A subject for the "ought" and "is," the State, was introduced; and this apparently slight change gives rise to a whole set of particularly difficult problems.

The State, or the polity, may be conceived as a set of rules or institutions through which individual human beings act collectively rather than individually or privately. That is to say, we may best describe what is normally called "the State" in terms that specify such rules and institutions. As we have previously emphasized, all attempts to make the State into more than this are regarded as falling entirely outside our frame of reference in this book. It seems unnecessary for us to compare our constructions with those of scholars who, at base, have adopted organic conceptions of collective life. A given set of rules describes a social organization, a political order. In discussing this order a useful, indeed an essential, line may be drawn between positive and normative theory. A positive science of politics should analyze the operation of an existing, or a postulated, set of rules for collective decision-making quite independent of the efficacy of this set in furthering or in promoting certain "social goals." A normative theory of politics should, by contrast, array the alternative sets of rules in accordance with their predicted efficiency in producing certain ends or goals which should be, if possible, made quite explicit. Normative theory must be erected upon and must draw its strength from the propositions of positive science, but it is only when this extension of normative theory is made that "reform" in existing institutions can be expected to emerge from specialized scholarship. Indeed the only purpose of science is its ultimate assistance in the development of normative propositions. We seek to learn how the world works in order to make it work "better," to "improve" things: this is as true for physical science as it is for social science.

Political science, normative or positive, is a science of human action; or, to adopt modern terminology, it is a behavioral science. The social order which is its subject matter consists, finally, in a network of human actions, human relationships. Moreover, individual behavior is not wholly predictable or predetermined, even when some allowance is made for stochastic variation. Individual human beings can make errors, and they can deliberately choose differently from the ways which, in fact, they do choose. Saying this, of course, commits us to a definite, but still debatable, philosophical position. However, the validity or the invalidity of presuming individual freedom of will is only indirectly relevant to the main point to be made here. This is that once individual behavior is introduced as a variable in the study of the social order under analysis, a second whole area of normative theorizing is opened. Moreover, as the whole history of political philosophy so amply demonstrates, it becomes very difficult to separate norms for the organizational structure—for the rules within which individual actions take place—from norms for regulating individual behavior itself.

The introduction of an analogy with the science of political economy may be useful in clarifying the distinction that is of central importance here. Here, as in politics, the study involves a social organization, the social order that relates the separate economic activities of individuals to each other. Here, also, a set of positive propositions may be derived, and, on the basis of these, normative propositions aimed at "improving" the working of the economy may be developed. However, students and scholars alike have continued to confuse this essentially appropriate normative theorizing with a second sort which relates to "improving" individual achievement in the operation of any specific economic setting. Many ill-informed scholars and students, especially those who work on the fringes of the discipline, conceive the study of economics to be aimed primarily at establishing norms for the earning of higher incomes by individuals and higher profits by business firms. The normative statements of economics are conceived to take the form of demonstrating to the individual what *he should* do (how he should behave) in order to further his own position in the economy vis-à-vis that of his fellows. Properly understood, this is not at all the subject matter of political economy: the latter is concerned with the norms for individual behavior only insofar as these norms determine individual action which, in turn, becomes data to the analysis of social organization.[1]

Having generated considerable confusion in economics, where by comparison the distinction is relatively straightforward, it is not surprising that the fully analogous but far more subtle distinction has been blurred in political theory. To compare the study of business administration with that of political obligation may appear ridiculous at first glance, but a moment's reflec-

1. The study of individual and business-firm behavior with a view toward establishing norms for improving strategic economic positions within a given organization of affairs is appropriately the task of "business administration." The point here is that this whole field of scholarship must be kept rigorously separate from that of political economy.

A similar analogy may be drawn from game theory, where the distinction has been more fully appreciated. The norms for individual-player strategy in a well-defined game must be kept quite distinct from the norms that may be advanced for "improving" the game itself through some change in the rules that describe it.

tion will reveal that methodologically the two are precisely analogous in their relation to economics on the one hand and to politics on the other. The science of politics, normative and positive, should be confined to the study of the political order. The positive aspects of this science should include the derivation of propositions that are conceptually refutable. The normative aspects should involve the construction of proposals aimed at securing "improvement" in the social organization (in the political order of affairs)—"improvement" being measured against some postulated set of goals derived, finally, from a fundamental ethical position. As with the science of economics, the behavior of the human actors in the process should be incorporated as data in the underlying positive analysis. There should be a sharp distinction made between the norms for ordering this individual behavior and those for improving or reforming the social order itself.

This basic distinction has never been made sufficiently clear. As a result the history of political theory-philosophy has been one of "politics *and* morals." Few modern theorists who discuss the underlying conceptual basis of polity have been able to free themselves of the compulsion to discuss political obligation. The obligation or the duty of the individual citizen to obey the law, to abide by the will of the majority, to act collectively in the "public" rather than in the "private" interest: these have occupied center stage in much of modern political philosophy.[2] These are, of course, vital and significant issues, but it should be recognized that they raise questions of *personal morality*. As problems, they do not belong properly in political theory. Political obligations, as accepted by the average citizen and as revealed in his political behavior, become (or should become) data to the political theorist. The task of the theorist here does not include the derivation of normative propositions relating to these duties of citizenship or these responsibilities of rulers. Along with the economist and other social scientists, the political theorist should take his human actors as he finds them.

It should once more be emphasized that this proposed separation of politics from morals does not suggest that the political theorist remain purely positivist. There remain normative aspects of political theory, quite apart from morals. These aspects relate to proposed "improvements" in the political order, in the institutions of politics, and *not* to improvements in individual behavior. Problems of social organization need not be moral problems.[3] The separation called for is not, however, so straightforward as the above

2. Cf. Isaiah Berlin, *Two Concepts of Liberty* (Oxford: Clarendon Press, 1958), p. 6.

3. Cf. Ludwig von Mises, *Human Action* (London: William Hodge, 1949), p. 2.

paragraphs might have initially suggested. The methodological breakthrough is complicated by the fact that questions or issues of political obligation (of personal morality) arise in two distinct places. First, there is the question concerned with individual obedience to or acquiescence to the sovereign will, independent of the manner in which this will is itself determined. Secondly, there are those questions concerned with the moral precepts to be employed in determining this will (in the making of the law): that is, the obligation, duty, or responsibility of the prince, the bureaucrat, the cabinet minister, the legislator, or even the ordinary elector, to act in a certain way in his capacity as decision-maker, law-giver, *for* the collectivity. Both of these obligations—that of citizen and that of ruler—involve moral issues, and both require the introduction of norms for individual behavior. It is relatively easy to see that if the State is conceived at base to be nothing other than a continuing embodiment of the sovereign will, and, further, if it is assumed that this will is the only meaning of law, any "improvement" or "reform" can only come through some change in the behavior of individuals. Under this conception of political order it becomes impossible to separate politics from morals.

The point to be made can be most clearly illustrated with reference to the genuinely absolutist ruler. Under such a regime, making the State what it "ought to be" in terms of any postulated ethical standard reduces quite simply and quickly to making the prince "behave" differently from the way that he does, in fact, behave. In this model it is not possible to separate the moral choices of the prince from the institutional setting within which these choices are made and implemented. There would be little point in making any attempt at separation in any case since, by hypothesis, the institutional setting itself can only be modified by the action of the prince himself.

The divorce of politics, as a science, from political obligation, as a moral problem, can only be accomplished if the institutions through which collective decisions are made are themselves subject to variation (to change) only as a result of a second or "higher order" kind of collective decision-making process. Only if the "constitutional" decision, as we have called it, can be separated from operational collective decisions (that is, from those decisions that are taken within predefined constitutional rules) can political science emerge independently from the rather murky discussions of political obligation. The achievement of this independence seems to have been one of the essential logical purposes or aims of the contractarian approach to political philosophy, despite its obvious shortcomings and despite the confusion that has served to obscure this aspect in modern discussion of contract theory.

As the political order is shifted away from absolutism and toward democracy, the distinction called for here can be more clearly made. A genuine "science of politics" can be developed that is almost wholly independent of moral philosophy. This "social" science can include both positive and normative elements, but the variables with which it deals are social institutions, rules of the political game, not human motives. Insofar as this science becomes normative, ethical questions must remain, but these do not pertain to precepts for ordering individual behavior in acceding to or participating in collective decision-making. Within "political science," so limited, the scholar who proposes to answer the question "What ought the State to be?" must first make an explicit ethical choice. The information that he provides to the external observer then becomes as follows: "Given these ends for society, the set of rules describing the political order that would come closest to achieving these ends is as follows. . . ." In this process the political scientist may specify the goals of social organization as broadly or as narrowly as he chooses. He may restrict himself to presenting his own personalized view of the "good" political society, always constructed from the behavior of real human beings rather than that of idealized "good" men. Or, by contrast, the political scientist may try, as best he can, to develop the normative implications of a set of ethical standards that he thinks should command widespread acceptance among all members of the social group. The point to be made is that, in either case, he must take men as they are, not as he would like them to be.

The normative aspects of the theory developed in this book are more restricted than either of those mentioned. We have tried to develop a "theory" of the political constitution. This theory is based on an analysis of specific rules for collective choice-making, given certain well-defined assumptions about human behavior in political action. On the basis of this analysis, we have then tried to answer the question: What set of rules *should* the fully rational individual, motivated primarily by his own self-interest, seek to achieve if he recognizes that the approval of such rules must embody mutual agreement among his fellows? Stated somewhat differently: What is the structure of the political constitution that will maximize "efficiency," in the broadest sense, for all individuals in the group, independently considered? As we have suggested earlier, the approach taken requires a minimum of ethical premises. We assume only that individuals are the relevant philosophical entities to be considered and that all individuals are to be considered equally capable of choosing. We have been concerned primarily with demonstrating the calculus through which constitutional decisions might be made, not with the precise configurations of the political institutions that might result from the calculus.

We have assumed that the individual whose calculus we have analyzed (the "representative" or the "average" individual) is motivated by self-interest, that his fellows in the constitutional decision are similarly motivated, and that, within the chosen set of rules for collective choice, individual participants are likewise directed. As we have suggested, this assumption about human motivation is perhaps the most controversial part of our analysis. It seems useful to repeat, in this methodological context, that, by making this assumption, we are not proposing the pursuit of self-interest as a norm for individual behavior in political process or for political obligation. The self-interest assumption, for our construction, serves an empirical function. As such, it may or may not be "realistic": this can only be determined by a comparison of some of the positive analytical implications with observable real-world facts.

From this rather elliptic discussion of the relation of political science to moral philosophy and the place of our own construction in this respect, we may now try to suggest some of those "classics" which seem congenial. It is perhaps clear that most of the so-called idealist theory-philosophy of political order is quite foreign to our approach. Writers in this tradition concern themselves more or less directly with questions of political duty or obligation. By our suggested classification these works belong in moral philosophy, and we should look to these, not for help in devising reforms in political institutions, but for guidelines of an individual ethic. It should not be surprising, therefore, that the most "sympathetic" or "congenial" works are to be found among the "realists" in the history of political doctrine. Initially we look to Glaucon in Plato's *Republic*, to Thomas Hobbes, and to Benedict Spinoza. Of these, and others within this tradition, only Spinoza's work seems to have much in common with our own, and only his seems deserving of special comment.

In his *Tractatus Politicus*, published posthumously in 1677,[4] Spinoza approaches the whole study of political organization in a way that seems surprisingly modern by our standards. First of all, men are assumed to be motivated solely by considerations of interest. This is an underlying assumption of the models through which Spinoza examines alternative organizational arrangements. He states, quite specifically, that human behavior is taken as an

4. Benedict Spinoza, *A Treatise on Politics*, trans. by William Maccall (London: Holyoake, 1854).

empirical fact and that he makes no attempt to attach either praise or condemnation to the behavior that he observes. Spinoza examines the various political institutions in terms of their efficacy in producing results which he holds to be desirable. To him, political institutions are variables subject to change and perfection, and he conceives the primary task of the political scientist to be that of analyzing the workings of alternative organizational structures and of making such recommendations for change as seem indicated. His work on the political order anticipates, in many respects, that of David Hume and that of Adam Smith on the economic order. Spinoza deliberately sets out to construct political institutions in such a fashion that individuals acting in pursuit of their own interests will be led, by the institutional structure within which such action takes place, to further the interests of their fellow members in the political group.

The constitutional and the operational levels of collective decision-making are clearly separated in Spinoza's work. For the latter, at least in his aristocracy model (his discussion of democracy was not completed), simple majority rule is acknowledged as appropriate for reaching decisions in legislative assemblies. For changes in the constitution, in the basic laws, "common consent" or relative unanimity is suggested. Spinoza's work, in many respects therefore, may be taken as the most appropriately chosen classical precursor to that of this book. It should be stated, however, that Spinoza's influence on our own ideas has been limited to his general and indirect effects on the Western intellectual tradition. In a specific sense, we have carefully reviewed Spinoza only after the completion of an initial draft of the main body of this book.

Although Spinoza is often described as a follower of Hobbes, we do not find Hobbes' work at all similar to Spinoza's in relation to our own construction. As we have suggested above, it seems essential that some separation of the constitutional and the operational level of decision be made before politics, as a social science, can be satisfactorily divorced from moral philosophy. If sovereignty is conceived as being necessarily undivided and indivisible, this essential separation cannot be made readily. The contractual apparatus, to Hobbes, becomes an excuse or a justification for political obedience of the individual and little more. Hobbes' construction is aimed at establishing a basis for political obligation, whereas Spinoza's construction becomes a genuine theory of political order that, more than most others, is largely divorced from all issues of obligation.

At this point, as elsewhere in this Appendix, it is necessary to refer to the work of David Hume. As we shall suggest in the following section, Hume did discuss issues of political obligation, and he made notable advances over the contractarian theorists in this respect. Hume recognized quite clearly, however, that the question of the obligation of the individual to obey the law was conceptually distinct from those questions that arise when alternative political orders are considered. He specifically divorces "political science" from "moral philosophy": indeed the title of one of his essays is "That Politics May Be Reduced to a Science."[5] In this essay he states that the purpose or aim of the checks and controls provided by the political constitution should be that of making it "the interest, even of bad men, to act for the public good."

RATIONAL CHOICE OF RESTRICTIVE RULES

As we have suggested, most of the important political philosophers have been concerned with the question of political obligation. In their discussions of this subject we may find points of departure that are helpful to an explanation of our work. John Locke and all of the writers who were responsible for developing the conception of "natural rights" made much of the distinction between the constitutional decision, which determines the rules for collective action, and the operational decision, which determines the shape of collective action within previously chosen rules. The individual, possessing certain inherent or natural rights, enters into a contractual relationship with his fellows, a relationship that is expressed in a constitution. The subsequent obligation of the individual to abide by the decisions made by the collectivity, so long as these are reached constitutionally, lies in his obligation to fulfill the contract once made. This basis of political obligation runs into immediate difficulty as soon as constitutional rules are made to apply to individuals other than those who might have been party to the original contract.

It is in this respect that the conceptions of David Hume appear most helpful, and they seem to have much in common with our own. Our basic analysis of the individual calculus that is involved in choosing among alternative organizational rules, in selecting a political constitution, has demonstrated that it will often be to the rational self-interest of the individual to select a particular rule that can be predicted to produce results on occasion that run

5. *Essays, Moral and Political: Selections*, included in *Hume's Moral and Political Philosophy* (New York: Hafner Publishing Co., 1948), pp. 295–306.

counter to the self-interest of the individual calculated within a shorter time span. By shifting the choice backward from the stage of the specific collective decision to the stage of the constitutional decision, we have been able to incorporate the acquiescence of the individual to adverse collective action into a calculus that retains an economic dimension and that can still be analyzed in nonmoral terms. In this respect our immediate precursor is Hume, who quite successfully was able to ground political obligation, neither on moral principle nor on contract, but on self-interest. Hume did this by resorting to the idea that the self-interest of each individual in the community dictates the observance of conventional rules of conduct. These rules, which may or may not have been formalized in contract, are necessary for the orderly conduct of social affairs. This argument, which does not base political obligation on contractual obligation, allows the primary difficulty of the contract theorists to be neatly surmounted. Not only is it to the initial interest of parties to agree on conventional rules if such rules do not exist, but it is also to the continuing interest of individuals to abide by the conventional rules in existence. Hume recognized, of course, that, *were it possible*, the individual's own interest would best be served by the adhering to the conventional rules of all other persons but himself while remaining free to violate these rules. However, precisely because such rules are *socially* derived, they must apply generally. Hence each individual must recognize that, were he to be free to violate convention, others must be similarly free; and, as compared to this chaotic state of affairs, he will rationally choose to accept restrictions on his own behavior.[6]

INDIVIDUALISM AS AN ANALYTICAL METHOD AND AS A SYSTEM OF SOCIAL ORDER

Many political philosophers, and especially those who have been concerned with the history of political doctrine, have not recognized the dual sense in which "individualism" may be employed as a descriptive noun identifying a theoretical-philosophical system. In the interest of clarity in discussion it seems useful to distinguish between individualism *as a method of analysis* and individualism *as a norm for organizing society*. The fact that, in the development of political theory, those who have adopted the individualistic method-

6. Henry D. Aiken seems to overlook this basic point in his otherwise excellent introduction to selections from Hume's writings. See Henry D. Aiken's introduction to *Hume's Moral and Political Philosophy*, p. xliv.

The relevant part of Hume's works is *Treatise of Human Nature*, Part II.

ology have tended for the most part to adopt individualistic norms for social organization has served only to compound this particular confusion.

Individualism as an analytical method suggests simply that all theorizing, all analysis, is resolved finally into considerations faced by the individual person as decision-maker. Regardless of the role of the individual in the actual social-choice structure—whether he be ruler or ruled—analysis reduces to an examination of his choice problem and of his means or opportunities for solving this problem. To this approach is opposed that which starts from the presumption that some unit larger than the single person, some group of persons that includes two or more members, is the entity whose choice problems are to be examined. In this approach the individual member becomes an integral and inseparable part of the larger entity, and an independent-choice calculus for the separate parts is presumed meaningless. The *individualistic* method of analyzing political and social action is contrasted with the *organic* method, and these methodological differences need not, indeed should not, necessarily carry particular implications concerning the normative rules for organizing society.[7]

One of the primary purposes of the contract theorists of political order seems to have been that of reducing the logic of collective organization to a logic of individual calculus, or, stated somewhat differently, of deriving a logic, an "idea of reason," as it was called by Kant, for collective organization from the individual-choice situation. These theorists asked the question: Can the existing organization of the State be "explained" as an outgrowth of a rational calculation made by individual human beings? In large part, the success or failure of the contract theorists should be assessed in these terms against their attempts to answer this question.

The individualist approach or method tends to obliterate any logical distinction or difference between the "public" and the "private" sectors of human activity. Collective action, along with private action, is motivated by individually conceived ends, and all action proceeds only after a mental calculus is performed by some individual or individuals. As decision-making or choosing bodies, individual human beings remain fundamentally invariant over the range of both private and public activity. All attempts of the political philosophers to distinguish sharply between "public right" and "private right" seem foreign to this approach.

7. For a discussion of "methodological individualism," see Ludwig von Mises, *Human Action*, pp. 41–44.

Our theory of constitutional choice is avowedly individualistic in this analytical-methodological sense. Therefore, we react sympathetically to the works of those political theorists who have most clearly discussed the logic of collective organization in terms of an individual calculus and who have specifically rejected the conceptual demarcation between public and private sectors of human activity in the analysis of this choice problem. Johannes Althusius, who wrote very early in the seventeenth century, must be noted especially in this respect, for he seems to have been the first scholar who attempted to derive a logical basis for collective organization from contractual principles that were held to be applicable to all forms of human association. Later writers of the seventeenth and the eighteenth centuries, within the general contractarian tradition, followed Althusius on this point, although the emphasis on the common logical basis for public and private association tends to become less pronounced in their works than it is in Althusius'.[8]

We find a similar emphasis in the writings of Christian Wolff in 1750. Wolff's work is also noteworthy because of his clear conception of the collective organization as a set of rules or institutions that are subject to analysis, to modification, and to reform. His method, like that of Spinoza, was that of examining *alternative* political institutions on which members of the community of rational individuals might agree jointly.[9]

The individualist methodology found another staunch defender more than a century later in A. Fouillée,[10] and his work is important for our purposes because he recognized, more clearly than most other writers, the distinction discussed in this section: that between individualism as a method of analysis and individualism as a norm for social organization. He recognized that there exists no logical inconsistency between *individualism* as a method of deriving principles of social organization and *collectivism* as a descriptive characteristic of this organization. As we have suggested, an individualistic approach is contrasted methodologically with an organic one. Either ap-

8. Althusius' basic work is *Politica methodice digesta* (1603–1610), ed. by C. J. Friedrich (Cambridge: Harvard University Press, 1932). I have also had the opportunity to consult in typescript a translation-in-substance of this work undertaken by Stanley Parry, C.S.C.

9. Wolff's ideas are discussed by J. W. Gough in his book, *The Social Contract* (2d ed.; Oxford: Clarendon Press, 1957), pp. 158–60. The original source is Christian Wolff, *Institutiones Juris Naturae et Gentium* (Halle, 1750).

10. Fouillée's work is discussed by Gough in *The Social Contract*, pp. 221–24. The particular work that seems directly relevant is A. Fouillée, *La Science Sociale Contemporaine* (1880).

proach may be employed conceptually as a means of presenting either *individualistic* or *collectivistic* ideas for social reform. Given certain underlying assumptions about human-behavior patterns, along with a specific ethical position, a collectivist political-economic order may be rationalized from a calculus of individual choice. Fouillée understood this, and he argued correctly that there was nothing internally contradictory in Fichte's position which tended to be both individualist (contractarian) and socialist (collectivist). In our terminology Fichte's position could be described as methodologically individualistic, up to a point, and normatively collectivistic. Among political thinkers Burke comes perhaps closest to representing the reverse position. As regards alternative systems of social order, Burke was anticollectivist. On the other hand, methodologically he was clearly anti-individualist, and he vigorously rejected all attempts to explain collective activity on the basis of rational individual choice.

It is perhaps not surprising that proponents of methodological individualism are to be found among French political theorists as a part of the reaction against the excesses committed in the name of Rousseau's conception of the "general will." Somewhat later than Fouillée we find the work of Leon Duguit. He rejected categorically the conception of "national sovereignty" as the foundation for a system of public law, and he attempted to construct an alternative system on the basis of the public-service State. Duguit saw the State, not as an organ of command exerting power over its subjects, but instead as a means through which public services may be provided to individuals. These services were said to be required because of the fact of social interdependence. To this point Duguit's approach is similar to our own, which, at base, defines the political relationship in terms of co-operation. Duguit failed, however, to recognize that different individuals and different groups may desire *different* "public services" from the collectivity. To him, "public utilities" assume an objective character which, presumably, reasonable men can discover without great difficulty. He did not consider, therefore, the problem of the proper extension of public services. As a result his conception of the "public-service" State can easily be employed to provide a theoretical foundation for the growth of what is sometimes called the "welfare State."[11]

11. See Leon Duguit, *Law in the Modern State*, trans. by Frida and Harold Laski (London: Allen and Unwin, 1921). Note especially the interpretation that Laski placed on Duguit's work in the Introduction.

REALISM AND RELEVANCE IN CONTRACT

The contract theory of the State can be interpreted as representing both an attempt to divorce political theory from moral philosophy and as an attempt to derive a logic of collective action from an analysis of individual choice. Since our own efforts embody both of these elements, it follows that our work falls within the broadly defined limits of the contractarian tradition. It seems useful, therefore, to discuss some of the criticisms that have been advanced to this conception and to try to relate these to our analysis.

Both the contractarians and their critics have been too much concerned with the origins of government. The contractarians have discussed the original formation of government out of the voluntary consent of rational, previously "free" men. Their critics seem to have considered the contractarians demolished when they showed that such an original contract was, for all intents and purposes, a purely intellectual construction with little or no basis in reality. The relevance of the contract theory must lie, however, not in its explanation of the origin of government, but in its potential aid in perfecting existing institutions of government. Moreover, viewed in this light, some version of contractarian theory must be accepted in discussion about matters politic.

The origin of civil government and the major influences in its development may be almost wholly nonrational in the sense that explanation on a contractual basis is possible. Societies form governments and change governments for a variety of reasons, many of which remain mysterious and far below the level of objective, scientific analysis. Political institutions, like languages, get changed, almost beyond recognition, by the gradual and largely unconscious modification imposed on them by the movement through time. In this sense political society can be said to develop and to grow organically; and, if the purpose of investigation is solely that of explaining such growth, there is perhaps little purpose in inventing anything like the contractual apparatus.

It is clear, however, that the uncontrolled and the uncontrollable process of historical development is rarely called on to explain *all* changes in political society. If all change, from some origin to the present and beyond, is presumed to take place independently of conscious direction, political science, as a positive-normative discipline, loses its purpose. If, in fact, political institutions are not considered to be subject to rationally chosen modification and change, it is surely wasted effort to try to explain uncontrollable change. On the other hand, if it is accepted that political society is "perfectible," that political institutions are subject to designed "improvement," the analysis of alternative possible changes and the selection of criteria through which actual or potential changes may be judged become highly important tasks. At this level the explanations of the origin of civil government and the reasons for the major nonrational developments of this government are almost wholly irrelevant. Discussion must be concentrated on the "margins" of variation in political institutions, not on the "totality" of such institutions, and the relevant question becomes one of criteria through which the several possible marginal adjustments may be arrayed.

The contract theory, in this context, may be interpreted as providing one such criterion. Adopting the criterion implicit in the contract theory, the analysis of political institutions asks: On what changes in the existing set of rules defining the political order can *all* citizens agree? This embodiment of the unanimity rule for all basic, structural reforms in political institutions, in the constitution, reflects the individualistic ethic in its broadest sense. Other criteria for judging changes in the political constitution may, of course, be advanced. These may range from the purely personal criterion of the scholar who asks: What changes in the existing set of political rules do I think should be made?—to the more complex criterion introduced by the scholar who asks: What changes in the existing set of political rules would be "best" for the "greatest number" of individuals in the group, as I interpret their interests? Note, however, that such criteria as these, and any others that might be employed, must introduce a stronger ethical postulate than the individualistic criterion that the contract theory embodies.

In this interpretation the contract theory of the State in political theory occupies a position that is analogous to the Pareto rule for assessing changes in the more technical discipline of modern welfare economics. It may be useful to recall the discussion of Chapter 12 in the text. To define a position as Pareto-efficient or Pareto optimal does not suggest that all changes that have moved the group to that position were themselves Pareto optimal. On the other hand, to define a position as nonoptimal does suggest that there exists a means of moving to an optimal position in a Pareto-optimal manner. Applying this fully analogous reasoning to the contractarian terminology, we may say that the definition of an existing set of political rules (the constitution) as reflecting consensus implies only that there exist no particular changes on which all citizens can agree. Analogous to the Pareto-optimality surface, which contains an infinity of points, the fact that an existing set of political institutions reflects consensus, so defined, does not in any way imply that this set, and this set only, is the only "optimal" or "efficient" government. There must exist also an infinite number (conceptually) of other institutional arrangements which would similarly embody consensus. By contrast, the definition of an existing set of institutions as nonoptimal in the sense that it does not reflect consensus means strictly that changes are possible on which *all* members of the group may agree.

This interpretation of the contract theory, which divorces the existence of consensus from the means through which the existing situation has been produced, allows Hume's criticism of the contractarians to be fully accepted without seriously weakening the usefulness of the construction itself in its provision of a meaningful criterion against which changes in political constitutions may be judged. Having advanced this "marginalist" interpretation of the contract theory, we do not suggest that an explicit statement of this interpretation is to be found in the writings of the contractarians. To our knowledge they did not make the essential distinction between the "total" and the "marginal" explanation of political constitutions. Strictly interpreted, therefore, their "theory" of government cannot be accepted. However, when an attempt is made to advance an alternative "theory," one which will provide a useful criterion for evaluating constitutional change that is, in fact, controllable, some modified "marginalist" version of the contract approach seems essential. It is in this latter sense that the constructions of this book may be classified as falling within the contractarian tradition.

THE ECONOMIC APPROACH TO A THEORY OF POLITICS

As we have suggested in Chapter 5, the relatively recent work of William J. Baumol[12] represents almost the only attempt to develop a theory of collective activity from the economic calculus of the individual citizen. Baumol's work, in one sense, developed the political implications of modern welfare economics, grounding the logic of State activity squarely and quite properly on the existence of external effects resulting from the private behavior of individuals. We believe that our work extends that of Baumol in two essential respects. First, as we have noted, the generalized-externality argument is applied to the constitutional problem, the choosing of decision-making rules. Secondly, the essentially economic approach embodied in the concentration on alternatives open for choice is more fully analyzed. The existence of exter-

12. William J. Baumol, *Welfare Economics and the Theory of the State* (Cambridge: Harvard University Press, 1951).

nal effects from private behavior has been shown to be neither a necessary nor a sufficient condition for collective action. A theory of collective action has been developed only after a careful consideration of the costs and the benefits expected to result from alternative organizational structures (alternative sets of rules).

In the literature of political theory-philosophy, a partial reading of which prompts this Appendix, it is not surprising that no narrowly conceived precursors to our work in this particular sense are to be found. The doctrinal developments in economics, on which our constructions are based, at least to some degree, have taken place during the period in which economics has existed independent of politics as a discipline. We do find, however, one rather neglected work in political theory that may be appropriately classified as being closely related to our own. It is again not surprising to discover that this work was written by one of the important figures of the Enlightenment and that it was completed during the last decade of the eighteenth century, although it was not published until a half century later. We refer to Wilhelm von Humboldt's *Ideen zu einem Versuch die Gränzen der Wirksamkeit des Staats zu bestimmen*.[13] Humboldt argued that the only legitimate sphere of collective action was that which included the provision of security to the individual against external attack and against the encroachment of his rights by his fellow men. The role of the State was that of removing or reducing the external costs of private action. As might be expected, Humboldt conceived the externality problem too narrowly. He rejected all efforts of collective action toward promoting the positive welfare of individuals. In so doing, he failed to recognize that, in an opportunity cost sense, the failure to take co-operative action when such is actually more "efficient" is precisely equivalent to the taking of positive private action that is detrimental to over-all "efficiency."

It is in his careful discussion of the logic of State action in those cases of demonstrable externality, however, that Humboldt reveals clearly what was, at base, an *economic* approach. He recognized that the mere existence of spillover or external effects resulting from private action did not justify State action: the decision must rest on a comparison of the costs, in terms of the greater limitation on individual freedom, and the benefits, in terms of the greater security provided by some collective limitations placed on private be-

13. Wilhelm von Humboldt (Breslau: Eduard Trewendt, 1851). English translation: *The Sphere and Duties of Government*, trans. by Joseph Coulthard (London: John Chapman, 1854).

havior.[14] He recognized that the function of theory in such cases cannot be that of laying down general rules; rather, this function must be that of "pointing out these moments of deliberation,"[15] that is to say, to outline the mental processes or calculus through which such decisions must be reached.

Humboldt seems almost alone in his very clear discussion of the voluntary arrangements that would tend to emerge to remove the external effects of private action—arrangements that we have discussed at some length in Chapter 5. He argued that, where possible, such arrangements are to be preferred to State action because of the unanimity that is implicit in all voluntary arrangements.[16] At the outset of his work Humboldt criticized other thinkers for their excessive concentration on the question concerning who should govern and their insufficient attention to the question concerning the proper sphere of government. He recognized clearly that these questions were closely related and that the first question was rather empty until and unless the second one was resolved. This criticism seems to hold with almost equal force against most of the modern works in political theory.

THE CLASSICAL CONCEPTION OF COLLECTIVE CHOICE

To our knowledge no political philosopher has approached the question of choosing among alternative decision-making rules in a manner that is similar to that which we have attempted to develop in this book. A partial explanation for this may lie in the very fact that those scholars who have been interested in political theory have been philosophers. As such, they have tended to think of collective decisions in terms of "will." If individuals differ in their desires for collective action, the decision-making rule must in some way determine whose "will" is to prevail. Individual or group interests, viewed in this way, tend to be treated as being mutually exclusive. Clearly the "will" of the majority and that of the minority cannot at the same time be prevalent. This whole approach to political process ignores or overlooks the possibility of quantifying individual or group interests. "Will" and "power" are terms that do not lend themselves readily to quantification.

By contrast to this "classical" approach, our approach is essentially economic, in that political decision-making is viewed, in the limit, as analogous

14. Ibid., p. 125.
15. Ibid., p. 126.
16. Ibid., p. 128.

to the determination of the terms of trade in an exchange. When individuals engage in trade, interests differ. Each individual desires to secure the most favorable terms of trade. However, no one draws from this the conclusion that the separate interests are mutually exclusive and that one must prevail over the other. Shall the "will" of the seller or the buyer prevail in a particular exchange? To the economist such a question is empty because "will" is meaningless unless specified more carefully. If it is defined as some maximum advantage from trade, the answer to the question must normally be that *neither* the "will" of the buyer or the seller prevails, although trade is observed to take place. On the other hand, if the term is defined as some improvement over an initial, before-trade position, the answer must be that *both* the "will" of the buyer and that of the seller prevail as a result of free exchange.

The point to be made here is that the very "vocabulary of politics" tends to focus attention too quickly on the particular problems presented under the existence of sharply defined and mutually exclusive alternatives. Choices at the ultimate constitutional level are interpreted as being of the "either-or" type. This is not to deny that such mutually exclusive choices do arise, and that when they do, decisions must be made. However, central to an economic approach to choice problems is the possibility of variation *at the margin*. If such variation is possible, choices become "either-or" only for small incremental changes; and, considering a total complex, *some* of *all* alternatives may be chosen. Interest in, or a desire for, a particular alternative becomes a function of its cost or price relative to the other alternatives available for choice. It is this functionally variable aspect that seems to have been almost wholly absent from the "classical" analysis of political decision-making. Practical politics has been traditionally recognized as consisting of the art of the possible—of the art of compromise. However, to our knowledge few political philosophers have recognized that once the necessity of compromise is acknowledged, alternatives are no longer considered as mutually exclusive, and the discussion that proceeds as if they were becomes largely irrelevant.

APPENDIX 2

THEORETICAL FORERUNNERS

by Gordon Tullock

INTRODUCTION

Although the theory presented in this book (as Appendix 1 indicates) had some foreshadowings in political science proper, its true intellectual roots lie in other areas. Economics and probability theory are its major sources, but it also owes a good deal to a series of investigations in a poorly defined field which I shall call the "strict theory of politics." It is with this latter field that the bulk of this Appendix will concern itself, largely because any more general discussion of the history of ideas in economics and in probability is beyond both my competence and my interests. Nevertheless, some remarks about the development of probability theory and economics will be of assistance in setting the theory in its proper place among the disciplines.

The theory of permutations and combinations, which eventually developed into statistics, game theory, and modern decision theory, started out with the analysis of games of chance. A game of chance in its pure form involves a device of some sort which produces various results with varying probabilities. The initial work in what we now call statistics was an exploration of the relative frequency with which various results may be expected to appear. It might be regarded as an attempt to determine the proper way to place bets. Among gambling games, however, there are a number in which the gains or losses of some given player depend not only on the performance of a device but also on the actions of another player. In such games, although simple probability calculations are normally of some assistance to a shrewd player, they cannot give a complete set of instructions on proper play.

In these "games of strategy," to use a modern term, if one party chooses a strategy, then this strategy will form part of the data which the other party should consider in choosing his own strategy. This is obviously true if each party announces his strategy, but it is also true if each party tries to conceal his strategy. In the latter case each will try to guess the other's strategy, while choosing a strategy for himself which will not be anticipated by his opponent. In each case an individual's choice of strategy depends on his opponent's choice or on his estimate of his opponent's choice. Examining the games with which they were familiar, the mathematicians discovered that any effort to specify the "correct" rules for a player wishing to win as much as possible led to an infinite regress. If the proper strategy for player A was strategy 1, then player B should take that fact into account and choose strategy 2, but if B chose strategy 2, then 1 was not the proper strategy for A, who should choose 3, etc. These early investigators, therefore, concluded that this type of problem was insoluble and confined their investigations to pure games of chance.

Since the investigations of these mathematicians developed eventually into the wonders of modern statistics, we can hardly criticize their decision, but other investigators had unknowingly found the clue to the solution of most strategic games. The presence of the infinite regress in games (in the old sense of the word, i.e., amusement games) is a contrived result. It comes from the fact that the games are human inventions and that the inventors aim at making games fair, interesting, and unpredictable. A well-designed game does lead to the infinite regress which disturbed the mathematicians, but there is no reason to believe that the real world has been carefully designed to be fair.[1] In the real world the process of adjustment to the strategies of the other players may well lead to a perfectly definite result. Returning to the example in the last paragraph, it may well be that after player B has chosen strategy 4 and A has responded by choosing 5, neither can better himself by shifting to another strategy. Strategy 4 may be the best response to 5, and 5 the best reply to 4. In this event the parties have reached a situation which is called a "saddle point" in modern game theory.

A set of cases where the individual "players'" attempt to adjust to the strategies chosen by other "players" lead to a determinate result was early discovered in the economic field, thus establishing the science of economics. The early economists discovered that if a large enough number of people were engaged in buying and selling something and each attempted to adjust his strategy to the strategy (guessed or observed) of the others, then this would lead

1. Sometimes, of course, games are not well designed. Checkers, for example, involves a very much more limited number of possible combinations than chess. In recent years expert players have learned these combinations so thoroughly that the principal determinant of victory is who has the first move. Thus, checkers tournaments among experts now consist of a large number of games, most of which are won by the first player, and the decision over the entire series depends on the possible occurrence of mistakes in the play of one or the other player. For ordinary players, the regress, if not infinite, is still so long that the existence of genuine "correct" strategies has no effect on the game.

to a perfectly definite result.[2] This result (the situation which would arise when each player had successfully adjusted his strategy to that of all the others, and no player still wished to make changes) was labeled by economists "equilibrium," a term which is really operationally identical to the game theorists' "saddle point." If we were inventing a terminology *de novo*, I would opt for "saddle point" rather than "equilibrium" as the name for this condition. "Equilibrium" is widely used in the biological and physical sciences, but with a rather different meaning. This leads to a good deal of unnecessary confusion. It was not normally assumed that equilibrium would ever be achieved —there were always too many endogenous changes for that—but a continuous tendency to approach a continually changing equilibrium point was demonstrated.

This made human behavior in certain areas reasonably predictable. It further turned out to be possible to investigate what type of equilibrium would result from various "rules of the game," and from this examination to decide which sets of such "rules" were most likely to lead to desired results. From this developed political economy, the science of improving social institutions. Economics progressed rapidly, and today it is by far the most highly developed of the social sciences. At the same time, the mathematicians were developing simple permutations and combinations into the wonder of modern statistics. Neither group appeared to recognize the existence of the relationship between the two fields that I have sketched above.

Eventually von Neumann discovered a solution for two-person games of strategy. Specifically, he discovered two special cases in which the efforts of two players to adjust their strategies to each other would not lead to an infinite regress. The first of these two special cases—strict dominance, in which one of the players has among his possible strategies one which is superior to any other, regardless of what the other player does—is of no great importance for our present purposes. Clearly, this leads quickly and easily to a determinate result.

2. One of the differences between the problem bothering the mathematician and the problem solved by the economist involves the number of independent actors in each "game." While I think that this is less important than the difference between contrived "fair" games and natural situations, it does have some importance. The fewer the independent actors, the more likely that their mutual attempts to adjust their strategies to those of the other players will lead to an infinite regress. The attempt of the probability theorists to solve a two-person game was, therefore, an effort to solve the most difficult case. This should increase the respect we have for von Neumann's eventual solution.

The second special case—the saddle point—is much more interesting. Assuming that there is no strict dominance, a game has a saddle point if the mutual efforts of the two players to adjust their strategy to each other would lead to a determinate result. This, of course, assumes that each player knows his opponent's strategy, and von Neumann, therefore, introduced a special and very interesting version of the economists' "perfect knowledge" assumption. Von Neumann advises each player to act on the assumption that his opponent will make no mistakes; specifically, if player A is able to decide that strategy 2 is the proper one for him, he should realize that player B will also figure this out and choose *his* strategy on the assumption that A's strategy is 2. Thus, strategy 2 can only be a good strategy for A if it is to his advantage, even assuming that B knows that A is using 2. It can be seen that all of this is simply a way of assuming perfect knowledge without using the magic words. In fact, the assumptions are much stronger than those used in economics since knowledge of another's intentions is normally not included in the area where information is "perfect" in the economic model.

The reader will have noted that my explanation of game theory differs somewhat from that normally given. This is principally the result of my desire to emphasize the similarities between it and economics. In spite of the different approach, it seems likely that anyone familiar with game theory will realize that my description is operationally identical to the conventional one. One difference between game theory and economics, however, deserves emphasis. Game theory studies the behavior of individuals in a "game" with given rules. Economics does the same, but the end or purpose of the investigation in economics is to choose between alternative sets of rules.[3] We study what the outcome of the "game" will be, but with the objective of making improvements in the rules.

Game theory normally accepts the "rules" as given. Under its assumptions the game with a saddle point does come to a perfectly determinate conclusion, and there is no infinite regress. This result, of course, comes from the structure of the game, and there is no implication that all games have a saddle point. If there *is* a saddle point, mutual adjustment of strategies will lead to a determinate equilibrium. Von Neumann, however, went further and demonstrated that a game which had no saddle point could be converted into a larger game in which the strategies of each party were decisions as to the type

3. As many economists will already have guessed, I am indebted to Professor Rutledge Vining for this point.

of randomized procedure which should be adopted to choose between the various strategies in the original game. This larger game has a definite saddle point in all cases, although it may be most difficult to calculate. These mixed strategies are most interesting ideas, although currently they can be computed for few real situations.

The application of this apparatus to the real world, begun by von Neumann and Morgenstern and since greatly expanded by numerous others, has been one of the more important intellectual roots of our present work. With economics, it provided the bulk of our intellectual tools. Fortunately we were able to avoid the problems raised by mixed strategies, and, equally fortunately, the most recent developments in economics were almost perfectly suited to our needs. In particular, the recent developments in the theory of choice have been basic to our work. Specifically, we are indebted to modern game theory and modern economics for a theoretical apparatus and for three major guidelines for our investigation. (1) Modern utility theory, which has largely been developed by economists but which has also benefited greatly from the work of the game theorists, led us to concentrate on the calculus of the individual decision-maker. (2) From game theory in particular, but also from our economic background, we were led into a search for "solutions" to well-defined "political games." (3) Political economy and the search for criteria in modern statistics led us into a search for the "optimal" set of "political rules of the game," as conceived by the utility-maximizing individual.

THE SEARCH FOR A MAJORITY RULE

In addition to these major fields of study, the much less well-known and undeveloped field which I have called "the strict theory of politics" has also influenced our work. In view of the rather limited number of people who are familiar with this field, it is necessary to discuss it in some detail. The strict theory of politics can be divided into three areas. The first of these, which has been named the "theory of committees and elections" by Duncan Black, will be the subject of this section. This will be followed by a section on the "theory of parties and candidates" and a final brief section on the "theory of constitutions." My knowledge in the first area, like the title I have given it, comes almost entirely from the work of Duncan Black.[4] I shall also follow his orga-

4. Duncan Black, *The Theory of Committees and Elections* (Cambridge: Cambridge University Press, 1958). The bulk of the theoretical material in this book was originally published in a series of articles in 1948 and 1949.

nizational example in separating the history of the subject prior to the mid-twentieth century from the modern period exemplified by Black and Arrow.

Black's book contains, as Part II, an excellent discussion of the early history of the subject. I will, therefore, merely indicate the general outline of the work done before Black revived the subject and refer the reader to Black's most excellent account for further details. The story begins with three French mathematicians and physicists writing in the period of the French Revolution. Borda opened the study and made important contributions. He was followed by Condorcet, who produced a study of the utmost importance which, unfortunately, was so badly presented that no one prior to Black appears to have understood it. Laplace added a few details to the structure as it stood. It should be noted that all of these men were much interested in the development of probability theory, and Condorcet presented his theory erroneously (this is the error which has led to his being so long misunderstood) as a branch of the mathematics of probability.

No one seems to have paid much attention to this work, and the only later development which Black was able to locate occurred in 1907 when E. J. Nanson produced a memoir on elections which clearly showed a familiarity with the work of Borda and Condorcet. His addition to the received theory was slight; the same can be said of the contributions of George H. Hallet and Francis Galton.

In the long interval between the development of the ideas of the three Frenchmen and their reappearance in the work of Nanson, another man had turned his mind to the problem. The Reverend C. L. Dodgson (Lewis Carroll), in addition to his work in formal logic and the *Alice* series, produced three pamphlets on voting methods. This subject is treated by Black in a particularly masterly manner, and I must refer the reader interested in the details to his account.[5] Only two matters should be referred to here. In the first place, Black has succeeded in proving that Carroll's work was entirely original; he had not taken his ideas from Borda or Condorcet. Secondly, it is clear that we have only fragments of Lewis Carroll's work in the field. He was writing a book which was never printed, but the pamphlets themselves show unmistakable evidence of being only part of a much larger body of knowledge.

But so far I have talked about who and when, and totally ignored the what. What, then, were these people investigating? From the fact that their work attracted so little notice and that it tended to be forgotten and then rein-

5. Ibid., pp. 189–238. The pamphlets are also reprinted there.

vented,[6] one might assume that it was not very important. In fact, I think that the tendency for the subject to be swept under a variety of rugs can be attributed to the importance of the challenge which it presented to traditional democratic doctrine. These investigators had found a problem which lay at the heart of traditional theory and which resisted all attempts to solve it. In a period in which democracy was almost a religion it is no wonder that most investigators turned aside.

Traditional democratic theory depends on majority voting. There are all sorts of problems about who shall vote (quorums, representation, etc.), but it is generally agreed that a majority of some group of people will eventually decide the issue. The problem which puzzled Condorcet, Carroll, Laplace, and Black was that involved in finding a system of voting which would lead to a majority which could reasonably be regarded as the genuine will of a majority of the group. To people who have not looked into the problem, this seems a foolish inquiry; it seems obvious that a majority is a majority and that is that. In reality the problem is a most difficult one.

In investigating the problem, all of the workers in this field used basically the same method. In the first place, they examined the problem of deciding an issue or group of issues in a single election. The investigation of logrolling, which interconnects different issues and different votes, was completely ignored by them. Presumably, they felt that this was more complicated than a single issue and hoped to develop a theory of logrolling after they understood the "simpler" problem. As we have shown in this book, logrolling eliminates the basic problem, so this whole line of investigation can now be regarded as simply an examination of the special case where there is no logrolling.

The second similarity in the methods of these investigators is that they all used the same mathematical device. They assume a number of voters confronted with a number of alternatives (candidates or bills), and they assume that each voter knows which of these alternatives he prefers. The more recent workers have used a matrix form of presentation in which each voter is represented by a vertical column and his order of preference by the place a given alternative occupies on that column.

V_1	V_2	V_3
A	C	B
B	A	C
C	B	A

6. Black also reinvented the subject.

Thus, voter v_1 prefers A to B and B to C. From matrices of this sort it is possible to work out the results of various voting procedures, and research has largely consisted of assuming various preference orders and then testing out specific voting procedures on the assumed matrix. The problem which has puzzled the workers in this field has been the difficulty of discovering a procedure which does not lead to paradoxes.

If a group of people are confronted with the problem of making a choice between a number of different ways of dealing with a given problem, it may be that a majority of them have one of the possible ways as their most preferred alternative. If this is so, no problem arises;[7] there clearly is a majority. More commonly, however, none of the possible courses of action is the first preference of a majority of the voters, a fact which is reflected in the popular view that democracy requires a willingness to compromise. If there are only two alternatives, of course, one will have a majority, and if there are only three, it is not unlikely that one will be preferred over all the others by a majority of the voters; but as the number of possible alternatives increases, the possibility that one will be preferred by a majority over all the others rapidly declines.

This being so, a number of procedures have been worked out for dealing with the problem of reaching a decision in cases where there is no alternative that is the first preference of a majority. These procedures may be divided into two general classes: those that reach a decision by some sort of manipulation of the votes but without a true majority; and those which restrict the choices confronting the voter in such a way that he is finally confronted with a choice between two, which naturally results in one or the other getting a majority. Two examples of the first type are: the system used to elect members of Parliament in England, where the candidate who receives the most votes is declared elected regardless of whether he has a true majority (this system is commonly called plurality voting); and, as our second example, each voter may mark his first, second, third, etc., preferences among the candidates. His first preference is then given, say, 5 voting points, his second 4, etc. The points are added and the candidate who has the most is declared elected.

The disadvantage of these systems is that they may elect people whom the majority of the voters dislike. To take an extreme example, suppose five men are running for some office. Candidate A is favored by 21 per cent of the voters; B, C, and D are each favored by 20 per cent of the voters; and E is favored

7. Lewis Carroll raised questions even about this case using an analysis which, in effect, contrasted an intense minority and an indifferent majority. (Ibid., pp. 216–17.)

by 19 per cent. A would be declared elected under the plurality system, although it might well be the case that 79 per cent of the voters would prefer B to A.[8] Clearly, this is an odd result, and it is extremely hard to argue that this is the rule of the majority. The second method mentioned above is also subject to this difficulty. It, too, is likely to elect a man who is regarded as worse than some other candidate by a majority of the voters. In fact, all of the systems which fall in this general classification are subject to this criticism and hence cannot really be called majority rule.

Among those systems which rely on restricting choice in order to force a majority vote, we can again examine two examples. The first will be a system not infrequently used in private-club elections in which all candidates are listed, a vote is taken, and the lowest is discarded. The process is repeated until only two remain, and one of these will then gain a majority over the other.[9] As in our previous examples, the result may be most unsatisfactory. It is quite possible for a candidate to be eliminated in the early stages who is preferred by a majority over the eventual victor. Again, is this majority rule?

All but one of the methods of forcing a majority by restricting choices are subject to this objection. The unique method which escapes this problem and which is used in almost all parliamentary bodies is to require that all votes be taken on a two-choice basis. Since only two choices are presented to the voters, one must get a majority of the votes cast. The rules of order are an elaborate and superficially highly logical system for forcing any possible collection of proposals into a series of specific motions which can be voted on in simple yes-no terms. In theory, all possible alternatives can be voted on in a series of pairs, each against each of the others, and the one which beats all of the others can reasonably be considered to have majority support. Unfortunately this process, which is the theoretical basis of all modern parliamentary procedure, leads directly into the worst of the voting paradoxes, the cyclical majority.

Suppose we have 101 voters who propose to choose among three measures, A, B, and C. Suppose further that the preferences of the voters among these measures are as follows:

8. This would certainly be so if the preference curves were single-peaked (see explanation below) on an array from A to E. As an example, simple plurality voting might have brought the Communists to power in France.

9. In an effort to be brief, I do not give examples of all of the types of problems which I discuss. The reader who doubts my statements about the possible outcome of some system of voting should consult Black, where one can find proofs and examples.

50	1	50
A	C	B
B	A	C
C	B	A

Now we put the matter to a vote, taking each issue against each of the others. In the choice between A and B, A wins; in the choice between A and C, C wins; but, unfortunately, in the choice between B and C, B wins. There is no choice which can be considered the will of the majority. Nor is this a special and unlikely arrangement of preferences. No general function has yet been calculated to show what portion of possible preference patterns would lead to this result, but it seems likely that where there is any sizable number of possible issues and voters this is very common—quite probably this is the normal case.[10]

In actual parliamentary practice we never find examples of this sort of thing occurring. The most likely explanation for this would appear to be quite simple: most decision-making bodies which follow Robert's Rules in taking decisions make a number of decisions, and consequently logrolling is possible. If logrolling is the norm (and it will be no secret to the reader that we think it is), then the problem of the cyclical majority vanishes. There are two other possible explanations for the absence of evidence of cyclical majorities in functioning parliamentary bodies, but they are both complicated and unlikely so I shall not attempt to discuss them here. However, one thing should be said: asserting that either of them was the correct explanation would, by logical implication, involve a very serious attack on the whole idea of democracy.

Thus the problem stood when Black took it up. Although he made some improvements in the analysis so far described, and produced the first comprehensive presentation of the matter, his principal contribution was his discovery of the "single-peaked preference curve."[11] It may be that the possible choices can be arranged on a single line in such a way that any individual will always prefer a choice which is closer to his own to any that is farther away. It seems likely that a good many of the issues in active political life are of that sort, particularly those that are involved in the familiar "left-right" continuum. Black demonstrated that in this situation no paradox develops. Voting

10. See Black's work (pp. 50–51, 125–40, 173–74, and chap. XVI) for a proof which demonstrates that there could almost never be a majority for complex issues.

11. I ignore chapters XII–XV and XVII in what follows, not because they are unimportant, but because they are not strictly relevant to our subject here.

on the issues in pairs, the normal parliamentary manner, simply leads to the alternative preferred by the median voter. Again, it is not obvious that this is "the will of the majority," but at least it is nonparadoxical.

Black thus demonstrated that many issues are decided on in a manner which can legitimately be called "majority" rule, but there still remained those issues which were not "single-peaked" and which, therefore, led to the paradoxes which we have discussed. It was at this point that Kenneth Arrow published the only work in this field which has had any significant effect on the scholarly community.[12] In spite of the difficulties of reading it arising from a quasi-mathematical style, Arrow's book is widely known. Since I shall be somewhat critical of the book, I should start by saying that this relative fame is, in my opinion, quite justified. In detail, I think Arrow's position is open to criticism, but he was the first to indicate, however vaguely, the real significance of the discoveries that we have been discussing.

All of the previous writers in this field have concerned themselves largely with attempts to develop procedures which would avoid the problems which we have been discussing. Arrow had the courage to say that they could not be avoided. Although his presentation was difficult and elliptical, the disproof of the "will of the majority" theory of democracy was implicit in his work. The impact of his book can readily be understood, and the rather forbidding format of his work, although it scared off potential readers, probably also gave it an appearance of rigor and logic which was very convincing. Altogether, the book was the sort which should have a wide impact, and it has had considerable effect.

Having said this, I wish now to turn to some criticisms of the book, at least as it now is interpreted. It should be noted that these criticisms do not go to the heart of Arrow's achievement. They are basically disagreements with certain interpretations of his basic argument rather than with the argument itself. Arrow sets up a number of criteria which he feels any decision-making system should fulfill, and then presents a demonstration that voting does not meet them.

To start our discussion with an examination of some of his criteria, Arrow has been severely criticized for requiring "rationality" in the voting outcomes.[13] His critics point out that any decision-making process is a device or

12. Kenneth Arrow, *Social Choice and Individual Values* (New York: John Wiley and Sons, 1951).

13. Particularly by my coauthor, James Buchanan, in "Social Choice, Democracy, and Free Markets," *Journal of Political Economy*, LXII (1954), 114–23. Reprinted in *Fiscal Theory and*

instrumentality. It has no mind, and therefore we should not expect rationality. As a methodological individualist, I agree with Arrow's critics, but, in the context of the time in which his book was published, the rationality or irrationality of the process was of some importance. It was published in 1951 at the end of a century in which democratic governments had steadily increased the proportion of decisions which were made by governmental means. At that time a large part of the intellectual community felt that the solution for many problems was that of turning operational control over to a democratic government.

If, however, governments are to serve this function of solving practically all problems and operating a very large part of the total economic apparatus, clearly they must function in a rational way. It is hard to argue that a given function should be transferred to the government if governmental decision processes are closely analogous to flipping coins. Thus, a person who believes in widespread government activities must at least be disappointed by irrationality in governmental decision-making processes. From the standpoint of the authors of this book, some irrational behavior on the part of the government is inevitable under any feasible decision-making rule. This fact should be taken into account in deciding whether or not to entrust a given activity to the government. Due to the predominance of processes in which votes are traded, where the particular type of irrationality described by Arrow is impossible,[14] the basic irrationality of governmental decision-making becomes less important, but the impact of Arrow's work on people whose views of the proper role of the government were more idealistic is readily understandable.

Arrow also says (p. 59): "Similarly, the market mechanism does not create a rational social choice." As Buchanan has shown,[15] this involves a misunderstanding of the nature of the market process. It does not produce a "social choice" of any sort, as such. Rationality or irrationality is here completely

---

Political Economy: Selected Essays (Chapel Hill: University of North Carolina Press, 1960). Duncan Black also has taken the position that rationality is a characteristic of rational beings, not of institutional arrangements. Arrow himself regards this criterion as weaker than his others (*Social Choice and Individual Values*, p. 60, footnote).

14. If votes are traded, then the order of preference of the individual voter becomes less important than the strength of his preferences. The cyclical majority, vital to Arrow's proof, results from the likelihood of certain orderings of preferences, together with the apparently obvious assumption that voters vote according to their preferences on each issue. Logrolling, which results in many voters voting against their own preferences on many issues, simply is not covered by Arrow's book.

15. James M. Buchanan, "Social Choice, Democracy, and Free Markets."

irrelevant. This is of considerable importance for our present work since democratic voting (in the view of the authors of this book) also does not produce a "social choice," as such. Hence, here also "rationality" is not to be considered an absolute requirement.

The second criterion postulated by Arrow is independence of irrelevant alternatives. In England it is frequently the case that the Liberal party has no chance of electing an M.P. from a given constituency; nevertheless, the decision by the Liberal party on whether or not to run a candidate may be decisive as between a Conservative or a Labour victory. Thus, the outcome is dependent upon the presence or absence of an "irrelevant"[16] candidate. In fact, this problem is simply the one we have discussed earlier: that a voting process may select a candidate who is considered less attractive than some other by a majority of the voters. Arrow chose to criticize the logical coherence of the result in keeping with his general approach. From our standpoint, the problem raised by these voting procedures is that they lead to results which are less desired by the majority than some other results.

Now it happens to be true that all voting procedures except the process prescribed by the rules of order, that is, taking all the feasible alternatives against each other in pairs, are subject to this problem.[17] This being so, the criterion rules out all but one method of voting. Since the one remaining method is subject to the problem of the cyclical majority, it is clear that no method is available which will work without flaws. Nevertheless, if we simply try to find the best method, not the perfect one, it seems likely that our most promising field lies among the systems which are not independent of "irrelevant" alternatives.

The last of Arrow's criteria which I wish to discuss is that the outcome should "not be imposed." Arrow obviously included this criterion in order to rule out any method which would decide policy without regard for individual preferences. Unfortunately, the wording he chose rules out all possible voting rules except unanimity if there is logrolling. I do not think this was de-

16. The word "irrelevant" does not seem to me too good a descriptive term, but I cannot think of a better one. Arrow apparently got the term from E. V. Huntington, "A Paradox in the Scoring of Competing Teams," *Science* (23 September 1938), 287–88.

17. For some reason Arrow does not prove this proposition which is indispensable to his general proof. In fact, he does not even mention it. The criterion of independence of irrelevant criteria is introduced and explained on pp. 26–28, but its vital importance in eliminating all forms of voting except those prescribed by Robert's Rules is never mentioned. Possibly he felt that it was obvious.

liberate on his part, but in any event it is true. If decisions are made by some voting rule of less than unanimity and if they result from logrolling, then "there will be some pair of alternatives, X and Y, such that the community can never express a preference for Y over X no matter what the tastes of all individuals are." By Arrow's definition, therefore, the result is imposed.

An example will make the matter clear. Suppose we return to the road model, but this time we assume that the 100 farmers live in northern Michigan. We shall assume that road-repair work is impossible in the winter, but, on the other hand, people are too busy in the summer-crop season to engage in "politicking." The normal procedure, therefore, is to vote on all road repairs in the winter but have the actual work done in the following summer. By early spring all the road-repair bills have been enacted, but none has yet been implemented. If the bargaining in the winter has proceeded to full equilibrium, then every individual farmer faces the prospect of spending more of his income in purchasing road repairs than he would freely choose. Suppose, at this point, it was proposed that 1 per cent less repairing be done on each road during the summer. On our assumptions this alternative would be unanimously approved if presented, but such an alternative could never be selected under simple majority rule.[18]

Thus, reaching decisions by a series of less-than-unanimous votes interconnected by logrolling violates the nonimposition criteria. Since we have pointed out at great length that the outcome will be nonoptimal, this does not disturb us greatly. It should be recognized that an imposed decision, in Arrow's terminology, may be the best available outcome. To sum up, all means of reaching decisions by voting will, in at least some cases, reach rather unsatisfactory results. This fact should be taken into account in deciding whether some given activity should be carried on under conditions requiring decisions by voting, but it is not an insuperable obstacle to democratic government.

Turning now to Arrow's proof of the general (im)possibility theorem, it should be noted that it is *general* possibility which is involved. Arrow is interested in the question of whether some given method of voting will, in every conceivable case, produce a satisfactory result. He proves that there is no vot-

18. This motion would be dominated by proposals to reduce repairs on 49 of the farmers' roads by 2 per cent. Further, if it were known in advance that this sort of thing would happen, then it would be taken into account by the people in constructing their logrolling bargains. They would offer 1 per cent more than they expected to pay and demand 1 per cent more than they expected to receive.

ing rule which will meet this test in choosing between three or more alternatives. He does not, however, disprove the existence of a voting rule which functioned unexceptionably for 99,999,999,999,999,999,999,999,999,999 cases out of each 100,000,000,000,000,000,000,000,000,000. I suspect that complex combinations of the sort invented by Nanson[19] can be built up to reduce the anomalies to any desired proportion. As in all other cases of successive approximations, the onerousness of the procedure would increase as a power of the accuracy.

The proof itself is extremely simple, although Arrow's presentation of it is not. He assumes (p. 58, 30-1-2) the preference pattern which leads to a cyclical majority, and then demonstrates that it leads to a "contradiction." (X is preferred to Y and Y is preferred to Z, but Z is preferred to X.) The form which he has chosen—discussion of the rationality of a nonthinking institution—is unfortunate, but it is still true that putting alternatives against each other in pairs does not lead to a final result if there is a cyclical majority. Of course, putting alternatives against each other in pairs is not the only method of voting. Arrow's whole "proof" (pp. 51–59) makes no sense if it is applied to voting methods other than pairwise comparisons. In fact, Arrow's insistence on "independence of irrelevant alternatives" eliminates all methods of voting except that used in his "proof." He never proves this nor does he even mention that it plays this part in his reasoning, but since it is, in fact, true, he can be forgiven for this omission. In any event much can be forgiven the man who took the nettle in his hand. Arrow was the first to dare to challenge the traditional theory of democracy by saying that no voting rule leading to rule by "the will of the majority" was possible.

THE BEHAVIOR OF POLITICIANS

The "theory of candidates and parties" treats politicians like entrepreneurs and parties like corporations or partnerships. It is based on the view that politicians want to get elected or re-elected, and that parties are simply voluntary coalitions of politicians organized for the purpose of winning elections. A corporation serves the individual economic ends of those who organize it, yet can be treated as a functional individual for some purposes. Similarly, a party serves the individual political interests of those who organize it, but can

19. See Duncan Black, *The Theory of Committees and Elections*, p. 187. See also Condorcet's system discussed by Black on pp. 174–75.

be considered as a unified body for some purposes. Altogether, this branch of investigation strongly resembles the "theory of the firm" in economics. In economics, of course, this was a relatively late development, coming long after political economy. Why it came early in politics, I do not know. It may merely reflect the fact that "strict political theory" has largely been developed in the fifteen years since the end of World War II, a very short period.

In any event this branch of political theory has been mainly developed by individuals whose basic training is in economics. The reasons for this are fairly clear. Although the subject matter is that normally studied by the political scientists, the methods are entirely economic. Almost any citizen of a democracy will know something about the subject matter of political science, but knowledge of the methodological technique of economics is not so universal. The average economist knows economic method and some political science, while the average political scientist has little facility with the mathematical techniques of the economist. Since the new field requires both a knowledge of economic method and political reality, it may be predicted that economists would come closer to possessing the desired combination of knowledge.

One can find certain foreshadowings of the "theory of candidates and elections" in the work of a number of modern economists. Hotelling[20] and Schumpeter,[21] in particular, made contributions. Basically, however, the theory has been developed by two people, Anthony Downs and myself. Since Downs' book[22] is fairly well known, even if not so widely read as might be hoped, while my contribution consists of a chapter in a book which has been circulated only in preliminary form,[23] I may perhaps be forgiven if I emphasize my own contribution.

The formal theory in this field has been largely based on Duncan Black's single-peaked preference curve. Although both Downs and I do discuss other possible structures, our basic picture of political preference can be equated to

20. Harold Hotelling, "Stability and Competition," *The Economic Journal*, XXXIX (1929), 41–57.

21. Joseph A. Schumpeter, *Capitalism, Socialism, and Democracy* (New York: Harper and Bros., 1942).

22. Anthony Downs, *An Economic Theory of Democracy* (New York: Harper and Bros., 1957). Downs studied under Arrow, and Arrow's influence on his work was significant.

23. Gordon Tullock, *A General Theory of Politics* (University of Virginia, 1958), privately circulated.

the left-right political continuum of the conventional political scientist. If we consider an individual candidate running for office, then both the desires of the voters for various governmental policies and the structure of the voting rules should be taken into account in determining his position on various issues. In working on this subject, I ignored the complex voting rules which have been developed by the theorists of committees and elections and confined myself to a few schemes. In one, the candidate must get 50 per cent of the votes to win, and it can readily be demonstrated that this will lead the opposing candidates to adopt closely similar positions on the issues. It also has a tendency to limit the number of active candidates in any one election to two.

Another possible scheme, much used in Europe, permits a number of candidates, say five, to be elected from each constituency. In this case, a candidate can insure his own victory by obtaining 20 per cent of the votes, and may win with less. Here, there is no tendency for the candidates to take similar positions; on the contrary, they will be spread over the full spectrum of voter opinion. These demonstrations carry over to party organizations too. The frequent lament that American and British parties are much alike, instead of representing different ideologies or, sometimes, classes, is thus a criticism of the voting rules rather than of our politicians. Further, although the European parties are ideologically different, government requires a coalition of such minority parties, and these coalitions are about as similar in their policies as are the two parties of the English-speaking world.

That the structure of the political alliances which we call parties is probably largely a reflection of the voting rules has been dimly realized in England since about the last quarter of the nineteenth century. Periodically, English scholars will argue that their system of single-member constituencies, with victory in the constituency going to whoever gets a plurality, leads to a two-party system. Undoubtedly it does have such a tendency, but the fact that since the last reform bill England has always had three parties, and that it has not infrequently been necessary to turn to coalitions between two of them to get a majority in Parliament, indicates that the tendency is merely a tendency. Still, it does seem likely that we would be able to deduce an “equilibrium” party structure from any constitutional voting scheme. Actually doing so with the rather complicated systems in use in most democracies must await further research. It would appear a particularly good field for an investigator looking for something important to do.

So much for my work, which covers a broad field rather lightly. Downs instead has covered a narrow field intensively. Basically he considers the British political system as it existed from 1945 to the date of publication of his book. From this system he removed the Liberal party, the House of Lords, and the University members, which will be generally accepted as only a minor simplification of the real world. He also made two structural changes of minor importance: elections occur at regular intervals instead of at the desire of the prime minister, and the Cabinet is elected directly by popular vote rather than indirectly through Parliament. Given the present organization of the parties in Great Britain, the latter is surely a permissible simplification, although it is startling at first glance.

Having produced this simplified model of what is already the simplest governmental system now in use in any democracy, Downs proceeds to analyze its functioning. Even at this highly simplified level,[24] he finds it necessary to introduce a set of functions referring to information held by individuals and the cost of obtaining more. This series of functions is also of considerable utility in economics, but the problem of inadequate information is less pressing there. One of Downs' more surprising conclusions is that a rational man will devote little effort to becoming well informed before voting. Since the mass of the voters clearly follow his advice, and since the traditional students of the problem continually call for more informed voting, it would appear that his approach is more realistic than those offered by the traditionalists.

This is a general characteristic of the Downs model—his conclusions are highly realistic. From a rather limited number of basic premises, most of which would not be seriously questioned, he produces by strictly logical reasoning a set of conclusions. These conclusions seem to fit the real world rather well, thus serving as a validation of the whole process. Among these conclusions are a number which we might call negative characteristics of democracy. These are matters, such as the relative lack of information of the voter, which have been widely noted but which have been regarded by traditional students as defects in the process. In the traditional view such defects result from failures on the part of the voters or politicians to "do their duty." As a result, throughout the history of political theory there has been much preaching aimed at "improving" the voter. Downs' demonstration that the voter was, in fact, behaving sensibly not only suggests why all of this preaching has been unsuccessful but also indicates that the preachers have been wrong.

24. In order to avoid misunderstanding, I should point out that, although Downs has obviously obtained his basic model by the process I describe, it has wide implications and is not merely a theory of the operation of the British government.

There seems to be no point in further summarization of Downs' main conclusions. He himself has included a summary after each chapter of his book and a final summary chapter listing all of his more important conclusions, and the curious reader can thus quickly gain the main points of his argument. If the summary leads the student on to read the whole book, so much the better. Discussion of possible further research in the field, however, does seem desirable.

In the first place, Downs' supersimplified model of party government, taken by itself, can no doubt be further investigated. It has the very great advantage of being the easiest possible research tool. Further, many conclusions drawn from this very simple model will also be applicable to all party systems. Nevertheless, investigation of more complex systems would seem called for. Both Downs and myself have done some work on multiparty systems such as the French, but this is merely a beginning. Introduction of more complicated models should eventually lead to a good understanding of party dynamics in almost all of the democracies.

The internal politics of parties is, strictly speaking, not part of Downs' basic model, but, in fact, he does discuss the situation of a minority within a party which is dissatisfied with the party policies. His conclusions fit the present crisis in the British Labour party very well, although they are far from a complete explanation. This field, however, is a particularly large one, and the connection between the individual active party member and the party itself should be a major area for further research. Again, it seems likely that investigation of systems more complex than that developed by Downs will be the eventual objective, but the pioneers would probably be wise to confine themselves to his supersimple model.

WE, THE PEOPLE

The "theory of constitutions" concerns itself with a discussion of the effects of various possible democratic constitutions. These constitutions, in the book to which this essay is an appendix, are evaluated entirely in terms of their effects on individual citizens. Now that the subject has been opened up, it does not seem unlikely that others will attempt to use the same system—but without our consistent individualism. Whether this will be possible or not cannot be foretold, but at the moment the system is entirely based on individual preferences. This individualistic position raises no particular problems in connection with the "theory of committees and elections" and only apparent problems with the "theory of candidates and parties."

In this book we have said little about parties[25] and elected decision-makers. Although there have been some exceptions, we have normally assumed that decisions are made by direct popular vote. Where we have discussed elected legislatures, we have assumed that the legislator simply votes according to the majority preference in his district. This is obviously a simplification of the real world, and it might seem inconsistent with the role of the politician in the theory of candidates and parties. In fact, there is no inconsistency. The details have not yet been fully worked out, but the two branches of the "strict theory of politics" merely amount to looking at the same phenomena from two different viewpoints. The theory of candidates and parties investigates the methods of winning elections with the preferences of the voters and the constitution taken as constant. The theory of constitutions, as we have used it, investigates the constitutional method of maximizing the extent to which the voter achieves his goals with the behavior of politicians as a constant.

The pattern of behavior on the part of politicians deduced by Downs and myself is taken into account in the theory of constitutions. Again, there are problems in detail, but a politician aiming at maximizing his support in the next election will follow a course of action which fits neatly into the theory of constitutions. The situation is similar to the relationship between general economics and the theory of the firm. General economics proves that a certain social organization will maximize the degree to which individual desires are met. The theory of the firm investigates how individual businessmen or corporations achieve their ends. The two theories integrate neatly because both are based on the same basic assumptions about human behavior. These assumptions are also those of the theories of candidates and parties, and of constitutions; hence we may expect all of these theories to fit together.

The basic forerunners of the theory of constitutions in the strict theory of politics have been found in the work discussed in the second and third sections of this Appendix. However, there have been some investigators who have done preliminary work directly in this area. Buchanan demonstrated

25. When we first considered undertaking this book, the possibility of thoroughly discussing parties was briefly considered. Generally speaking, the addition of formal parties does not change the conclusions we have drawn but adds a complicating factor to the reasoning. Further, in the United States, party discipline is very weak, and use of a monolithic-party model would have been completely inappropriate. Use of a weak-party model would have complicated the reasoning beyond endurance without changing the final conclusions much. Since the book showed signs of being too long anyway, we decided to put this matter off for future consideration.

that the State must be considered as merely a device, not an end in itself.[26] A State, qua State, does not have either preferences or aversions and can feel no pleasure or pain.[27] Samuelson went on to point out that every citizen would agree to the establishment of the State because it provides a method of providing services needed by all.[28] He also pointed out that this universal agreement would extend to an agreement to coerce individuals who attempted to obtain the advantages of membership in the State without paying the cost.

Another investigation relevant to the theory of constitutions was carried on by Karl A. Wittfogel.[29] Although his principal field of investigation lay outside the area in which democracy has developed, the contrast between the "hydraulic" State and the "multicentered" State with which our own history deals greatly increases our understanding of our own institutions. From our standpoint, the main lesson to be learned is that the State should not have a monopoly of force. The oriental states were "too strong for society," and we should do everything in our power to avoid a similar situation. The State should have enough power to "keep the peace" but not enough to provide temptation to ambitious men. The State should never be given enough power to prevent genuinely popular uprisings against it.

The work of Rutledge Vining had a major effect on both of us, largely through his emphasis on the necessity of separating consideration of what "rules of the game" were most satisfactory from the consideration of the strategy to be followed under a given set of "rules."

A further area in which quite a bit of research has been done and which can, in a sense, be taken as supporting the position we have taken in this book is the statistical study of voting behavior. With the great modern development of statistical methods, it was inevitable that investigators would eventually turn to voting records as a source of information about politics. A great deal of work has now been done in this field, and a vast literature now exists consisting of statistical investigations of the influence of various factors on voting. We have not made any thorough attempt to survey this literature, but

26. James Buchanan, "The Pure Theory of Government Finance: A Suggested Approach," *Journal of Political Economy*, LVII (1949), 496–505.

27. In nondemocratic states the preference schedule of an individual may be what the State device is intended to maximize; but the king is not the State, regardless of what Louis XIV said, and the State itself has no "welfare function."

28. Paul A. Samuelson, "The Pure Theory of Public Expenditure," *Review of Economics and Statistics*, XXXVI (1954), 387–89.

29. Karl A. Wittfogel, *Oriental Despotism* (New Haven: Yale University Press, 1957).

from what reading we have done it would appear that this work largely supports our basic position and contradicts the traditional view.

In addition to these investigations which influenced our work, we have found two clear-cut cases of previous work directly in the "theory of constitutions." The first of these, by Wicksell,[30] involves a fairly sophisticated discussion of an important constitutional problem together with recommendations for specific constitutional changes. The particular problem he discussed is now "one with Nineveh and Tyre," but his approach is still of considerable interest. The second example is an article by J. Roland Pennock,[31] a most elegant example of what can be done in this field. It had no influence on our work, but only because we had overlooked it when it first appeared and just found it recently.

Both Wicksell and Pennock overlooked the problem of the costs of decision in choosing the optimal constitutional rule. We are not in a position to criticize them on this point since we both made the same mistakes in our own earlier work. In Buchanan's "Positive Economics, Welfare Economics, and Political Economy" and my "Some Problems of Majority Voting"[32] the costs of decision-making are ignored, although these two articles clearly deftly fall within the "theory of constitutions."

In summary, although good work has been done in the field, the "strict theory of politics" is still an underdeveloped area. One of the purposes of this book is to attract resources, in the form of research work, into the field. There are few more promising areas for original work.

30. Knut Wicksell, *Finanztheoretische Untersuchungen* (Jena: Gustav Fischer, 1896).

31. J. Roland Pennock, "Federal and Unitary Government—Disharmony and Frustration," *Behavioral Science*, IV (April 1959), 147–57.

32. This article reappears in a somewhat modified form as Chapter 10 of this book.

INDEX

References to bibliographic information appear in italics.

The typeface used for the text of this book is Galliard, an old-style face designed by Matthew Carter in 1978, in the spirit of a sixteenth-century French typeface of Robert Granjon.
The display type is Meta Book, a variant of Meta, designed by Erik Spiekermann in the 1990s.

This book is printed on paper that is acid-free and meets the requirements of the American National Standard for Permanence of Paper for Printed Library Materials, z39.48-1992. ♾

Book design by Richard Hendel, Chapel Hill, North Carolina
Typography by G&S Typesetters, Inc., Austin, Texas
Printed and bound by Thomson-Shore, Dexter, Michigan

CHAPTER 13

PARETO OPTIMALITY, EXTERNAL COSTS, AND INCOME REDISTRIBUTION

We have shown that, if full side payments are allowed to take place, *any* decision-making rule for collective action will lead to positions that may properly be classified as Pareto-optimal, although Pareto optimality may not characterize the process or processes through which the positions are attained. Because of the latter, nothing can be said concerning the "desirability" or the "undesirability" of the changes embodied in the operation of any given decision-making rule short of unanimity. Recall that the definition of a Paretian P-point is as follows: a position from which no change can be made without harming at least one individual in the group. This suggests that, when such a position is attained, no external costs are being imposed on the individual by other individuals. Economists are familiar with the fact that one of the necessary conditions for Pareto optimality is the absence of such externalities. Moreover, as we have previously shown, the presence of external costs is equivalent to the existence of "mutual gains from trade," which can, by definition, be secured to the advantage of all parties.

The introduction of full side payments into the model of collective choice seems to imply, therefore, some restrictions on the applicability of the external-costs function developed in Chapter 6. This function, you will recall, relates the expected external costs on the individual to the decision-making rules. The value of the function decreases as the rule becomes more inclusive, but this value remains positive throughout the range. The relevance of this construction has been demonstrated for the individual constitutional calculus when full side payments are not present. Any rule for collective choice embodying less than full consensus must impose some external costs on the individual since resources will tend to be allocated "inefficiently" because of the choice mechanism. If, however, the introduction of full side payments should negate the relevance of this external-costs function, our analysis of constitutional choice would be rather severely limited.

In this chapter we shall try to show that the individual, at the stage of constitutional choice, will expect collective activity to impose some external costs on him, even if full side payments are allowed to take place in the process of